Foucault and Liberal Political Economy

PHILOSOPHY, POLITICS, AND ECONOMICS

Ryan Muldoon, Carmen Pavel, Geoffrey Sayre-McCord, Eric Schliesser, Itai Sher
Series Editors

Published in the Series

The Open Society and Its Complexities
Gerald Gaus

A Theory of Subjective Wellbeing
Mark Fabian

Intelligent Democracy
Jonathan Benson

The Social Cost of Carbon
J. Paul Kelleher

Foucault and Liberal Political Economy

Power, Knowledge, and Freedom

MARK PENNINGTON

To Mike

With thanks for your courage

Mark Pennington

OXFORD
UNIVERSITY PRESS

OXFORD
UNIVERSITY PRESS

Oxford University Press is a department of the University of Oxford. It furthers the University's objective of excellence in research, scholarship, and education by publishing worldwide. Oxford is a registered trade mark of Oxford University Press in the UK and in certain other countries.

Published in the United States of America by Oxford University Press
198 Madison Avenue, New York, NY 10016, United States of America.

CIP data is on file at the Library of Congress

ISBN 9780197690529

DOI: 10.1093/9780197690550.001.0001

Printed by Marquis Book Printing, Canada

The manufacturer's authorized representative in the EU for product safety is Oxford University Press España S.A., Parque Empresarial San Fernando de Henares, Avenida de Castilla, 2 – 28830 Madrid (www.oup.es/en).

MIX
Paper | Supporting responsible forestry
FSC® C103567
FSC
www.fsc.org

In loving memory of those who made me
Joyce, Walter, Elizabeth, and Isaac

Contents

Series Editors' Foreword

Philosophy, Politics and Economics (PPE) is coming of age as a distinct area of research of high social relevance. Modern societies face numerous complex challenges, including those associated with immigration, inequality, trade, environmental degradation, pluralism, and technological change. These cannot be completely understood through any single disciplinary lens. By fostering a more robustly interdisciplinary approach to these challenges, PPE as a field of study will help uncover opportunities that have been missed due to existing disciplinary blinders.

OUP and the editors aim for the series to be a home for scholarly monographs at the cutting edge of PPE research as well as for books aimed at broader audiences looking to learn about PPE and the perspectives it brings to pressing questions and issues. We are interested in research that integrates the disciplines of philosophy, political science, and economics to tackle or solve important policy and research problems. We are also interested in work that develops new theories and approaches that *synthesise* the different fields and offer a means to integrate them into something new.

We welcome original, boundary crossing new work that incorporates insights from all the social sciences, not just political science and economics. We intend for work in the series to be ecumenical about its potential scope and rigorous about its methods. We believe that an integrated approach to PPE can range very broadly, and we are excited to explore its frontiers.

Acknowledgements

I owe special thanks to the editors of this series for showing faith in this project; to the John Templeton Foundation who provided the financial support through grant number 81823 (The Political Economy of Knowledge and Ignorance) which gave me the space and time to complete the manuscript; and to Bryan Cheang for administrative and moral support. Helpful comments have been received throughout from colleagues in the Department of Political Economy at King's College London and from the Centre for the Study of Governance and Society. Thanks to Danielle Guizzo, Erwin Dekker, and Daniel Bell for extensive comments on early drafts of the opening chapters which were presented at the annual PPE Society Conference in New Orleans in November 2022. My appreciation is also due to Lynne Kiesling, Niclas Berggren, Vincent Geloso, and Emily Skarbek who offered comments on later drafts presented at the annual Public Choice Society meeting held in Dallas, 2024, and to Carlos Palacios who gave helpful comments on Chapters 1–4. I have also presented different aspects of the arguments presented here at events organised by colleagues and friends at New York University and the University of Lincoln to whom I also owe my thanks. Finally, I offer my lasting appreciation to two departed friends: Jeffrey Friedman whose unique contribution in creating and editing *Critical Review* has been one of my greatest influences; and Walter Grinder—who offered me an invitation in 1994 that changed the course of my life.

Mark Pennington, 1 May 2024
Upholland, Lancashire

1
Introduction
Foucault and Liberal Political Economy

Introduction

The French social theorist Michel Foucault has been one of the most influential voices in contemporary political thought. Inspired by his 'postmodern' critiques of enlightenment rationalism, complex analyses of power and technologies of government, and his attack on the idea of the autonomous individual subject, many Foucauldians are deeply sceptical of liberal political economy. While the latter relies heavily on discourses that emphasise individual freedom, Foucault's followers often see liberal institutions as systems of social control that limit experimentation with alternative modes of life and conceptions of individuality. Late in his life, however, Foucault demonstrated a now well-documented, and some have suggested,[1] sympathetic interest in liberal political economy, notably in the *Birth of BioPolitics* lectures and in his discussions on 'governmentality'.[2]

This book aims to present the first major discussion of Foucault's work from a standpoint sympathetic to liberal political economy. By 'political economy' is meant an approach to social theory recognising that the economic and political elements of decision-making cannot easily be separated. By 'liberal political economy' is meant an explanatory social theory emphasising the role of individual agency in shaping personal and social outcomes and a normative theory that sees the protection of that agency as requiring limitations on governmental and private power. The primary purpose in these pages is not, however, to establish whether Foucault had sympathies with liberal political economy so understood or to add to the already voluminous intellectual history on his vast output. Rather, the intention is to show how Foucault's ontological and epistemological

[1] For example, Behrent, M. (2009) 'Liberalism Without Humanism: Michel Foucault and the Free Market Creed, 1976–1979', *Modern Intellectual History*, 6 (3): 539–68. See also the essays in Zamora, D., and Behrent, M., eds. (2016) *Foucault and Neo-Liberalism*, Cambridge: Polity Press; Sawyer, S., and D. Steinmetz-Jenkins, eds. (2019) *Foucault, Neo-Liberalism and Beyond*, London: Rowman and Littlefield.

[2] Foucault, M. (hereafter MF) (1979/2008) *The Birth of BioPolitics*, New York: Palgrave/Macmillan.

Foucault and Liberal Political Economy. Mark Pennington, Oxford University Press. © Mark Pennington 2025.
DOI: 10.1093/9780197690550.003.0001

framework and his ethical focus on freedom as a practice of self-creation in the face of cultural power relations are compatible with what will be described throughout as a 'postmodern liberalism'. The book might thus be interpreted as an attempt to open a mutually enriching conversation between those inspired by Foucault and liberal political economists, which Foucault attempted to initiate but has since never been engaged.

One reason for this failure may reflect the response of some Foucauldians to *The Birth of BioPolitics*. Though the lectures contain no sustained attempt to critique the different schools of liberal political economy they identify,[3] a significant number of writers influenced by Foucault have projected onto his discussion the critical genealogical method and the unmasking of various 'power effects' that characterised much of his output throughout the early-mid 1970s. These projections have since spawned an entire academic industry that focuses on pathologies of 'neo-liberal' discourses and the contemporary modes of governance to which these discourses are held to have given rise.[4]

For their part, the lack of engagement from liberal political economists both with *The Birth of BioPolitics* and, indeed, with the entirety of Foucault's intellectual output[5] may reflect a more widely held perception that Foucault was a figure of the radical left who worked within a Marxist or at least Marxisant intellectual milieu, inherently hostile to liberalism and its commitments to human agency and individual rights. While this characterisation is understandable, it is a lazy one nonetheless. It is true that for a brief time Foucault was a member of the French Communist Party and that for a period in the early 1970s his work was infused by rhetoric not dissimilar to that found in Marxist writings. Equally, however, many of Foucault's contributions are highly critical of Marxist concepts and not merely from a standpoint sympathetic to Marxism,

[3] For a discussion of this lack of critique see, e.g., Dean, M., and Zamora, D. (2021) *The Last Man Takes LSD: Foucault and the End of Revolution*, London: Verso.

[4] For example, Brown, W. (2015) *Undoing the Demos: Neoliberalism's Stealth Revolution*, New York: Zone Books; Brown, W. (2019) *In the Ruins of Neoliberalism*, New York: Columbia University Press; See also Harcourt, B. (2011) *The Illusion of Free Markets: Punishment and the Myth of Natural Order*, Cambridge, MA: Harvard University Press. On the wider literature, see, e.g., Birch, K. (2017) *A Research Agenda for Neo-Liberalism*: Cheltenham: Edward Elgar.

[5] The only exception here is the seminar held between Harcourt, Becker, and Ewald at the University of Chicago. The focus of this seminar was largely on Becker's work and did not represent a systematic engagement with the broader tradition of liberal political economy—see (2012) 'Becker on Ewald on Foucault on Becker and American Neoliberalism and Michel Foucault's Birth of Bio Politics Lectures', *Coase-Sandor Working Paper Series on Law, and Economics*, Chicago University, 614. Elsewhere, there are brief hints of possible engagement in Lavoie, D., and Chamlee-Wright, E. (2001) *Culture and Enterprise*, London: Routledge. By contrast, there has been somewhat more notable engagement with Foucault from social democratic liberals represented in the work of Richard Rorty and William Connolly—e.g. Rorty, R. 'Moral Identity and Private Autonomy: The Case of Michel Foucault', in Rorty, R. (1991) *Essays on Heidegger and Others*, New York: Cambridge University Press; Connolly, W. (1993) 'Beyond Good and Evil: The Ethical Sensibility of Michel Foucault', *Political Theory*, 21 (3): 365–89.

but from one that by the latter part of the 1970s was discernibly hostile to that project and to socialism more broadly.[6] One of the frustrating or attractive aspects of Foucault's thought, depending on one's point of view, is that there are 'many Foucaults' reflected in the shifting emphases, styles of analysis and reinterpretations of his own works, and in the multiple and often contradictory interpretations placed on them by his numerous readers and followers. As Foucault himself once put it, 'No, I am not where you seek me, but over here, looking on and laughing'.[7]

Though Foucault's engagement with liberal political economy in *The Birth of BioPolitics* provides the context of this book, the content of those lectures is not the primary focus. Rather, the aim is to identify, to examine, and to develop a series of connections, equivalences, and grounds for productive interplay between the broad sweep of Foucault's intellectual oeuvre and a neglected 'postmodern' strand of liberal thought.[8] Liberal political economy is not a unified church; rather, it has significant differences between a modernist or rationalist branch, which seeks to identify the institutions that will secure individual freedom from an essentialist, universalist account of human nature, and a scientific approach to institutional design, and a non-rationalist branch which emphasises cultural and economic pluralism, as well as radical limits to human knowledge about self and society. It is the latter branch which has the potential for creative dialogue with Foucault's oeuvre. This potential arises from a social ontology based on a culturally situated individualism; a philosophy of social science deeply sceptical of positivistic, 'scientistic' modes of analysis and 'expert rule'; and a shared focus on freedom as an open-ended process of self-creation in the face of cultural power relations.

What emerges from the dialogue presented in these pages will be a distinctively 'Foucauldian liberalism', critical of the dominant modernist liberalisms in political economy and political philosophy and the institutional regimes they promote or justify. This liberalism will be one that may not currently be recognisable *either* to Foucauldians *or* to liberals alike. In brief, the book will present an explanatory and normative political economy combining the tools of Foucault's critical social theory with liberal political economy to explore how and why contemporary 'liberal societies' might be considered 'over-governed' or 'insufficiently liberal'.

[6] Dean and Zamora, *The Last Man Takes LSD.*

[7] MF (1969) *The Archaeology of Knowledge*, Paris: Gallimard, 28.

[8] The term 'postmodern liberal political economy' has not to this author's knowledge been used previously. Richard Rorty has described himself as advocating a 'post-modern bourgeois liberalism' but his advocacy of this stance is not rooted in the type of integrated political economic analysis offered here. See Rorty, M. (1983) 'Post-Modern Bourgeois Liberalism', *Journal of Philosophy*, 80 (10): 583–9.

Why Foucault?

Given the absence of engagement with Foucault's thought from liberal political economists, it might reasonably be asked why such engagement is warranted and why it matters. Though its achievements in securing unprecedented reductions in poverty and improvements in human health should not be underestimated,[9] there is currently a profound sense that the liberal order as we know it may be exhausted as a political project. While there seems little appetite for returning to the state socialisms that rose to prominence in the twentieth century, the combination of financial crises, growing ecological and public health concerns, and the rise of an increasingly conflictual identity-based politics is fuelling a sense that liberal welfare state capitalism is in crisis. Contemporary liberal societies are characterised by seemingly contradictory tendencies where political movements express disillusionment with what they see as chronic power imbalances and the failures of a technocratic elite while simultaneously demanding stronger leadership and greater regulatory control across multiple domains. Under the surface of this general mood is a highly influential set of ideas within the academy that views the intellectual case for the liberal order as based on a philosophically flawed social science and an impoverished conception of human freedom. In an environment such as this, the future of liberal institutions such as open markets, freedom of contract, freedom of association, freedom of the press, and 'limited government' should not be taken for granted.

Against this background, by far the most important reason for liberals to learn from Foucault is that although his political commitments were ambiguous, he can be read as chiding modern 'liberal' societies and their supporting philosophies for failing to appreciate the full range of threats to freedom.[10] If a central concern of liberalism has been the problem of 'over-government', then one of Foucault's most important contributions has been to expose the multiple sources and potential forms of this 'over-government' in modern societies and how these threats to freedom have been neglected by, and in some cases resulted from, the dominant strands in liberal thought. Understanding whether there are resources within liberal political economy to address these challenges is an important undertaking if its freedom-loving credentials are to be sustained and if potentially dangerous forms of *illiberal* rule are to be avoided. There are several defining aspects of Foucault's critical social theory where such an engagement

[9] See, e.g., McCloskey, D. (2016) *Bourgeois Equality*, Chicago: University of Chicago Press. McCloskey shows that incomes in broadly liberal societies have increased by *3000%* since the Industrial Revolution.

[10] For example, Rajchman, J. (1985) *Michel Foucault: The Freedom of Philosophy*, New York: Columbia University Press.

may help clarify important differences within the liberal tradition about the nature of freedom and the threats to it.

The first reflects Foucault's ontological critique of the rational autonomous subject. This conception of the individual informs the dominant strands of 'modernist' liberal political economy and social science such as neo-classical economics and rational choice theory, as well as normative theories of liberalism such as rights-based libertarianism, Rawlsian egalitarianism, and luck egalitarianism that emphasise a set of rights derived from an underlying human essence and an autonomous rationality. For Foucault, beyond perhaps some very broad biological parameters, there is no underlying human nature or essence and no underlying rationality that exists prior to or independent from a specific cultural-historical context. The sense of individuality or subjectivity experienced by people is an *effect* of the social discourses and power relations they find themselves in and the perceptual frames, 'grids of intelligibility', and 'the regimes of power and truth' that characterise a specific cultural milieu.

Second, liberal theories work from an impoverished conception of power and of 'government', which understands it as an authority granted to a political entity by individuals in the form of a contract, or as a state of affairs imposed on one individual by another, or by a sovereign ruler or group. While not denying the existence of such power, Foucault emphasises instead the importance of 'decentred' manifestations of power. This power is not held by specific individuals or groups in the way that territory or a political office may be held but operates instead through a web-like process of interactions that affect what is considered acceptable or otherwise within a culture. Subjects 'acted upon' in this way behave differently than they otherwise might.[11] The 'discursive power' that limits actions and imprints on people an identity and social positionality 'circulates' or 'flows' through people and organisations and is modified by them in multiple and strategic 'power/knowledge' games where people attempt to 'conduct the conduct' of others.[12] What concerns Foucault is that when various discourses in circulation align or crystallise with each other and with the formal apparatus of government, they may rigidify an otherwise fluid, plural, or fractured set of power relations into a state of domination.[13] Freedom is the capacity to recreate oneself in the face of power relations, while a state of unfreedom occurs when people are locked into a particular identity by a stabilised set of discourses and institutions. This does not mean that people should be forced to change their conceptions of themselves if they are to be free, but it does require drawing attention to the

[11] MF (1982) 'The Subject and Power', *Critical Inquiry*, 8 (4): 777–95, quote at 786.

[12] For example, MF (1980) *Power-Knowledge: Selected Interviews*, ed. Gordon, C., New York: Pantheon.

[13] Ibid.

social processes that may block or limit the capacity of people to identify and to experiment with alternative ways of being.

Third, one of the primary exemplars of this decentred power and its potential to constitute a form of over-government arises from scientific discourses. Where modernist versions of liberalism tend to see the application of the scientific method as contributing to the growth of knowledge and the advance of freedom, Foucault sees the reach of these methods, especially in the human and social sciences, as at best ambiguous and at worst as a potential form of freedom-threatening power over individuals' capacities for self-creation. For Foucault, it is through the application of various scientific 'gazes' or forms of 'objectivation' in modern society that people *acquire* a sense of their individuality. By 'objectivation' Foucault refers to the process by which people become the objects of scientific analysis and of 'truth claims' that seek to govern them in accordance with the underlying nature of their selfhood and of their environment. As these claims circulate, they in turn generate processes of 'subjectivation' where people come to see or to understand themselves through the relevant conceptual grids. The latter may limit freedom by routinising as totalising or objective truths what are often partial and subjective perspectives. Objectivation and subjectivation processes may thus operate as a constraint on freedom and at worst as a form of domination, imposing fixed notions of subjectivity that may limit the scope of people to craft alternative identities and values.[14]

This critique of scientific rationality is most clearly expressed in the analysis of 'disciplinary power' and 'bio-power' which Foucault associates with discourses that emerged from the Enlightenment. Discipline works through hierarchical observation combined with normalising or moralistic judgements that classify individuals in relation to norms then used as the basis for the application of 'corrective' measures, enforced through a combination of social punishments and internalised 'self-control'.[15] These power/knowledge classifications that link scientific claims to 'know' others with the power to 'discipline' them have in Foucault's view led to the subjugation of people defined by social discourses, as well as the experts that propagate them, as sexually perverted, insane, criminal, or deviant in various respects.[16]

Bio-power on the other hand, operates through social technologies that classify social, economic, or environmental conditions as the objects of intervention and manipulation and is justified in the name of improving 'population health' or providing 'security'.[17] States throughout many parts of the world have recently enforced unprecedented restrictions on personal liberties to control a

[14] Ibid.
[15] MF (1977) *Discipline and Punish*, New York: Vantage.
[16] MF (1976/1998) *The History of Sexuality*, vol. 1, London: Penguin.
[17] MF (1977–78/2007) *Security, Territory and Population*, New York: Palgrave/Macmillan.

global pandemic in precisely these terms and in the process have exercised what Foucault describes as the power to 'make live and let die'.[18] While the measures deployed to monitor and control the new coronavirus were a more extreme form of this power, the monitoring by economists, public health professionals, and other experts of social states, for example, of levels of unemployment, inequality, and pollution on the one hand, to the prevalence of smoking, obesity, and alcohol consumption on the other, are all examples of classifications intertwined with the surveillance of behaviours in contemporary regulatory-welfare states. The production of statistics and reports documenting what are described as societal 'imbalances' or 'crises' are correspondingly used to acquire powers and in turn grant status to those who claim the requisite knowledge to operate them in the social interest.

Finally, where many in the liberal and in the socialist traditions have understood freedom in terms of a set of institutions, rights, and resources that can 'liberate' an authentic individual essence, for Foucault it is precisely those discourses that view human beings as having an underlying 'truth' that run the risk of trapping people in socially constructed categories. Normative theories of liberalism, such as libertarianism and Rawlsian egalitarianism, for example, which see states as contractually obliged to respect negative rights to 'non-interference' or positive rights to 'bundles of resources', owed to rational autonomous agents, fail to recognise that there may be no neutral or impartial standpoint from which to judge the rationality of action or the rights and resources agents should have.

In Foucault's view there can be no freedom 'outside' of power relations because subjects are always the *products* of various technologies of power. Freedom is not to be achieved by eliminating such technologies but by ensuring that they do not rigidify and that they remain open to challenge and contestation, so that people have the capacity to *recreate* themselves. Insofar as they judge individuals and societies against a 'power-free' notion of truth or rationality, liberal discourses may inhibit this freedom because of their tendency to classify observed behaviours as being more, or less, rational and to propose corrective measures for 'failures' of rationality at the individual or at the societal level. The very commitment to rationalism and an ethics of 'truth' in modernist theories generates 'power effects' that result in multiple interventions and potentially stifling forms of social control. This does not mean that Foucault's approach implies the endorsement of an entirely unbounded conception of pluralism and freedom; instead, it should be seen as a warning about the potentially *illiberal* consequences that may arise from the deployment of seemingly neutral categories such as 'rationality' or 'reasonableness' to set the relevant boundaries.

[18] *The History of Sexuality*, part 5.

Why postmodern liberal political economy?

Though these Foucauldian critiques have a well-specified target in the dominant modernist forms of liberalism, the analysis offered here shows that they have their equivalents in a subordinate or minority discourse *within* liberal political economy itself. This 'postmodern' liberalism has not previously been coherently articulated, but strands of it are detectable in the writings of F. A Hayek, those of Deirdre McCloskey, and elements of the contemporary Austrian school of economics, as well as in the context of political philosophy apart from Hayek in the works of Michael Oakeshott, Gerald Gaus, and Chandran Kukathas.[19]

The aim of this book is to bring together these strands of thought, to enunciate the elements of a postmodern liberalism, and to show how this perspective might engage in a productive conversation with Foucault in ways that expose the *illiberalism* of contemporary societies and the dominant forms of social science and political philosophy that contribute to this state of affairs. While there is no suggestion that these authors would identify as postmodernists or that they would agree with all the arguments presented here, there is a discernible 'family resemblance' between liberal approaches that question essentialist understandings of the relationship between self and society that has significant overlaps with the postmodern themes in Foucault's thought.

First, the liberalism explored and developed here shares Foucault's concern not simply with 'sovereign' forms of power centred in the state but with the 'decentred' entanglements of actors in the interlocking realms of civil

[19] Representative works include Hayek, F. A. (1948) *Individualism and Economic Order*, Chicago: University of Chicago Press; Hayek, F. A. (1957) *The Counter-Revolution of Science*, Indianapolis, IN: Liberty Fund; Hayek, F. A. 'The Pretence of Knowledge', in Hayek, F.A. (1978) *New Studies in Philosophy, Politics, Economics and the History of Ideas*, London: Routledge; McCloskey, D. (1990) *If You're So Smart*, Chicago: University of Chicago Press; McCloskey, D. (2022) *Beyond Behaviourism, Positivism and Neo-Institutionalism in Economics*, Chicago: University of Chicago Press. In the wider 'Austrian school' they include Buchanan, J., and Vanberg, V. (1991) 'The Market as a Creative Process', *Economics and Philosophy*, 7: 167–86; Lachmann, L. (1986) *The Market as an Economic Process*, New York and Oxford: Basil Blackwell; Lavoie, D. (1985) *National Economic Planning*, Washingtonm DC: Cato Institute; O'Driscoll, G., and Rizzo, M. (2015) *Austrian Economics Re-Examined: The Economics of Time and Ignorance*, London: Routledge; Shackle, G. (1972) *Epistemics and Economics*, Cambridge: Cambridge University Press; Storr, V., and Arielle, J. (2020) *Cultural Considerations Within Austrian Economics*, Cambridge: Cambridge University Press. In political science examples include Aligica, P. (2014) *Institutional Diversity and Political Economy: The Ostroms and Beyond*, Oxford: Oxford University Press; Friedman, J. (2019) *Power Without Knowledge*, Oxford: Oxford University Press; Ostrom, V. (1997) The *Meaning of Democracy and the Vulnerability of Democracies*, Ann Arbor: University of Michigan Press; Wagner, R. (2016) *Politics as a Peculiar Business*, Cheltenham: Edward Elgar. In political philosophy, apart from Hayek's works, they include Oakeshott, M. (1975/1990) *On Human Conduct*, Oxford: Clarendon Press; Gaus, G. (2016) *The Tyranny of the Ideal*, Princeton, NJ: Princeton University Press; Gaus, G. (2021) *The Open Society and Its Complexities*, New York: Oxford University Press; Kukathas, C. (2003) *The Liberal Archipelago*, Oxford: Oxford University Press; Muldoon, R. (2016) *Social Contract Theory for a Diverse World*, London: Routledge; see also Tebble, A. (2016) *Epistemic Liberalism*, London: Routledge.

society, markets, and public authority that produce the patterned though *unintended* social phenomena that influence subjectivity. The diverse and dispersed strategies adopted by agents to pursue wealth and cultural and political status are understood to be simultaneously affected by cultural norms, the behaviour of market participants, and expectations about the regulatory and distributive role of public bodies, and these strategies in turn generate evolving power relations through spontaneous ordering processes. Such orders are the 'result of human action but not of human design', and given their complexity, they cannot be directed by any individual or group or by a sovereign point of economic or political authority.

Second, this postmodern liberalism concurs with Foucault's deep scepticism of social scientific and philosophical approaches grounded in the possibility that objectively 'true knowledge' about individual selves or the social world is attainable. Faith that the contents of a universal human nature and distinctions between truth and falsehood can be discerned through scientific reasoning constitutes an important *threat* to freedom because it leads to the view that such knowledge can be centralised and human behaviour subject to control by an organised intelligence. That this stance characterises the prevailing neo-classical paradigm in liberal economics and in political philosophy is evident in the substantial role granted to social scientific expertise as a guarantor of justice and 'positive freedom' in the dominant liberal egalitarian paradigm. From a postmodern liberal perspective, however, it is precisely the decentralised, partial, and subjective character of the knowledge pertinent to social order that warrants a profound scepticism of scientistic planning, regulation, and control. A commitment to freedom and pluralism implies a rejection of rationalist and scientistic modes of thought whether expressed in the name of efficiency or justice or in the name of liberalism, socialism, or any other political project.

Third, the liberalism presented here agrees with Foucault's contention that freedom does not exist 'outside' of culture and power relations. Its central concern is not to eliminate power and authority but to divide it and to make it harder for any one equilibrium of evaluative standards to become established or for any one lens of objectivation or cultural gaze to dominate the social order. Institutions such as private property, market competition, and political and legal decentralisation are favoured not because they reflect the rational means to the achievement of social welfare, or fundamental moral rights commensurate with an underlying rationality or human nature, but as tools through which to resist and to destabilise power relations—whether these originate in civil society, private enterprise, or in the state. It is the cultural-economic creative destruction that may be exercised in such settings that continually disrupts existing modes of thought and of being.

While the similarities between this liberalism and Foucault's analysis should be apparent, the case for it to engage with Foucault's thought goes well beyond these equivalences. Postmodern liberal political economy is an open-ended research program, and this book will show that a synthesis with Foucault's work can enrich that program and its critique of contemporary modes of governance by paying much greater attention to the role that 'discourse' plays in shaping and giving effect to power relations. A suitably postmodern liberalism should focus not only on the epistemic pretensions of modern states but also on the freedom-limiting and potentially dominating effects on their subjects' identities exercised by the discourses that govern them. Though not necessarily in opposition to all forms of state regulation or redistribution, this liberalism recognises how discourses that justify the monopoly of public agents to control currency, to tax, to regulate terms on which people trade, to determine which markets 'fail' or 'succeed', to specify which foods should be bought and sold, and that attempt to insulate people from various risks may involve processes of objectivation that position some subjects as incapable or inferior and embody power/knowledge claims to epistemic authority at multiple levels. Similarly, discourses of social justice that propose to equalise opportunities or to eliminate the effects of 'brute luck' implicitly or explicitly presuppose a network of bio-political surveillance techniques that connect the family, school, workplace, and state—and through which people will be monitored and classified in ways that may profoundly affect their identities, capacity for agency, and sense of self-worth.

The importance of developing a postmodern liberalism with an appreciation of the relationships among freedom, discourse, and power is particularly pressing because many of the issues shaping contemporary life are so closely associated with the cultural power dynamics that were Foucault's concern. Social exclusions around race, class, gender, and sexual identities continue to illustrate the relevance of his account of how power 'circulates' and 'governs' behaviour outside the formal apparatus of government. Localised expressions of racial or sexual stereotypes, insensitive policing tactics, or curricular decisions in educational institutions may multiply micro-level events to produce macro-level outcomes where large numbers of people may experience marginalisation *without* any single agency or group being 'in control' or intending to produce the relevant outcome. The contemporary salience of these issues to public debate about 'structural' or 'systemic' inequalities around matters such as race and gender norms offers an important opportunity for a postmodern liberalism to engage with Foucauldian analysis through an understanding of these exclusions as 'spontaneous order' phenomena that do not originate from any one locus of authority. Specifically, an engagement with Foucault's work can develop a liberal political economy with a more nuanced account of the relationship between these phenomena and human freedom. While some in the liberal tradition have been at the forefront in showing how spontaneous orders such as markets enable people to exercise freedom by limiting their dependence on any sovereign centre, they have often allowed their enthusiasm for these processes to downplay the extent to which potentially dominating constraints on individual freedom may themselves arise spontaneously.

On the other hand, the liberal understanding of cultural power relations as 'complex phenomena' that cannot be consciously 'grasped' or 'dismantled' by any actor or group may complement the Foucauldian analysis by highlighting the difficulties of attempting to modify what Foucault would understand to be 'decentred' or 'systemic' forms of power through centralised or disciplinary forms of 'correction'. A Foucauldian or postmodern liberalism would be alert to the challenges that face private, civil, and public agencies in seeking to reduce social exclusions without thereby introducing new disciplinary objectivations and margins of exclusion. This is a particularly significant task because Foucault's work highlights threats to freedom that may arise from institutional procedures central to modern states that tether people to group identifications, rather than enabling them to cross boundaries and create *new* identities. Foucault's understanding of freedom as self-creation requires that subjects expose themselves to new possibilities or 'limit experiences', and this leads to a suspicion of the procedures in contemporary political economies that privilege group identifications, a suspicion with many affinities to a radically liberal individualism. Seen in this light, the attempts by some on the political right to associate or to even to blame Foucault for what they see as the excesses of contemporary identity or 'woke' politics are particularly misguided.[20] The intolerance and attempts to silence alternative views, in other words 'cancel culture', are the antithesis of a perspective that stands for radical openness and where no identities are privileged or protected from contestation.

Elsewhere, with the contemporary impetus to the extension of 'bio-political' states, Foucault's accounts of the relationship between scientific authority and political power and their potential effects on the identity and freedoms of human subjects has never been more relevant. Having implemented unprecedented emergency restrictions on personal and enterprise freedom to address a global pandemic, states across the world are now being encouraged to consider far-reaching measures to address a 'global climate emergency'. This creates an important opportunity for a postmodern liberalism to ally with Foucault's thought not by denying the threats or emergencies concerned and the need for some sort of discourse around them but by problematising the underlying epistemic assumptions, by emphasising the importance of discursive and evaluative pluralism, and by showing how certain narratives and framings may be pregnant

[20] For example, Murray, D. (2022) *The War on the West*, New York: Harper Collins.

with threats to that very pluralism. Such an approach does not abandon scientific rationality per se but aims at what Foucault referred to as a 'rational critique of rational analysis' and which Hayek described as 'using reason to understand the limits of reason'.[21]

If there are compelling reasons for liberals to engage with Foucault, there are similarly important reasons for Foucauldians to engage with liberal political economy and especially the postmodern variant enunciated here. Many 'critical left' followers of Foucault in the post-structuralist tradition equate liberalism with rational choice theory and with modernist forms of political philosophy, seeing these perspectives as discourses of freedom and choice that disguise how liberal institutions entangle people and their subjectivity in a network of disciplinary and bio-political controls. By failing sufficiently to appreciate the significant differences between modernist and postmodern variants of liberalism, however, these critics chronically fail to distinguish those forms of liberal political economy and philosophy guilty of the modernist rationalism they reject from those that derive liberal conclusions from critiques of this very rationalism.[22]

Consider education, where public policy in Anglophone countries has sought to promote parental choice and to facilitate the exercise of such choice through 'league tables' that measure pupil achievements against national standardised examinations. These policies have often been promoted on rational choice and utilitarian grounds, as a way of 'incentivising' improvements in educational standards, and on liberal egalitarian or social justice grounds, as a way of increasing choice to the least advantaged and of equalising opportunities. For some Foucauldian and radical left critics, such measures represent a clear example of states having been captured by a managerialist discourse that objectivates parents and pupils as consumers and that acts as a form of disciplinary power both for educators who must submit to a parental 'gaze' and for those very parents who come to judge their own and their children's performance against the gaze of national educational standards.[23]

The problem here, however, is that this line of critique is consistent with a postmodern liberalism which sees such reforms as a species of scientistic planning and control that threatens evaluative pluralism. A 'free market' in education would have little or no place for curricular or other national standards against which the performance of all pupils and schools would be judged. Neither would such a market presuppose that education should be conducted in

[21] MF (1998) 'Structuralism and Post-Structuralism', in Rabinow, P., ed. (1998) *Aesthetics, Method and Epistemology*, New York: New Press, 441; Hayek, F. A. (1958) 'Freedom, Reason and Tradition', *Ethics*, 68 (4): 229–45, quote at 241.

[22] For example, Brown, *Undoing the Demos* and *In the Ruins of Neoliberalism.*

[23] Ball, S. 'Management as Moral Technology', in Ball, S., ed. (1990) *Foucault and Education*, London: Routledge.

disciplinary institutions known as 'schools' as opposed to other locations such as at home, online learning networks, or even places of employment. While such a regime would not eliminate the potential for capillary networks of disciplinary power across different educational sites, the capacity for these networks to exercise a totalising power/knowledge over educators, parents, and students alike might be harder to sustain than when all or most educational institutions are administered by the gaze of the state and its satellite agencies.[24] Indeed, it may be an inevitable aspect of a state that tries to incentivise improvements and to equalise opportunities that it will require a decentred network of disciplinary surveillance to monitor and to 'police' the relevant, incentives, standards, and opportunities.

By engaging with this postmodern liberalism, left social theorists might thus be encouraged to incorporate some appropriately liberal understandings of how to limit the potentially dominating effects of power into a 'left-governmentality' that may avoid the more pervasive forms of domination associated historically with socialist regimes.[25] In 1979 Foucault chided socialism for 'having no governmentality of its own' and for merely intensifying the forms of disciplinary power and bio-power experienced under liberalism.[26] More than forty years later, the radical left continues to lack a persuasive account of how highly complex socio-economic systems can be successfully coordinated without the widespread reliance on a market-based spontaneous order. Similarly, post-structuralist and critical left thinkers have failed to explain how their commitments to social justice can be achieved in the absence of networks of surveillance that seek to control the incomes, choices, and identities of people through state-organised forms of objectivation. Radical critics of the contemporary 'liberal order' might thus profit from an engagement with a postmodern liberalism that challenges contemporary political economies for being *insufficiently liberal*.

The structure of the book

Part I of the book will highlight the connections, equivalences, tensions, and possibility for productive interplay between the Foucauldian and postmodern liberal political economy perspectives to build a Foucauldian liberalism focused

[24] For example, Pennington, M. (2014) 'Against Democratic Education', *Social Philosophy and Policy*, 31 (1): 1–35. See also Tooley, J. (1995) *Disestablishing the School*, London: Routledge.

[25] See, e.g., Zamora, D., 'Finding a Left Governmentality: Foucault's Last Decade', in Sawyer and Steinmetz-Jenkins, *Foucault, Neo-Liberalism and Beyond*. See also Dean, M., 'Foucault, Ewald, Neo-liberalism, and the Left', in Zamora and Behrent, *Foucault and Neo-Liberalism*.

[26] *The Birth of Bio Politics*, 93–4.

on freedom as an open-ended practice of self-creation and re-creation in the face of power.

The elements of a Foucauldian liberalism

Chapter 2 focuses on social theory, showing that Foucault's anti-essentialist ontology of the subject is compatible with that put forward by Hayek, Oakeshott, Gaus, and key thinkers in the modern 'Austrian' tradition who reject the mechanistic and atomistic individualism of the dominant rational choice paradigm in liberal social science. Outside basic biological parameters, subjects are understood to have no underlying nature or essence but acquire their identity and categories of thought from an environment of cultural-economic power relations. While individuals are 'produced' by these cultural-economic processes, they are not determined by them. Rather, subjects can *reshape* their surroundings 'at the margin' through creative acts of 'resistance' (Foucault) or entrepreneurship (postmodern liberalism), which challenge or reinterpret the categories that constitute them and that introduce instability or disequilibria into the social realm. To deny the autonomy of the subject is not, therefore, to deny the capacity for personal agency. The chapter proceeds to show that while Foucault has an account of cultural power relations, he lacks an adequate theory of social coordination to explain how the systemic qualities of power he identifies may arise and be challenged. The latter may be afforded by attention to the signalling processes and evolutionary selection effects identified by the postmodern liberal perspective. The postmodern liberal understanding of the relationship between institutions and agency may however itself be enriched by a Foucauldian appreciation of the way that discourses whether scientific or philosophical may work to limit agency and how they can be deployed creatively as a form of entrepreneurial action.

Chapter 3 turns to epistemology and philosophy of social science, showing that Foucault and postmodern liberals share a social constructionist stance critical of positivist attempts to discern objective truths and law-like relationships in the social world. It argues that Foucauldians have reason to embrace the postmodern liberal critique of utilitarian socio-economic planning and regulation as at one with their challenge to the modernist rationalism of mainstream liberal social science. This critique offers a 'scientific' challenge to 'expert rule' thus avoiding Foucault's tendency to deny the possibility of having *any* useful knowledge about people and the world. Its post-foundational or pragmatist standpoint recognises that *all* experiences of the world must be interpreted through theories that prove themselves not in relation to an absolute conception of truth but as contingently 'better' guides to action. Accordingly, it advocates a form of competitive or fractured political economic arrangement that allows multiple truth claims—*including its own*—to be continually contested against rivals. Equally, however, this postmodern liberalism may be complemented by a Foucauldian focus on how institutionalised discourses of scientific rationalism may generate power effects that privilege claims to expert authority in ways that may limit the capacity for people to engage in entrepreneurship and opportunities for self-governance.

In their different ways the Foucauldian and postmodern liberal analyses are explicitly anti-normative or amoral in orientation. Foucault's conception of freedom is focussed on shattering pre-existing moral foundations so that new standards might emerge. For postmodern liberals meanwhile, justice does not refer to any societal end state but to institutions that facilitate the creation not only of the means to achieve specific ends but the open-ended creation of the ends themselves as well. As such, chapter 4 argues that both perspectives imply a deep scepticism towards the claims by mainstream liberal philosophy to neutrality between conceptions of the good when the institutions these liberals favour presuppose a form of ethical monism instead of an open-ended process of ethical creative destruction. In addition to threatening freedom by narrowing the scope for such experimentation, the chapter shows that the commitment to positive rights in the egalitarian liberal canon cannot be separated from the widespread use of surveillance techniques and objectivating forms of bio-power where some assume the authority to speak 'for or above others'. Though such processes are unlikely to be eliminated in *any* society, institutions that protect largely negative rights may be comparatively well placed to sustain and generate gaps in the nexus of bio-political technologies and facilitate resistance against their power effects.

Foucauldian liberalism and social critique

With the elements of a Foucauldian liberalism in place, part II of the book develops a critical political economy exploring how overlapping discourses of socio-economic scientism and positive rights that characterise contemporary governance practices may represent potentially *illiberal* constraints on freedom. These 'pastoral' or 'bio-political' *dispositifs* are based on the desire to compare, rank, and grade both people and socio-economic states, as well as justify empowering some actors to 'correct' the conduct of others. Though there are strong epistemic reasons to believe that these efforts will fail, *even on their own terms*, alignments between these discourses and between states and private and civil actors may generate 'power effects' that constrain people in socially constructed categories. This tendency is evident across multiple domains of contemporary governance and is reflected in a complex web of practices that view individual people and entire populations as variables to be observed, measured, and regulated and that discursively position some actors with the epistemic authority to do the relevant classifying and regulating. While forming classificatory schemes may be a basic aspect of how the human mind works and that people must use to navigate an uncertain environment, a Foucauldian liberalism emphasises the threats to freedom from a *monopolisation* of the classificatory and evaluative process, the practices through which correctional monopolies may arise, and the scope for them to be undermined.

Paradoxically, one area where the tendency to seek new ways of 'correcting' people and populations has arisen from the social movements that have historically fought emancipatory struggles *against* scientific constructions of race, class, gender, and sexuality. The mobilisation of civil rights, feminist, and LGBT rights movements informed by standpoint epistemologies has challenged some of the most severe forms of social domination, and this has encouraged many analysts to favour a form of 'group differentiated' democracy to reallocate resources and social status towards historically disadvantaged groups.[27] Chapter 5 argues that the danger to freedom here is that privileging group-differentiated democracy as the vehicle for the expression of identity risks the formation of internal classificatory monopolies where elites and/or majorities *within* the relevant groups use managerial power techniques to objectify and discipline individuals failing to conform to prescribed thoughts and actions. These correctional processes may limit discursive competition and work to ossify and cartelise identities both within groups and in how group members are labelled by external actors in ways inimical to the 'boundary crossing' and 'limit experiences' that Foucault saw as integral to freedom. This cultural fluidity, while not excluding group-based processes, may be dependent on maintaining a broader institutional framework for self-representation where entrepreneurs, voluntary associations, and political jurisdictions compete by offering new combinations of goods, services, and ideas that facilitate a kaleidoscope of new and shifting identity configurations.

Chapter 6 turns to a different set of threats associated with 'bio-political' efforts to manage public health. From decisions to smoke, vape, consume alcohol, or eat fatty or sugary foods, many societies have witnessed an amoeba-like growth of regulatory initiatives which it is claimed will enable individuals to 'improve' their health and that of the general population. This 'lifestyle epidemiology' has increasingly overlapped and allied itself with the newly influential discourse of behavioural economics. The latter suggests that people may not fulfil their 'true' or 'real' preferences owing to various decision-making biases that demand corrective regulatory action. The chapter argues that these discursive alliances

[27] For example, Young, I. (2000) *Inclusion and Democracy*, Oxford: Oxford University Press.

illustrate the ongoing power of scientistic modes of thought in contemporary liberal societies and the threat to pluralism and freedom they represent. The public health *dispositif* may best be understood as a form of power/knowledge that privileges regulators' understandings of what rationality requires and that may stifle the potential for ethical self-creation and self-government—threats that were especially evident during the COVID-19 pandemic.

Elsewhere, the threat to freedom from correctional *dispositifs* is nowhere more significant than in the emergent discursive coalitions that construct the problem of human-ecological order. The modern environmental movement is heavily influenced by naturalistic discourses that construct human agents as disturbing otherwise stable ecological systems, and these discourses may lead to the labelling of individuals and entire populations as 'guilty' of crimes against nature and humanity alike. Chapter 7 argues for a Foucauldian liberal scepticism of this scientific naturalism, emphasising instead the prevalence of disequilibrium and sometimes dramatic change in both the human and the non-human world that defies attempts to engage in a 'predict and control' model of socio-ecological management. This view also emphasises the importance of sustaining a discursive and institutional pluralism that allows the coexistence of rival understandings of ecological dilemmas and that sustains awareness of different ways they might be governed. Such pluralism is however threatened by what many perceive as a global environmental crisis and the bio-security state that may emerge in its wake. Whether such a state is required to ensure human and ecological welfare cannot easily be established, but should a global bio-security apparatus emerge in this regard, it may exercise unprecedented forms of bio-power, which, for good or ill, will limit the vistas that can be explored in ways deeply ambiguous in their implications for human freedom.

The power to classify certain actions as criminal, to limit the freedoms of those defined as criminals, and to subject them to correctional measures is an important illustration of how objectivation and subjectivation processes may reflect power relations between those who define criminal acts and those subjected to these definitions. Within this context, the explosion in the prison population and the growth of the 'prison-industrial complex' occurring across many liberal democracies are of significant concern because it is questionable how societies that imprison large shares of their populations, often to punish consensual acts such as the trade in and use of drugs, can be considered 'liberal' or 'free'. While some Foucauldians have argued that 'neo-liberal' discourses that seek to defend private property relations underlie the growth of the carceral state,[28]chapter 8 explores an alternative explanation which points to the role played by a scientistic bio-power and centralised- and monopolistic-funding mechanisms that

[28] For example, Harcourt, *The Illusion of Free Markets.*

shield the power/knowledge claims of politicians and criminal justice services with respect to the costs of criminalising activities.

With its critique of classificatory and pastoral monopolies, the critical liberal political economy developed in this book must, however, be wary of imposing its own gaze to determine when and where the most significant threats to freedom may arise and how they might be mitigated. Traditionally, liberals have looked to the state both as a significant threat to human liberty and as an important tool through which to protect that liberty. Similarly, for a postmodern or Foucauldian liberalism, while the state is not necessarily the source of the discourses and technologies that endanger freedom, the entanglement of those discourses and technologies with the powers that many contemporary states possess represents a uniquely significant threat to that freedom. Identifying which of the multiple entanglements among the public, private, and civil spheres are most dangerous is, however, a scientistic temptation that should be resisted. While this book will consider threats to freedom and the possible institutions that might limit them, an engagement with Foucault's perspective may require a liberalism that shifts away from global or total forms of critique to those more modest and local in their ambitions. This may mean that in the task of identifying and resisting the relationships most threatening to freedom, liberals might pay more attention to the localised struggles of entrepreneurs and civil associations that seek to run faster than those that strive to pursue and discipline them.

PART I

THE ELEMENTS OF A FOUCAULDIAN LIBERALISM

2

The Death and Life of the Subject

Power, Agency, and Liberal Political Economy

Introduction

Liberal political economy has long been challenged by 'critical theories' for grounding its social theory and philosophy on a conception of the rational, autonomous individual and for ignoring how individuals are shaped or even determined by socio-cultural forces. Many identifying with this intellectual lineage see Foucault's proclamation of 'the death of the subject' as confirmation that his oeuvre is deeply at odds with the liberal tradition. This view may also explain why liberal political economists have largely ignored Foucault's work, seeing it as at one with fundamentally 'anti-liberal' and 'anti-humanist' perspectives that deny the explanatory and the ethical significance of individual agency.

Against this background the present chapter will show that far from denying its explanatory role, a conception of individual agency is central to Foucault's analysis of power. Liberal political economy on the other hand is not defined by a belief in an autonomous rationality. The 'post-modern' stream in liberal thought understands reason as a cultural and historical product with subjects who have the potential for agency but *not* for autonomy. A proper appreciation of Foucault's ontological stance and that of this postmodern liberalism shows that both are committed to an account of 'situated agency' that challenges a clear separation between 'agency' and 'structure'.

The analysis begins by sketching Foucault's challenge to the autonomous subject in the different phases of his oeuvre. It proceeds to identify the postmodern strand in liberal political economy focussing on its conception of mind as an extension of culture and of culture as a form of evolutionary 'spontaneous order'. Subsequent sections synthesise the Foucauldian and postmodern liberal positions. Foucault's analysis is shown to offer an account of power without a properly developed theory of the processes that allow multiple nodes of power to connect and to generate systemic effects. As such, it may be strengthened by incorporating liberal political economy's focus on evolutionary processes and a greater recognition of the role that non-discursive institutions may play in facilitating or blocking cultural fluidity. For its part, postmodern liberalism has

Foucault and Liberal Political Economy. Mark Pennington, Oxford University Press. © Mark Pennington 2025.
DOI: 10.1093/9780197690550.003.0002

paid insufficient attention to 'discourses' as spontaneous order phenomena and may profit from a Foucauldian appreciation of how these 'grids of intelligibility' may affect the positionality and identity of subjects. Outlining the terms of this synthesis sets the scene for subsequent chapters that will focus on alignments between discourses and institutions that may threaten freedom, evaluative pluralism, and the exercise of creative human agency.

Foucault on the death and life of the subject

Perhaps no statement captures Foucault's contribution to debates about human agency better than his pronouncement in *The Order of Things* on the 'death of man'. There Foucault suggests that the capacity to understand oneself in distinction to others and how to act in relation to oneself and to others are constituted by historically contingent processes operating as a form of power over the individual. The latter is understood as an 'effect' of such power with no stable essence outside of these 'power-effects'. For Foucault therefore, the concept of man is an 'invention of recent date', and one that might soon be 'erased, like a face drawn in sand at the edge of the sea'.[1]

In emphasising the constitutive role of socio-cultural processes on human subjects Foucault's views must be understood in the context of wider debates within postwar continental philosophy. On one side of these were Sartre's existentialism[2] and the hermeneutic and phenomenological traditions represented by Husserl, Schutz, and Merleau-Ponty.[3] On the other were the emergent structuralist schools influenced by Marxism.[4] In Foucault's view, the former traditions saw individual actors as *autonomous* generators of meaning[5] about themselves and the external world, while the latter traditions rejected the idea of the autonomous individual in favour of a structural determinism where patterns of thought could be traced back to underlying material causes. Foucault, by contrast, rejected *both* the idea of the subject as an autonomous generator of meaning and the materialist determinism of Marxism. For Foucault, the subject is formed by a complex and often unstable and accidental set of practices operating at multiple

[1] Foucault, M. (hereafter MF) (1970) *The Order of Things*, New York: Random House, 387.

[2] Sartre, J. P. (1956) *Being and Nothingness*, New York: Washington Square Press.

[3] Husserl, E. (1970) *The Crisis of the European Sciences and Transcendental Phenomenology*, Evanston, IL: Northwestern University Press; Merleau-Ponty, M. (1962) *The Phenomenology of Perception*, London: Routledge; Schutz, A. (1967) *The Phenomenology of the Social World*, Evanston, IL: Northwestern University Press.

[4] Notably, Althusser, L. (1969) *For Marx*, London: Allen Lane.

[5] It might be argued that Foucault's critiques of phenomenology are overdone, with theorists such as Husserl and Merleau-Ponty also emphasising the inherently situated and *intersubjective* aspect of meaning rather than seeing this in narrowly individualist terms.

levels that they can never fully understand or control and yet which make possible their own thought and sense of being.

The subject and archaeology

In his 'archaeological' period from the mid-1960s through the early 1970s, Foucault focussed on how large-scale systems for the organisation of knowledge provide the historically contingent conditions that constitute thought. The Kantian *a priori*, understood as templates of order that classify experience and that persist through time, is replaced with the *historical a priori* where the forms of order structuring experience are the product of specific historical-cultural periods.[6] While the patterns that have ordered thought in the past may be discerned, it is *not* possible to project these systems forward to future historical periods. The archaeological approach thus exposes the ruptures or breaks between the various 'epistemes' that have organised knowledge across different epochs and, in the process, challenges the autonomy of the subject in the following ways.

First, Foucault emphasises the historical role that 'discourses' play in constituting the conditions of experience. Though concepts such as madness or sex refer to 'real' human phenomena, the *experience* of such phenomena cannot be separated from the discursive framework within which they are understood and 'known'. Foucault is concerned specifically with whatever it is that makes people in a historical period take certain statements about the relationship between a linguistic 'signifier' and what is 'signified' seriously. Statements about the world only have meaning against a background of other statements which themselves only have meaning as part of a broader 'discursive formation' that specifies 'truth conditions'. Discursive formations in Foucault's account *create* the objects of which they speak[7]—*including human subjects*. Such formations are not reducible to individual speech acts but are united by rules governing the formation of statements and objects such as those concerning questions of madness, gender, or sexuality—rules of which the participants to discourse are largely *unaware*. It is not, therefore, subjects who give meaning to discourses but discourses that constitute people's awareness of themselves and of the world.

[6] This period covers *The Order of Things*; *The Archaeology of Knowledge* (1972) New York: Harper and Row; and *The Birth of the Clinic* (1973), New York: Vintage Books. For discussions of this period see Dreyfus, H., and Rabinow, P. (1983) *Michel Foucault: Beyond Structuralism and Hermeneutics*, Chicago: University of Chicago Press, esp. chaps. 2–4; Prado, C. (2006) *Searle and Foucault on Truth*, Cambridge: Cambridge University Press, esp. chap. 3, 72–6. See also Oksala, J. (2005) *Foucault and Freedom*, Cambridge: Cambridge University Press; and McNay, L. (1994) *Foucault: A Critical Introduction*, Cambridge: Polity.

[7] MF *The Archaeology of Knowledge*, 47.

Archaeology thus 'unearths' and describes the discursive rules that have governed different historical periods. The rules in question are not those of grammatical structure (langue) or surface speaking (parole) but refer to the way that different statements relate to each other and that affect what kind of statements can be uttered and listened to. They are not transcendent features conditioning the formation of acceptable statements across *all* periods of time, as in structural determinist analysis such as classical Marxism.[8] Rather, they are historically *specific* with different rules operative in different epochs or epistemes. Crucially, each historical-cultural period is characterised by only *one* episteme—and it is the rules of the relevant epistemes which explain why seemingly disparate and autonomous fields of enquiry such as biology, political economy, and linguistics develop similar conceptual and argumentative structures. Thus, in each of these fields or their antecedents the renaissance episteme reasoned through rules of resemblance; the classical episteme was governed by rules of difference reflected in systems of tabulation and classification that compared the 'essences' of various objects; and the modern episteme is characterised by a focus on organic structures related to each other through functional or law-like regularities.

Second, by emphasising 'epistemic breaks' between different epochs, archaeology demonstrates that the evolution of thought is not one of linear progression. Perceptual structures are reflective of more, or less, arbitrary shifts and reconfigurations of the discursive formations through which thought is organised and expressed. These shifts mean that subjects born into different epochs use different and incommensurable forms of reasoning. Medical practitioners in the Renaissance era, for example, worked with categories for the understanding and treatment of disease that were scarcely comprehensible to those occupying such roles in the classical era that dawned only a few decades later.

Third, by emphasising the scale of these ruptures Foucault highlights the difficulty of attributing the movement from one episteme to another, to a particular originator or set of originators. That there is no subject or group of subjects that can be designated as causing the relevant epistemic shifts brings out the possibility that the process of social change may be *autonomous* from the purposes, actions, and beliefs of subjects.

[8] *The Order of Things* is often depicted as a quasi-structuralist work, but Foucault vehemently rejected the structuralist label seeing the search for underlying historical laws as grounded in the discourse of the modern episteme. Hence the quip that Marxism belongs in the nineteenth-century episteme 'as a fish in water'—chap. 8, 262. Nonetheless, in his own attempt to discern specific 'blocks' of history governed by orderly 'epistemes', Foucault might be considered to swim in a mode of thought that seeks to find stronger 'ordering' processes than might in fact be operative. Those who emphasise a greater level of conceptual contestation and question the existence of singular epistemes might be considered more consistently 'postmodern' or 'post-structuralist' than Foucault himself. In his conversations with Dreyfus and Rabinow, Foucault concedes that in this period his work may have been unduly haunted by the presence of structuralism, in *Michel Foucault*.

In drawing attention to the historically specific categories operative 'above' individuals in this way, Foucault's archaeologies have been widely criticised for downplaying pluralism *within* the historical periods they analyse.[9] The notion of *singular* epistemes has been extensively challenged with critics demonstrating the existence of competing and overlapping systems of thought in the eras examined, albeit often within the context of dominant traditions.[10] Others have questioned the idea of epistemic 'breaks', emphasising how some concepts and patterns of thought have retained significance *across* historical periods.[11] Finally, and perhaps most important, the exclusive focus on discursive formations has been challenged for suggesting that there is nothing 'outside of discourse' and for failing to appreciate the role that *non-discursive* practices, institutions, and events may have on discursive evolution.[12] In their influential exegesis, endorsed by Foucault himself,[13] Dreyfus and Rabinow argue that the account of discursive formations is circular. If the rules of a discourse are as significant as the archaeological method suggests then the concept of change let alone an epistemic break cannot be explained. Either the rules of the episteme determine its future development such that an epistemic break becomes impossible to conceive or it must be admitted that discursive rules may be reorganised in response to factors that cannot themselves be explained by such rules. Foucault makes the error of equating observable regularities with rules that generate these regularities—and since there is nothing outside of discourse, the rules of discourse somehow regulate themselves.

The subject and genealogy

Perhaps because of these difficulties Foucault's work shifted in the mid-late 1970s to the role played by a more fragmented, plural though interconnected set of discourses in fields such as criminology, sexuality, and public health. Though the focus on an historical-discursive context was maintained, this was no longer considered to operate in a strictly rule-governed manner. Moreover, the works of this period focus explicitly on the relationships between 'discursive practices' and the social and economic institutions, or 'non-discursive practices', with

[9] For an account of these critiques see, e.g., Gutting, G. (1989) *Michel Foucault's Archaeology of Scientific Reason*, Cambridge: Cambridge University Press.

[10] For a summary see, Merquior, J. (1985/91) *Foucault*, Hammersmith and London: Fontana Press, chap. 5.

[11] Ibid.

[12] This line of critique is developed forcefully by Dreyfus and Rabinow, *Michel Foucault*, esp. chap. 4.

[13] Foucault's endorsement of *Beyond Structuralism and Hermeneutics* reads: "This book presents a very clear and intelligent analysis of the work I have attempted to do. Resolving many misunderstandings, it offers an accurate, synthetic view."

which they interact and how these are infused with the exercise of power. The latter is seen as a key factor influencing the development of discourse rather than discursive evolution floating above social institutions and practices. Though operating at a lower scale of analysis, the resultant genealogical studies continue nonetheless to question the autonomy of the subject by focussing on how discourse is 'deployed' as part of 'strategies of power and government' to influence others and the often unintended 'power effects' that these strategies generate.[14]

Throughout his genealogies Foucault highlights the 'objectivating' role of 'disciplines' associated with discourses that emerged from the Enlightenment era in an attempt by various actors to 'govern' or to 'conduct the conduct' of others at multiple different scales. 'Government' here refers to *all* attempts to influence the mentality, behaviour, and bodily comportment of others whether in the home or family, academic disciplines, places of employment, or specific territorial spaces. Many of the relevant techniques, such as those documented in Foucault's account of the modern prison, had historical antecedents in the practices of monasteries, military barracks, and schoolrooms but with the emergent techniques 'folding back' into these other domains. For Foucault, what distinguishes the period of Enlightenment or modernity is a shift from predominantly religious conduct-shaping to a 'disciplinary power' informed by 'knowledges' or 'savoirs' that attempt to generate regularised behaviours or 'docile bodies' often geared towards increasing productivity and wealth, improving hygiene, or maintaining public order. Employers, for example, have often adopted the disciplinary techniques found in military establishments or in the prison system to eliminate theft and to increase worker productivity. Similarly, examinations in schools to grade and distinguish individuals are often mirrored in the physical separation of ability groups into different rooms or buildings or across different schools—much as the classification of the mentally ill has often led to their physical separation in asylums.

Hierarchical observation and differentiation against a norm are central to these techniques and work by continually comparing categories such as good and bad citizens, the productive and the unproductive, the sane and the insane, the healthy and the unhealthy, and normal and abnormal expressions of sexuality. These 'dividing practices' distinguish people from one another, often in fine detail, by placing them within a classificatory or statistical grid, and this leads in turn to processes of 'subjectivation' which generate the sense of self. Crucially, the power exercised by these techniques is 'economised' because as disciplines and their associated discourses become entrenched in the social landscape and

[14] The genealogical period refers mostly to *Discipline and Punish* (1975/77) New York: Pantheon; the first volume of *The History of Sexuality* (1976/1998) London: Penguin; and to various interviews and essays compiled in *Power-Knowledge: Selected Interviews and Other Writings* (1980) New York: Pantheon.

the sense of being watched, whether real or imagined, is omnipresent, subjects increasingly enforce the relevant disciplines upon themselves through a form of routinised action—which unintentionally perpetuates the norms in question. In Foucault's view power is exercised over subjects primarily in the form of these routines.

In emphasising routinised processes Foucault does not suggest that they merely attach or bolt themselves on to an underlying or core identity but that the position of individuals in relation to these 'technologies of government' is what *constitutes* their very subjectivity. As he explains:

> The individual is not to be conceived as a sort of elementary nucleus . . . on which power comes to fasten . . . In fact, it is already one of the prime effects of power that certain bodies, certain gestures, certain discourses, certain desires, come to be identified and constituted as individuals.[15]

This view does not deny the existence of biology per se but maintains that there is no unchanging essence or human 'nature' *separable* from the effects of discourse and power.[16] The latter point distinguishes Foucault's account from Marxist and some rational choice theories. Where such theories understand power as an imposition on an underlying essence, for Foucault the individual historically subjugated by a particular disciplinary-discursive regime is also a *product* of that very regime. Excepting a thin set of biological parameters, there is no authentic essence that can be said to have been 'repressed'. Power is a productive force that *creates* the sense of individuality. As discourses and disciplines gain currency, the identities, and positionalities they imprint on subjects through the actions they allow, prohibit, or correct, become habituated and internalised to the point that they may be *experienced* by individuals *as if* they reflect an essential or natural aspect of themselves or of the world. Power is also productive in the sense that it entails practices that may enable people to achieve things (such as being effective athletes or productive workers) that might not otherwise be possible.

Though discursive power arises from multiple attempts to exert influence over others, Foucault's account is not functionalist in the manner of neo-Marxist and rational choice theories, which interpret the discursive realm as an epiphenomenal effect of underlying or real interests. Having briefly adopted Marxist-sounding categories prior to *Discipline and Punish,* Foucault rejects

[15] MF (2000) *Michel Foucault the Essential Works*, vol. 3: *Power*, ed. Gordon, C., London, Allen Lane: Penguin Press.

[16] For a recent discussion of this distinction see Bagg, S. (2021) 'Beyond the Search for the Subject: An Anti-Essentialist Ontology for Liberal Democracy', *European Journal of Political Theory*, 20 (2): 208–31.

a 'hermeneutics of suspicion' where actors deliberately hide the true or 'real' meaning of their actions. The genealogical period sees subjects and their interests emerging from more, or less, historically accidental discursive and behavioural practices and their interaction with other such practices. In market economies for example, there is no real or underlying capitalist or proletarian interest apart from the different and perhaps contradictory discourses and techniques that constitute those interests.[17] Practices become established through historical accidents that may then work to shape or *produce* the interests and identity of a particular class or group, and once established they may be used to defend or advance those interests. Thus, members of the emergent eighteenth-century bourgeoisie that sought the introduction of factory discipline over the working class had themselves been constituted as subjects by similar techniques which led them to a particular understanding of the value of work discipline and an 'orderly' life. Similarly, the working class were able to evade for a significant period the discipline associated with the '*dispositif* of sexuality', which the ruling classes had first 'tried out on themselves' under the influence of a science of sexuality propagated by new groupings of experts.[18]

On the decentred character of power

If Foucault's genealogies question the autonomy of the subject, then so too they challenge the role of individual or collective agency in the operation of power regimes. Foucault defines power as 'the name one attributes to a complex strategic situation in a particular society'.[19] Crucially, the character of this 'complex strategic situation' cannot be attributed to the intentions and actions of any single 'originator' or to any specific locus or 'origin'. Three aspects of the resulting 'decentred' understanding of power thus emerge.

First, power is not held by specific individuals or groups but works through chain-like or network effects. As people adopt certain discourses and disciplines, they work *impersonally* to condition the available actions of others, often without those concerned being aware of these effects. In the case of education and employment for example, the ability of educators in schools and universities to exercise discipline over students is dependent on the attitudes and routines of parents and on the actions of employers in recognising approved qualifications in their hiring practices—and vice versa.

[17] On this point see MF (1976) *Society Must Be Defended*, London: Penguin, esp. 32–3.
[18] Foucault, *The History of Sexuality*, 162.
[19] Ibid., 93.

Second, the power manifested in such networks does not emanate from any single point in the social order. Rather, it emerges from multiple 'decentred', and at times contradictory, attempts by actors to assert their place in society and to 'conduct the conduct' of others through various forms of 'governmentality'.

Third, though power relations emerge in part from goal-oriented action by specific people or groups, there is no identifiable 'author', institution, or place to which they can be traced. The discourses and disciplines producing people's patterns of thought, positionality, and interests are largely *unintended consequences* of multiple attempts to affect the conduct of others. While the interests of subjects are constituted at the intersection of discursive and non-discursive practices as people advance those interests *within* these practices, they also work in decentred vein to *reshape* them in *unanticipated* ways. Power 'circulates' or 'flows' through people and is modified by them in multiple strategic plays or relays.

Foucault uses the term microphysics or micro-analytics of power to explain how power *morphs* as it interacts with the agents subject to it and with small variations in the details of the environment in question.[20] He also speaks of 'non-subjective intentionality' and of power 'being on manoeuvres' to describe the 'swarming processes' through which power relations emerge and re-emerge as disciplines and techniques are copied, adapted, and spread.[21] What matters is that while some such attempts to spread disciplines are driven by goal-oriented actions, only *some* of their results will be intended. Management consultants, for example, may not anticipate how the uptake of their practices in education and local government may mutate within those systems and how these mutations may spill out to generate new practices beyond. Localised strategies played out within specific discourses and disciplines may 'swarm' from multiple points linking to generate an overlapping chain of practices that have *not* been formulated by anyone but that may be experienced by others as a form of empowerment or constraint, depending on their positionality within the system of practices. Foucauldian power then has effects *over and above* those attributable to discrete individual actions and cannot be reduced to a mere sum of such actions. A corollary is that while power relations may have the *appearance* of a coherent structure, there is no single purpose, intention, or meaning that underlies this structure.

[20] Ibid.

[21] For a discussion see, e.g., Pickett, B. (2006) *On the Use and Abuse of Foucault for Politics*, Oxford: Lexington Books.

Agency, power, and interaction effects

Critics of Foucault maintain that his analyses give such prominence to discourses and disciplinary practices in constituting subjects that they cannot account for the significant variations in the beliefs and actions of those similarly positioned in the same discursive or disciplinary formations.[22] Likewise, many argue that it is untenable to make use of metaphors such as 'tactics', 'deployments', and 'manoeuvres' of power while denying that any group of actors is responsible for bringing about specific 'strategic' or 'systemic effects'.[23] On this reading, the admission that he had previously "insisted too much on ... techniques of domination" rather than techniques of 're-subjectification' or 'self-creation',

> which permit individuals to effect a certain number of operations on their own bodies, on their souls, on their own thoughts, on their own conduct, and this in a manner so as to transform themselves

was an abandonment by Foucault of his earlier 'anti-humanism' and a belated acknowledgement that the autonomy of 'the subject' must be kept alive in some capacity.[24]

Now, while there can be no doubt that choice-oriented action receives greater emphasis in Foucault's final works, the suggestion that this represented an ontological volte-face is to confuse rejecting the autonomy of the subject with that of rejecting human agency per se. As Oksala argues, the common thread connecting *all* Foucault's work, whether the archaeologies, the genealogies, or the final works on the 'care of the self', is that subjects are formed by cultural categories *not of their own making*. What Foucault continued to reject is the notion of an underlying human essence distinguishable from the effects of culture and history.[25] The self, created through techniques of 're-subjectification', is one where the elements refashioned are the *products of power* and not of an 'authentic' or 'underlying self'.[26]

To recognise the 'downward causation' effects of culture, history, and discursive power relations in this way is, however, fully compatible with actors making creative and nondetermined moves *within* the boundaries set by the 'strategic

[22] For example, Bevir, M. (1999) 'Foucault and Critique: Deploying Agency Against Autonomy', *Political Theory*, 27 (1): 65–84.

[23] On this critique, see esp. Taylor, C. (1984) 'Foucault on Freedom and Truth', *Political Theory*, 12 (2): 152–83.

[24] Quoted in Miller, J. (1993) *The Passion of Michel Foucault*, New York: Simon and Schuster, 321–2.

[25] Oksala, *Foucault and Freedom*, 78–81. See also Bagg, 'Beyond'.

[26] On this see Foucault's critique of Sartre on the meaning of self-creation, in Dreyfus and Rabinow, *Michel Foucault*, 237.

field' of power and thus to generate processes of 'upward causation'. While subjects face cultural-discursive constructs that constitute themselves and their environment, much as they face a physical environment, they can manipulate and *subvert* that environment either deliberately or by accident in ways that may work *incrementally* to transform it. Indeed, the whole notion of a micro-analytics of power is concerned with the way that discourses and disciplines *morph* in a decentred vein as they pass *through* subjects, a morphing that would not be possible if there was no agency involved.[27] More broadly, while supra-individual practices work to constitute individuals, those ideas and practices are given life *by* individual agents. Discourses *do not act*—different 'bits' of discourses are interpreted and transmitted between individuals in families, schools, and workplaces. To suggest otherwise would imply the existence of a sovereign site from which all the elements of a discursive formation can be seen and acted upon.

What becomes explicit in the essay 'The Subject and Power' is how multiple acts of 'resistance' generate fluidity and disequilibrium in power relations.[28] Foucault is clear here to distinguish between states of slavery or imprisonment, which eradicate the scope for subjects to exercise agency, and power relations that are applied to 'free agents'.[29] Were *Discipline and Punish* gives the impression that 'technologies of government' align into a deterministic, 'total system' of domination or a 'carceral archipelago', power relations are now understood as complex and fragile with discourses and disciplines establishing themselves through highly contingent and often accidental circumstances that could have turned out differently. Correspondingly, there are usually sufficient gaps, anomalies, or ambiguities within a discursive formation to allow for creative challenges to the status quo. Thus, many gays and lesbians whose sexuality has been categorised as deviant or unnatural have sought to appropriate the discourse of scientific naturalism to make a case for the natural basis of homosexuality.[30] Irrespective of whether these claims are 'true', they illustrate that subjects can work creatively to shift the terms of a prevailing discourse *from within* to secure greater recognition and status. Foucault refers to this process as the 'tactical polyvalence of discourses',[31] wherein normalisation strategies continually generate resistance from those labelled as deviant or subordinate, and these acts may shift the boundaries of what is considered normal or deviant. What is resisted, as well as who is resisting, is subject to constant change, with new boundaries

[27] Bagg's 'Beyond' is especially clear on this point.
[28] MF (1982) 'The Subject and Power', *Critical Inquiry* 8 (4): 777–95.
[29] Ibid., 790.
[30] On this, see, e.g., Lemke, T. (2019) *Foucault's Analysis of Modern Governmentality*, London: Verso, 324–9.
[31] Foucault, *The History of Sexuality*, 100–2.

generating further and unexpected directions of resistance in a constant tussle between equilibrating and disequilibrating forces.

By contrast, states of domination arise when an otherwise fluid, plural, or contradictory set of discourses align or crystallise with each other and with the juridical powers of states. While states have no stable 'essence' outside the discourses in circulation, should their juridical powers be colonised by a particular discourse or coalition of discourses, this may lead to the emergence of a more stable 'governmentalisation of power', or *dispositif* that narrows the scope for challenge. In the case of sexuality, for example, wherever same-sex relationships are not only marginalised by dominant discourses but are also outlawed by them, then resistance against such discourses may be that much harder.

To focus on the role of states in this context does not, however, contradict the decentred account of power. As Dean and Villadsen argue, the accounts of sovereign power which Foucault criticises are ones that understand the sovereign's power as exercised *according to his own will.*[32] By contrast, Foucault highlights the micro-level or 'ascending processes' that *connect* decentred forms of power with sovereign or state authority. In his discussion of the emergence of disciplinary power in eighteenth-century England and France, for example, Foucault, shows that many mechanisms of social control arose initially from spontaneous groupings in civil society operating *outside* the state judicial system, and it was these 'policing mechanisms from below' that provided the breeding ground for the subsequent state-controlled apparatus of order, hygiene, and discipline. Similarly, in many instances, the spread of these practices followed demands *from decentralised agents* for the state to enforce disciplines that *could not* effectively be sustained by the actors themselves.[33] As Foucault understands his work on prisons, madness, and sexuality, what was involved

> was always the identification of the gradual, piecemeal but continuous takeover by the state of a number of practices, ways of doing things, or if you like, governmentalities. The problem of bringing under state control, of 'statification' (*etatisation*) was the heart of the questions I have tried to address.[34]

Positioning his work 'beyond structuralism and hermeneutics', Dreyfus and Rabinow argue that Foucault was searching for a form of situated agency which neither reduces social phenomena to structural determinants exercising causality independent of human agency nor reflects a similarly reductive focus on

[32] Dean, M., and Villadsen, K. (2016) *State Phobia and Civil Society: The Political Legacy of Michel Foucault*, Stanford: Stanford University Press, 60–1.
[33] Ibid.
[34] MF (1978–79/2008) *The Birth of Bio Politics*, London: Palgrave Macmillan, 77.

subjective individual meanings and intentions as the *sole* generators of social order.[35] What Foucault's 'analytics of power' highlight is the importance of *interaction effects* combining 'upward' *and* 'downward' forms of causation, where the latter are understood as nondeterministic, *supra-individual* phenomena that emerge as *unintended consequences* from the localised strategies of multiple actors.[36] *All* acts have unintended consequences for the actions of others, and this is what makes it hard to discern any originating agency underlying social phenomena, in general, and power relations, in particular. As such, Foucauldian ontology shows some striking similarities with an important strand in liberal political economy, and it is these affinities that will now be examined.

Postmodern liberalism and the non-autonomy of the subject

Though developing in the context of different debates, the focus on situated agency and unintended social phenomena indicates the potential for a close affiliation between Foucault's thought and aspects of the liberal tradition. Establishing this potential is an important element in making the case for a Foucauldian or postmodern liberalism because it is often assumed that liberal social theory depends on a conception of the autonomous individual whom Foucault utterly rejects.

Foucault's oeuvre is typically positioned at the radical end of 'critical left' perspectives, challenging the ontology of liberal political economy and the normative implications often derived from it. Specifically, Foucauldians evince a scepticism of the rational actor or *Homo economicus* models that dominate liberal social science. In the latter, outcomes are explained as equilibria arising from the interaction of individuals, each of whom maximises their interests and preferences—which in turn reflects an autonomous rationality and an underlying nature *pre-existing* any social context. Social institutions such as property rights, democracy, and law affect the capacity of actors to secure their preferences by shaping the incentives that people face, but these institutions are the product of conscious rational choice where those designing or choosing them fully anticipate their effects or where the range of any uncertainty is also subject to rational calculation on probabilistic lines. The effects in question may be those anticipated by a group or class of rulers that adopts rules to sustain its capacity to maximise its interests by exploiting those over whom it rules. Alternatively, they may reflect a more benevolent anticipation that a set of rules will prove conducive

[35] Dreyfus and Rabinow, 'Introduction', *Michel Foucault*.
[36] Prado, *Searle and Foucault on Truth* (77–81) is especially clear on the role of unintended consequences in Foucault's social theory.

to the maximisation of the general welfare.[37] From a Foucauldian perspective, however, far from representing a universally valid account of human action, this model of the maximising individual is likely to be a product of the discourses of possessive individualism and consumerism routinised and institutionalised in Western capitalist societies.

Mind and culture

Though the theories frequently criticised by Foucauldians in this way have played a significant role in liberal thought, they stand in sharp contrast to what will be referred to here as the postmodern strand in liberal political economy. The components of this tradition are most discernible in Hayek's writings and others in the modern 'Austrian' tradition, such as Ludwig Lachmann, Don Lavoie, Deirdre McCloskey, Emily Chamlee-Wright, and Virgil Storr, and outside of economics in the works of the political philosophers Michael Oakeshott, Gerald Gaus, and Chandran Kukathas. Though there are important differences between these contributors, all work with a *culturally conditioned* view of the subject that rejects what Hayek dubs as the 'bogey of the economic man' and Oakeshott refers to as the 'unencumbered intellect',[38] of the *Homo economicus.* This postmodern tradition is explicit in recognising that outside basic biological needs such as those for food, shelter, and sex, the tastes, values, and preferences that motivate action are *not* a reflection of underlying human essences but are acquired from the socio-cultural environment through a partially *unconscious* process of imitation and emulation.[39] Crucially, it is not only tastes and interests that are so constituted but also much of the capacity to engage in reasoned thought.

Postmodern liberals reject the Cartesian conception of mind, where knowledge is considered to reflect 'internal' mental states, favouring an 'externalist' conception where both the physical and cultural environment are understood

[37] There are numerous works encompassed by this general description. Representative examples include North, D., and Thomas, R. (1973) *The Origins of the Western World*, Cambridge: Cambridge University Press; North, D., and Weingast, B. (1989) 'Constitutions and Credible Commitment: The Evolution of Institutions of Public Choice in 17th Century England', *Journal of Economic History*, 49: 803–32; and more recently Acemoglu, D., and Robinson, J. (2013) *Why Nations Fail*, London: Profile Books. Most works within public choice theory are explicitly formulated in these terms—see, e.g., Buchanan, J., and Tullock, G. (1962) *The Calculus of Consent*, Ann Arbor: University of Michigan Press; Olson, M. (1967) *The Logic of Collective Action*, Cambridge, MA: Harvard University Press.

[38] Hayek, F. A., 'Individualism: True and False', in Hayek, F. A., *Individualism and Economic Order*, Chicago: University of Chicago Press. Oakeshott, M. (1962/1991) *Rationalism in Politics*, Indianapolis, IN: Liberty Fund.

[39] See also Hayek, F. A., 'The Non Sequitur of the Dependence Effect', in Hayek, F. A. (1967) *Studies in Philosophy, Politics and Economics*, London: Routledge. Hayek, F. A. (1960) *The Constitution of Liberty*, London: Routledge, chaps. 2–4.

as causal determinants of the content of individual brains. As does Kant, this view sees the mind as a complex classification system with an innate capacity to categorise and order experience. Unlike Kant, however, postmodern liberals share Foucault's view that the classifications the mind deploys are *historically specific* to the socio-cultural environment into which it is born and in which it continues to be immersed.[40] Rather than encoding everything themselves, the capacity for agents to operate in the world is augmented by drawing on a rule-guided or extended cultural intelligence. People are embedded in overlapping systems of rules, symbols, and signs that guide and constrain their behaviour—often unconsciously—and which they unintentionally perpetuate. This propensity to follow rules and routines, even when their character is not fully comprehended, is illustrated by such phenomena as the ability to speak a language intelligibly *without* consciously knowing the rules of the relevant grammar.

This emphasis on unconscious rule-following and of systems of rules developing beyond the immediate apprehension of those immersed within them is thus highly congruent with Foucault's archaeological contention that social participants are often *unaware* of the rule-governed nature of the modes of thought that constitute their subjectivity. People are understood to follow discursive and non-discursive practices and traditions they find 'given' in the environment and that seem to be successful for neighbouring agents as a way of coping with uncertainty. In the case of norms of gender and sexuality, for example, though sex differences may be 'real' the clothes that people wear, the bodily comportments they adopt, and the roles they play in socio-economic life will to a large extent be picked up from the social environment rather than reflecting some underlying truth or essence. Styles of dress identifying a person as 'male', or a particular 'type of male' may, for example, reduce the likelihood that people seeking sex will be rebuffed. This rule-following/routinised behaviour allows agents to operate in the world without the need to start from scratch in creating the basis for social interaction. This postmodern liberal view thus has a close affinity with Judith Butler's Foucauldian account of gender and sexual performativity where people are 'scripted into' or 'take up' roles such as 'masculine', 'feminine', 'heterosexual', or 'homosexual' rather than these necessarily reflecting 'who or what they are'.[41] Crucially, however, the relevant rules are not necessarily chosen for a specific purpose. People are born into rules, techniques

[40] See, Hayek, F. A. (1952) *The Sensory Order*, Chicago: University of Chicago Press. Hayek, F. A. (1967) 'Rules, Perception, and Intelligibility', in *Studies in Philosophy, Politics and Economics*. For accounts of Hayek's externalist view of mind see Burczak, T. (1994) 'The Postmodern Moments of F. A. Hayek's Economics', *Economics and Philosophy*, 10: 31–58. On the similarities between Hayek and Oakeshott in this regard, see Marsh, L. (2012) 'Hayek and Oakeshott: Situating the Mind', in Franco, P. and Marsh, L., eds. (2012) *A Companion to Michael Oakeshott*, University Park: Penn State University Press.

[41] Butler, J. (2006) *Gender Trouble*, London: Routledge.

of thought and cultural practices, and it is the practices themselves that enable them to make choices and that set parameters around those choices—or in Foucauldian terms, they discipline choices. Culture conditions what is thought possible and chosen but is not itself consciously chosen.

Where Foucault sees thought as shaped, though *not determined* by discursive formations, postmodern liberalism views the mind as a classification system constituted by multiple and often competing 'streams of tradition'.[42] This focus on competing 'streams' places its analysis closer to the more fractured account of discourse offered by the genealogical Foucault. Individuals are not autonomous agents with a rationality separate from their cultural milieu. Neither however, are they determined by that milieu. Agents can *choose* whether to act as 'docile bodies' merely accepting and perpetuating the traditions in which they are embedded, or they can *challenge* or *resist* aspects of them through entrepreneurial action. Creative agency can be exercised *within and across* traditions as individuals 'play' with the culturally acquired practices that structure and organise thought, and as they encounter new or anomalous events and experiences such agency may generate mutations and variations that contribute to the evolution of new discursive and non-discursive patterns.

The concept of the extended, or external, mind does not therefore imply the presence of some collective group subject that pursues ends separate from those of its members. Owing to the limits of human intelligence, subjects must always rely on and work within rules and practices *not of their own making*. As in Foucault's decentred account of power, while the rules and categories structuring individual action are socially constituted, they cannot be reduced to the actions, meanings, and intentions of specific individuals or groups or projections from a sovereign centre of control. Institutions such as language, norms of gender and sexuality, money, private property, and market prices have no 'author'. Such institutions are neither natural *nor* artificial—they cannot be reduced to individual intentions or meanings but are social precisely because they emerge as the result of no one's intentions and meanings. This idea is encapsulated in the recognition that a significant class of phenomena are *the results of human action but not of human design*, and they have effects distinct from the actions of the elements from which they are composed. As Hayek puts it,

> The mind is embedded in a traditional impersonal structure of learnt rules, and its capacity to order experience is an acquired replica of cultural patterns which every individual mind finds given ... To put it differently, mind can exist only as part of another independently existing distinct structure or order, though that

[42] For example, Hayek, F. A. (1958) 'Freedom, Reason and Tradition', *Ethics*, 68 (4): 229–45. See also his *The Constitution of Liberty*, chaps. 2–4.

> order persists and develops only because millions of minds constantly absorb and modify parts of it.[43]

Not only does this perspective reject the atomism of rational choice theory and the holistic structuralism of Marxism, but it also challenges *all* social science accounts that posit a divide between agency and structure. Postmodern liberalism is thus at one with Foucault and contemporary 'continental' social theorists, such as Bruno Latour,[44] in maintaining that there is no independent structure that can be separated from the effects of agency and there is no agency that can be separated from the effects of structure—where the latter is understood as an emergent and unintended property of multiple individual acts.

Returning to the example of gender and sexuality, on this view individuals who describe themselves as 'queer' or 'non-binary' may be considered as 'norm entrepreneurs' who challenge the socially routinised categories of homosexuality and heterosexuality or who disrupt performative stereotypes of male and female 'normalcy'.[45] While none of these individual rebellions may work to transform the relevant norms whole cloth, the effect of any one challenge may make it easier for subsequent challenges to proceed, with multiple such acts contributing incrementally to the emergence of new and often *unanticipated* sexual-ordering practices. Recognising the role of individual agency in this sense does not, therefore, imply that the relevant norms can be traced to a specific 'author' or 'inventor'.

Similar processes are captured in the understanding of market-based coordination and disruption. Faced with a prevailing set of market prices, some people may act as routinised price 'takers' unintentionally reproducing a given market structure, while others may exercise creative agency by challenging or disrupting established prices. An entrepreneur may perceive a creative gap in a market and by acting on this perception may create new knowledge that otherwise might not have been produced. The profits (and losses) generated by such actions may also set in motion 'swarming processes' as neighbouring actors imitate profitable ventures and avoid loss makers. The resulting coordination represents a 'rough-and-ready' patterning rather than a general equilibrium or fully integrated system that Foucault terms a 'carceral archipelago', precisely because competition between entrepreneurs occurs under uncertain conditions where agents cannot fully anticipate the actions of their exchange partners or of

[43] Hayek, F. A. (1982) *Law, Legislation and Liberty*, London: Routledge, 157.

[44] See esp. Latour, B. (2005) *Reassembling the Social: An Introduction to Actor-Network Theory*, Oxford: Oxford University Press.

[45] See, e.g., Pils, R., and Schoenegger, P. (2021) 'On the Epistemological Similarities Between Market Liberalism and Standpoint Theory', *Episteme*, online, https://doi.org/10.1017/epi.2021.13. See also Malamet, A., and Novak, M. (2023) 'Gender as a Discovery Process: Social Construction, Markets and Gender', *Cosmos and Taxis*, 11 and 12: 1–15.

other actors in the social environment.[46] This is a profoundly different account of market coordination from that offered by the dominant rational choice model in neo-classical economics. While the latter is consistent with viewing coordinative processes as a series of decentralised relationships, it views decision-making as mechanical in character. Paradoxically, in rational choice models agents do not 'choose'. Each node is presented with decentralised but objective data about costs, prices, and substitutes, with utility-maximising actors 'computing' clear solutions to constrained optimisation problems that at both micro- and macro-levels yield a determinate equilibrium state. As Shackle puts it:

> Conventional economics is not about choice, but about acting according to necessity. Economic man obeys the dictates of reason, follows the logic of choice. To call this conduct choice is surely to misuse words, when we suppose that to him the ends among which he can select and the criteria of selection are given, and the means to each end known . . . Choice in such a theory is empty.[47]

In contrast to this micro-level structuralism, the postmodern liberal view understands actors as creative, and this creativity engenders a 'kaleidic' quality to socio-economic relations where ordering or patterning forces, though identifiable, are temporary.[48] This account thus provides a socio-economic parallel to Foucault's later analysis of how resistance generates cultural and discursive fluidity. Far from a seamless equilibrium, markets offer arenas of contestation and struggle. Consumers, for example, are not merely passive agents submitting to and reproducing the effects of advertising but may challenge entrepreneurial expectations by rearranging their consumption plans in unexpected ways. Likewise, while many entrepreneurs may passively accept current market prices or management practices, others may challenge or 'resist' them in ways

[46] Hayek's account of market coordination and its differences with neo-classical conceptions are set out in the essays 'Economics and Knowledge', 'The Use of Knowledge in Society', and 'The Meaning of Competition', all contained in the collection *Individualism and Economic Order.* See also, Hayek, F. A. 'Competition as a Discovery Process', in Hayek, F. A. (1978) *New Studies in Philosophy, Politics, Economics and the History of Ideas*, London: Routledge.

[47] Shackle, G. (1969) *Decision, Order and Time in Human Affairs*, Cambridge: Cambridge University Press, 272–3.

[48] Representative works here include Lachmann, L. (1970) *The Legacy of Max Weber*, London: Heinemann; Lachmann, L. (1986) *The Market as an Economic Process*, Oxford: Basil Blackwell; Lavoie, D. (1985) *Rivalry and Central Planning: The Socialist Calculation Debate Reconsidered*, Cambridge: Cambridge University Press; Lavoie, D. (1985) *National Economic Planning: What Is Left?* Cambridge, MA: Ballinger Press; Shackle, G. (1972) *Epistemics and Economics*, Cambridge: Cambridge University Press. See also in this vein O'Driscoll, G., and Rizzo, M. (2015) *Austrian Economics Re-Examined: The Economics of Time and Ignorance*, London: Routledge; Buchanan, J., and Vanberg, V. (1991) 'The Market as a Creative Process', *Economics and Philosophy*, 7 (2): 167–86; Buchanan, J., and Vanberg, V. (2002) 'Constitutional Implications of Radical Subjectivism', *Review of Austrian Economics*, 15 (2–3): 121–9.

that reorientate the competitive environment—often in ways that they do not anticipate.

This is why the neo-classical concept of perfect competition wherein no actor or firm can exert a significant impact on a market is rejected as both an inaccurate depiction of market processes and as an inappropriate normative standard against which to judge them. Perceptions of market opportunities are dispersed in a lumpy and uneven manner, and it is through the *unequal* impact of the creative strategies of different actors that a process of imitative learning, where entrepreneurs and firms discover which production models to follow and which to avoid, is set in train. This process mirrors Foucault's 'tactical polyvalence of discourses' wherein inequalities generated by a set of power relations result in attacks on those relations which in turn prompt further strategic moves to defend, to re-establish them, or to create new margins of inequality. Unequal influence should not, therefore, be equated with the ability to control or to dominate a market. The generation of 'super-normal' profits, for example, typically generates a competitive response as rivals attack the source of these profits, which in turn generates further disequilibrating and equilibrating moves.

Where Foucault sees power as having no centre and as radiating from multiple points that complement or contradict one another to varying degrees, so this postmodern liberalism understands 'society' as a complex and evolving network or archipelago of micro-orders that may have varying degrees of overlap with other such orders.[49] The influence of these nodes or networks will differ, with some becoming more influential in terms of economic or cultural power through swarming processes, but where even the most powerful or influential of networks, such as those constituting modern states, are unable to direct society as a whole.

The creative aspect of agency emphasised here applies as much to the *production of subjects* as it does to the production of goods. Political economies continually remake the socio-economic world *and those within it.*[50] Consumer preferences, for example, while not determined by advertising are nonetheless *constituted within markets* as rival producers present people with options for consumption which they may not have conceived of until confronted with them. Similarly, a political economy may contain many different organisational types (including those of an authoritarian or disciplinary nature). The competing forms of political organisation, business organisation, management routines, divisions of labour, training programmes, advertising and consumption

[49] Dopfner, K., Foster, J., and Potts, J. (2004) 'Micro-Meso-Macro', *Journal of Evolutionary Economics*, 14: 263–79.

[50] Burczak, 'Postmodern Moments' (47–50) is especially clear on this point.

practices, and the various niches within the social ecology work to produce a diversity of personal styles, cultural dispositions, and aptitudes.

Crucially, while different political economies allow for different forms of creative agency, their effects can never be *reduced* to the role of such agency, because the rules of the political economy also generate *downward causation* effects.[51] The capacity for people to calculate in terms of comparative costs and prices and in the process to coordinate their actions (however temporarily) is *not* a property of individuals but of *rule-based interactions*. Similarly, the production of different subjects and the processes that enable learning and the acquisition of capacities is dependent on a set of rules that facilitate mutation and imitation. The wealth, skills, and cultural norms generated are not merely an aggregate effect of individual agency but a *supra-individual* or interactive effect of specific institutional configurations.

Evolutionary selection and entangled political economies

Where this liberal social theory departs from Foucault is in the use of evolutionary concepts at multiple levels to explain how patterned though unintended social formations emerge. Evolutionary explanations in biology rely on replication, variation, and selection to account for the evolution of species in a context of limited resources, where those whose traits are best adapted to the selection environment or to changes within it prosper relative to others. Organisms pass on their characteristics through their genes which are the replicators selected according to their phenotypic effects and where small variations as they are passed from one generation to the next are selected for or against. In cultural theories of evolution by contrast, such as those of Hayek,[52] Gaus, and Dawkins, the relevant units are concepts, ideas, and practices—sometimes referred to as 'memes'—with the vehicles for their transmission being the individuals and groups that adhere to the relevant practices.[53] Selection occurs through the effects the practices have on the survival, prosperity, or status of those following them such as, for example, the ability of a business enterprise to secure customers and profits relative

[51] On downward causation in 'Austrian' economics see Lewis, P. (2014) 'Notions of Order and Process in Hayek: The Significance of Emergence', *Cambridge Journal of Economics*, 39 (4): 1167–90.

[52] Hayek makes use of evolutionary concepts in various works—notably in *The Constitution of Liberty* and *Law, Legislation and Liberty*, as well as in his final work *The Fatal Conceit* (1988) London: Routledge. Dawkins elucidates these concepts in Dawkins, R. (1989) *The Selfish Gene*, Oxford: Oxford University Press.

[53] See, e.g., Distin, K. (2005) *The Selfish Meme*, Cambridge: Cambridge University Press; Goodenough, W. (1999) 'Outline of a Framework for a Theory of Cultural Evolution', *Cross-Cultural Research*, 33 (1): 84–107; Mokyr, J. (2016) *A Culture of Growth*, Princeton, NJ: Princeton University Press.

to its rivals. The selection environment meanwhile consists of the background economic and technological conditions, institutional rules, feedback processes, and the separate though overlapping preferences and beliefs of actors.

At the societal or macro-level Hayek and Gaus deploy notions of 'group' or 'cultural selection' where those adhering to certain institutions and rules, either by conscious choice, force, or more often by historical accident, prove to have greater survival value than others. This selection does not imply that the rules in question are optimal but that they have performed relatively better than available alternatives. Moreover, it is not the groups as such that are selected, but the rules and institutions with groups acting as a *vehicle* for the transmission of the relevant rules that act upon them. Groups that resolve disputes through violent combat, for example, might fair less well than those following nonviolent practices of dispute resolution.[54] Such group selection exercises *downward causation*, influencing the behavioural practices and routines that survive relative to others.

Unlike biological or Darwinian explanations that emphasise the transmission of inherited characteristics, Hayek and Gaus argue that cultural evolution *simulates* Lamarckism where the characteristics in question can be acquired from an *indefinite* number of actors through associative learning or reflexivity. These explanations should not, therefore, be confused with socio-biological theories that posit a connection between biological traits and culture. While humans have a genetic capacity for culture, culture itself is *not* genetically controlled, and this is why cultural evolution proceeds much more speedily than biological evolution.[55] Rather than genetic transmission the primary mechanism for the transmission of cultural practices is *imitation*. This need not be based on a full understanding of what it is about the practices in question that leads to their success but only that what is imitated *sufficiently* corresponds to what produces the effect concerned. The transmission of a firm's management

[54] For useful discussions of Hayek's account of group selection see Schaefer, A. (2021) 'Hayek's Twin Ideas: Reconciling Methodological Individualism with Group Selection', *Cambridge Journal of Economics*, online, https://doi.org/10.1093/cje/beab036; see also, Whitman, G. (1998) 'Hayek Contra Pangloss on Evolutionary Systems', *Constitutional Political Economy*, 9: 45–66; Zywicki, T. (2000) 'Was Hayek Right About Group Selection After All?', *Review of Austrian Economics*, 13: 81–95. Some have argued that Hayek's commitments to methodological individualism and group selection are mutually incompatible—e.g., Vanberg, V. (1986) 'Spontaneous Market Order and Social Rules: A Critical Evaluation of F. A. Hayek's Theory of Cultural Evolution', *Economics and Philosophy*, 2 (1): 75–100.

Schaefer offers a rebuttal to this view. He shows that group selection does *not* presuppose a group actor but that what Hayek refers to as 'groups' are individuals linked through various network effects—it is the networks that are subject to group selection processes and that generate a form of 'downward causation', but the formation of the relevant networks remains explainable in agency-oriented terms.

[55] On these points and on Hayek's rejection of 'Social Darwinism' see esp. *The Fatal Conceit*, 25. For a discussion see also Gaus, G. (2021) *The Open Society and Its Complexities*, New York: Oxford University Press, chap. 2.

practices, for example, need not depend on its rivals knowing what it is about them that enhances profitability for the practices to be copied successfully.

As Gaus has emphasised, neither should these analyses be confused with functionalist accounts or with teleological reasoning. Evolution is *nonlinear and purposeless*, and while institutions perform 'functions', they are not there *because* they perform a specific function. Rules that allow for economic growth, for example, do not exist to perform this function but because they may have secured an advantage in the context of a competitive-evolutionary environment which happened to select for this particular 'trait'. Similarly, in market settings firms by accident or design may adopt Foucauldian disciplinary mechanisms that instil 'team spirit' into their employees and which discourage narrowly selfish or 'free-riding' conduct in ways that influence their competitive success. Markets themselves are framed by rules of property and contract; some of which may be provided by political jurisdictions, such as states, or alternatively through private associations or clubs—and all of which may be subject to competition from other rule-making bodies whether these are states or private actors. Competition, therefore, does not necessarily involve 'competitive behaviour' but may entail 'competition' between different forms of 'cooperation' and/or 'disciplined conduct'. Neither need those involved be aware that they are 'competing'. Competition refers to differences in individual and organisational practices and in techniques of government operating within a selective environment constituted by differing rules of property and contract.

On this postmodern liberal view, cultural evolution is open-ended and has no tendency towards an optimal or fixed set of practices. The standards, norms, and values witnessed in a society will be those that have survived an evolutionary process and will reflect all manner of historically contingent categories such as those based on gender, race, class, or social status that may advantage some actors and practices over others. Insofar as certain sex or gender divisions of labour may have enabled those that practiced them to flourish, this does not mean that the rules were consciously chosen because of this effect—and neither does it imply that practices that may have held such an advantage at one point in time will do so in the future. Rules and institutions should be analysed in terms of their propensity to allow for an open-ended process through which new standards and practices develop, as well as for their propensity to limit, close down, or rigidify in favour of that which currently exists. An evolutionary approach does not, therefore, imply an uncritical acceptance of whatever has evolved but focuses attention on the processes that may sustain fluidity and those that may rigidify into 'dead ends'.

Rather than pure institutional types, political economies should be understood as complex 'entanglements' between different decision rules, and where the selection effects operative under these different rules may conflict.[56] Thus, if price controls have a competitive advantage in attracting the attention of voters as a way to reduce the cost of living or inequality, and such proposals spread in popularity with those seeking political power, they may disrupt the coordinative properties of the market price system. Likewise, if commercial enterprises use their revenues to invest in political campaigns to hobble potential competitors by raising barriers to entry, and if such strategies are copied by incumbent market leaders, the wider dynamism of commercial practices may be impeded. There is no automatic tendency towards the selection of the most efficient or wealth-generating practices in part because people may not know what these are and because their motivations are often mixed and complex. Some agents may, for example, prefer status and positionality—'being a big fish in a small pond'—over absolute wealth and may seek to block actions that threaten their position and status. There is no pure or 'power-free' market economy independent of other forms of decision-making such as, for example, systems of democratic rule where the dyadic interactions found in markets are replaced with triadic relations where two or more parties may impose terms on a third. Neither is there a pure planned economy that operates 'free' from commercial influences—with all 'really existing' socialist economies having relied on at least some elements of market exchange. The properties of 'entangled political economies' will reflect the relative strength of a complex mix of rules, practices, and the techniques of government selected within them. The structure of power, meanwhile, will be affected by a combination of 'bottom-up' and 'top-down' influences that will in turn affect the extent to which power relations remain fluid/competitive or rigid/monopolistic.

Foucault, evolution, and entangled political economy

It should now be evident that the social theories advanced by Foucault and by postmodern liberals work with a conception of the subject, which limits the role of essentialism to a thin set of biological characteristics. Similarly, while not denying purposeful or goal-oriented conduct both perspectives reject 'sovereign' views of social order in favour of non-anthropomorphic explanations. Equally important in both traditions is an attention to *interactive or emergent patterning* phenomena that *cannot* be reduced to the effects of individual agency but that operate to generate 'downward causation' on the character and form of subjectivity. The Foucauldian and postmodern liberal accounts also reject

[56] On 'entangled political economy' see Wagner, R. (2016) *Politics as a Peculiar Business: Insights from a Theory of Entangled Political Economy*, Cheltenham: Edward Elgar.

equilibrium perspectives, favouring a disequilibrium focus on fluidity and nonlinearity that recognises the capacity of individuals to exercise creative agency manifested in acts of resistance (Foucault) and entrepreneurship (postmodern liberalism) and that operate as a form of 'upward causation'. Correspondingly, there is a shared focus on the processes that may stifle this creativity and block processes of contestation.

While these similarities should be clear, Foucault's account of discursive power arguably lacks a convincing explanation of the coordinative processes through which patterned social relationships develop, solidify, and how they may be destabilised. Indeed, it might be argued that Foucault has a theory of power but *without* an adequate theory of socio-economic coordination and disruption. As such, this section considers how Foucault's social theory may be strengthened by understanding power relations as evolutionary, spontaneous orders within different though interlocking institutional rules and the role of such non-discursive institutions in generating coordinative or systemic effects. The evolutionary perspective of postmodern liberalism, is not however, without weaknesses of its own. Where Foucault analyses power without an account of systemic coordination, postmodern liberalism has an account of socio-economic ordering without sufficient appreciation of discourses as spontaneous orders that activate or constrain different forms of subjectivity and agency. The subsequent section will thus explore how postmodern liberalism may incorporate a Foucauldian appreciation of the relationship between agency and discourse into its political economy of institutions and decisions.

Foucault, power, and spontaneous order

Foucault's decentred analysis of power shows how interlinking 'technologies of government' may give the *appearance* of an overarching order of power relations *without* any sovereign actor or group being in control. As such, his approach must be distinguished from what Nozick describes as conspiracy theories or 'hidden hand' explanations in social theory.[57] The latter refer to situations where there may be an *appearance* of no one being in control, but where the outcome in question has been *engineered* by the conscious though *hidden* manipulation of a controlling group or groups. Foucault's theory however is closer to an 'invisible hand' or 'spontaneous order' explanation such as Hayek's, where patterns of coordination that may *look* as though they have been 'designed' in fact *lack* a relevant designer. As Foucault, puts it:

[57] Nozick, R. (1994) 'Invisible Hand Explanations', *American Economic Review*, 84 (2): 314–8.

> Power relations are both intentional and non-subjective. If in fact they are intelligible, this is not because they are the effect of another instance that 'explains' them, but rather because they are imbued through and through with calculation: there is no power that is exercised without a series of aims and objectives. But this does not mean that it results from the choice or decision of an individual subject, let us not look for a headquarters that provides over its rationality.[58]

If they are to be successful, however, such accounts must specify the selection or patterning principles allowing the relevant regularities to form *without* a 'hidden hand'. For Foucault networks of power simply emerge as an unintended consequence of multiple acts, but the basis for the resultant order is never explained. As Dean points out, while Foucault's decentred approach to power aims to 'cut off the head of the king' in social theory, this raises the question of 'how it is possible that this headless body often behaves as if it indeed had a head'.[59] What is missing is a focus on the environmental 'filtering processes' that operate under different non-discursive institutional configurations and that may signal the relative 'success' or 'failure' of the practices in question, with these signals or symbols operating as attractors or detractors that generate coordinated or systemic effects.

In contemporary political economies there are several such filtering processes that may account for the patterned emergence of norms, practices, and technologies of government. Perhaps the most important is economic calculation and profit-and-loss accounting. Whether by accident or design, should the introduction of new disciplinary techniques that shape the conduct of those within a business enterprise such as, for example, Taylorism, performance-based pay, or a social media strategy that drives brand loyalty enhance their relative profitability, this may encourage the entrepreneur or organisation in question to expand their reach with profits providing the necessary means to do so. These profits may also attract the attention of rival businesses or those in overlapping fields in pursuit of improvements to their own profitability. Profit signals may then generate a series of imitation and selection effects that produce a coordinated swarm of actions that was *not* intended by anyone in the relevant chain.

Important though they may be market signals are not the only such filters. The production of goods not directly marketed may also generate selection effects facilitating the emergence and spread of governmental practices *without* this

[58] *The History of Sexuality*, 94–5.

[59] Dean, M. (1994) *Critical and Effective Histories: Foucault's Methods and Historical Sociology*, London: Routledge.

being the deliberate intent of any one actor or group. Systems of political federalism or inter-jurisdictional competition may, for example, generate positive and negative 'swarming processes' as people and resources move towards some jurisdictions and away from others to secure what they perceive as better access to various territorially based goods. These shifts in the distribution of people and tax revenues may in turn prompt imitators to adopt or adapt the techniques to govern the production of both people and public spaces in what are perceived as the most successful jurisdictions. Competitions for political office may also operate through similar processes with the parties and organisations that develop the most effective vote-winning techniques or discursive memes attracting imitators. Equivalent effects may be prevalent in interest group politics and social movements as well, with the flow of people and resources towards groups that prove more effective in garnering citizens' attention, generating the relevant signals of attraction.[60]

In all these examples, though the creative agency exercised by individuals, organisations, and groups generates mutations in techniques and associated discourses that may then be selected according to their results, it is *not* necessarily the actors themselves that are selected but *the practices they adhere to*—practices that may be passed on to an indefinite number of other agents through imitation. This means that elements of the social structure or system can persist even as the individuals occupying it change. In an important sense, therefore, the socio-cultural structure is *distinct* from the specific individuals working within it—individuals are 'the foci in the network of relationships'[61]—and it is these networks that are subject to selection processes.

The latter understanding may best account for the emergence of what Foucault understands to be impersonal 'strategies of power' even when there is no 'strategizing agent' behind them. A disciplinary dividing practice, meme, or discursive trope that generates profits in private industry may, for example, be adopted by other enterprises and perhaps public authorities to facilitate winning elections, collecting taxes, or enforcing regulation—and vice versa. In this way techniques of government might be said to *acquire* actors and to morph as goal-following agents either consciously or unconsciously adopt practices that may give them some strategic advantage in the pursuit of wealth, power, or status—whether in commercial or political competition or the interaction between the two—and to assume the *appearance* of having a strategic or systemic purpose that shapes the decision environment of others.

[60] For example, Novak, M. (2021) *Freedom in Contention: Social Movements and Liberal Political Economy*, London: Rowman and Littlefield.

[61] Hayek, F. A. (1957) *The Counter-Revolution of Science*, Indianapolis, IN: Liberty Fund, 50.

Foucault and evolutionary theory

Foucault said little about the relevance of such explanations to his account of power, but the few comments he made about evolutionary theories were *not* favourable. The reason for this appears to have been an elision of evolutionary accounts with naturalistic and teleological views that imply the existence of a progressive direction towards a societal end state, and the potentially homogenising quality of such explanations. Societal equivalents of ecological theories that explain how an initially heterogenous environment may generate a 'climax ecology' are an important example in point. Thus, Foucault explicitly challenged the social relevance of early theories of biological evolution for their focus on 'destiny', the identification of a 'continuous line', and for the 'projection of teleologies';[62] and he was emphatic in noting that 'genealogy does not resemble the evolution of a species and does not map the destiny of a people'.[63] Rather, 'it operates on a field of entangled and confused parchments, on documents that have been scratched over and recopied many times'.[64]

Foucault also expressed concerns about explanations rooted in the mistaken search for 'originating' acts and for an 'originating subject' with a clear 'line of descent', when it is the 'multiple beginnings' and the complex concatenation of events, discourses, and agency that prevent the attribution of power relations to any causal 'originator' or 'author'. This would seem to speak directly against what Hayek refers to as the 'compositive method' in social theory, the very purpose of which is to explain chains of events that spread or ripple out from individual acts of entrepreneurship within institutional rules.[65] Thus:

> How do you see change, or let us say revolution at least in the scientific order and in the field of discourses, if you link it with the themes of meaning, project, origin, return, constituting subject, in short the entire thematic that ensures for history the universal presence of the Logos?[66]

This view was expressed in the early 1970s, and it is not clear whether Foucault held to it as his oeuvre developed. It is the contention here, however, that if he did, Foucault was misguided in rejecting a form of explanation highly complementary to his account of power relations. Three points are worthy of attention in this regard.

[62] *The Archaeology of Knowledge*, 209.

[63] MF (1977) 'Nietzsche, Genealogy, History', trans. Bouchard, D. and Simon, S., in Bouchard, D. F., ed. (1977) *Language, Counter-Memory, Practice*, Ithaca, NY: Cornell University Press, 146.

[64] Ibid.

[65] Hayek discusses this method most extensively in Hayek, *Counter-Revolution*.

[66] Foucault, *The Archaeology of Knowledge*, 209.

First, evolutionary explanations *do not* imply a teleological view wherein selective dynamics lead to a homogenising and stable set of practices or a universal subject. As Atterton notes, Foucault himself was aware that unlike the earlier theories of biological evolution that he criticised, the Darwinian approach marked a focus *not* on continuity and teleological progress but on *discontinuity*.[67] Indeed, as Prado argues with its focus on randomly discontinuous perpetuation, rather than an attempt to discern an underlying and organised continuity to history, Foucauldian genealogy is *itself* thoroughly Darwinian in character.[68] Moreover, contemporary theories of evolution, far from emphasising stability, equilibrium, and climax, focus on more, or less, constant and open-ended processes of variation, change, and disequilibrium with patterns and regularities being at most *temporary*—so Foucault should perhaps have recognised the compatibility of this focus on radical discontinuity and the coordinated though 'kaleidic' quality of socio-economic life with his own social theory.

In the context of political economy specifically, the non-Darwinian theory of cultural evolution espoused by Hayek and Gaus emphasises that while stability with respect to basic rules such as property, contract, and relatively peaceful forms of dispute resolution might be explained with respect to their *long-run* survival value, such rules are compatible with a diversity of shifting cultural norms and practices. Indeed, there are likely to be evolutionary advantages for institutions and cultural practices that produce a *diversity* of subjects—precisely because such diversity facilitates adaptation to *unforeseen* changes and events. While it is perhaps understandable that Foucault may have been troubled by the apparent 'naturalism' of evolutionary theories—those espoused by Hayek and Gaus explain social processes in terms that are *neither* 'natural' nor 'artificial/constructed'. Rather, they see the social constructs that constitute power relations as a form of unplanned order that as Foucault puts it 'lacks a headquarters'.[69]

Nor do these theories imply that the evolutionary process follows a continuous path or line. While socio-cultural mutations must have some 'fit' with the current environment if they are to be selected, many small incremental shifts and adaptations in consumption habits, business or political routines may *transform* that selection environment (such as, e.g., the preferences of agents, their organisational routines, and the discursive power relations which they reflect or to which they give rise) so that it is not possible to trace a clear or continuous 'line of progress'. Moreover, while evolutionary processes may account for *strands*

[67] Atterton, P. (1994) 'Power's Blind Struggle for Existence: Foucault, Genealogy and Darwinism', *History of the Human Sciences*, 7 (4): 1–20. For a similar argument see also Solinas, M. (2017) 'Foucault's Darwinian Genealogy', *Genealogy*, 1 (9): 1–17.

[68] Prado, *Searle and Foucault on Truth*, 76–7.

[69] The History of Sexuality, 94–5.

of order, these are unlikely to point in the same direction. In the entangled institutional mixes constituting most political economies there are likely to be overlapping but at times *contradictory* selection criteria in operation– such as, for example, those that may generate success in commerce and in politics.

Second, the compositive method does not imply an excessive focus on the 'originating' role played by specific individuals and groups, and neither does it presuppose a constituting subject. Any given act of entrepreneurship may be dependent on and may have arisen from a complex historical concatenation of cultural-economic events or what Foucault refers to as 'multiple beginnings' that are *outside* the entrepreneur's control. As Hayek explains:

> While we are sometimes able to trace the intellectual processes that have led to a new idea, we can scarcely ever reconstruct the sequence and combination of those contributions that have not led to the acquisition of explicit knowledge; we can scarcely ever reconstruct the favourable habits and skills employed, the facilities and opportunities used, and the particular environment of the main actors that has favoured the result.[70]

All that the compositive method elucidates is how human *agency* that produces variations and that operates in an environment that generates signalling and selection effects may lead to the formation of temporary regularities, patterns, or strands of order. The process that Hayek describes is open-ended; it is *not* shaped by any single 'originator' or 'author', and as Burczak points out, it might even be understood as an essentially meaningless and purposeless, 'process without a subject'.[71]

This understanding is consistent with a Foucauldian focus on the micro-analytics of power, where power relations arise from localised contingencies or variations that may have ripple or network effects elsewhere, and where actors though constituted by dispersed social practices exercise agency *within* these practices. Indeed, the 'compositive method' seems thoroughly at one with Foucault's commitment to a 'decentred' or 'ascending' analysis, wherein power relations do not reflect the projections of a single centre of control but arise through complex and dispersed 'linking processes' with separate though overlapping decision-making nodes generating more, or less, stable chains of decisions, much in the way that Hayek explains the systemic process of price formation and change in a market setting. Foucault's genealogies and Hayek's compositive method do not seek to predict the future evolution of events. Rather

[70] Hayek, *The Constitution of Liberty*, 34.

[71] Burczak, 'Postmodern Moments' (55) uses this phrase drawn from Althusser—one of Foucault's mentors—to describe Hayek's understanding of a market economy.

the narratives they present illustrate the *type of process* through which strands of power relations or market structures may develop and evolve. Where Foucault's account may usefully be accompanied by one such as Hayek's is by recognising the role of individual agency in a context of signalling processes and institutional selection effects, as well as the role of these in generating patterned relationships.

The third reason why Foucault's approach may benefit from engaging with evolutionary theories is that while focused on the fluidity of relationships they also highlight the possibility of 'dead-ends' where the process of open-ended change is rigidified, halted, or *blocked*, and they may draw attention to the type of institutional contexts where fluidity is more likely to be sustained.

Foucault recognises that while cultural power struggles occur in *all* societies, some societies may be more likely to facilitate resistance and cultural fluidity than others, but he does not expound an explicit theory to explicate what the relevant institutional factors may be.[72] From a postmodern liberal standpoint, however, the fluidity of discursive power relations will be affected by how much room *non-discursive* institutions allow independent *action* and that afford what Foucault understands to be sites of cultural 'resistance' or 'heterotopia' that may unsettle established routines and ways of thinking.[73] Whether from acts of deliberate or accidental resistance, the potential for transformational mutations to arise is likely to have some association with the number of decision points that different configurations of institutional rules allow. Unexpected actions that upset established routines and power relations may happen under *any* institutional regime—including the most authoritarian and disciplinary (witness the collapse of the former Eastern bloc countries), but they may be more likely to fuel an open-ended process of change and adaptation in a social ecology that has multiple independent nodes—as in largely market-driven economies and systems of inter-jurisdictional competition—where a higher proportion of decisions are taken *without* the permission of a central hierarchy or large numbers of other actors.

Insofar as they have an independent sphere of action, individuals, civil associations, and firms may engage in acts of resistance against current market prices and the normalisation strategies of other actors by engaging in what Foucault refers to as 'counter-conducts'. While these conducts may occur in the discursive realm, a more important manifestation may arise through *actions* that provide exemplars that other agents may subsequently emulate. According to Hayek, the human capacity to learn by imitation *preceded* the capacity to express actions and concepts in the form of words.[74] People were able to copy proven,

[72] Foucault, 'The Subject and Power', 780.
[73] MF (1967) 'Of Other Spaces', *Diacritics*, 16 (1): 22–7.
[74] Hayek, F. A., 'The Primacy of the Abstract', in *Studies in Philosophy, Politics and Economics*.

successful techniques in hunting or in early forms of husbandry and to observe property rights and territory *before* having acquired the ability to communicate these practices verbally. It follows that while discursive challenge is an important mechanism for the destabilisation as well as the transmission of existing ideas and power relations, equally if not more important may be the learning and potential for destabilisation that arises from *seeing* the results of others *acting* in a particular way—results that may then prompt a change in the concepts that are expressed and classified in discursive terms. In a cultural context imbued with sexist or gendered stereotypes or categorisations, for example, a business with the freedom to challenge these norms through its hiring practices and that generates high profits may destabilise the cultural status quo, prompting other actors to shift their interpretive horizon.[75]

Though the scope for decentralised nodes to take independent action may be important to the fluidity of power relations, it offers no guarantees of maintaining fluidity where what economists refer to as "network effects" may operate. When the value of certain goods and cultural practices (such as computer software, social media platforms, or human language) is affected by the number of people using them, there may be significant coordination problems in switching alternatives. Concentrations of economic, political, and cultural power may thus arise and persist that have little relation to the qualities of the goods or practices on offer because competition may select according to more, or less, random factors, such as being the first to establish a foothold in a certain market or cultural-associational setting.[76] Such 'lock-ins' have particular relevance in the context of the power relations generated at the intersection of commerce, culture, and politics. Language presents perhaps the clearest example: the speakers of 'minority' languages often choose second languages according to the extent of the language's economic or social network and the associated benefits that it might offer them.[77] Similarly, in order to be heard in politics, individuals, organisations, or groups may have to express their interests and demands in terms of the discursive concepts that have the greatest currency if they are to have any chance of success—actions which may reproduce the dominance of the concepts, categories, and routines in question.

While lock-ins may occur in commerce and civil association, notably today in areas such as social media and platform economies, the postmodern liberal perspective urges particular attention to the role played by the juridical

[75] Lavoie, D., and Chamlee-Wright, E. (2001) *Culture and Enterprise*, London: Routledge.

[76] David, P. (1985) 'Clio and the Economics of QWERTY', *American Economic Review*, 75: 32–7. On the limitations of network effects see Leibowitz, S., and Margolis, S., (1994) 'Network Externality: An Uncommon Tragedy', *Journal of Economic Perspectives*, 8: 133–50.

[77] Reksulak, M., Shugart, W., and Tollinson, R. (2004) 'Economics and English: Language Growth in Economic Perspective', *Southern Economic Journal*, 71 (2): 232–59.

powers of states and their agencies and the relationships between 'top-down' and 'bottom-up' forms of power in *fostering or reinforcing* such effects. Specifically, the capacity to use sovereign political authority to limit or to block competition may institutionalise routinised practices by limiting the scope for subjects to be exposed to alternative practices that might destabilise the status quo. Though they may not be the source of specific discourses and though they may not control their evolution, states, and, increasingly, international bodies such as the European Union, the International Monetary Fund, the World Bank, and the International Panel on Climate Change do have significant power to project discourses throughout the wider society and to reinforce routinised conduct. This also means that they may become a target or focal point, attracting swarms of commercial and civil actors seeking to 'conduct the conduct' of others.

As in Foucault's account, states should not be understood as unitary actors guided by a sovereign goal or purpose but as comprising a plurality or decentred network of culturally constituted interests. Competition between such networks is, however, often limited with some coalitions, or organisational nodes exercising a disproportionate influence if they capture the juridical-coercive powers that governments hold. Just as states may interact with private agents in ways that limit market competition by privileging certain firms or business practices, so too they may generate a form of discursive or cultural monopoly power. Limits on competition may come from the bottom up as well as from the top down as coalitions use sovereign political authority to enforce rules and practices that protect their position in ways that might not be possible without the use of such authority. These processes may account for the emergence of what Foucault refers to as a ruling *dispositif* and for the 'governmentalisation of power relations', which are not explicitly provided in his own accounts.[78] In short, the more that discourse, rulemaking, and enforcement come to be focussed on state structures, the greater may be the need for actors in business and civil society to orient themselves towards these institutions and the discourses they project. Correspondingly, the greater the likelihood that the discourses they deploy to advance their interests will link with each other and with the apparatus of formal government to create a more stable 'block' reproducing dominant discursive coalitions or strategies and morphing a plural and mobile set of power relations into a more rigidified pattern.[79]

[78] MF (1977–78/2007) *Security, Territory and Population*, New York: Palgrave.

[79] On institutional sclerosis see Olson, M. (1982) *The Rise and Decline of Nations*, New Haven, CT: Yale University Press.

Postmodern liberalism, discursive power, and entangled political economy

Where Foucault's analysis of power relations can be strengthened by incorporating the evolutionary analyses set out above, liberal social theory may be enriched by paying much greater attention to the role that Foucault's notion of discourse plays in shaping and constraining the character and evolution of political-economic entanglements. Postmodern liberalism recognises that language is a particular form of spontaneous order and one that can have important effects in constituting individuals as subjects. Hayek, for example, writing in distinctly Foucauldian vein refers to language as

> the most important instance of an undesigned growth, of a set of rules which govern our lives but of which we can say neither why they are what they are, nor what they do to us.[80]

He also notes in similarly Foucauldian terms that

> what many think of as 'human nature', is in fact largely the result of those moral conceptions which every individual learns with language and thinking.[81]

More recently, the institutional economists Denzau and North emphasise the importance of 'shared mental models' in generating path-dependent outcomes,[82] and Shiller has shown how narratives and metaphors often influence people's loose thinking and actions to the point where they become one of the primary reasons for action that then feeds through to socio-economic outcomes and decisions.[83]

Notwithstanding such references, however, postmodern liberals have largely neglected the role that discourse may exercise as both an enabling and a constraining form of spontaneous order—as indeed has the dominant rational choice tradition in liberal political economy. Burczak attributes this failure to a desire to avoid positing the existence of autonomous social structures working *above* the individual.[84] While postmodern liberalism subscribes to a socially situated individualism rather than an atomistic one, it remains committed to an

80 Hayek, *The Constitution of Liberty*, 64.
81 Ibid., 65.
82 Denzau, A., and North, D. (1994) 'Shared Mental Models', *Kyklos*, 47 (1): 3–31.
83 Shiller, R. (2019) *Narrative Economics*, Princeton, NJ: Princeton University Press.
84 Burczak, 'Postmodern Moments', 53.

individualist perspective nonetheless, precisely because it avoids explanations that *essentialise* the role of social structures as determinants of action. Yet, it is entirely possible to recognise the role of macro-level social phenomena *without* essentialising their role as 'determinants' in this way. Indeed, as noted earlier, the notion that social traditions and institutions, such as property and prices, exercise *downward causation* on subjects while *not* determining their actions is an important illustration of non-reductionist spontaneous order analysis. In the specific case of Foucault's discourse theoretic perspective, it is possible to recognise that the emergent way individuals and society are *described* in discourse may significantly influence the content of political-economic entanglements. 'Discourses', while not themselves 'caused' by underlying determinants, once they are established may nonetheless shape or 'discipline' the field within which individuals conceive of themselves and their interests, the ways that different people are positioned in relation to one another, and the effect of such positioning in facilitating or constraining their sense of agency or empowerment.[85]

To illustrate how a discourse may 'produce the object of which it speaks' in the Foucauldian sense, consider the possible impact the description of entrepreneurship and business activity in politics and the media may have on the phenomenon of income inequality. To the extent that public discourse attributes such inequality to wealth acquired through illegitimate or corrupt means rather than through innovation and alertness to mutually advantageous opportunities, then the effect of this discursive construction may discourage subjects who do not identify with such descriptions from entering business life or encourage them to shift their entrepreneurial activity to other fields. Correspondingly, as the number of business entrepreneurs lessen, the financial returns for those remaining might rise—thus exacerbating the inequality targeted by the discourse. While it is possible for people to resist such a discourse by, for example, using their agency to invest in forms of counter-conduct that challenge the construction of entrepreneurs as corrupt, it remains the case that the discourse would operate as a *constraint* on their options for action, much as the range of available technologies may constrain, though not determine, the range of production methods possible at a particular point in time.

[85] Surprisingly, Burczak suggests that though compatible with a hermeneutic postmodernism, Hayek's perspective it is not compatible with Foucault's views on the subject. Burczak reaches this conclusion on the basis that Foucault's perspective amounts to a form of cultural or discursive determinism that precludes 'choice-oriented subjectivity'. For the reasons explored throughout this chapter, Foucault's perspective *does not* endorse such a view. For Foucault, although agents are 'produced' by their culture, they are also able to exercise creative agency *within* it. Foucault puts it thus: "Power is exercised only over free subjects, and only insofar as they are free. By this we mean individual or collective subjects who are faced with a field of possibilities in which several ways of behaving, several reactions and diverse comportments may be realised," 'The Subject and Power', 790.

Within this context, McCloskey's account of what has enabled liberal democracies to increase incomes by a factor of thirtyfold in the last 200 years highlights the inadequacies of explanations that ignore the discursive dimension.[86] The dominant explanation for income growth offered by liberal political economy focuses on the significance of private property rights and the increased security of those rights in the period prior to the Industrial Revolution.[87] According to this rational choice view, increases in the security of property generated 'high-powered incentives' that encouraged investment and work effort as individuals felt more confident that gains from their efforts would not be appropriated by public and private predators. For McCloskey, however, since security of property barely changed prior to the Industrial Revolution neither of these explanations is satisfactory. What mattered was the interaction of these non-discursive institutions with a gradual but marked change in the character of public culture arising from multiple discursive nodes in literature, art, religion, and politics, from one that described innovation and enterprise as a threat to an established order to one where such enterprise initially came to be tolerated and was eventually celebrated. Similarly, rather than being reserved in the hands of a narrow elite, public discourse increasingly emphasised an openness to enterprise from wider and wider spheres of the population. The mere presence of market institutions was *not* therefore sufficient to account for the 'great enrichment' since a public culture that decries innovation or limits its exercise to elite members is not one where agents are empowered to put those institutions *into effect*. In Foucauldian terminology, for agency to be so empowered required a discursive shift to *activate or produce* an entrepreneurial- and innovation-friendly subjectivity that celebrated those who challenged the status quo.

While McCloskey's account emphasises the role of discursive change as a facilitator of a more dynamic, entrepreneurial, and egalitarian social order, Foucault's analysis of discursive and disciplinary dividing practices might be viewed as a potentially countervailing set of narratives. Consider, for example, how discourses of economic competition in many societies intersect with heavily gendered dividing practices in ways that may lead to and reproduce unequal forms of economic participation. The free market is frequently described as a competitive 'dog-eat-dog' environment where the characteristics to effectively operate are discursively associated with 'maleness'. The effect of these intersecting discourses may discourage women from entering commercial activity or confine them to what are depicted and perceived as fields that value 'female' traits (e.g.

[86] McCloskey, D. (2016) *Bourgeois Equality: How Ideas, Not Capital or Institutions Enriched the World*, Chicago: University of Chicago Press.

[87] For example, North and Weingast, 'Constitutions and Credible Commitment'.

cooperative, less aggressive, unassuming, etc.), for example in the public or charitable sectors.[88] Similarly, by maintaining a binary between 'competitive' and 'cooperative' sectors and between distinctively 'male' and 'female' characteristics, these discourses may obscure the extent to which competitive commercial activity depends on cooperation and the forms of competitive conduct that occur in voluntary and public sector settings. Relatedly, they may, of course, constrain the scope of different conceptions of femininity and masculinity to evolve.

Elsewhere, the Foucauldian analysis of disciplinary-dividing practices may have considerable relevance to understanding multiple other inequalities in contemporary mixed and heavily regulated or 'entangled political' economies. While disciplinary techniques may enable high productivity, they may also work to constrain entrepreneurial agency, to limit competition, and to generate inequalities through the way that different subjects are culturally produced and positioned within regulatory practices that compare, rank, and grade people, as well as empower some actors to do the relevant 'grading'. Racialised and gendered dividing practices have been, for example, used historically by coalitions of business and labour interests to restrict access to markets and to limit or to 'manage' competition as part of 'rent-seeking' or cartelisation strategies to secure wealth or to preserve status and position.[89] These 'grading narratives' may intersect with markets, civil society, and public policy and include, among others, discourses of occupational licensure, employment regulation, urban and land use planning, public health, and the regulation of finance and banking.

Existing work in rational choice political economy and especially public choice theory has examined how regulatory rent-seeking may increase material inequalities by, for example, raising entry barriers to low-cost producers that block competition, privilege established businesses, and a regulatory class of public bureaucrats.[90] Though not inconsistent with such findings, a Foucauldian perspective would emphasise that discourses of regulation may generate inegalitarian structures by constraining who is *authorised* to act as an entrepreneur and what constitutes legitimate entrepreneurship in multiple domains. It is not simply that some actors may be unable to afford the costs of setting up in a particular line of enterprise but that the very idea of entrepreneurship may be discursively limited or even delegitimised by regulatory-disciplinary discourses that cut across significant swathes of economic life. Consider, for example,

[88] Horwitz, S. (1995) 'Feminist Economics: An Austrian Perspective', *Journal of Economic Methodology*, 2 (2): 259–79.

[89] On racialised rent-seeking see Hutt, W. (1964) *The Economics of the Colour Bar*, London: Andre Deutsch; Higgs, R. (1977) *Competition and Coercion*, Cambridge: Cambridge University Press; Lundahl, M. (1989) 'Apartheid: Cui Bono?', *World Development*, 17 (6): 825–37. On gendered rent-seeking see Ogilvie, S. (2003) *A Bitter Living*, Oxford: Oxford University Press.

[90] For a recent discussion on such regulatory capture see Lindsey, B., and Teles, S. (2017) *The Captured Economy*, Oxford: Oxford University Press.

how entrepreneurial activity in what is still referred to as the 'informal' or 'unregulated sector' in many countries has often been ignored or delegitimised by discourses that describe it as 'petty trading' or borderline criminal activity, notwithstanding its huge importance to the livelihoods of many low- and middle-income people—often disproportionately women.[91] Such discourses, while not precluding agency, may nonetheless work to constrain it by preventing people from deploying the significant capital assets they hold and expanding their enterprises because formal legal systems either refuse to recognise their existence or view them as illegitimate.

Elsewhere, the prospect of securing profits in markets might provide an incentive or signal to act, but whether one area of activity or another is *perceived* as a possible source of profits will be affected by the discursively constituted and routinised meanings prevalent in a society. If the very idea of certain market exchanges—whether in drugs, sex, human body parts, or in child-rearing—is described in discourse as repulsive or repugnant, then irrespective of whether these activities are legally prohibited, this may affect the incentive for people to respond to any profit opportunities that exist and it may also affect which people engage in such trades and the character of the market concerned. When markets are delegitimated in public narratives, then they may be more likely to be populated by agents who have themselves been marginalised or delegitimised.

A Foucauldian focus on the importance of discourse in activating and constraining agency and the limits of narrowly formal institutional explanations would also understand the extent to which people engage in positive-sum interactions rather than negative-sum 'rent-seeking' as *activated* by the *stories* that citizens and their governments tell each other, as well as how these discourses frame unfolding socio-economic events.[92] Understanding agency through the lens of the incentives provided by formal rules ignores how those incentives are discursively constituted. Thus, even in settings that provide relative security of property, if the narratives of would-be parties to trade portray one another as untrustworthy or narrowly opportunistic, then potential gains from trade may fail to be realised if people avoid trading relationships for fear of exploitation, or they may behave in an exploitative way themselves. In the former Soviet Union for example, the discursive description of market activity during the communist period as corrupt, opportunistic, or criminal, combined with the legacy of an institutional regime that left many people relying on black markets

[91] On this see esp. Easterly, W. (2007) *The White Man's Burden*, Oxford: Oxford University Press; Easterly, W. (2014) *The Tyranny of Experts*, New York: Basic Books.

[92] Choi, G., and Storr, V. (2019) 'A Culture of Rent Seeking', *Public Choice*, 181: 101–20; Chamlee-Wright, E., and Storr, V. (2011) 'Social Capital as Narratives and Post-Disaster Community Recovery', *Sociological Review*, 59 (2): 266–82; See also the collection Grube, L., and Storr, V. (2015) *Culture and Economic Action*, Cheltenham: Edward Elgar.

that lacked the protections of contract law, may have generated a subjectivity that *reproduced* these very forms of behaviour when market institutions were formally legalised.[93] Such explanations may account for why changes in formal rules may not lead to significantly different outcomes because the images lodged in people's minds and that constitute their subjectivity may be as much of a factor influencing how they behave than changes in legislation.[94]

The latter point suggests a need for a more fundamental recasting of how incentives are conceived in political economic analysis. The dominant rational choice paradigm in liberal political economy understands incentives as objective or structural characteristics of the 'choice situation' facing agents and extrapolates from these 'micro-foundations' to account for macro-societal outcomes. Foucault's discourse theoretic approach recognises that agents are purposeful and often strategic actors and thus does not rule out the potential significance of incentives. Unlike rational choice theories, however, Foucault works with a much thinner conception of rationality where the specific content of means-ends reasoning, and hence what the incentives are, varies according to the historically and discursively constituted framings of those concerned. Discourse always shapes political-economic action and can be deployed to shape it, so it is hard to disentangle any incentives that exist prior to or separate from the relevant discourses. In the context of political action, for example, how different players are described or constructed in public narratives may exercise a significant influence on their ability to secure political economic success by making certain thoughts and actions more, or less, costly to express, and this may affect the range of strategies available to them. Consider here how the financial power of industry groups is sometimes countered by the social circulation of dividing practices that represent the interests of some groups as 'virtuous' or 'public spirited' and others as potentially 'corrupt' or 'greedy', as is often the case in confrontations between environmental campaigners and commercial-housing developers. In such cases the way that certain activities or interests are labelled in discourse may be a key factor in the relevant 'incentive structure'.[95] Indeed, some of the categories deployed by public choice theory itself may be understood to work in a similarly strategic vein. The description of certain political lobbying activities with the negative coding 'rent-seeking'. for example, may be understood as a discursive attempt to undermine the legitimacy of a category of actions and to make it more difficult for other players in the game to

[93] Pejovich, S. (2003) 'Understanding the Transaction Costs of Transition: It's the Culture Stupid', *Review of Austrian Economics*, 16 (4): 347–61.

[94] Boettke, P., Coyne, C., and Leeson, P. (2008) 'Institutional Stickiness and the New Development Economics', *American Journal of Economics and Sociology*, 67 (2): 331–58.

[95] On this, see Rydin, Y., and Pennington, M. (2001) 'The Discourses of the Prisoners' Dilemma', *Environmental Politics* 10 (3): 48–71; Forsyth, T. (2003) *Critical Political Ecology*, London: Routledge.

undertake such actions. Similarly, public choice depictions of civil servants as empire builders may be interpreted as a rhetorical or discursive strategy to undermine regulatory-dividing practices that portray private businesses as selfish while describing public agents as selfless guardians of the public good.

If discourses frame or 'discipline' incentives in this way, then it follows that agents looking to change their position within any strategic field of power relations must seek to change the prevailing discourse. Postmodern liberals of the Austrian school recognise this point in emphasising the persuasive function of advertising in market settings under conditions of uncertainty where consumers are alerted to new possibilities for consumption and reminded of them through various forms of marketing. On this view, advertisers need to be aware of trends in the prevailing consumption culture to position new products, and in successful cases the persuasive role of advertising may enable new entrants to undermine the position of dominant market players. These persuasive-discursive functions are highly significant, with McCloskey and Klamer,[96] suggesting that they account for a large part of measurable, let alone non-measurable, economic activity.

Though this analysis is well placed to account for persuasive activities *within* a market, it may also be used to understand the entrepreneurial deployment of discourse by agents seeking to promote change to the cultural norms and the governance or legislative framework within which markets operate or which may affect the capacity for a market to exist. The incorporation of a Foucauldian concern with the way that discourses might be deployed entrepreneurially in attempts to 'conduct the conduct' of others at multiple different levels would thus widen the understanding of the complex entanglements across markets, civil society, and politics. Consider, for example, the discursive activity of entrepreneurs currently seeking to promote trade in what were previously constructed as 'repugnant' or 'noxious markets'. Kuchar has shown how entrepreneurs seeking to create at least partial legitimacy for commercial surrogacy markets in the United States sought to deploy discourses of contract and consent that are prevalent in US culture in an attempt to neutralise opposition to what are often seen by conservative religious groupings, and indeed much of the wider population, as repugnant 'baby-selling' practices.[97] Elsewhere, Sotikaropoulos shows how the promoters of various 'crypto-markets' that use blockchain technologies have sought to deploy the currency of a discourse that emphasises privacy, individual rights, and transparency to contrast their systems of anonymous peer-to-peer

[96] McCloskey, D., and Klamer, A. (1995) 'One Quarter of GDP Is Persuasion', *American Economic Review*, 85 (2): 191–5.

[97] Kuchar, P. (2016) 'Entrepreneurship and Institutional Change', *Journal of Evolutionary Economics*, 26 (2): 347–79.

reviewing with the opacity of underground or 'black markets' and with the threat of surveillance from the state.[98] Those seeking to curtail or to close down such markets, meanwhile, have deployed narratives that portray them as populated by corrupt actors who routinely operate at the edge of the law. Attempts to block or to delegitimise emergent discursive strategies will often be an important tool in the armoury of those seeking to preserve the status quo.

These examples illustrate how entrepreneurial agents may work creatively and strategically within discursive contexts *not of their own making* to find overlap with congruent narratives or to counteract rival narratives in seeking to advance their goals. Attention to the diverse ways agents 'pick up' and 'deploy' discursive strategies, or what Foucault refers to as 'cynicisms of power',[99] is thus essential to any interpretive political economy concerned with the shifting entanglements across markets, civil society, and the state. This approach is not incompatible with public choice theories which examine processes of governmental capture by specific groups, but it does require that these theories recognise the crucial role of persuasion and discourse in constituting group interests and in seeking to advance such interests. Persuasive activities are hard to account for in rational choice models where actors are already assumed to know what their preferences are and to have full information, or a proxy for it, in pursuit of those preferences. Indeed, any change or cultural fluidity is hard to conceptualise in a rationalist framework that understands individuals as existing in a state of permanent equilibrium not only with themselves but also with other individuals and the institutions they inhabit.

Conclusion

The social ontology associated with Foucault's 'death of the subject' is often considered fundamentally at odds with the 'individualism' of liberal political economy. The previous pages have shown, however, that an important though subordinate postmodern strand in liberal social theory rejects the idea of the autonomous individual and shares with Foucault a 'situated' conception of human agency. In such a political economy, discourses, traditions, power relations, markets, public policies, and the interactions across these phenomena are understood as *structured though indeterminate* fields that both produce and are produced by the choices of agents; where pattered relationships are both created and disturbed by evolutionary selection processes not under the control

[98] Sotikaropoulos, N. (2018) 'Crypto-Markets as a Libertarian Counter-Conduct of Resistance', *European Journal of Social Theory*, 21 (2): 189–206.
[99] Foucault, *The History of Sexuality*, 95.

of a sovereign centre of authority; and where attention is paid to the processes through which institutional and discursive blockages may freeze an otherwise mobile or fluid set of socio-economic relations and cultural/discursive constructions. What emerges from this postmodern social theory is the notion of an 'entangled political economy', encapsulating the idea of markets, civil society, and the state as complex and interacting institutional and discursive arenas that constitute the interests of diverse actors and that are continually reconstituted by actors working creatively within them. The extent to which socio-economic power relations are prone to 'freeze' or 'rigidify' will depend on a complex array of factors, including the characteristics of the mix across commerce, politics, and the sovereign powers of the state, as well as their interaction with various discursive framings.

One such set of framings is provided by the discourses of scientific rationalism in political-economic theory that continue to exercise a highly significant influence on public policy in contemporary liberal societies. The next chapter will thus synthesise the Foucauldian and postmodern liberal perspectives to examine how the contours of contemporary political economies may be shaped by these scientistic discourses. The subsequent chapter will explore the potential 'power effects' arising from the normative discourses of rights, freedom, and conceptions of the subject that characterise contemporary liberal political philosophy. In both these analyses attention will focus on the sources of a potentially *illiberal* 'governmentalisation of power' and the threats this may pose to the exercise of creative human agency.

3
Scientism, Science, and Expert Rule
Power/Knowledge and Liberal Political Economy

Introduction

Foucault's social theory and that of the postmodern strand in liberal political economy were shown in the previous chapter to share an anti-essentialist ontology, a situated account of human agency, and a non-reductionist understanding of social order. This chapter turns to epistemology, the philosophy of social science, and the relationships among scientific discourses, power, and agency. It will show that the postmodern stream in liberal political economy shares with Foucault a social constructionist stance questioning the scientific status of positivist and natural science methods that attempt to discern law-like relationships in the social world and that justify a form of utilitarian expert rule.

Important though these similarities are, they represent a 'family resemblance' rather than a tight equivalence between the Foucauldian and postmodern liberal traditions. Foucault's critiques of scientific rationalism focus on the sciences of individual behaviour, though they may be equally relevant to the utilitarian discourses of 'bio-power' such as those of modern economic theory, examined late in his career. Postmodern liberal critiques of social scientific 'scientism', by contrast, focus primarily on those utilitarian discourses that justify expert-centred modes of socio-economic regulation. Within this context, the chapter has two major objectives. The first is to defend Foucault's social constructionism against the charge of extreme relativism by incorporating the post-foundational and evolutionist view of science from the postmodern liberal tradition and the distinction it makes between the capacity to discern law-like relationships in 'simple' versus 'complex' phenomena. The second is to synthesise the Foucauldian and postmodern liberal perspectives, developing a shared critique of scientism in modernist political economy. Bringing together the Foucauldian and postmodern liberal perspectives in this way may help expose otherwise hidden examples of potential *illiberalism* in contemporary political economies by considering the 'power effects' generated by the bio-political discourses that sustain regimes of expert authority.

The analysis begins by setting out the Foucauldian and postmodern liberal critiques of modernist science in their respective contexts. It proceeds to develop

Foucault and Liberal Political Economy. Mark Pennington, Oxford University Press. © Mark Pennington 2025.
DOI: 10.1093/9780197690550.003.0003

the post-foundational view of scientific truth and its implications for the social scientific and normative aspects of the Foucauldian framework. Finally, it explores how the Foucauldian concept of discursive 'power effects' may be incorporated into a liberal critique of scientistic regulation in contemporary political economies.

Foucault on the human sciences and power/knowledge

Foucault's work can be situated within a family of social constructionist approaches in the philosophy of social science deeply sceptical about the applicability of 'modernist' natural science methods to the analysis of human phenomena.[1] Supporters of scientific naturalism hold that it is possible through scientific reasoning to arrive at objective knowledge based on universal laws and that law-like knowledge about the social world can be achieved if these techniques are sufficiently replicated in the study of human phenomena.[2] Closely related is the positivist view that the goal of scientific knowledge is predictive power. While there may be difficulties in securing the data that will enable fully accurate predictions natural science methods allow the discernment of a predictable range of actions that can inform decision-making—a range that will be become increasingly specified through the acquisition of more and better data. In turn, such predictive power facilitates the manipulation and control of background causal factors to secure valued social outcomes and to avoid negative ones. A corollary of this stance is that there is a division of labour between those with the time and/or technical skill to gather and to analyse such data and those who are both the objects of these data-gathering exercises and the subjects of the decisions and policies informed by them. Though it is compatible with different ethical positions, there is a tendency implicitly or explicitly for this outlook to align with a utilitarian frame that seeks to use the relevant data to maximise an aggregate conception of welfare.

[1] This family of approaches includes the hermeneutics of Hans Georg Gadamer and Paul Ricoeur—see, e.g., Gadamer, H. G. (1975) *Truth and Method*, New York: Seabury Press; Ricoeur, P. (1984–88) *Time and Narrative*, 3 vols. trans., McLaughlin, K. and Pellauer, D., Chicago: University of Chicago Press; the pragmatism of Richard Bernstein—e.g., Bernstein, R. (1978) *The Restructuring of Social and Political Theory*, Philadelphia: University of Pennsylvania Press; the humanist-interpretivism of Charles Taylor—e.g., Taylor, C. (1985) *Human Agency and Language*, Cambridge: Cambridge University Press; and the critical theory of Jurgen Habermas—e.g., Habermas, J. (1984) *The Theory of Communicative Action*, vol. 1, Boston: Beacon Press. For a detailed discussion of these approaches see Bevir, M., and Blakely, J. (2018) *Interpretive Social Science*, Oxford: Oxford University Press.

Foucault's social constructionism is positioned as one of the more radical or 'postmodern' members of this family given its emphasis on the inseparable relationship between power and knowledge.

[2] Hempel, C. (1942) 'The Function of General Laws in History', *The Philosophical Journal*, 39 (2): 35–48.

In general, scepticism of this scientific naturalism derives from a rejection of the Cartesian proposition that human beliefs have some causal, mechanical relationship to the external world.[3] Unlike the natural sciences which examine 'mind-independent' phenomena existing prior to their conceptualisation by science, social constructionists, such as Foucault, believe that human agents engage *creatively* with the world around them and are at least partly responsible for *constructing* or *producing* that world through the beliefs, theories, and practices to which they adhere. On this view, predictive power is not in the gift of the social sciences with the patterns that form the very stuff of social scientific investigation seen as the historically contingent and temporary effect of a set of overlapping beliefs and practices rather than the strongly correlated or deterministic relationships between dependent and independent variables found in the natural sciences. While social science lacks the capacity to predict the future according to past correlations and associations, attempts to enforce policies and institutions based on such models may work nonetheless to constrain human agency and the evolution of social norms and practices. Thus, one of the tasks of a critical social theory is to emancipate people from reductive understandings that narrow human possibilities by presenting as natural or inevitable what may be contingent social constructs.

Foucault's social constructionism developed primarily as a critique of disciplines such as psychology, psychiatry, and criminology that understand phenomena such as mental illness, sexuality, and crime as subject to law-like regularities. He presents a 'rational critique of rational analysis',[4] using reason and evidence to 'destabilise' the claims of modernist science. His purpose is to develop a 'critical ontology' of ourselves and our present 'with the objective of questioning what is necessary and what is contingent in the identities by which we have come to know ourselves and the relations of power in which we find ourselves and thus to open the possibility of thinking and acting differently'.[5] The resultant focus on 'destabilisation of the present' is reflected in three different strands of argument.[6]

In the first, the archaeological and genealogical methods offer detailed historical accounts challenging the notion of a progressive movement from a state of ignorance to one of greater knowledge about humans *as* humans. In *Madness and Civilisation*, for example, Foucault reveals that understandings of people who engage in random outbursts of disorderly or foul language considered

[3] Descartes, R. (1968) *Discourse on Method and the Meditations*, London: Penguin Classics.

[4] Foucault, M. (hereafter MF) 'Structuralism and Post-Structuralism', in Rabinow, P., ed. (1998) *Aesthetics, Method and Epistemology*, New York: New Press, 441.

[5] Dean, M., and Villadsen, K. (2016: 11) *State-Phobia and Civil Society: The Political Legacy of Michel Foucault*, Stanford: Stanford University Press.

[6] For a summary of Foucault's critiques see, e.g., McIntyre, J. (2021) *The Limits of Scientific Reason: Habermas, Foucault and Science as a Social Institution*, London: Rowman and Littlefield.

'mad' are *variable* social constructs.[7] Where in the classical era Europeans viewed such behaviours as a moral failing that could not be 'cured' but only isolated or contained, the modern era came to understand madness as an 'illness', governed by biological and psychological *laws* that allowed for appropriate 'treatment'. Elsewhere, *Discipline and Punish* documents a shift associated with the Enlightenment era from an approach to crime focussed on spectacular, brutal, and highly public forms of punishment, which sought to deter future transgressions, to a 'disciplinary power' focussed on the scientific surveillance of criminal 'types' that could be subject to analysis, treatment, and rehabilitation.[8] *The History of Sexuality* meanwhile evidenced a shift from seeing sex as a pleasurable act subject to excess and worthy of moral censure to one where various 'perversions' or 'abnormalities' such as homosexuality could be discerned and 'treated' through scientific means.[9] Crucially, these shifts did not represent movements from less to more rational understandings of madness, crime, and sexuality but illustrated *ruptures* or *discontinuities* between one conception of rationality and another. Recognising the potency of these ruptures should similarly work to destabilise contemporary 'taken-for-granted' or routinised understandings of other societal phenomena.

Where the analysis of these shifting constructions destabilises the idea of a progressive growth of knowledge, Foucault opens a second line of critique challenging the existence of natural types or essences that can be subject to scientific manipulation. Thus, Jeremy Bentham's model of the prison as panopticon, where inmates were subject to constant surveillance by a central and all-seeing control tower from which their behaviour could be scientifically studied and remodelled, did not in fact lead to a reduction in recidivism. Similarly, the introduction of mental 'hospitals' did not lead to a reduction in mental illness, and homosexuality was not 'cured' by the subjection of 'perverts' to the techniques of psychiatry and sexology. Though often failing *on their own terms* what these scientific 'gazes' of 'objectivation' resulted in were corresponding processes of 'subjectivation' as those classified as mentally ill, criminal, or homosexual internalised these labels in their very identity as people. This is what Foucault describes as both the 'totalising' and the 'individualising' power effects of modernist discourses. They are totalising because they come to encompass an ever-expanding range of people in the scope of scientific surveillance, and they are individualising in that people increasingly come to identify themselves with and to be 'imprisoned' by their imagined positions in the relevant classificatory grids.[10] Resistance against

[7] MF (1961) *Madness and Civilisation*, New York: Vintage. See also Gutting, G. 'Foucault and the History of Madness', in Gutting, G., ed. (2003) *The Cambridge Companion to Foucault*, Cambridge: Cambridge University Press.

[8] MF (1977) *Discipline and Punish*, New York: Vantage.

[9] MF (1976/1998) *The History of Sexuality*, vol. 1, London: Penguin.

[10] Ibid.

these constructions requires acts of 'refusal' or 'transgression' as when gays and lesbians adopt comportments and behaviours challenging stereotypes of homosexuality in a manner that may reveal the possibility of a 'new economy of bodies and pleasures' that crosses classificatory boundaries.[11]

The third and related strand of Foucault's critique suggests that scientific authority and knowledge are inextricably enmeshed with the exercise of power—hence the coupling power/knowledge. Attempts to 'know' others, to label them and to place them in classificatory grids, arise from a Nietzschean 'will-to truth' reflecting the desire to exert influence and authority over others by imposing a particular social construction or interpretation upon them. Thus:

> What types of knowledge are you trying to disqualify when you say that you are a science? What speaking subject, what discursive subject, what subject of experience and knowledge are you trying to minorize when you say: 'I speak this discourse, I am speaking a scientific discourse, and I am a scientist'.[12]

Foucault's power/knowledge concept must however be distinguished from the Marxian tradition of 'ideology-critique' and its distinction between true and false or manipulated knowledge. For Foucault the relevant scientific constructions are not necessarily 'wrong' in some externally objective sense, but if they achieve sufficient social currency and especially if they align or crystallise with political authority, they may exercise 'power effects' that limit the scope of creative agency by affecting what is considered true, *irrespective of whether it is true*. Crucially, while such alignments may work overtly to thwart resistance by legal prohibitions, they may also limit opposition as people come to see themselves and their position in society through routinised assumptions. Such 'power effects' are especially likely to arise when there is close to a discursive monopoly across civil society and the state that limits exposure to alternatives possibilities and constructions.

In line with his wider account of power, Foucault recognises that scientific objectivations are not necessarily imposed from a sovereign centre but often emerge in decentred vein as discourses or new areas of scientific expertise attain increasing currency from multiple points, colonising more and more of society, including the apparatus of the state. While scientific rationalism was not 'invented' to serve the 'interests of experts' per se, once established its interlocking discourses may shape or produce those interests and be deployed strategically to 'police the truth'. Thus, the response of Enlightenment prison reformers to the failure of the modern prison to reduce recidivism was not to

11 Ibid. 157–9.
12 MF (1976/2004) *Society Must Be Defended*, London: Penguin, 10.

question its social value but to propose further prison models based on more fine-grained classifications of offenders such that it became increasingly unclear whether the aim was to address the problem of crime or to serve the interests of those deriving status from supervising classificatory schemes.

It is not only the actions of those claiming scientific expertise that may contribute to this phenomenon, however. Scientific truth claims may exercise further 'power effects', assuming a life of their own, as they are taken up, disseminated, reinterpreted, and recirculated by multiple nodes in the economy and civil society through many small 'cynicisms of power' in strategic attempts to extract economic or political advantage.[13] In the *History of Sexuality*, for example, Foucault explains how far from suppressing public discourse about sexual conduct the '*dispositif* of sexuality' in the nineteenth century was drawn upon as an *incitement* to discourse about sexual behaviour and hence as a stimulant to the regulatory techniques that might be invoked to manage it.

The emergence of what Foucault terms 'bio-power' is part of a broader process whereby experts identified new anomalies and classifications in order that they might be 'governed by science', and these developments led to new conceptualisations of the state.[14] According to Foucault, European states had previously operated through a 'Raison d'Etat' where the sovereign's power was tied to the capacity to maintain territorial integrity and to protect the citizens from external attack. Outside of mobilising for war and collecting taxes, the sovereign paid little attention to the lives of its citizens. The rise of bio-power, however, reflected a new form of 'police power' where the sovereign saw its own authority as closely aligned with the 'welfare of the population'. Where the disciplinary power associated with Bentham's panopticon focuses on identifying anomalies in the conduct of individuals, scientific bio-power targets the whole population in its gaze. Instead of seeking to 'reform' or to 'treat' anomalous individuals, bio-power works on the environmental background within which large numbers of people act to induce behavioural changes that may lead to desired outcomes such as the elimination of disease.[15] Foucault understands this bio-power as a modernist mutation of an earlier Judaeo-Christian 'pastoral power'. With the modernist 'Cartesian moment' this religious pastorship mutated from a 'power of care' for

[13] *The History of Sexuality*, 95.

[14] The first references to bio-power are in the lecture series published as *Society Must Be Defended* and in *The History of Sexuality*, vol. 1, published shortly thereafter. It is discussed in greater detail in the posthumously published lecture series: MF (1977/2007) *Security, Territory and Population*, New York: Palgrave.

[15] As an example, Foucault refers to the role of medicine: "Medicine is a power-knowledge that can be applied to both the body and the population, both the organism and biological processes and it will therefore have both disciplinary and regulatory results," *Society Must Be Defended*, 252.

the 'salvation of the flock', to a 'government of life and populations' backed by science. As Foucault explains:

> Western man was gradually learning what it meant to be a living species in a living world, to have a body, conditions of existence, probabilities of life, an individual and collective welfare, forces that could be modified, and a space in which they could be distributed in an optimal manner.[16]

The practitioners of bio-power focus on disequilibria in the rate of births and deaths, indicators of population 'health' and levels of environmental risks; and the exercise of their 'scientific pastorship' is associated with attempts to 'conduct the conduct' of others through techniques such as the production of statistics, surveys, and scientific reports. Notions such as 'the population' are social constructs or 'objects' *created* or made visible by the production of statistics and a 'gaze' that purports to 'know them' in order that they might be 'governed' and 'regulated'. Though bio-power is distinct from disciplinary power and juridical or sovereign power, with its focus on population-level anomalies such as variations in sexual behaviour, it may incorporate these other power mechanisms to monitor societal states and to organise and enforce appropriate interventions or 'treatments' that try to 'administer, optimise and multiply life' by subjecting it to 'precise controls and comprehensive regulations'.[17]

In the *Birth of BioPolitics* Foucault considers economic expertise as an emergent and increasingly influential form of this bio-power. In the nineteenth century and beyond notions of 'the economy' were constructed through the production of statistics deployed to analyse relative states of economic 'health', and these discourses were closely associated with the rise of utilitarian philosophies focused on 'social welfare'. While trade and exchange between people and states had been present for centuries, the notion of 'the economy' as a manageable 'object' only came into view with the ascent of these bio-political discourses and their coalescence with the apparatus of the modern state.

Socio-economic expressions of bio-power come, however, in a variety of forms with different positionings of subjects in relation to the claims of the relevant expertise. On the one hand, a totalising form of bio-power which centres the knowledge and ability to manipulate background environmental conditions characterises totalitarian systems of socio-economic planning in both its fascist[18]

[16] *The History of Sexuality*, 142.

[17] Ibid., 137.

[18] On fascism and Nazism: "We have then, in Nazi society something that is really quite extraordinary: this is a society which has generalised bio-power in an absolute sense, but which has also generalised the sovereign right to kill. The two mechanisms—the classic, archaic mechanism that gave the state the right of life and death over citizens, and the new mechanism organised around

and socialist forms,[19] where the power to induce changes to behaviour through penalties and rewards is tightly aligned with the disciplinary and sovereign powers of the state—including the right to kill. Alternative bio-political discourses, however, have characterised broadly liberal forms of government and these emphasise to varying degrees the *limits* of any sovereign bio-power. Such discourses open a space where instead of constantly expanding the reach of direct social controls, those concerned with the health and wealth of the nation recognise the efficiency of a loosening of *some* such controls and of 'governing at a distance'. These mechanisms include potentially self-regulating processes, such as the operation of the price system, that allow for coordination *without* central control, as well as more centralised efforts to 'stimulate' or 'incentivise' desired changes in behaviour such as taxes, subsidies, and performance-related pay that nonetheless work 'through' the subject's freedom to respond to the relevant stimulants.[20] The concept of 'governmentality' is invoked by Foucault to refer to the shifting configurations of a 'triangle of power' with sovereign power, disciplinary power, and various stimulatory mechanisms representing the different 'corners' of this triangle.

Within this context, the bio-political discourse of modern economic theory examines the extent to which 'the economy' is a self-regulating system where disequilibria between supply and demand are speedily corrected via decentralised processes in markets and civil society, or whether such disequilibria persist and require 'corrective' intervention by public authorities. Thus, Keynesian theories and some microeconomic perspectives emphasise multiple 'failures' of efficiency in markets and civil society but the different strands of 'neo-liberal' political economy question the capacity of states to act in this corrective role.[21] Modern economic bio-power then is a form of 'governmentality' concerned with a utilitarian 'optimisation' of the balance between control and decontrol and in Foucault's view has become one of the most significant mechanisms for governing the population 'through science'.

discipline and regulation, or in other words the new mechanisms of bio-power—coincide exactly," *Society Must Be Defended*, 260.

[19] On socialism: "Ultimately, the idea that the essential function of society or the State, or whatever it is that must replace the state, is to take control of life, to manage it, to compensate for its aleatory nature, to explore and reduce biological accidents and possibilities . . . it seems to me that socialism takes this over wholesale. And the result is that we immediately find ourselves in a socialist State which must exercise the right to kill, or the right to eliminate, or the right to disqualify," ibid., 261.

[20] The concept of 'governing through freedom' and of 'governing at a distance' is discussed at length in Rose, N. (1999) *Powers of Freedom: Reframing Political Thought*, Cambridge: Cambridge University Press. For Rose, 'governing at a distance' is a key feature of 'advanced liberal government'.

[21] MF (1979/2008) *The Birth of BioPolitics*, New York: Palgrave/Macmillan.

Postmodern liberalism on socio-economic scientism and the pretence of knowledge

Where Foucault's social constructionism presents a 'rational critique of rational analysis' postmodern liberals of the 'Austrian' school[22] offer a parallel critique of socio-economic scientism that 'uses reason to understand the limits of reason.'[23] This analysis developed from debates within economic theory and political economy that Foucault describes as bio-political discourses. Though postmodern liberal political economy is part of this family of discourses, what distinguishes its contribution is a social constructionist, anti-Cartesian critique of the dominant modernist schools of twentieth-century economic thought.

For Hayek in particular, because the world is more complex than can be directly perceived by cognitively limited agents, human viewpoints must *always* be to some degree *partial or perspectival.* Contrary to Ernst Mach and other positivist theorists,[24] there are no pure sense data that the mind experiences as 'brute facts'—such data must be perceived, classified, and interpreted through a theoretical or cultural lens. The unmediated stance required by positivist theories implies that people can extract themselves from their local and culturally filtered experiences to view the world from an objective or omniscient 'gods-eye' perspective.[25] The closest approximation to such a perspective may arise in the analysis of 'simple' phenomena where it may be possible to predict the outcomes generated by the application of a stimulus into a closed system and to establish stable linear relationships between variables. Scientific problems in some (though by no means all) parts of physics are of this type, and they may allow for the derivation of predictive, quantitative regularities by scientific analysts. 'Complex phenomena', by contrast, refer to systems where the elements making

[22] The suggestion here is not that members of this school identify as 'postmodern' but that their analyses draw on social constructionist arguments that might be considered 'postmodern.' Though there is considerable overlap between perspectives within the Austrian school, there is a schism between those such as Murray Rothbard who follow the praxeological and aprioristic method of Von Mises and those who, under the influence of Hayek, describe themselves as radical subjectivists. The term 'postmodern Austrian' in this context refers to radical subjectivist thinkers such as Ludwig Lachmann, Don Lavoie, and George Shackle and more recently is reflected in the work of Virgil Storr and Emily Chamlee-Wright. For an account reintegrating the praxeological approach with the hermeneutic or interpretivist method see Lavoie, D. (2011) 'The Interpretive Dimension of Economics: Science, Hermeneutics and Praxeology', *Review of Austrian Economics*, 24 (1): 91–128. Some of James Buchanan's writings might also be included in the postmodern liberal grouping—notably in the methodological essay collection—Buchanan, J. (1979) *What Should Economists Do?*, Indianapolis, IN: Liberty Fund—see esp. the essay 'Natural and Arti-Factual Man.'

[23] In the late 1940s Hayek worked on the 'Abuse of Reason' project, essays from which are published in his methodological collection originally published in 1952 as *The Counter-Revolution of Science*, Glencoe, IL: Free Press—and subsequently republished by Liberty Fund, Indianapolis (1957). See also the essay, Hayek, F. A. (1958) 'Freedom, Reason and Tradition', *Ethics*, 68 (4): 229–45, quote at 241.

[24] Mach, E. (1902) *The Analysis of Sensations*, Chicago: Open Court.

[25] On this see esp. Hayek, F. A. (1952) *The Sensory Order*, Chicago: University of Chicago Press.

up a greater whole do not interact in linear fashion and where the number of elements and the character of their interaction may be too vast to be captured synoptically by any observing mind.[26]

In Hayek's account the human mind is *itself* a complex order lacking the capacity for a complete understanding of its *own* operations. The phenomenon of mind arises from neural networks and synaptic connections within the brain.[27] The latter are formed via an iterative process as the mind experiences sensations from the external world grouping or classifying them in relation to previous experiences that have themselves been grouped or classified. These classifications are not, however, an objective representation of the world but a theoretical or interpretive *construction* of that world derived in part from a process of cultural conditioning. The mind is a complex and linked network of overlapping constructions reflecting both historical-cultural representations and emergent constructions as new experiences unsettle previous interpretations.

On this account, there are no autonomous sensations—all sensations are embedded in a web of relations to other sensations that constitute a complex 'sensory order'. Though there is some order in the mind such that it does not experience the world as chaotic, this does not equate to a stable equilibrium. The minds' categories of perception are subject to disintegration and recombination as new experiences and anomalies prompt a process of reclassification. Thus, Hayek destabilises the idea of an orchestrating Cartesian mind or self that consciously controls its own operation. The self is not a 'unity' as in models which treat mind as a computer-like machine but an emergent property from a complex assemblage of overlapping and sometimes conflicting micro-orders within the brain that generate a state of consciousness *without a designer*. While it is possible to understand the general principles through which mind works, it is not possible for the mind to reconstruct the complex network of neural firings that constitute its state of consciousness and being.[28]

This problem of explanation is magnified in settings involving the complex interaction between *multiple minds*. Understanding why agents behave as they do, requires access to the subjective interpretations and theories that guide their everyday actions. The term subjective here should not, however, be confused with the existence of isolated or pre-social mental constructs. As the previous

[26] On simple and complex phenomena see, Hayek, F. A. 'The Theory of Complex Phenomena', in Hayek (1967) *Studies in Philosophy, Politics and Economics*, London: Routledge.

[27] Hayek's *Sensory Order* is a recognised forerunner of 'connectionist' theories of the mind, theories which retain considerable influence in theoretical psychology and cognitive science. For a discussion see, Smith, B. 'The Connectionist Mind: A Study of Hayekian Psychology', in Frowen, S., ed. (1997) *Hayek: Economist and Social Philosopher: A Critical Retrospect*, London: St Martin's Press.

[28] See Dempsey, G. (1996) 'Hayek's Terra Incognita of the Mind', *Southern Journal of Philosophy*, 34 (1): 13–41. See also Horwitz, S. (2000) 'From the Sensory Order to the Liberal Order: Hayek's Non-Rationalist Liberalism', *Review of Austrian Economics*, 13 (1): 23–40.

chapter showed, these are derived from the socio-cultural environment and *not* from an autonomous subjectivity. Nonetheless, the exercise of creative agency *within* that environment introduces a kaleidic quality to the social construction of reality with periods of relative orderliness prone to disintegration, before cascading into a new pattern or order. For Hayek and 'radical subjectivists' such as Lachmann, Lavoie, and Shackle, this undermines scientific attempts to predict the behaviour of statistically 'representative agents' because it is acts of creativity or in Foucauldian terms 'resistance' by entrepreneurial *outliers* that drive social change. Even in the more limited probabilistic sense of predicting a range of possible outcomes, success requires that modellers can access the dynamic and often contradictory constructions in the minds of multiple actors. In the absence of such mind-reading skills, however, the goal of successful prediction is chimerical because 'tomorrow's new knowledge renders obsolete and can destroy all our present ideas'.[29] These ideas will not typically be destroyed anew 'every day', so there are *some* regularities that may be captured by statistics and that may aid day-to-day coordination through a form of educated guesswork. Without such regularities people would be unable to operate in what would appear to them as a state of chaos. The ongoing exercise of creative agency, however, means that longer term statistical predictions are of limited value since reliable models require knowledge of the constructs that will shape the future in advance of their emergence. There is no 'law of large' numbers in human relationships because these are characterised by creative novelty—not fixed laws of nature around which random perturbations cancel or average each other out. Social life is not a truly 'mass phenomena' because each actor differs in subtle ways that cannot be 'measured' or 'controlled' for.[30]

This conception of the 'knowledge problem' leads to a comprehensive critique of social scientific 'scientism', Benthamite utilitarianism, and of institutions and policies informed by these attitudes. Where Foucault's genealogies destabilise the behavioural classifications and naturalist personality types of the human sciences, postmodern liberals destabilise the static equilibrium relationships between 'variables' in modernist political economy that underpin bio-political and utilitarian attempts to develop a 'predict and control' model of socio-economic life. Their critiques of socialist proposals for central economic planning and support for the milder forms of such planning in liberal economics that flow from the modernist epistemology of twentieth century neo-classical thought are paradigmatic of this discourse.[31]

[29] Shackle, G. (1973) 'Keynes and Today's Establishment in Economic Theory: A View', *Journal of Economic Literature*, 11 (2): 516–19.

[30] Weimer, W. (2023) *Epistemology of the Human Sciences*, London: Palgrave, 24.

[31] Prominent examples are Neurath, O. (1917/2004) 'The Economic Order of the Future and the Economic Sciences', in Uebel T., and Cohen, S., eds. (2004) *Economic Writings: Selections 1904–1945*,

The modernist, utilitarian perspective that has dominated postwar economic theory purports to explain how socio-economic life might be coordinated in one of two ways. In the first 'socialist model', the postulate of full information equilibrium suggests the possibility of a panoptic all-seeing and all-knowing social planner who at zero cost can inform production units and households about the demand and supply of different goods in accordance with a totalising social welfare function.[32] Or, where a central bureaucracy sets rules and targets, 'governing at a distance' occurs to align the actions of decentralised plant managers with those of social welfare while allowing them to use their own knowledge to meet these targets.[33]

In the second 'market friendly' or liberal model, the data necessary to achieve economic coordination are considered too costly for any single agency to search for or to collect, and where it may be more efficient to devolve decision-making to self-interested individuals and a network of decentralised panopticons, engaged through acts of market exchange. On this view, market prices transparently communicate objective economic 'facts' in a decentralised manner by way of incentives that 'tell' actors what to do and that punish a failure to obey mechanistic economic laws.[34] Nonetheless, while some decisions may be more efficiently carried out in markets, there are others where the costs of coordinating through them may remain higher than when relying on a central hierarchy or panopticon. Similarly, there are assumed to be certain goods whose objective characteristics—such as their 'non-excludability' and propensity to generate 'free-riding' or 'collective action problems', make them *inherently* unsuitable for decentralised supply. Efficient resource allocation, therefore, implies the existence of an optimal balance between decentralised exchange in markets and hierarchical systems of control—a balance accessible to those with the appropriate economic expertise.

For the postmodern liberals, however, both these models err. First, because it is a 'pretence of knowledge' to suggest that the generation and interpretive processing of the relevant 'data' can be centralised in 'the head' of an

Dordrecht: Springer; Tinbergen, J. (1956) *Economic Policy: Principles and Design*, Rotterdam: North Holland. For a discussion of the relationship between economics and public policy in this regard see Blaug, M. (1992) *The Methodology of Economics*, Cambridge: Cambridge University Press, 128–9.

32 The omniscient agent is the 'Walrasian auctioneer'.

33 This is what is envisaged in 'market socialist' models where decentralised public firms are instructed to meet targets in such a way that price equals marginal cost. For example, Lerner, A. (1944) *The Economics of Control*, New York: Macmillan.

34 Stigler's work illustrates the optimal decentralisation approach which retains influence in the broadly 'pro-market' Chicago school—for example Stigler G. (1961) 'The Economics of Information', *Journal of Political Economy*, 69 (3): 213–25. Stiglitz also works within the 'optimal decentralisation' approach though with notably less 'market friendly' conclusions, see, e.g., Stiglitz, J. (1994) *Whither Socialism?*, Cambridge, MA: MIT Press.

all-encompassing economic sovereign.[35] No actor or organisation has access to a 'social welfare function'—there are only the fragmentary, subjective, and often contradictory interpretations of economic conditions held in the imaginations of multiple dispersed agents. The optimal decentralisation model is, however, scarcely more plausible. The economic problem is not one of searching for and aggregating decentralised but objective knowledge but of matching the way that multiple, subjective, and shifting social constructs of relative resource scarcity are continually adjusted to one another through the competitive and interpretive guesswork within the market process.[36] Learning in such a context is not captured by the mechanical process depicted in 'Bayesian models' where actors update their prior information as they encounter new information and where they cannot initiate anything not already implied in pre-existent data. Such models do not recognise the role of interpretation and creativity generating new possibilities in the face of the unforeseen. Specialist entrepreneurs must 'read' and interpret prices in their part of the market while non-specialist market actors adjust to the decisions of others *without* having to know all the factors that generate the need for such adjustments. It is not that there is no economic expertise in such an order, but no one necessarily knows where such expertise may lie. Neither is objective knowledge of the costs and benefits of different levels of hierarchy and decentralisation available to any centre of control. The boundary between the 'spontaneous order' of 'the market' and of the 'planned' or 'designed order' of hierarchical or disciplinary organisations such as the business firm or of governmental bureaucracies is itself subject to uncertainty with the relevant costs and benefits emergent from the process of competition. This view does not, therefore, reject a role for public or governmental agencies per se but maintains that where they do operate such bodies should remain open to competition, actual or potential, from private or non-governmental suppliers.

For this postmodern economic theory prices do not provide objective incentives that 'tell' economic agents what to do and neither do they operate through a network of decentralised panopticons.[37] Rather, prices, profits,

[35] Hayek, F. A. 'The Pretence of Knowledge', in Hayek (1978) *New Studies in Philosophy, Politics, Economics and the History of Ideas*, London: Routledge.

[36] Lachmann, L. (1986/2020) *The Market as an Economic Process*, Oxford, Basil Blackwell/Arlington, VA, Mercatus Center, George Mason University enunciates this perspective. See also, Lavoie, D. (1985) *Rivalry and Central Planning: The Socialist Calculation Debate Reconsidered*, Cambridge: Cambridge University Press.

[37] The neo-classical full information equilibrium model, were it to reflect social reality, *would* be one of decentralised panoptic control or what Foucault refers to in the first editions of *Discipline and Punish* as a 'carceral archipelago'—with each actor perfectly overlooked by neighbouring actors even though there is no central actor perfectly overlooking everybody else. By contrast, the Austrian subjectivist model suggests a world where *even at the decentralised level* actors have only a limited capacity to oversee and to anticipate the actions of those with whom they interact. On the Austrian view a carceral archipelago is as much of an epistemic impossibility as is a market in full information equilibrium.

and losses, operate as useful though 'noisy' aids to the mind. They are never witnessed in their totality by any actor or organisation but present themselves as overlapping and *non-transparent* 'bits' of data that both affect and are affected by a process wherein rival readings of the beliefs and values of other actors come into contestation. This is why the 'knowledge problem' is not primarily one of access to computational power. Even with 'big data' or 'artificial intelligence' the data will not 'speak for themselves'. Technological developments may increase the complexity of the tasks that any actor can perform and the amount of information any individual or organisation may access, but the data in question will remain open to interpretation, and it is because readings of data are no more than social constructs that maintaining an environment where these constructs are open to competitive challenge is paramount. This is why prices should be distinguished from statistics or statistical aggregates. Where prices, profits, and losses emerge like language from multiple and continually changing interpretations by agents of their 'circumstances of time and place'—whether aided by machines or otherwise—statistical classifications abstract away from these particulars in favour of a unitary scheme imposed from outside.[38] To use Foucauldian terminology, statistical accounting suppresses or subjugates knowledge, much of which is tacit or inarticulate and is embedded in the daily routines and creative practices of multiple enterprises, investors, workers, and consumers.

Though some writers influenced by Foucault have suggested that similar subjugations may occur under the 'scientific management' practices that characterise large corporations,[39] this misses the point that *unless these practices are protected from competition by public authority*, they cannot easily block challenges from those drawing on alternative models emphasising less hierarchical conceptions of knowledge.[40] It is the suppression of competition that explains the observed incapacity of centrally directed models that dispense with private property and the profit-and-loss system in favour of statistical accounting to match the *dynamic and reflexive* properties of economies that rely predominantly on competition and market-generated prices. Centrally controlled systems cannot reflect the current state of socially distributed knowledge, and their operation may block the creative emergence of *new social constructs*. No objective 'economic fundamentals' exist, and much of the knowledge that the market coordinates would not be produced under a model that limits private ownership and that suppresses decentralised competition. Where Foucault sees the

[38] Hayek, F. A. (1945) 'The Use of Knowledge in Society', *American Economic Review*, 35 (4): 519–30.

[39] See, e.g., Scott, J. (1998) *Seeing Like a State*, New Haven, CT: Yale University Press—though he distances himself from Hayek, Scott's critique of high modernist social engineering is almost entirely Hayekian or Austrian in spirit.

[40] On Scott's failures in this regard see De Long, B. (1999) 'Seeing Ones Intellectual Roots: A Review Essay of James C Scott's *Seeing Like a State*', *Review of Austrian Economics*, 12 (2): 257–64.

colonisation of the state by the human sciences and their disciplines subjugating 'deviants' and blocking the creative emergence of a 'new economy of bodies and pleasures' so this postmodern liberal stance sees the coalescence of a socio-economic scientism with the administrative powers of the state blocking the 'creative economic destruction' that continually 'strikes at the foundations and very lives' of existing economic organisations,[41] categories, and routines. Such systems freeze the socio-economic order into a classificatory grid reflecting only the limited imagination of the planners' gaze.

Foucault and postmodern liberalism on bio-power, knowledge, and scientific truth

It should now be apparent that the Foucauldian and postmodern liberal perspectives offer social constructionist perspectives that in their different contexts challenge the authority of modernist expertise. Few postmodern liberals have engaged with the 'psych' disciplines, but of those doing so, Tomas Szasz's critiques of modern psychiatry have many commonalities with Foucault's analysis of the 'dubious sciences' and of any claims to political authority based on them.[42] Elsewhere, the postmodern liberal recognition of the complex interrelations between human subjects and their environments—of the complexity of the 'nature and nurture' interchange is consistent with Foucauldian scepticism of any scientific capacity to discern an underlying and naturalistic human essence. These arguments echo many of the earlier claims made by feminist liberals such as Mary Wollstonecraft and John Stuart Mill who doubted whether observed differences between men and women reflected naturalistic laws as opposed to the effects of social conditioning.[43] For present purposes, however, it is with Foucault's concept of bio-power and especially its economic manifestations where the most significant possibilities for a dialogue between the Foucauldian and postmodern liberal perspectives lies.

The focus on bio-power arose relatively late in Foucault's career and refers to power/knowledge claims based on the ability to identify and to correct societal disequilibria. Just as Foucault was profoundly sceptical that an underlying nature of those labelled homosexual, criminal, or insane could be 'known by science' so too one might expect a similar scepticism of claims by economists and would-be social planners to 'know' entire populations and to manipulate

[41] Schumpeter, J. (1942) *Capitalism, Socialism and Democracy*, New York: Harper and Row.
[42] Szasz, T. (1961) *The Myth of Mental Illness*, New York: Harper and Row.
[43] Wollstonecraft, M. (1792/2008) *A Vindication of the Rights of Woman and a Vindication of the Rights of Men*, Oxford: Oxford University Press; Mill, J. S., 'The Subjection of Women', in Mill (1869/1996), *On Liberty and the Subjection of Women*, Ware: Wordsworth.

and control their environments in accordance with scientific laws and utilitarian calculations. It would be strange if an author dedicated to destabilising the idea of a unitary Cartesian self 'accessible to science' were to favour a unitary conception of society accessible to a macro-level form of scientific expertise. Similarly, it would seem incongruent if a theorist concerned with how resistance to power may be limited and alternative knowledges subjugated when claims to scientific authority become entangled with state power were to endorse the totalising and hierarchical power/knowledge claims implied by schemes for centralised socio-economic control.

Within this context, several commentators have suggested that Foucault's interest in twentieth-century economic theory and liberal political economy arose from a recognition that *some* bio-political discourses focus on the *limits* to disciplinary and sovereign forms of power and thus open a potential space for new forms of freedom and agency to be exercised. The postmodern liberalism of the Austrian school demonstrates the impossibility of a fully disciplinary society, and its critiques of central planning highlight the consequences of a state colonised by panoptic notions of scientific management. This analysis might also imply a critique of Foucault's early-mid-career emphasis on the scale and effectiveness of panopticism as a form of social control. While the Austrian account recognises that the exercise of disciplinary power by organisations such as firms, schools, and public bureaucracies may give *some* shape to individual behaviour, it also emphasises that given the cognitive limits of such organisations their capacity to monitor behaviour and to control it through surveillance is strictly limited, and, correspondingly, that the scope of the internalised self-discipline generated by such techniques should not be overemphasised.

Nonetheless, the Austrian critique of panoptic technique is compatible with a Foucauldian recognition that while they may not 'work' the attempt, to use such techniques may place people in situations that exercise profound 'power effects' on how they see themselves and others through processes of objectivation, subjectivation, and the social positionalities they generate. Scarcity may be a time invariant aspect of the human condition, but how that scarcity is *experienced* may be affected by the institutional and discursive setting. In the context of the formerly 'planned economies' for example, plant managers, workers, and consumers alike were regularly placed in a situation of either submitting to the objectivating requirements of 'the plan' or of statistically determined 'prices' and thus subordinating their own situated knowledge to those in authority; or, acting in accordance with their own knowledge to secure their needs and wants in informal or illegal markets, at the risk of disciplinary sanction.[44] In the former

[44] For an account of the Soviet economy see Roberts, P. (1971) *Alienation and the Soviet Economy*, Albuquerque: University of New Mexico Press.

instance, conforming to the planner's gaze may have produced subjectivities characterised by a sense of inferiority or dependence on bureaucratic officialdom. In the latter case, while resistance to the socialist gaze in informal markets helped sustain the 'planned economy', the criminalisation of entrepreneurial conduct may have exercised profound subjectivation effects on those labelled 'deviants', 'speculators', and economic 'traitors' for participating in these markets.[45]

The potential congruence between Foucault's concerns here and the postmodern liberal analysis might also be understood in terms of the wider Foucauldian focus on decentring.[46] While the latter refers to an understanding of discursive power as arising from multiple nodes or points rather than its projection from a sovereign centre, it also refers to the project of destabilising discourses that though not originating from any one site, centre authority in various forms of scientific expertise. Postmodern Austrians and their predecessors such as Adam Smith challenge the very idea of a sovereign or 'god-like' point of view from which self and society can be surveyed, and thus offer a form of expertise that *decentres the experts' point of view*. Referring to these traditions Foucault explains:

> Economics is an atheist discipline, economics is a discipline without God, economics is a discipline without totality, economics is a discipline that begins to demonstrate not only the uselessness, but the impossibility of a sovereign point of view, of a point of a sovereign's point of view, upon the totality of the state that is his to govern.[47]

[45] For example, Pejovich, S. (2003) 'Understanding the Transaction Costs of Transition: It's the Culture Stupid', *Review of Austrian Economics*, 16 (4): 347–61.

[46] Several prominent accounts emphasise this connection and see it as part of a move towards a provisional acceptance of liberalism in the final years of Foucault's life. Having suggested in the early to mid-1970s that 'eastern bloc' economies had simply adopted practices that had been earlier perfected by 'liberalism' (see, e.g., MF [1991] *Remarks on Marx*, New York: Semiotext, 160), Foucault backed away from this conclusion in apparent recognition (a) of the many gaps that exist between circuits of power in liberal societies and (b) the more totalising alignment between state sovereignty, disciplinary power, and bio-power found in planned socialist economies. See, e.g., Paras, E. (2006) *Foucault 2.0: Beyond Power and Knowledge*, New York: Other Press; Audier, S., 'A Grand Misunderstanding: Foucault and German Neo-Liberalism, Then and Now', in Sawyer, S., and Steinmetz-Jenkins, D., eds. (2019) *Foucault, Neoliberalism and Beyond*, London: Rowman and Littlefield; Dean and Villadsen, *State-Phobia and Civil Society*; Behrent, M. (2009) 'Liberalism Without Humanism: Michel Foucault and the Free Market Creed, 1976–1979', *Modern Intellectual History*, 6 (3): 539–68.

[47] *The Birth of BioPolitics*, 282. It is not clear whether Foucault endorses the Austrian analysis since *The Birth of Bio Politics* is largely descriptive. One reason to suspect that Foucault *was* moving towards at least a modest endorsement of the liberal position follows from his critique of scientific 'gazes' such as those analysed in *The Birth of the Clinic*. *The Birth of BioPolitics* recognises that whilst liberal economics can itself be considered a form of bio-political 'gaze', it is a peculiar one precisely because it sees the possibility of a totalising and sovereign gaze as *chimerical* and thus seeks to undermine the idea of a sovereign power-knowledge—see esp. his discussion on pages 279–81.

Not only might this political economy be seen as less totalising than a fascist or socialist form of bio-power, but it might also be judged more modest in its scientific claims than strongly modernist and utilitarian forms of liberal political economy such as neo-classical economics and Keynesianism that claim the expertise to identify and correct multiple disequilibria or 'failures' in markets and in civil society to 'improve' the 'welfare of the population'.

Relatedly, this discourse does not entail extensive objectivation processes that purport to 'know' the nature of individual selves, and neither does it claim to distinguish actions which are more, or less, rational and to propose their 'correction' from an externally objective standpoint. Furthermore, and this is a point not recognised by Foucault, this discourse does not presuppose a unitary or fixed self. Unlike neo-classical economics, there is no assumption that agents are self-interested and focussed on maximising a stable set of preferences. Rather, agents are considered uncertain about what their interests are and even of *who they are* and similarly uncertain about how to coordinate with others to achieve whatever goals and purposes they may have—*irrespective* of whether these are self-interested or other-regarding.

With its suggestion that prices and market signals provide for only a rough and ready coordination as opposed to the tight equilibria emphasised in neo-classical accounts, the postmodern liberal analysis may also ameliorate potential Foucauldian concerns that subjects may be prone to a manipulative form of 'scientific control' or 'stimulus response' through the cultural production of a *Homo economicus* that responds predictably to prices and market signals.[48] Put simply, in a market economy there is no one 'stimulator' and neither is there any singular or representative 'response' to any given 'stimulant'.

Finally, one might expect Foucault to have some sympathy for a liberal, market-based social order and what Schumpeter referred to as its 'gales of creative destruction'. Foucault's greatest influence, Friedrich Nietzsche, drew on Greek mythology distinguishing the different characters of the sons of Zeus—Dionysus and Apollo. Dionysian characters are associated with an unpredictable, dreaming, and rebellious spirit who push boundaries and engage in 'limit experiences' that generate new paradigms and modes of thought. Apollonian characters, by contrast, favour harmony, order, and the exercise of logic to perfect established modes of thought and ways of being.[49] Though Nietzsche did not value either of these traits more than the other—with artistic beauty arising from

[48] This possibility is discussed in the conversation between Becker, G., Ewald, F., and Harcourt, B.—see (2012) Becker on Ewald on Foucault and Becker and American Neo-Liberalism and Michel Foucault's Birth of Bio-Politics Lectures, Coase-Sandor Working Paper Series on Law and Economics, 614. See also the discussion in Dean, M., and Zamora, D. (2021) *The Last Man Takes LSD: Foucault and the End of Revolution*, London: Verso, 164–5.

[49] Nietzsche, F. (1872/1993) *The Birth of Tragedy*, London: Penguin.

the creative tension between the two—there is a concern found in Nietzsche, Foucault, and in other postmodern writers that Enlightenment rationalism and the disciplines it has spawned are excessively Apollonian and unduly limit creativity. From a postmodern liberal standpoint, it is precisely the Dionysian drives or 'animal spirits' of entrepreneurs that strive to create something new and different that are given space in a dynamic market economy and that periodically shatter established routines, practices, and economic categories. Such an economy is not a static equilibrium that reproduces existing social constructs but works instead to continually *destabilise* them. In comparison, an excessively Apollonian or more heavily regulated political economy may work to freeze subjects into a static understanding of self and society alike.

Significant though these complementarities are, what must be established are the more specific terms on which the Foucauldian and postmodern liberal perspectives might be brought into dialogue. One area where the postmodern liberal perspective might address weaknesses in the Foucauldian tradition is by making clearer the epistemic status of its critical claims. If a modernist science of society is to be rejected, then this raises the question of whether there is *any* alternative basis through which to establish notions of scientific 'truth' that can be distinguished from those of a mere 'power/knowledge'. This challenge is especially pertinent for Foucault whose work has regularly been accused of undercutting the basis of its own critical analysis. If *all* knowledge is reflective of an arbitrary 'will-to-truth', then what of Foucault's own 'truth claims'?[50]

The latter problem afflicts both the account of discursive power relations where Foucault arguably fails to explain why his analysis of modern power is to be favoured over alternatives and his critique of scientific power/knowledge regimes. While it is sometimes suggested that Foucault is not interested in normative evaluation per se but in understanding the mechanisms through which different 'regimes of truth' are enforced or 'policed', this reading is hard to sustain given the moral indignation he expresses at the 'intolerable' effects disciplinary gazes have had on the experience of groups marginalised or subjugated by them. Such indignation is, however, itself hard to square with the tight coupling between power and knowledge Foucault expounded in midcareer.[51] If all truth claims are understood as merely a way of exercising power over others, then how are people to know which if any of the 'intolerable' practices they find themselves in are worth challenging or resisting, let alone what might replace them.

[50] Well-known critiques include Fraser, N. (1981) 'Foucault on Modern Power: Empirical Insights and Normative Confusions', *Praxis International*, 3: 272–87; Habermas, J. (1985/1990) *The Philosophical Discourse of Modernity*, Cambridge: Polity Press.

[51] MF (1980) *Power/Knowledge: Selected Interviews and Other Writings*, New York: Pantheon.

Towards the end of his life, however, notably in essays such as 'What Is Enlightenment?', Foucault softened the power/knowledge coupling, adopting a stance that does not deny that there are better and worse forms of argument or that there are some more or less valid forms of knowledge; rather, he emphasises the importance of uncertainty, of keeping all truth claims under scrutiny, and of being aware of the routinised social processes that might block that very scrutiny.[52] There are in this regard important similarities between the Foucauldian perspective and that of Kuhn who analysed the way that the power relations sustaining 'normal science' may block innovation and new forms of understanding.[53] It is here that the concern to decentre expertise and to undermine the arrogance of modernist science might best be situated. What Foucault seems to favour is an environment that preserves a 'pluralism of rationalities' so that people might remain alert to the possibility of multiple ways of their being governed and not being frozen into a particular classificatory grid and the roles and positions it creates.[54] This stance opens a space that allows normative distinctions between different institutions and power regimes to be made—though Foucault himself never articulated a basis for these distinctions.

Postmodern liberalism, by contrast, is much clearer about the appropriate form in which social scientific truth claims and their normative implications might be scrutinised. It argues for a post-foundational, pragmatist, and evolutionist science focused on the comparative plausibility of competing narrative explanations.[55] This perspective recognises human experience as a potential source of knowledge in a context where all experiences of the world must be interpreted through theories and webs of belief that prove themselves not in relation to absolute truth but as contingently better guides to action than available alternatives. In the remainder of this section, it will be argued that this account may be best placed to distinguish the socio-economic contexts where scepticism of the relationship between science and power is especially warranted from those where people may have good reason to accept *at least in a provisional*

[52] MF 'What Is Enlightenment?', in Rabinow, P., ed. (1984) *The Foucault Reader*, New York: Pantheon Books.

[53] Kuhn, T. (1962) *The Structure of Scientific Revolutions*, Chicago: University of Chicago Press.

[54] MF (1982) 'The Subject and Power', *Critical Inquiry*, 8 (4): 777–95.

[55] This account is not from any single text, although many elements are evident in Hayek's methodological work *The Counter-Revolution of Science*, in *The Sensory Order*, and in the essays Hayek 'The Theory of Complex Phenomena' and 'Rules Perception and Intelligibility', both in Hayek, *Studies in Philosophy, Politics and Economics*. See also 'The Primacy of the Abstract' in Hayek, *New Studies*.

Perhaps the clearest statement of the scientific case for interpretive methods in economics and political economy is Lachmann, L. (1970) *The Legacy of Max Weber*, London: Heinemann. See also Madison, G. (1989) 'Hayek and the Interpretive Turn', *Critical Review*, 3 (2): 169–85; Madison, G. (1990) 'Getting Beyond Objectivism: The Philosophical Hermeneutics of Gadamer and Ricoeur', in Lavoie, D., ed. (1990) *Economics and Hermeneutics*, London: Routledge.

sense the conclusions of the relevant science. The subsequent section draws out the residual value of Foucault's power/knowledge concept, exploring how its incorporation into the postmodern liberal perspective may strengthen the latter's understanding of the threat to human agency represented by the scientistic discourses that dominate policy debates in contemporary liberal political economies.

Theory and experience

Foucault's social constructionism demonstrates the instability of truth claims by showing how these are conditioned by historically specific modes of thought (archaeology) and attempts to exert power and authority over others (genealogy). As such, it challenges foundationalist philosophies of science that posit the existence of external, objective truths accessible to the human mind. This leads to a radical suspicion of scientific representations of reality especially in the human and social sciences. In Foucault's view the experience actors have of the world cannot be separated from the theories that construct those experiences, and those theories are shot through with the contingent effects of history and power.

Postmodern liberalism agrees with Foucault that there is no theory-free experience, and that the theories people hold about the world have no necessary connection to an underlying reality. As such, it joins Foucault in challenging the foundationalist claim that agents can have fully justified or certain beliefs on which to ground their actions. While there may be an external reality separate from the theories people hold, given their cognitive limitations and the culturally situated nature of all thought, people may never know if they have a proper grasp of that reality.

Nonetheless, postmodern liberalism does not see the construction of the world in *purely* discursive or theoretical terms, arguing that people's thoughts and constructions may be modified as they interact with that world, in response to various experiential anomalies and acts of human creativity that prompt theoretical reflection. This interplay between theory and experience unfolds with respect both to understandings of the physical world and to the process of making sense of one's own existence and that of other human agents. Hayek, for example, subscribes to a post-foundational view where the ideas people hold are not seen as entirely arbitrary but as representing their attempts to comprehend their environment and to navigate it under conditions of uncertainty. It is precisely from its explicit recognition of the role of experience that postmodern liberalism problematises positivist and behaviouralist conceptions of human action being subject to law-like 'prediction'. While the possibility of accurately predicting the future cannot be ruled out, the *repeated experience* of engaging with and observing other human beings suggests that outside of the routines, traditions, discourses, and disciplines,[56] that give some more or less weakly patterned texture to social life, human behaviour is *not* subject to law-like regularities and that people are to a large degree *predictably unpredictable*.[57]

If human behaviour is neither 'chaotic' nor 'law-like' then everyday social understanding and coordination requires people to navigate the world through the construction of dynamic and evolving *narrative guides* that interpret why those they interact with behave as they do.[58] This requires what Gadamer refers to as a 'fusing of horizons' with the meanings and beliefs of other agents to enable a degree of at least *temporary* overlap across the relevant horizons.[59] Business entrepreneurs must, for example, operate with 'stories' about why consumers value their products while also having stories about their interactions with suppliers when making judgements or guesses about the future reliability of their logistics operations. To act successfully, however, it is insufficient to focus on any belief in isolation from the background web of cultural meanings and traditions within which that belief is situated. In the case of an entrepreneur trying to interpret consumer demand, this is because perceptions about the potential value of new products or technologies will be influenced by the wider web of historical consumption practices in a community and whether any innovation is perceived to 'fit' those practices. Successful action requires engagement in an interpretive or 'hermeneutic circle' where beliefs regarding a particular dimension of conduct are related to a wider network of supporting beliefs and practices and checked for their consistency or compatibility with them. A corollary is that if an unexpected event or an act of creative agency works to unsettle a particular belief—whether in the value of a product, mode of organisation, or social norm or institution—this may have wider destabilising consequences that ripple through an interconnected set of beliefs and practices. Though people always reason from a culturally situated standpoint, the cultural background is rarely static. To operate successfully, therefore, actors must engage in a constant and open-ended process of forming and reforming narratives about the relationship between themselves and others.[60]

[56] Note that though the traditions or disciplines within which agents are situated give some *general* shape to social interactions, this does not imply that people 'schooled' in such traditions and disciplines are predictable in other than a very weak sense. Thus, while a trained boxer may be more predictable in the moves he or she makes than an untrained street-brawler, when faced with a similarly trained opponent, success will depend at least in part on the ability to *surprise* the opponent in question. Similarly, even the most intense drilling by the boxer's trainer will not enable the latter to control or predict the moves that their charge makes when faced with the opponent's actual as opposed to hypothetical combinations.

[57] On this, see esp. Shackle, G. (1972) *Epistemics and Economics*, London: Routledge.

[58] On this, see esp. Lachmann, *The Legacy of Max Weber*, chap. 2.

[59] Gadamer, *Truth and Method*.

[60] Ibid. See also Madison, 'Hayek and the Interpretive Turn'.

An important implication here is that while they are unlikely ever to fully represent reality, the beliefs people hold must have *sufficient* correspondence with that reality to enable them to act satisfactorily in the physical and human world. As Bevir explains,

> Snake catchers in South India cannot treat cobras as harmless or they will be poisoned; they cannot conceive of venomous snakes and non-venomous snakes alike as objects they can pick up without precautions.[61]

Within this context, one reason why there is likely to be at least a *limited* correspondence between people's beliefs and the world they inhabit is because of the effect of evolutionary processes. Hayek and Gaus argue that cultural rules, practices, and belief systems have an evolutionary survival value where certain practices may enable people to survive *better than the available alternatives* but the practices in question may be based on 'false' beliefs. Thus, it is not necessary for snake catchers to properly understand the distinctions between cobras and non-venomous snakes for them to act successfully, and indeed the distinctions they do make might even be 'false'—such as the belief that certain snakes have magical properties that prevent them from harming humans. What matters is that those holding to the belief that there is a distinction between types of snakes are more likely to survive than those who fail to make such a distinction. Similarly, in the economic realm, it is not necessary for a successful enterprise to have a full understanding of what it is about its products that makes them popular with those who buy them. Such an enterprise might have a faulty understanding, but so long as its theories lead it to produce saleable goods, it may be more likely to survive than enterprises whose interpretations exhibit a lesser correspondence with consumer valuations.

A further implication of this pragmatist and evolutionary epistemology is that people may have greater confidence in a particular belief or practice the longer it has been successfully adhered to and the more open it has remained throughout to contestation. While it does not guarantee that beliefs and practices will accurately reflect reality, an environment where those practices are subject to ongoing and pluralistic challenges will be one where there is more likely to be at least some correspondence between what people think about the world and the reality of that world, than if the relevant processes of contestation are blocked or are absent.

[61] Bevir, M. (2022) *Life After God: An Encounter with Post-Modernism*, Leiden: Brill, 110.

Post-foundationalism, narrative interpretation and social scientific truth

Though operating at a higher level of generality, this post-foundational stance suggests that social scientific explanation is simply another form of the everyday narrative interpretation that people must use to navigate and coordinate their interactions with others. Such explanation involves the construction of 'theories about theories',[62] or the 'interpretation of interpretations',[63] in accounting for societal patterns and the intended and unintended consequences of interacting individual and organisational plans. It attempts to construct narratives or stories to understand how more local-level narratives may overlap with each other to generate a wider *trans-subjective social order*, of how such orders may be stabilised, and of the processes through which they might be destabilised. The postmodern liberal analysis of the dynamic and coordinative properties of a market economy constitutes a narrative explanation in this sense. It offers an account of how, in a context where people's beliefs and values sustain a system of private property and contract law, the dispersed and often contradictory economic expectations of multiple agents may be brought into a form of at least temporary overlap through the generation, interpretation, and response to price signals. Foucault's account of discursive power relations and of the emergence of power/knowledge complexes might also be understood as a narrative explanation in this regard. He offers an account of how a set of power relations may emerge as an unintended consequence of multiple dispersed attempts by agents to exert influence and positionality over others and of how overlapping discursive and non-discursive practices may generate a network of cultural norms and expectations that constrain and facilitate certain actions.

This focus on narrative understanding is based partly on the recognition that scientific explanations focussed only on observable aspects of human behaviour are inadequate. One cannot, for example, distinguish monetary exchange from acts of social punishment by merely observing the transfer of small metallic discs between persons without also having an interpretive grasp of what the transfer of such discs may *mean* to those concerned. Similarly, one cannot satisfactorily explain the decision of people not to participate in some form of collective action by invoking *objective* incentives to 'free-ride' without attempting to understand how the relevant actors may *perceive* the incentives in question. Such an approach must recognise that even if they appear to be false or mistaken from an external vantage point, effective explanation of people's actions must recognise

[62] Hayek, *Counter-Revolution.*
[63] Geertz, C. (1973) *The Interpretation of Culture*, New York: Basic Books.

that 'the facts of the social sciences are subjective'—*they are what people think they are*.[64]

Narrative explanation is also the properly scientific mode where theories cannot be subject to falsification via predictive 'tests'. If knowledge prompting action may change between the date of prediction and the date to which the prediction applies, theories that predict how people will respond to changes in otherwise constant environments *cannot* be tested. To 'test' such theories would require an external observer with access to the 'state of knowledge' held by the relevant actor and to discern which part of this knowledge is utilised when a decision is made. Yet since the state of knowledge is continually changing as agents learn from others and from their own experiences, there are no unchanging parameters against which to determine the effect of a change in any specific parameter.[65] In these circumstances, the scientific quality of a theory should *not* be considered against its capacity to predict outcomes but in terms of its *inter-subjective plausibility vis à vis, alternatives*. Just as people in their daily lives are involved in a 'hermeneutic circle' enabling them to act by checking beliefs and theories for consistency with related beliefs so too must social scientists engage in a circle of interpretation about explanations for wider trans-subjective forms of social order. Rival theories and explanations can then be compared, evaluated, and checked for their consistency or plausibility in the light of shared facts or at least shared beliefs about the facts.[66] This stance does not preclude the use of statistics or quantitative methods as part of narrative construction. Such methods may be used to evaluate the plausibility of different narratives and to check for the presence of various patterns. If, for example, a narrative maintains that public expenditure has been reduced but the available descriptive statistics show significant increases in that expenditure, the plausibility of the narrative may be questioned. Similarly, inferential statistics might be used to ascertain whether there has been a patterned association between 'variables' that may have held in a specific period. What the interpretive or narrative method questions is the use of statistical inference to pinpoint the specific causes of events in a 'law-like' or mechanical manner and to predict future events from these historical associations.

In Hayek's view scientific explanations of the narrative kind are appropriate even in some fields of *natural* science where the character of what is being explained prevents the evaluation of theories through falsifying 'tests'.[67]

64 Hayek, *Counter-Revolution*, 44.

65 Lachmann, *The Market as an Economic Process*, 27–31.

66 Bevir and Blakely, *Interpretive Social Science*, provide a recent account and defence of this method. Lachmann, *The Legacy of Max Weber*, provides a comparable account in economics and political economy.

67 Hayek's approach thus remains distinct from Popper's falsificationist—'weak positivist' views—see, e.g., Popper, K. (1959/2002) *The Logic of Scientific Discovery*, London: Routledge. Hayek accepts

In biology and ecology, for example, the data pertinent to processes of evolutionary change are so vast and dynamic that they could not possibly be gathered in such a way as to statistically 'test' predictions derived from evolutionary theories.[68] The scientific status of the theory of evolution, therefore, derives *not* from any predictions based on it, but owing to the *plausibility of the story*, it tells about the process of natural selection compared to alternative accounts of biological and ecological order, such as those emphasising 'intelligent design'.

In the social sciences similar 'explanations of process' or 'predictions in principle', which come in the form of qualitative stories rather than attempts to specify measurable magnitudes, are all that can be offered when the relevant 'data' are the changing thoughts, imaginations, and interpretations of human actors. The postmodern market process theory of the Austrian school is paradigmatic of such 'explanations of principle'. The latter does not 'predict in detail' how entrepreneurs, workers, or consumers will respond to a particular shift in economic conditions but tells a story about the *type of process* through which adjustments to changing conditions might arise in a context characterised by the private ownership of property and of contract law, and of how such a process of adjustment and change may differ from contexts where these institutions and the beliefs sustaining them are absent. Foucault's understanding of power relations as a complex strategic situation involving both equilibrating and disequilibrating processes might be understood in a similar vein—especially so when combined with the evolutionary perspective set out in the previous chapter. His is not a theory that can be subject to falsifying tests, but it is one that offers a narrative account of the type of process through which cultures convey advantages and disadvantages on certain speaking positions and how the pattern of such advantages and disadvantages may shift as an unintended consequence of strategizing by multiple different agents or, alternatively, how a culture might become rigidified or frozen.

that scientific theories must be falsifiable but questions whether falsification should be confined to 'predictive tests'. When exploring 'complex phenomena' it is not possible to know whether a predictive test is properly calibrated for what it purports to be testing. The form of 'testing' must, therefore, be looser than when examining simple phenomena. Though he does not name it as such, the method Hayek favours is closer to that of 'inference to the best explanation'. In this method a theory is 'tested' not through the falsification of predictions but in terms of its capacity to explain an empirical phenomenon relative to an alternative account of the same phenomenon. Thus, Darwin inferred the hypothesis of natural selection not from biological evidence but on the grounds that natural selection provided the best explanation of that evidence. For a discussion see Lipton, P. (2000) 'Inference to the Best Explanation', in Newton Smith, W. H., ed. (2000) *A Companion to the Philosophy of Science*, Blackwell: Oxford. Integrating this view with the interpretive method of the postmodern/postfoundationalist Austrians would require entering a hermeneutic circle where what counts as 'the best explanation' might be the theory most compatible with a wider web of beliefs that people currently have reason to share.

[68] For example, Botkin, D. (1990) *Discordant Harmonies*, Oxford: Oxford University Press.

Post-foundationalist science and postmodern liberal truth claims

It should be evident from this account that the post-foundational pragmatist view of science does not imply a retreat into relativism or the suggestion that all claims to knowledge are *merely* a form of power. From a hermeneutic or interpretive perspective not all stories and narratives should be considered equally plausible given the background beliefs that social theorists and laypersons alike may share. Owing to the widely shared experience that humans are fallible, limited in their cognitive span, and capable of creative agency, for example, the postmodern liberal narrative of why 'really existing market economies' tend to generate a greater level of dynamic coordination than 'really existing planned economies' might be considered *more plausible* than alternatives that interpret market phenomena as the product of historical laws, conspiratorial design by a controlling mind or group, or of perfectly informed responses to objectively 'given' data about tastes and relative resource scarcities. Similarly, given the complex character of contemporary societies and the multiplicity of decision points within them, Foucault's decentred account of the emergence of socio-cultural power relations might be considered *more plausible* than theories reducing the exercise of power to the control of economic resources or to holding positions of political office. Foucault's perspective also offers a plausible narrative to explain why the effects of power may not be confined to the *overt* suppression of others knowledge but may also work through less readily observable mechanisms where the authority conveyed on certain discourses and speaking positions operates as a form of cultural habituation, limiting the consideration of alternative problem constructions and blocking or constraining open-ended creativity.

On the view advanced here, it is in the context of the intersubjective plausibility of their respective theories that the postmodern liberal and Foucauldian perspectives might also ground normative critiques of political economic regimes that centre decision-making authority with those claiming modernist expertise. While a consistently post-foundationalist philosophy of science cannot rule out the possibility that future experience may challenge the contention that human creativity renders law-like predictions about individuals or populations unattainable, it suggests that there are plausible *scientific reasons* to be highly sceptical of such methods and to resist attempts to combine them with the exercise of administrative state power.

Recast in terms of this post-foundational stance, the terms on which Foucault might offer normatively relevant distinctions between different power regimes may be brought more clearly into view. In short, if we understand human beings as 'complex phenomena' in the Hayekian sense, then given uncertainty about the boundaries between the effects of nature and those arising from discourses and disciplines in creating the sense of self, there is justifiable scepticism of power regimes that align claims to scientifically 'know' the essence of human selves or of populations via the juridical powers of states. Foucault's analysis of the unpredictable shifts or ruptures in understandings of humans as humans, of how claims to scientific knowledge have been entwined with attempts to exert power over others, and of the potentially negative consequences for those subject to various scientific gazes offers a compelling though contestable narrative that may inform peoples actions when faced with those claiming scientific authority to govern them. Though disciplinary power and bio-power are not *necessarily* negative in their consequences, there are reasons to be especially wary of *totalising* power regimes that align their truth claims with state power because of their greater potential to lock or to freeze people in a particular form of self-understanding. This might in turn lead Foucauldians to offer at least tentative support for broadly liberal market economies. While networks of expertise are omnipresent throughout such societies, they do not exercise the same degree of power over people, witnessed historically in, for example, fascist regimes, the former Eastern bloc countries, or regimes such as contemporary North Korea.

In the case of economic bio-power specifically, concepts such as 'market economy' and 'planned economy' are discursive or ideational constructs that may not necessarily reflect a definitively 'true' representation of that which they describe. Nonetheless, if they value economic creativity and the material prosperity it brings, then at least *where they have had experience of them*, people have reason to make a distinction between social institutions that centralise decision-making authority from those, such as private property and contract law, that operate with a relatively more decentred understanding of knowledge about self and society. This is a provisional or fallibilist truth claim about the value of broadly 'market economies' that Foucauldians concerned with maintaining a pluralism of rationalities might endorse. The enforcement of institutions based on these distinctions will inevitably be entwined with the exercise of power, but this does not mean that these claims to knowledge can be *reduced* to the exercise of such power. The 'bio-power' of postmodern liberalism is explicit in recognising that *all* truth claims, *including its own*, should be exposed to ongoing contestation. Its scientific and normative objection to a planned economy is precisely that such models block the evolution of knowledge through a totalising form of 'bio-power' that grants public agencies the authority to determine what is true.

The relative absence of such a power is best illustrated at the global level where there is no governmental arbiter of truth; and where the existence of states such as Cuba, Bolivia, North Korea, Venezuela, and Iran; and the possibility for future democratic socialist, authoritarian, and theocratic experiments of this kind afford space for discursive-institutional claims about the advantages of predominantly market systems to be *continuously* challenged and to become more, or less, robust. In Foucauldian terms the international order offers examples of 'heterotopias' or 'dystopias' where, faced with a vision of how they should be governed, subjects can form alternative conceptions which might enable them not to be governed 'like that, by these people, and at that price'.[69] Experiments with *non-totalising* forms of planning are also permissible, but the open-ended production of knowledge is only possible in settings where no monopolistic agency has the authority to determine which experiments should proceed and how their results should be interpreted. Similarly, a post-foundationalist endorsement of market institutions does not imply rejecting all forms of 'intervention' or 'regulation' in them or an endorsement of all aspects of 'capitalism as we know it'. It recognises that markets are not 'natural' phenomena and that they can be governed in different ways. What it problematises are centralised or monopolistic forms of 'intervention' and 'regulation' grounded in claims of modernist expertise.

Power effects and socio-economic modernism in liberal political economies

The foregoing analysis has shown that there are scientific, non-relativist grounds for scepticism of bio-political regimes that claim to know the nature of individual selves and to scientifically manage complex socio-economic phenomena. Both the postmodern liberal and Foucauldian perspectives favour a plural-rationalities approach alert to the processes through which alignments between modernist scientism and state power may limit that pluralism. The postmodern liberal stance emphasises how these alignments may stifle the identification of opportunity costs and the creation of alternative forms of production, consumption, and regulation. The Foucauldian perspective on the other hand emphasises the importance of 'power effects' that may limit people's capacity to explore alternative conceptions of themselves and ways of being governed. As well as the overt mechanisms that may impede the exploration of alternative constructions, Foucault highlights the *less perceptible* ways that the exercise of power may block the process of evolution or may constrain the paths on which it proceeds. It is here that a focus on the 'power effects' of socio-economic scientism may offer an important complement to the postmodern liberal analysis by highlighting the more, or less, subtle processes through which alignments between bio-political discourses and state authority may insulate themselves from experimental challenge.

[69] MF 'What Is Critique?', in MF, ed. (2007) *The Politics of Truth*, trans. Hochroth, L., and Porter, C., Los Angeles: Semiotext, 75.

While the threat to creative agency from a scientistic bio-power may be greatest under regimes of centralised socio-economic planning, milder threats to pluralism may also occur in the context of broadly liberal though 'entangled political economies' where modernist forms of economic theory predominate. Indeed, it may be especially important to explore the possible workings of these processes in such regimes precisely because they rely less extensively on 'command and control' techniques and their 'power effects' might be correspondingly harder to detect. The purpose of analysing the relevant policies and discourses is not to demonstrate that they are objectively 'wrong' but to show that even in contexts where there is a relatively greater dispersal of decision-making authority, alignments between modernist discourses and state power may work to *restrict pluralism*. To illustrate the relevance of these potentially illiberal 'power effects', the final part of this chapter considers two modernist bio-political *discourses* highly influential in postwar political economies: the 'science of aggregates' in macroeconomics and the 'science of incentives' in microeconomics.

Modernist liberalism and macroeconomic bio-power

Foucault uses the term *dispositif*, or apparatus, to refer to an interlinking set of philosophical and scientific understandings that set the acceptable boundaries for public discourse and the conduct of government. Within this context, the *dispositif* of modern macroeconomics refers to an interlinking set of discourses, concepts, and theories that analyse 'the economy' in terms of the interaction between aggregate variables. For much of the postwar period Keynesianism was pre-eminent in this tradition before it was challenged and temporarily replaced by monetarist and new classical doctrines in the 1980s. What emerged in the mid-1990s, however, and has persisted beyond the financial crisis of 2008, is a hybrid between Keynesian and monetarist/new classical theories; the distinguishing feature of which is a commitment to the use of 'stimulus' measures, whether a fiscal or monetary kind, based on assumptions about the predicted response of 'representative economic actors' to the relevant stimuli.[70]

[70] Note, the rational expectations school remains critical of this perspective. It maintains that 'stimulus' is ineffective because businesses, consumers, investors, and taxpayers will already incorporate the future impact of these decisions into their current behaviour and adjust accordingly—by for example curtailing current spending in anticipation of future tax rises. It arrives at this view from a different scientistic assumption—namely that representative economic agents carry in their heads an accurate understanding of the effects of current government policies on future rates of taxation and interest. The work of Robert Lucas is exemplary of the rational expectations school—see, e.g., Lucas, R. (1972) 'Expectations and the Neutrality of Money', *Journal of Economic Theory* 4 (2): 103–24; Lucas, R. (1976) 'Econometric Policy Evaluation: A Critique', *Carnegie Rochester Conference Series on Public Policy*, 1: 19–46.

Understood in Foucauldian terms this *dispositif* operates through a discursive and decentred power network connecting economics as a social scientific discipline with the major institutions of state such as treasuries and central banks, as well as various industrial and financial interests, and much of the public and private media.[71] This network emerged not through deliberate design or conspiracy but in a decentred vein through a concatenation of events that gradually aligned economic expertise with state authority. Specifically, the socio-political status of economics as the pre-eminent social science arose in the historical context of the interwar and postwar periods when natural science methods were seen as the pinnacle of scientific advance, and with economics perceived to be the social science most closely linked to such methods. This identification has subsequently been maintained by the exercise of disciplinary power within the economics profession, 'policing' the scientific credentials of work for its adherence to mathematical formalism and the application of econometric techniques. The demand for such work has in turn been sustained by a network of analysts in private industry and more important by officials and politicians in governments, central banks, and treasuries, whose own prestige and claims to expertise are closely aligned with macroeconomic discourse.[72] In many cases this discourse has been entangled with a particular set of institutional privileges and monopoly powers such as, for example, the power to issue currency, to regulate financial transactions, to issue public debt, and to levy taxes.

Central to the macroeconomic *dispositif* is a metaphor of the economic order as a smoothly running machine usually in a steady equilibrium but one prone to periodic 'break-downs'.[73] Though the different schools of macroeconomics disagree about the source of these 'break-downs' and the appropriate technical 'fixes' for them, what unites the *dispositif* is a modernist belief in the desirability of order, control, and predictability and a related belief that macroeconomic 'engineering' in the face of disequilibria enables the delivery of such control. In the case of Keynesianism, the disequilibria in question are instabilities in 'aggregate

The current 'new classical' and 'New Keynesian' synthesis retains the view that expectations must be accounted for by policymakers but emphasises 'rigidities' in the informational environment in which economic agents act—it is these 'rigidities' that are held to allow for policy interventions to make a difference and to have 'corrective' effects.

[71] Thornton, T. (2016) *From Economics to Political Economy: The Problems, Promises and Solutions of Pluralist Economics*, London: Routledge. See also in the specific case of Keynesianism, Guizzo, D. (2016) 'Keynes, Keynesianism and the Political Economy of Power of the Post-War World', PhD thesis, Federal University of Parana, Brazil.

[72] Thornton, *From Economics to Political Economy*; Guizzo, 'Keynes, Keynesianism'. See also Marcussen, M. (2009) 'Scientization of Central Banking: The Politics of A-Politicization', in Marcussen, M., and Dyson, K., eds. (2009) *Central Banks in the Age of the Euro: Europeanization, Convergence and Power*, Oxford: Oxford University Press.

[73] For a discussion of this metaphor see Wagner, R. (2020) *Macroeconomics as Systems Theory*, London: Palgrave.

demand' arising from 'weaknesses' or 'excesses' of consumer and investor 'confidence' that generate 'output gaps' between what could be produced with current resource endowments and what is in fact produced. Deficit finance measures are the favoured tool to redress these 'imbalances' with tax cuts and/or public expenditure increases favoured during a slump to 'stimulate' aggregate demand and tax hikes and/or public expenditure cuts preferred during a boom to lower 'irrational exuberance'. For new classical and monetarist theorists on the other hand, 'disturbances' in the circulation of money are judged as the primary cause of instability in an otherwise stable economic order, with the manipulation of interest rates and control of the money supply the principal tools to address instability by lowering rates during deflationary downturns and raising rates when the threat of general inflation looms.

A liberal-Foucauldian analysis of this scientific *dispositif* would not deny that the situational logics analysed by modern macroeconomics *may* reflect 'real' phenomena leading to unsatisfactory outcomes such as prolonged unemployment, deflation, or inflation. Nonetheless, it would question the capacity of the macroeconomic gaze to properly diagnose the causes of economic fluctuations and to 'correct' them accordingly. Keynesian attempts to smooth fluctuations in 'total demand' for example, rely on aggregate-level statistics that abstract from the often contradictory time- and place-specific interpretations that inform multiple individual and organisational decisions. This 'government by statistics' may obscure or erase ongoing shifts in the distribution of demand across different markets with measures to 'stimulate' demand and to eliminate 'output gaps' potentially freezing what might otherwise be a dynamic process for the reallocation of labour and capital between alternative lines of production. Similarly, monetarist proposals for the targeting of monetary aggregates to discern the appropriate rate of money growth assume that it is possible for those in charge of the relevant authorities to dispense with localised and context-specific understandings that may influence the willingness of actors to issue credit and to hold cash. More broadly, all modernist macroeconomic theories that attempt to manipulate economic aggregates face a significant 'knowledge problem' in predicting how these actions will affect the subjective expectations of heterogenous agents whose *diverse* interpretations of localised economic conditions cannot be reduced to those of 'representative actors'.[74] Even post-Keynesian theories which share with postmodern Austrians a focus on the significance of radical uncertainty

[74] Keynes's views do not necessarily conform to the modernist label. With his emphasis on radical uncertainty both reflecting and generating 'animal spirits', Keynes might even be described as a 'postmodern liberal'. Where Keynes differs from the position enunciated here is by centring policy experts' capacities to promote coordination by manipulating 'animal spirits'. For an account emphasising Keynes's anti-modernist credentials see Parsons, W. (1997) *Keynes and the Quest for a Moral Science*, Cheltenham: Edward Elgar.

emphasise the use of aggregate concepts as 'scientific tools' for macroeconomic management and thus downplay the problems that may arise from *differential* interpretations of what the relevant aggregates 'mean' or consist of, as well as how diverse agents may respond to centralised attempts to manipulate them.[75] The central contradiction of Keynesian and post-Keynesian theories alike is the suggestion that the 'non-scientific' creative drives or 'animal spirits' of entrepreneurs and investors can be subject to a predictable form of stimulus response. As one critic puts it:

> As long as the world is not entirely totalitarian . . . neither the objective data of the future nor the subjective reactions of millions of individuals can be predicted.[76]

Within this context and notwithstanding the massive data-generating exercises informing what has become in many countries an immense apparatus of taxing, spending, and regulatory and money-printing powers, there is little or no clear evidence that such measures have contributed to the reduction of economic fluctuations.[77] The question might thus be raised as to why these governance regimes have remained relatively stable for such a prolonged period. It is here that a liberal-Foucauldian perspective would highlight the interaction between the more overt ways that the macroeconomic *dispositif* may work to limit pluralistic contestation and to 'police the truth' and the subtler processes through which it may conceal some of its own 'power effects'.

Turning first to the most visible manifestations of macroeconomic power/knowledge, both the postmodern liberal and Foucauldian perspectives would emphasise the problem that people face in evaluating the 'truth claims' of economic experts when these claims are so closely linked with the

[75] The leading post-Keynesian is Hyman Minsky—e.g. Minsky, H. (1986) *Stabilizing an Unstable Economy*, New York: McGraw Hill. See also Davidson, P. (2017) *Who's Afraid of John Maynard Keynes?*, New York: Palgrave-Macmillan. Post-Keynesians follow Keynes in suggesting that a 'somewhat comprehensive socialisation of investment' may reduce uncertainty. For postmodern Austrians, however, since the relevant 'big players' in the state agencies charged with this investment will be as prone to error as anybody else, such a move may *increase* uncertainty as market participants must continually second guess the systemic consequences of the 'big players' actions—see Butos, W., and Koppl, R. (1993) 'Hayekian Expectations: Theory and Empirical Applications', *Constitutional Political Economy*, 4 (3): 303–29.

G. L. S Shackle, who is included here in the postmodern Austrian camp, is sometimes considered a 'post-Keynesian' owing to his focus on the 'kaleidic' quality of markets and their resultant instability and for his support of public works schemes. What distinguishes Shackle from post-Keynesians is that he did not see these measures as a superior coordinating procedure but as ameliorating the hardships brought about by an economic instability with no obvious 'cure'.

[76] Hahn, A. (1949) *The Economics of Illusion: A Critical Analysis of Contemporary Economic Theory and Policy*, New York: Squier.

[77] For example, Selgin, G., Lastrape, W., and White, L. (2012) 'Has the Fed Been a Failure?', *Journal of Macroeconomics*, 34 (3): 569–96.

exercise of legislative power. Macroeconomic scientism goes hand in hand with a centralisation of decision-making in central banks and treasuries that privileges the speaking position of economic experts in 'grading' different states of the world and in judging their own actions in a manner that may reduce opportunities for those subject to these decisions to witness alternative possibilities or counterfactuals. This problem may be exacerbated in a context where the social status and positionality of macroeconomic managers may be dependent on there not being significant disagreement between the relevant experts less this undermines their claims to expertise. Once power/knowledge claims have been made by 'big players' in the financial system, these may act as a focal point for finance ministries and central banks in other countries, 'seeking cover' for their own expertise by aligning with measures adopted elsewhere. In the aftermath of the financial crisis of 2008, for example, central bank officials and finance ministers in many Western democracies seized new financial and regulatory powers and judged *themselves* to have 'saved the international financial system' from what they claimed would otherwise have been an economic cataclysm[78] if large financial institutions had been allowed to fail.[79] The problem here, however, is that *any* macroeconomic intervention can be justified on the grounds of the 'disorder' predicted to prevail without the intervention, but the very exercise of these powers may reduce the scope of the social constructions that underlie these discourses from being challenged by alternative interpretative frames, such as, for example, those emphasising the capacities of people to reshuffle resources and to generate new patterns of saving, consumption, and employment. It is precisely such entanglements between macroeconomic discourse and legislative authority that may make it difficult for people to conceive of challenges to the explanatory categories of the *dispositif* and to consider alternative possibilities for action.

In addition to these more overt 'power effects', Foucault's perspective would also emphasise the possible role of less readily perceptible limitations on pluralism arising from the impact the macroeconomic *dispositif* may exercise on the routinised expectations of those immersed within its constituent discourses. Of particular importance here may be the power of metaphors such as 'the economy as machine'. Judging the outcomes of economic processes against such a metaphor may subtly privilege the case for granting powers to those who would impose a particular interpretation of what the 'ideal' or 'normal' rate of growth, monetary circulation, spending, and employment should in fact be. Such 'normalising' discourse may be understood as equivalent to the disciplinary power exercised

78 Koppl, R. (2018) *Expert Failure*, Cambridge: Cambridge University Press.

79 In Berger and Luckmann's view such tactics are a common strategy to cajole populations into acquiescence with expert opinion—see Berger, P., and Luckmann, T. (1966) *The Social Construction of Reality*, New York: Anchor Books, 68.

against individuals who exhibit what have historically been considered 'disruptive' or 'deviant' behaviours. In the context of macroeconomic bio-power, the relevant 'normalising' assumption is that economic 'stability' is *inherently* desirable and that economic events or actions departing from this norm require some form of 'treatment' or 'intervention'.[80] Yet, if market economies are understood as a cauldron of ceaseless change where values, preferences, and expectations are in a state of flux, then the very idea of a 'normal' rate of growth, investment, monetary circulation, spending, and employment against which any given state might be judged needs to be problematised. Though some stability in the rules of interaction between people may be required to sustain socio-economic life, such as those of property and contract, unless human creativity is eliminated then the relevant rules are unlikely to generate stable outcomes. To evaluate the performance of the socio-economic order against the ideal of a stable 'machine' may thus be to generate a near permanent demand for 'interventions' in its operations—a demand that might be interpreted as a 'power effect' of this very discourse. Similarly, the discursive representation of 'the economy' as a unitary entity that can be surveyed and managed from a 'governing site', as circulated repeatedly in both official and everyday macroeconomic 'talk', may conceal from view that what is targeted by macroeconomic decision-makers are not necessarily 'real' phenomena but congeries of statistics and projections, which have no necessary correspondence to the multiple and often contradictory social constructions that inform the day-to-day decisions of workers, consumers, and investors.

Crucially, these 'power effects' may operate not only on the conceptual frames through which people perceive economic problems but also on how actors see *themselves and others* through processes of objectivation and subjectivation. While postmodern liberalism suggests that socio-economic uncertainty cannot be eradicated in the context of a complex and advanced economic order, Foucault's approach would emphasise that how such uncertainty is *experienced* by agents and the relationships they have with others may be affected by the prevailing discursive frame and the positionality it confers on different speaking positions. Keynesian discourses, for example, posit a division between the great mass of economic actors considered prone to at least short-term 'irrationality' or 'rigidity' and a set of 'economic physicians' in central banks and finance ministries who are assumed to be fully rational, or at least 'more rational', and thus better positioned to identify 'output gaps' and close them accordingly. Where the prevailing discourse implies that absent 'stimulus measures' entrepreneurs,

[80] On the centrality of 'stability' to the macroeconomic *dispositif* see the discussion by Abolafia on macroeconomic advisers' rationales for responding to the financial crisis of 2008—Abolafia, M. (2020) *Stewards of the Market*, Cambridge, MA: Harvard University Press.

savers, and consumers *cannot* through their independent actions make necessary adjustments to 'market instabilities'—or at least not in 'sufficient time'—then many such agents may no longer *see themselves* as capable of adjusting to shifting economic sands without some form of 'stimulus', and they may come to 'demand' or expect such measures as the required response to economic perturbations. The latter is a possible illustration of what Hacking refers to as a 'looping phenomena' where the very way that people are described by the macroeconomic gaze may change the way that they behave and their self-understanding.[81] Note, however, that the emergence of a widespread routinised belief in such measures and an alignment between the views of economic experts and those who will be subject to them need not increase the likelihood that the policies concerned will 'work'. Actors sharing a belief in the need for certain macroeconomic policies are still likely in their daily consumption and investment decisions to behave in ways that may counteract the intentions of those implementing the relevant policies.

Looping effects are not necessarily a top-down phenomena but may arise in a decentred vein as macroeconomic management tropes are taken up by actors in markets, civil society, and the media to advance certain worldviews or interests. Consider in this context how in the aftermath of the 2008 financial crisis, automobile corporations and unions in the United States mobilised Keynesian theories about the need to maintain confidence and to avoid 'downward spiralling' when lobbying for government bailouts of major automobile businesses. Elsewhere, monetarist discourses have increasingly been adopted by many players in financial markets to lobby for the continuation of the quantitative easing measures originally adopted after the crisis of 2008—measures that have often disproportionately delivered funds to actors in asset markets and that may have generated or produced a set of interests who now associate their economic well-being with the continuation of such measures. Many of these actors had earlier succumbed to the hubristic and scientistic belief that risk had effectively been eliminated from these markets, or at least had been 'accurately priced' by complex financial-modelling instruments, but they were quick to mobilise discursive tropes favouring a form of government intervention perceived as beneficial to their interests when the hubris was revealed.[82]

The point here is not to suggest that the macroeconomic policies in question are *necessarily* 'wrong' or that it is impossible for them to 'improve' on economic patterns that would otherwise be established. Rather, the suggestion is that

[81] Hacking, I. (1999) *The Social Construction of What*, Cambridge, MA: Harvard University Press. An empirical example of this phenomena is documented by Holmes who explores how the self-understanding of central bankers is influenced by concepts derived from economic theory—see Holmes, D. (2013) *Economy of Words: Communicative Imperatives in Central Banks*, Chicago: University of Chicago Press.

[82] On this see, e.g., Dowd, K., and Hutchinson, M. (2010) *Alchemists of Loss: How Modern Finance and Government Intervention Crashed the Financial System*, Chichester: John Wiley.

dominant macroeconomic discourses and their alignment with state power may affect how economic fluctuations are *experienced* by actors and may influence what is considered true about such fluctuations, *irrespective of whether it is true.* They may for example, lead people to assume that avoiding severe downturns requires submission to an apparatus of taxing, spending, and money-printing powers and that those seeking to resist such powers are a disruptive threat to the social order. Human agency is not eliminated by such legislative-discursive alignments, because it remains possible for contrarian actors to perceive the situation differently. Nonetheless, where discursive currency and the authority of the state combine, they may habituate people into a particular cognitive frame that makes it *more difficult* for them to conceive of and to witness alternative scenarios for how they might be governed. Such habituation effects may be particularly powerful when legislative or sovereign power prevents those with contrarian perspectives who do wish to 'resist' the dominant narrative from *acting* on their beliefs, as is the case when, for example, public agencies prohibit the issuance of alternative currencies.[83]

Modernist liberalism and microeconomic bio-power

The discursive dominance of modernist economic theory in its macroeconomic form has also been evident in a corresponding alignment between many public policy institutions in liberal political economies and its microeconomic sibling—the 'discourse of incentives'. Where macroeconomic modernism focuses on aggregate variables, microeconomic modernism turns its gaze to the 'incentive structures' held to affect the performance of markets and of the agencies often charged with regulating them.

Traditionally, this analysis focused on the incentives leading to market 'efficiency' and to market 'failure'. The former is held to predominate when competition incentivises property owners to internalise the costs of their decisions and where equilibrium prices reflect all relevant cost-benefit margins. By contrast, market 'failures' predominate where the 'non-excludability' of certain goods or various information asymmetries between buyers and sellers allows some actors to externalise costs onto others. In this narrative the regulatory role of the state is to change the incentive structure facing the relevant actors; internalising costs by modifying market prices through regulations, taxes, or subsidies; and by regulating the terms of trade between private parties. With the 'public choice revolution' of the 1980s, however, the scope of the discourse of incentives widened

[83] On the public suppression of parallel or alternative currencies see White, L. (2014) 'The Troubling Suppression of Competition from Alternative Monies: The Case of the Liberty Dollar and E Gold', *Cato Journal*, 34 (2): 281–301.

to include analyses of 'government failures', as well. Here, actors in governmental agencies are also understood to be self-interested, and their propensity to act in ways that might 'correct' market failures will be dependent on their incentives to do so. Government bureaucracies may, for example, have monopoly powers that enable them to impose costs on others, they may use informational advantages over citizens to extract 'rents' from the public purse, and they may be captured by business and labour lobbies to the detriment of consumer welfare.[84]

Though mainstream microeconomics differs in the relative weights it attaches to market and government failures, what unites the microeconomic *dispositif* is the belief that economic experts can identify the relevant 'incentive structures' and where necessary *redesign* incentives to produce desirable outcomes. A recent manifestation of this stance is represented by the 'mechanism design' theories developed by Hurwicz and his followers that purport to account for the respective failures of markets and states by designing the right 'mix' of incentives.[85] This attitude is also evident in the widespread adoption of the 'field experiments' and 'randomised control trials' pioneered by Banerjee and Duflo.[86] The latter is less focussed on the comparative qualities of markets and governments per se, favouring instead a 'problem-based' approach that seeks to identify 'what works' in solving specific problems—such as improving educational outcomes in schools. Nonetheless, it is characterised by the belief that economic analysts can use quasi-experimental methods to objectively identify the relevant causal factors and manipulate them to produce better outcomes through a social engineering model. The economist is constructed and positioned as akin to a physician or plumber—able to diagnose and offer a technical 'fix' to a clients' problems—though not necessarily a fix that the 'client' has been consulted about or directly asked for.

While the extent to which the growth of the regulatory state can be attributed to this discourse remains in doubt, there are few public policy interventions that have not been justified in these terms, with multiple policy domains in liberal democracies drawing at least loosely on the narrative that 'incentives matter', and with economics sustaining a reputation as the pre-eminent 'policy science'. The proximity of this science with state institutions and their capacity

[84] Public choice theory is now more widely recognised, but in the dominant centres of economics education and in the most frequently adopted textbooks it remains a *minority* discourse. Recent studies suggest that textbook coverage typically allots five to ten times as much space to 'market failure' analyses as it does to 'government failure' analyses. See, e.g., Eyzaguirre, H., Ferrarini, T., and O'Roark, J. (2016) Textbook Confessions: Of Failures, Markets and Government, *Journal of Economics and Finance Education*, 15 (2): 60–71.

[85] For example, Hurwicz, L., and Reiter, S. (2006) *Designing Economic Mechanisms*, Cambridge: Cambridge University Press.

[86] Banerjee, A., and Duflo, E. (2011) *Poor Economics: A Radical Rethinking of the Way to Fight Global Poverty*, New York: Public Affairs; Duflo, E. (2012) 'Human Values and the Design of the Fight Against Poverty: Paternalism Versus Freedom?', Tanner Lecture, Harvard University, 2 May.

to communicate, project, and circulate these discourses may in turn have exercised an important influence driving the gradual expansion in government power. The implications inferred from microeconomic discourse have varied over time with alternating bouts of nationalisation and privatisation, and with moves to regulate, deregulate, and re-regulate markets; but the overall trend has been one marked by a significant though gradual expansion of public authority.[87]

Now, from a postmodern liberal/Foucauldian perspective, what needs to be problematised here is not so much the idea that 'incentives matter' but the scientistic assumption that knowledge of the incentives in question is accessible to those claiming the relevant expertise to engage in the necessary acts of 'treatment' or 'institutional design'—and the possible impact that being subject to the designers' gaze may have on peoples' identities and their capacities for action.

Consider here the analysis of the 'collective action problems' and 'information asymmetries' that play such a prominent role in modern microeconomic theory. The depiction of agents in these discourses as narrowly self-interested presents an essentialist logic where goods or services deemed to exhibit the objective quality of 'non-excludability', or a particular level of technical complexity, will not be supplied or at least not in 'sufficient' quantities or qualities without intervention by government agencies. From a social constructionist standpoint, however, whether a good has the characteristics of a collective good will often be contingent on the discourses, traditions, and cultural beliefs of the actors concerned and their relative propensities to consider 'free-riding' as an option. It may also be affected by the creativity of those in question to solve collective action challenges should they in fact arise. Similarly, whether the participants to various exchanges are likely to take advantage of information asymmetries to the detriment of other parties is not an objective property aligned with the characteristics of specific goods or services but will be affected by the cultural, moral, and professional values of those concerned and their creativity in responding to any contexts where such asymmetries are perceived as problematic. Seen in this light, the totalising logics of modern microeconomic theory and its scientistic methods ignore or erase the plural rationalities and the subjective, situational knowledge of actors about their own capacities and motives, as well as those of others in their environment.

87 Haldane documents the consistent expansion of regulation even during periods that have been characterised as 'de-regulatory'. In the UK financial sector, for example, there was one regulator employed for every 11,000 employees in financial services for the year 1979, but by 2011 this ratio had increased to one regulator for every 300 financial services employees—even though total employment in financial services had increased only marginally during this period. See Haldane, A. (2012) 'The Dog and the Frisbee' speech, Federal Reserve Bank of Kansas City's 366th economic policy symposium, 'The Changing Policy Landscape', Jackson Hole, Wyoming, 31 August, pp. 13–14, https://www.bis.org/review/r120905a.pdf.

In the latter context and commensurate with Foucauldian genealogy, authors in the Austrian and Coasian traditions have 'unearthed' numerous forgotten examples of alleged collective action dilemmas, from the supply of lighthouses to television signals, and from sewage systems to the provision of streetlights, where far from displaying an objective 'essence', entrepreneurial creativity had enabled 'collective goods' to be supplied without the assistance of centralised public authority.[88] Similarly, the hundreds of case studies examined by Ostrom have uncovered a multiplicity of governance arrangements that have managed goods predicted by neo-classical economics to suffer from free-riding dynamics.[89] Crucially, not only have these arrangements managed to avoid or to overcome such dynamics, but they also have done so through a mosaic of governance arrangements involving complex mixes of private, communal, and public rights that transcend the binary of 'private' and 'public' ownership or regulation—none of which were anticipated by mainstream economic models as viable options for managing the relevant assets and resources. Elsewhere, numerous markets predicted by microeconomic models not to function owing to information asymmetries have been found to operate without central regulation and have evolved complex governance arrangements to deal with issues of trust that were not anticipated by economic theorists.[90] Correspondingly, many of the behaviours predicted to arise in government agencies by public choice theorists have often failed to materialise. This is not necessarily because public choice theory is wrong about the importance of incentives, but because many of those devising the relevant public choice models simply lack the situational knowledge to assess what the incentives are in a plurality of agencies and different cultural-institutional settings.[91]

Given this modernist and scientistic insensitivity to local context, microeconomic discourses have often contributed to the imposition of classificatory schemes or explanatory grids on people that do not correspond to the structure of the choice situations perceived by the actors themselves. Ostrom's work offers numerous cases of attempts by expert bodies to impose rules for the management of what they deemed to be goods subject to depletion owing to the free-rider problem that led to worse outcomes than those prior to the introduction of the rules concerned. In many such cases those most familiar with the resource base were faced with a choice of submitting to a set of externally imposed rules alien to the decisional context as they saw it, and thus of having to act in the manner of subordinates, or, alternatively, of breaking the rules in question at the

[88] Spulber, D., ed. (2001) *Famous Fables of Economics: Myths of Market Failure*, London: Wiley.

[89] Ostrom, E. (1990) *Governing the Commons*, Cambridge: Cambridge University Press.

[90] Spulber, *Famous Fables of Economics*.

[91] Rubin, E. (2002) 'Public Choice, Phenomenology and the Meaning of the Modern State', *Cornell Law Review*, 87 (2): 309–61.

risk of disciplinary sanction. Similar dynamics have arisen following attempts to introduce 'performance targets' and other 'new public management' techniques in public sector environments. In settings ranging from schools and universities to police departments, those subject to these techniques have been placed in a position of subordinating their experiential knowledge of what matters to those they serve to meet quantitative performance metrics analogous to those adopted by socialist regimes to induce managerial accountability to planning targets. As in such systems these centralised attempts to 'improve incentives' have often been accompanied by efforts to 'game the system' as producers focus their activities on what can be measured to avoid disciplinary action—to the neglect of more qualitative dimensions of service quality.[92]

From a Foucauldian perspective, however, the latter dilemmas may be only one manifestation of the possible 'power effects' arising from a setting where a scientistic economic narrative attains a kind of cultural currency and where it is assumed that economic experts have or can attain clearly defined answers to multiple socio-economic problems. First, when prevailing discourses centre the knowledge of economic experts to attend to matters of institutional design, then the potential for localised agency and creativity may be erased, lost, or denuded. The more time subjects must spend satisfying bureaucratic rules and quantitative targets, the less time they may have for creativity or innovation that breaks from established routines.

Second, and relatedly, the institutionalisation of economic narratives surrounding phenomena such as free-riding, externalities, and information asymmetries may work to *produce* a subjectivity of helplessness on the part of many people—a situation where the possibility of successful private action or of community self-governance is *experienced* as a practical impossibility, and where it may become the norm to accept or even to demand recourse to centralised solutions to multiple problems constructed in terms of these logics.

Third, these discourses might be mobilised by actors outside of the relevant science to seek power over others. Nowhere may this phenomenon have been more pronounced than in the deployment of the concept of externalities. When little or no objective data may be available to assess the sizes or directions of externalities or whether private or communal actions are sufficient to internalise them, then power/knowledge claims may assume considerable significance with 'externalities' used as a rhetorical device in Foucauldian 'cynicisms of power' to redistribute rights and resources between actors. Grow Sun and Daniels refer here to the important role played by 'externality entrepreneurs' in private interest groups and public bureaucracies labelling certain activities as the generators of externalities or as other forms of market failure to secure power and resources at

[92] Muller, J. (2015) *The Tyranny of Metrics*, Princeton, NJ: Princeton University Press.

the expense of other actors.[93] Such entrepreneurship may in turn have generated a mimetic or discursive currency multiplying demands for regulatory action in many different fields. McCloskey, for example, documents over one hundred alleged externality problems or other forms of market 'imperfection', most of which, though cited as justifying state action, have never been subject to empirical scrutiny.[94]

None of the above implies that the scenarios referred to in neo-classical micro-theory are of no relevance to *some* real empirical phenomena, and neither does it imply that there are effective solutions to such challenges that might be found without publicly organised institutional designs informed by such expertise. What the analysis does suggest, however, is that wherever there is a strong alignment between public policy and these discourses, then it may be hard to discern the extent to which the problems they depict are 'real' or 'discursively generated'—and that the dominance of such discourses may diminish the possibility for people to create their own responses, if and when they have the capacity to do so.

Conclusion

This chapter has argued that Foucault's concern to limit the subjugation of people by systems of expert rule and his social constructionist analysis of modernist bio-power may have a close affinity with postmodern liberal critiques of regulatory regimes which suppose that people and populations can be 'known by science'. These critiques, it was suggested, may also be strengthened by an appreciation of the 'power effects' that alignments between scientistic discourses and state power may exercise on subjects in constraining their potential for creative agency. This combined Foucauldian and postmodern liberal position points towards a deep scepticism of modernist economic and philosophical approaches, often though not exclusively associated with utilitarianism, which presuppose that 'the welfare of the population' can be secured by a form of 'expert rule'. The pages that follow turn now to the dominant discourses of freedom and rights in liberal political philosophy that work outside of an exclusively utilitarian framework, which from a Foucauldian and postmodern liberal standpoint are also reliant on rationalistic assumptions and a set of 'dividing practices' that represent a further source of potential 'over-government' in contemporary political economies.

[93] Grow Sun, L., and Daniels, B. (2016) 'Externality Entrepreneurism', *University of California Davis Law Review*, 50: 321–403.

[94] McCloskey, D. (2022) *Beyond Positivism, Behaviourism and Neo-Institutionalism in Economics*, Chicago: University of Chicago Press, chap. 3.

4
Freedom and Rights
Power/Knowledge and the Social Construction of Liberal Justice

Introduction

The discussion so far in this book has established important commonalities between the Foucauldian and postmodern liberal perspectives in their understanding of agency and structure and of threats to human freedom from alignments between scientific discourses and the juridical authority of states. Building on these analyses of the relationships between discursive and non-discursive institutions, this chapter focuses on discourses of rights, justice, and freedom in the liberal tradition and their potential 'power effects'.

Foucault's philosophical stance is often associated with deep scepticism of liberal rights because they neglect the significance of discursive power relations *outside* of the law, and because they are often construed by liberal discourses as the expression of a universal human nature and rationality that Foucault rejects. Late in life, however, Foucault recognised the scope of rights to work as potential tools of freedom but without specifying any principles to inform which rights might satisfy this role. The following pages thus engage Foucault's understanding of freedom with the competing conceptions of rights offered by the dominant egalitarian tradition in contemporary liberal political philosophy and those of a postmodern liberalism. They argue that Foucault's conception of freedom should tilt towards the embrace of largely negative rights because, while these do not directly address asymmetries in power, such rights reduce the likelihood that decentred power relations will align with sovereign or state power. By contrast, the extensive positive or welfare rights favoured by egalitarian liberals presuppose a potentially *illiberal* apparatus of disciplinary and bio-political surveillance that aligns decentred power relations with sovereign power in ways that may narrow the scope of subjects to exercise creative freedom.

Developing these points, the first section presents Foucault's conception of freedom as self-creation and his understanding of the potential sources of unfreedom. This is followed by an outline of the role that positive conceptions of rights and freedom play in some of the major contributors to liberal egalitarian

Foucault and Liberal Political Economy. Mark Pennington, Oxford University Press. © Mark Pennington 2025.
DOI: 10.1093/9780197690550.003.0004

thought. Subsequent sections develop a Foucauldian and postmodern liberal critique of the disciplinary and bio-political tendencies prominent in these discourses paying particular attention to their potential 'power effects' and exploring how negative rights may be better placed to sustain a Foucauldian 'pluralism of rationalities'.

Foucault on freedom, self-creation, and power

Foucault on freedom as self-creation

One of Foucault's most distinctive contributions to political thought is his understanding of freedom. Given his view that subjects are fabricated by power, freedom for Foucault does not equate to a state where a true or underlying self finds its authentic expression. Rather, freedom is understood as a 'critical practice' where people engage creatively with their culture, drawing on techniques or strategies they find *within it* to explore alternative possibilities or 'limit experiences' that push, challenge, or transgress the classificatory boundaries in which they are situated.[1] A subject whose mind and body has been disciplined in their familial and work environments may, for example, draw on other disciplinary techniques they observe in the social environment, such as a sporting discipline, a psychological or sexual technique, or religious practice to *refashion or re-subjectify* themselves and to explore alternative forms of selfhood.[2]

In his later works on personal ethics and 'care of the self', Foucault sees human subjectivity as an emergent 'work of art'—not in the sense of being 'free from government' but of engaging in a process of ongoing critique and finding alternative ways of being governed to those within which one currently lives and that mark out ones individuality.[3] While people are always the products of 'technologies of the self' that 'govern' them, they also have scope to consciously adopt certain techniques to take 'care of the self' and to exercise a form of self-mastery.[4] This process of self-government should not, however, be confused with one where agents discover an 'inner' truth but as an open-ended 'art of living'. It is precisely

[1] Foucault, M. (hereafter MF) (1993) 'About the Beginnings of the Hermeneutics of the Self', *Political Theory*, 21 (2): 198–227; See also MF 'What Is Enlightenment', in Rabinow, P., ed. (1984) *The Foucault Reader*, New York: Pantheon Books, 45.

[2] MF (1988) 'The Ethic of the Care of the Self as a Practice of Freedom', in Bernauer, J., and Rasmussen, D., eds. (1988) *The Final Foucault*, Cambridge, MA: MIT Press; see also MF 'What Is Critique?', in Lothringer, S., and Hochroth, L., eds. (1997) *The Politics of Truth: Michel Foucault*, New York: Semiotext.

[3] MF (1984) *The History of Sexuality*, vol. 3: *The Care of the Self*, London: Penguin.

[4] MF 'On the Genealogy of Ethics: An Overview of Work in Progress', in Rabinow, P., ed. (1997) *Ethics, Subjectivity and Truth*, New York: New Press.

those discourses that view human agents as having an underlying truth that risk constraining them within contingently constructed categories.[5] Thus, 'the target nowadays is not to discover who we are but to refuse who we are'.[6]

Within this context, Foucault's conception of freedom does not specify the practices to which people should adhere to be free. In an important sense, therefore, Foucauldian freedom is close to a 'negative' conception. So long as subjects may act or comport themselves differently, they are to be considered 'free', irrespective of whether or how they use that freedom.[7] Given his decentred account of power relations operative *outside* of the law, however, Foucault's understanding precludes the identification of freedom as the complete *absence* of 'interference' or of 'government'. Since subjects can never exist 'outside' of power, freedom is not the absence of social 'interference' but is exercised *in relation to various attempted forms of interference.* While the power relations emergent from multiple efforts to 'conduct the conduct' of others are exercised only over 'free agents' and should not be confused with slavery or states of domination, they are forms of government nonetheless and not a 'power-free' realm. Asymmetries of power, however, are *not* in themselves a threat to freedom, and indeed it is precisely by challenging such asymmetries and of taking risks when doing so that people may *exercise* their freedom.[8] In this sense freedom refers to an active state. Exercising freedom is to *refuse a state of passive acceptance*, to expose oneself to risk and to place one's identity on the line. This account comes to the fore in Foucault's discussion of *parrhesia*, or free speech, where freedom is the act of standing up and confronting power directly—as did the dissidents in Eastern Europe speaking out against socialist regimes.[9]

In the middle stages of his career the idea of 'resistance' in Foucault's thought seemed to imply an imperative for 'total innovation' with subjects needing to engage in a more, or less, constant process of revolt against their current conceptions of themselves and institutions. Setting aside the exhausting quality of this demand for permanent reinvention and the state of paranoia about the effects of power it might generate, this phase of Foucault's work seems deeply at odds with any practicable notions of self-creation and functioning social institutions. How might subjects have any appreciation of themselves as a 'work of art' if every aspect of what they are is ripe for destabilisation from one day to the next? Similarly, how might subjects have any confidence that what they are

[5] For example, MF (1984) 'Polemics, Politics and Problematizations: An Interview', in Rabinow, *The Foucault Reader*, 383–5. For discussion on this aspect of Foucault's thought see also McNay, L. (1994) *Foucault*, Cambridge: Polity Press, esp. chap. 4; Ocksala, J. (2006) *Foucault on Freedom*, Cambridge: Cambridge University Press, esp. chaps. 7–9.

[6] MF (1982) 'The Subject and Power', *Critical Inquiry*, 8 (4): 777–95, quote at 785.

[7] Ibid., 790.

[8] MF (2011) *The Courage of Truth*, London: Palgrave.

[9] MF 'Fearless Speech', in Pearson, J. ed. (2001) *Fearless Speech* New York: Semiotext.

creating will be protected when the institutions they must draw on to build their lives and to engage with others are open to constant attack?[10]

Later in life, however, Foucault's emphasis shifted towards one of 'immanent criticism', with no implication that people should engage in endless bouts of self-criticism or that *all* social institutions should be subject to permanent destabilisation. Thus,

> We know from experience that the claim to escape from the systems of contemporary reality so as to produce the overall programs of another society, of another way of thinking, another culture, another vision of the world, has led to the return of some of the most dangerous traditions. I prefer the very specific transformations that have proved to be possible in the last twenty years in a certain number of areas that concern our ways of being and thinking, relations to authority, relations between the sexes, the way we perceive insanity or illness.[11]

What appears to be favoured by the later Foucault is a personal and social ethic and an institutional setting keeping open the possibility for incremental challenge to the status quo on multiple different margins for those who wish to engage in such challenge.[12] Inspiration is drawn from ancient Greek ethics with its focus on the exercise of freedom within a *limited set of binding rules* that allow for the process of personal experimentation and self-creation to proceed. There is no suggestion here of 'going back' to the specific practices of the Greeks but of drawing on them as a historical inspiration to a different type of morality. As Foucault explains:

> The few great common laws—of the city, religion, nature—remained present, but it was as if they traced a very wide circle in the distance, inside of which practical thought had to define what could rightfully be done . . . Therefore, in this form of morality, the individual did not make himself into an ethical subject by universalising the principles that informed his action; on the contrary he did so by means of an attitude and a quest that individualised his action, modulated it, and perhaps even gave him a special brilliance by virtue of the rational and deliberate structure his actions manifested.[13]

[10] This tension is also evident in Nietzsche. Thus, 'enduring habits . . . I hate and feel as if a tyrant has come near me and the air around me is thickening when events take a shape that seems inevitably to produce enduring habits'. Yet, on the other hand, 'the most intolerable, the truly terrible, would of course be a life entirely without habits, a life that continually demand improvisation—that would be my exile and my Siberia'. See Nietzsche, F. (2008) *The Gay Science*, Cambridge: Cambridge University Press, 168.

[11] MF 'What Is Enlightenment', 46–7.

[12] Ibid.

[13] MF (1984) *History of Sexuality*, vol. 2: *The Use of Pleasure*, London: Penguin, 62.

Foucault on freedom, rights, and domination

The freedom Foucault envisages then is one embedded in critical practices, and it defines unfreedom, domination, and abuse in terms of the *suppression of those practices*. This can be overt through laws and institutions that block certain actions, such as curtailments on speech, but it can also operate in a more decentred vein through the institutionalisation of routinised assumptions that circulate in discourses and disciplinary practices. The capacity for people to reflect critically on themselves and their environment and to engage freely in re-creative acts is dependent on maintaining a pluralism of rationalities, while the latter is itself sustained by the ongoing willingness of subjects to use their freedom to transgress classificatory boundaries. Thus, Foucault is concerned to avoid 'strategic codifications' of power where these refer to alignments between power relations operating in civil society, the economy, and the state, such that the contradictions, gaps, and ambiguities that characterise a more pluralistic set of social relations are excessively narrowed.

Consider here the practice of veiling by Muslim women.[14] If this occurs under a secular state or a religious state where religious pluralism is tolerated and in a commercial society, then, while it may reflect a form of patriarchal domination, it is also possible that Muslim and perhaps also non-Muslim women might adopt the veil as form of *critical practice* or *self-fashioning*. Though this setting would not constitute a 'power-free' environment—with pressure from both commerce and religious normalisation representing the relevant 'power effects'—neither would it represent a state of 'domination'. Those subjectified within religious power relations might, for example, see in certain commercial and secular practices the scope to challenge or to reformulate what had previously been 'taken-for-granted' aspects of their religion, while those seeking to engage critically with commercial practices and discourses might turn to religion to do so. Women may veil as an act of resistance against the effects of commercial objectivation, and even those who do not might be alerted to its possible effects through exposure to those who do veil. By contrast, should veiling occur under a theocratic state that threatens violence and that controls employment and consumption practices as well as religious expression—then this might be considered a 'strategic codification'. Domination might also prevail under a secular state outlawing religious practice and controlling all processes of production and consumption.

[14] This example draws on one from Valdez, I. (2016) 'Non-Domination or Practices of Freedom? French Muslim Women, Foucault and the Full Veil Ban', *American Political Science Review*, 110 (1): 18–36. See also Mahmood, S. (2012) *Politics of Piety: The Islamic Revival and the Feminist Subject*, Princeton, NJ: Princeton University Press.

Though concerned to avoid such states of domination, Foucault was wary of seeking to eliminate power asymmetries per se. The reasons for this are illustrated by his critical engagement with radical left accounts of revolution. For theorists of the Frankfurt school such as Horkheimer and Adorno, freedom is the 'liberation' of an 'alienated' or 'authentic' human nature from the repressive effects of social institutions and, in particular, those of capitalism.[15] Similarly, Habermas identified freedom as a perfectly transparent and 'power-free' form of communication between citizens, with money and commerce seen as the primary 'distorting' influences.[16] For Foucault, however, since there is no authentic self or rationality 'outside' of power, the idea of a 'power free' or 'transparent' environment is chimerical, with claims to know which institutions and policies will 'liberate' such an essence—another example of a 'will to knowledge' or power/knowledge claim.[17]

Moreover, since power operates largely through decentred cultural processes, attempts to 'free' subjects by seizing control of state agencies are dangerous. This is because if the discourse of those with state power does not align with discursive power relations elsewhere in society, it is unlikely to generate a transformation without the widespread use of violent and/or authoritarian powers such as those witnessed under communist and fascist rule. Dean and Villadsen emphasise that Foucault associates these excesses with the institutionalisation of claims to speak 'for others' or 'above others'. In the former instance, his targets are the representational claims of totalising political entities that purport to embody the 'true' voice of the people—such as those of Leninist vanguard parties and those forms of parliamentary socialism claiming to represent the 'true' interests of the proletariat. When referring to those who speak 'above others', his targets are institutionalised claims to knowledge manifested in networks of appointed experts and organised science that derive their backing from state authority.[18]

Such risks from state domination are, however, heightened wherever the discourse of state *does* align with dominant discourses elsewhere. Here state power may simply *reinforce* power relations in civil society and the economy, further reducing the scope for challenge and transgression. The threat of domination then can arise from both 'above' and 'below' and is at its greatest when 'ascending' and 'descending' forces combine. In seeking to avoid such domination, however, it is important not to seek a 'power-free' setting. Thus,

[15] Horkheimer, M., and Adorno, T. (1944/1972) *The Dialectic of Enlightenment*, New York: Herder and Herder.

[16] Habermas, J. (1984) *The Theory of Communicative Action*, Boston: Beacon Press.

[17] On the debate between Foucault and Habermas, see Ashenden, S., and Owen, D., eds. (1999) *Foucault Contra Habermas*, London: SAGE.

[18] Dean, M., and Villadsen, K. (2016) *State-Phobia and Civil Society: The Political Legacy of Michel Foucault*, Stanford: Stanford University Press, 60–1.

> I don't believe there can be a society without relations of power, if you understand them as means by which individuals try to conduct, to determine the behaviour of others. The problem is not trying to dissolve them in the Utopia of a perfectly transparent communication, but to give oneself the rules of law, the techniques of management, and also the ethics that will allow these games of power to be played with a minimum of domination.[19]

For all this, Foucault was conspicuous in failing to explain what the 'rules of law', the 'techniques of management', and the 'ethics' might be[20]—because there is no explicit theory of institutions such as the state in the Foucauldian oeuvre. Rather, the state is interpreted as a mobile plane or complex assemblage of 'technologies of government'. Though they may be generated from within the state, power techniques such as hierarchical observation and individualisation against a norm often develop initially in localised sites such as hospitals, which then become templates for adoption in other settings such as schools and prisons, adapting themselves to the educational and penal purposes in hand. As these techniques and discourses cohere into a more general strategy of social organisation or *dispositif*, they may colonise the state apparatus such that it mirrors the society in which it is embedded.

For much of his career Foucault was also sceptical if not hostile to liberal notions of rights because the decentred character of 'governmental activity' *outside* formal law renders them irrelevant to the problem of power, and indeed discourses of liberal rights may cynically operate to obscure the operation of such power. Rights to 'non-interference' or to 'bundles of resources' may, for example, conceal from view that groups such as women and homosexuals are already subjugated by discursive power relations operative within the home and in civil society. Moreover, the discourse of Enlightenment liberalism draws on a form of abstract philosophical reasoning that centres the philosophers' views on human nature, rationality, and the rights that flow from it, thus concealing its perspectival character—much as the social scientific rationalism discussed in the previous chapter centres the experts' points of view and masks its 'power effects'.

This scepticism towards liberal rights appears, however, to have moderated in the later 1970s with Foucault's involvement in the campaigns of East European dissidents and public support for the Polish Solidarity movement. Similarly, having appeared sympathetic to the Iranian Revolution of 1979 as a spiritual uprising against the modernist gaze of the Shah, Foucault was chastened by

[19] MF 'The Ethic of the Care of the Self', 18.

[20] MF in Dreyfus, H., and Rabinow, P. (1983) *Michel Foucault: Beyond Structuralism and Hermeneutics*, Chicago: University of Chicago Press, 231–2.

the emergence of a theocratic state that crushed religious and other freedoms, suppressed women, and culminated in the execution of 'deviants'—such as homosexuals.[21]

Insofar as he subsequently endorsed rights, however, by, for example, campaigning as a gay activist, Foucault never saw these rights as the moralised recognition of an underlying or natural essence. Protections for those engaging in same-sex practices were warranted not to free a 'gay essence' but because allowing 'gay' people to live their lives more openly might alert people in general to a greater set of creative possibilities for human relationships and forms of sexual expression. This is at one with Foucault's 'anti-normative' or 'postmodern' stance which sees the institutionalisation of any one set of ethical or rational standards not as a protection of freedom but as a 'normalising society', stifling freedom and the processes of social contestation that allow new evaluative standards to emerge.

Nonetheless, Foucault did not offer an account of the relationship between coercive state power and decentred power and of the role of rights in maintaining a pluralism of rationalities. Neither was the plural rationalities approach explicated with respect to matters of economic resource distribution that cut across sociocultural power relations. The liberal tradition, has by contrast, been much more specific in considering the relationships among rights, resource distribution, and state power but with significant differences between the emphasis on positive welfare rights in the discourse of high-modern and egalitarian liberalism and the focus on predominantly negative rights,[22] in the classical liberal, libertarian, and what is defined in this book as the postmodern liberal tradition. The next section turns to the relationships among positive welfare rights, freedom, and public authority in the most influential strands of liberal egalitarian thought.

Egalitarian liberalism on positive rights, freedom, and non-domination

Contemporary liberal political philosophy uses different terminology than Foucault, but its case for rights protections is oriented towards a framework that may facilitate the exercise of individuals' creative powers and avoid states of unfreedom that is potentially compatible with Foucault's search for 'the rules of law, techniques of management, and the ethics that minimise domination'. John

[21] In 1979 Foucault visited Iran to report on the revolution—for an analysis and critique of his coverage see Afary, J., and Anderson, K. (2005) *Foucault, Gender and the Iranian Revolution*, Chicago: University of Chicago Press.

[22] The distinction is discussed by Berlin, I. 'Two Concepts of Liberty', in Berlin, I. (1969) *Four Essays on Liberty*, Oxford: Clarendon Press.

Rawls, for example, focuses on the conditions that enable individuals to freely exercise their 'moral powers', and Ronald Dworkin works with a 'choice-oriented' conception of freedom. Elsewhere, the radical egalitarianism of Gerald Cohen favours structures that allow individuals to freely pursue their 'self-realisation', while the capabilities approach of Amartya Sen and Martha Nussbaum examines the substantive freedoms that enable individuals to make use of their 'creative capacities'.

The concern for individual freedom within the liberal egalitarian tradition is associated with support for a range of state-guaranteed rights to wealth or resources and the capacity to use such resources that go well beyond the 'negative rights' to 'non-interference' favoured by classical liberals and libertarians. Central to these narratives is a 'positive' conception of freedom, where wealth is seen as a 'ticket' that gives its holder access to otherwise unattainable possibilities and that opens new creative horizons.[23] Wealth may also lessen a person's dependence on others and reduce their likelihood of being subject to a state of servility or domination. In this regard, liberal egalitarians share the concerns of republican theorists, such as Pettit, that people may be unfree or dominated even if they are *not* subject to direct interference—it is the possibility that someone *could* be subject to interference that may lead them to subordinate themselves to others, and freedom from such domination requires access to resources guaranteed by a public system of justice.[24] Thus, a worker with a state-guaranteed income need not cater to their employers' whims for fear of losing their job and being reduced to destitution. Similarly, a woman with a secure and independent income may be less likely to be dominated by her spouse and confined to traditional gender roles or subject to domestic violence than an equivalent woman lacking an income.

Though wealth is an important component of freedom so too, however, is a culture of equal respect ensuring that people are not unduly inhibited in using their freedom by social norms and traditions. A gay or lesbian child guaranteed an education that teaches principles of equal respect across different sexualities may, for example, be more likely to take the opportunities afforded by their freedom than one taught that homosexual people are inferior or morally degenerate. It follows that if people are to be free from the constraints of material deprivation or of social tradition, then sovereign state action must extend beyond the protection of mere 'non-interference' rights to guarantee the resources and background culture that will ensure whatever negative freedoms people have are freedoms 'worth having'.

[23] See, e.g., Cohen, G. (1995) *Self Ownership, Freedom and Equality*, New York: Cambridge University Press, 58–9.

[24] Pettit, P. (1997) *Republicanism: A Theory of Freedom and Government*, Oxford: Oxford University Press.

Positive rights, impartial justice, and egalitarian liberalism

The liberal egalitarian approach finds its most influential expression in Rawls's *Theory of Justice*, where the thought experiment of the original position is deployed to derive impartial rules separate from the powers and interests that drive day-to-day political economic bargaining.[25] The Rawlsian approach aims to neutralise factors such as the value of talents or the effect of cultural or familial background that are outside of an individual's control but may impact the 'fair value of their liberty'. The logic of this experiment is that if people do not know their position in society, their talents, social advantages, or the conception of the good that they will pursue, they will favour a set of rights that would willingly be entered into by *all* agents *irrespective* of their social position. Reframed in terms of Foucault's freedom as self-creation, if one does not know what kinds of self might be possible, then one might favour institutions that allow the greatest scope for any actor to engage in the process of self-creation.

What emerges from this reasoning are Rawls's two principles of justice. The first, which has priority, is the principle of basic liberty, including freedom of religion, freedom of occupation, freedom of the press, as well as non-discrimination, and political freedoms such as voting rights and the right to join political parties. The second, the 'difference principle', states that inequalities in access to primary goods such as food, clothing, healthcare, and education that are relevant to the 'social bases of self-respect'—are justified only if they work to the maximum advantage of agents from the least-advantaged class. Such inequalities are themselves only justifiable if they arise from a position of 'fair equality of opportunity' which addresses differences in family background and wealth.

'Fair equality of opportunity' is also central to the 'luck egalitarian' liberalism pioneered by Ronald Dworkin.[26] In his view, the Rawlsian approach is insufficiently 'choice sensitive' because it fails to grant adequate scope for human agency. For Rawls, even decisions to work hard or to take risks are attributed to 'morally arbitrary' factors that make it hard for any actor to be said to have deserved or to have chosen anything. Couched in Foucauldian terms, though people are not responsible for the culture that 'produces' their subjectivity, this does not imply that they have no scope to exercise creative agency or resistance. In Dworkin's view, however, by effectively denying a role for such agency, the application of the difference principle discriminates against those who prosper through certain choices they make and against those who find themselves in the least-advantaged class through factors beyond their control.

[25] Rawls, J. (1971) *A Theory of Justice*, Cambridge, MA: Harvard University Press.

[26] Dworkin, R. (1981) 'Equality of Resources', *Philosophy and Public Affairs*, 10 (4): 283–345; Dworkin, R. (2000) *Sovereign Virtue: The Theory and Practice of Equality*, Cambridge, MA: Harvard University Press.

Dworkin's 'luck egalitarianism' favours instead welfare rights that track the principle of 'equality of resources' and the distinction between 'option luck' and 'brute luck'. The former refers to risks that people may consider when making choices or investments such as pursuing a particular career path or business deal with a given bundle of resources. Also included are ambitions or acquired preferences that may arise from having made certain choices or sets of choices. Inequalities reflecting such agency are justifiable and should not be seen as legitimate targets for redistributive action. Inequalities reflecting 'brute luck', by contrast, should be subject to compensatory action through a system of public justice. People whose freedom is constrained by their genetic makeup or by a lack of material wealth or cultural capital should be entitled to compensation for their relative misfortune. Similarly, impartiality requires that the beneficiaries of brute luck should compensate those who find their freedom constrained by circumstances beyond their control.[27]

The different inequalities legitimated by Rawls and Dworkin are, however, both seen as incompatible with a properly impartial stance by Gerald Cohen. Cohen is informed by a radical socialist ethic but works within the parameters of egalitarian or positive/welfare rights liberalism. According to Cohen, the inequalities in wealth and freedom justified by Rawls are unduly biased by the assumption that people are predominantly self-interested and require inequalities in access to consumption goods if they are to be motivated to produce the wealth necessary to maximise the positive freedom of the least advantaged. Similarly, though Dworkin's luck egalitarianism tracks 'socialist equality of opportunity', it assumes that people will not ameliorate let alone eliminate inequalities arising from the choices and risks they voluntarily assume. Yet, in Cohen's view it should not be assumed that people cannot be moved towards 'the fullest realisation of their nature', and to embrace a 'socialist principle of community' that does not place selfish motives above the welfare of the least advantaged.[28] Rawls's and Dworkin's understandings of impartiality are biased by the discourses and behaviours that dominate contemporary capitalist welfare states and that present themselves as natural or unchangeable aspects of the human condition—or in Foucauldian terms they reflect and indeed may reinforce 'capitalist subjectivations'.

To illustrate the impartial value of socialist equality of opportunity and socialist community, Cohen draws on the practices embodied in a camping

[27] Given the role that equality of opportunity plays in the Rawlsian and Dworkinian approaches, the key disagreement is that where Dworkin sees no case for redistribution once starting points have been equalised, Rawls believes that the difference principle should also be applied to inequalities emergent from a condition of fair equality of opportunity.

[28] Cohen, G. 'Incentives, Inequality and Community', in Darwall, S., ed. (1995) *Equal Freedom: Selected Tanner Lectures on Human Values*, Ann Arbor: University of Michigan Press; Cohen, G. (2008) *Rescuing Justice and Equality*, Cambridge, MA: Harvard University Press.

trip—where the participants pool all of their property, where all work as hard as is required for the trip to go well, where food and goods are held in common and shared freely, and where there are no contribution-based distinctions in access to goods or status.[29] The impartial character of these values and behaviours is, Cohen suggests, indicated by the fact that most people—including those living in capitalist societies, would recognise that their experience of camping would change for the worse if people behaved as they do in private markets, where a competitive spirit reigns, where goods are privately appropriated, where skills and aptitudes are rewarded differentially, and where there are marked differences in wealth and status.

Positive rights, pluralism, and political liberalism

The commitments to positive rights by Rawls, Dworkin, and Cohen stem from a deontological philosophical stance aiming to identify universal standards of freedom and justice derived from impartial reasoning. In recent years, however, these 'comprehensive' approaches have been joined by one that grounds the case for positive rights and freedoms not from a universalist position but from a convergence on certain institutional rules and principles that may be supported by plural perspectives—not dissimilar to Foucault's 'pluralism of rationalities'.

In *Political Liberalism* Rawls himself played a significant role in these developments, suggesting that his principles could form the basis for a stable and 'well-ordered society' sustained by an 'overlapping consensus' between agents with a plurality of differing though 'reasonable' worldviews.[30] Though members of a political community may in their private lives hold to very different morals or 'comprehensive doctrines', their public lives as citizens require convergence on a set of political principles. On this view, there needs to be a stable framework of *public morality* that governs interactions that must be acceptable to *all* citizens irrespective of wealth, social status, culture, or religious background—not determined by bargaining and power politics. These principles are democratic and participatory in spirit and embodied in the notion of 'public reason', and it is citizens committed to such reasoning who endorse Rawlsian justice. The latter reflects the principle of public reason while sustaining the conditions (basic democratic freedoms, fair equality of opportunity, and maximising the position of representatives from the least-advantaged class) that prevent the process of public deliberation from being dominated by those with wealth or power.

[29] Cohen, G. (2009) *Why Not Socialism?*, Princeton, NJ: Princeton University Press.

[30] Rawls, J. (1993) *Political Liberalism*, New York: Columbia University Press; Rawls, J. (2001) Justice as Fairness: A Restatement, in Kelly, E., ed (2001) *Justice as Fairness: A Restatement*, Cambridge, MA: Harvard University Press.

This focus on democratic participation in the later Rawls also finds expression in the 'capabilities' approach of Amartya Sen[31] and Martha Nussbaum.[32] For Sen and Nussbaum, it is insufficient to focus on the resources and freedoms that subjects have as these are reflected in the law without also paying attention to their 'capacities' to exercise these freedoms in ways that enable them to live creative and fulfilling lives. 'Substantive freedoms' are related to wealth and resources that may be guaranteed through positive rights, but they cannot be reduced to having such rights. Poverty may prevent people from exploring their capacities, but so too may a state of ignorance; oppression by public or private actors; or being trapped in a particular frame of mind, ideology, or what Foucault would understand as a totalising discursive formation. In this sense Sen, Nussbaum, and Foucault all echo John Stuart Mill's concerns about the decentred role of culture and public opinion in constraining freedom. As Mill, puts it,

> Protection, therefore, against the tyranny of the magistrate is not enough; there needs protection also against the tyranny of the prevailing opinion and feeling, against the tendency of society to impose by other means than civil penalties, its' own ideas and practices as rules of conduct on those who dissent from them; to fetter development, and if possible to prevent the formation of any individuality.[33]

Within this context, capability for Sen refers to the capacity of agents to achieve valuable 'functionings'. Eating, starving, and fasting are all 'functionings', but *capacity* is the ability to choose between these different states. A destitute person does not choose to starve even though there may be no difference in the observable state of a starving person and someone who is fasting. Similarly, a woman confined to a life of domestic servitude owing to a lack of education or because of an education that naturalises such roles for women does not choose such a state compared to a woman preferring domesticity in full awareness of what she might achieve by pursuing a professional career. In Sen's view, therefore, freedom is the capacity to exercise self-mastery or choice over the direction of one's life, and as for Foucault, understanding an agents' freedom must go beyond observing the 'revealed preferences' of the subject to examine the cultural context within which such preferences are formed and exercised.

[31] For example, Sen, A. (1999) *Development as Freedom*, Oxford: Oxford University Press; Sen, A. (2004) 'Elements of a Theory of Human Rights', *Philosophy and Public Affairs*, 32 (4): 315–56.

[32] For example, Nussbaum, M. (1994) 'Human Functioning and Social Justice: In Defence of Aristotelian Essentialism', *Political Theory*, 20 (2): 202–46; Nussbaum, M. (2000) *Women and Human Development: The Capabilities Approach*, Cambridge: Cambridge University Press; Nussbaum, M. (2003) 'Capabilities as Fundamental Entitlements: Sen and Social Justice', *Feminist Economics*, 9 (2): 41–4.

[33] Mill, J. S. (1981) *On Liberty*, ed. Gertrud Himmelfarb, New Yok: Penguin, 63.

Nussbaum's approach also overlaps with Foucauldian concerns about the decentred operation of power 'outside' of the law and was developed through a feminist analysis of gendered power-relations in the home. Nussbaum follows Susan Moller Okin, criticising the Rawlsian distinction between the private realm of family life and the public world of justice, rights, and resource distribution.[34] For Nussbaum resource distribution is relevant to the attainment of capacities with different actors requiring different levels of resourcing to achieve equivalent levels of capacity. A childbearing woman may, for example, require more resources to develop the same capacities as a single man. Equally though, women's capacities may also be affected by cultural expectations that they should look after the elderly and disabled and be responsible for unpaid work in the home—expectations that may narrow their capacity to live richer and more varied lives. Nussbaum's focus on cultural power relations thus draws attention to how a subject's capabilities reflect not only their *internal* capacities but also the discursive conditions within which those capacities are fostered or stifled.

Though recognising the importance of wealth, Nussbaum does not equate freedom with wealth because achieving certain capabilities may be in tension with the production of more goods—as for example where pollution impairs people's health or where capacities to appreciate the wonders of the natural world may be impeded in a cultural-discursive context saturated by materialistic values. Nussbaum thus joins Sen in challenging narrowly output- based measures of development such as GDP per capita growth that neglect the complex and multifaceted character of human capabilities and freedom.

In their various contributions Sen and Nussbaum working in almost a Foucauldian vein reject an essentialist reading of human nature that identifies external criteria of human flourishing and an abstract set of institutions considered most compatible with that flourishing.[35] Rather, their focus is on the substantive freedoms and opportunities that have been *historically experienced* by subjects living under different institutional regimes and the processes of interpersonal reasoning through which they might come to evaluate these different states of the world. On this view, claims about human nature and social institutions are part of a process of public reasoning from which we neither can nor need to operate 'outside of' to make evaluative judgements. There is no need to have a theory of an idealised state of freedom to recognise that, for example, South Korean institutions do better in promoting substantive freedoms than do those in North Korea.[36]

34 Moller Okin, S. (1989) *Justice, Gender, and the Family*, New York: Basic Books.

35 Nussbaum describes her approach as Aristotelian essentialism. She does not support naturalist, teleological views, favouring instead an 'internalist essentialism' which rejects any claim 'that there is a determinate way the world is apart from the interpretive workings of the cognitive faculties of living beings'—see Nussbaum, 'Human Functioning and Social Justice', 206.

36 Sen, A. (2009) *The Idea of Justice*, London: Allen and Lane.

What emerges from the capability approach is a complex account where the scope to exercise choice or self-government depends on multifarious combinations of contextual factors that cannot be reduced to one dimension such as wealth or access to a particular set of services or opportunities. Rather than the maximum advantage of the worst off, or strict equality substantive freedoms are seen in terms of the attainment of some minimum threshold. Nussbaum lists the various capabilities required for what she sees to be a creative and fulfilling life but does not offer any quantitative weighting of the different components, suggesting only that some threshold level should be attained for people's freedom to be honoured.[37] Sen is even less prescriptive, insisting only that processes of democratic deliberation allowing for a properly open process of public reasoning are the most basic elements of freedom—and they require that people have access to some threshold level of capacities to participate in the democratic process that must be guaranteed by the system of public justice.[38]

The over-governed subject and egalitarian liberalism I: Impartiality, positive rights, and pastoral power

By focussing on resource distribution and power relations inside and outside the law, the liberal egalitarian approaches highlighted above may be considered better attuned to Foucault's emphasis on the complex constraints facing subjects than classical liberal or libertarian discourses that conceptualise freedom more narrowly as the mere absence of 'coercive interference' with rights to person, property, and contract. It will be the contention here, however, that such a conclusion may be unwarranted. Far from preserving spaces for freedom as self-creation, egalitarian discourses have the potential to 'over-govern' these spaces owing to their propensity to speak 'for or above others'. The ethical standards these discourses advance, though claiming to reflect 'impartial' or 'public' forms of reasoning, are in fact partial perspectives that were they to be institutionalised may curtail the ethical reflexivity central to a Foucauldian 'pluralism of rationalities'. Moreover, the means egalitarian liberals propose to secure positive freedoms and capabilities implicitly or explicitly depend on disciplinary and bio-political classification mechanisms that may lock people into socially

[37] The list includes the capacity to live a normal length of life; possession of bodily and mental health; the right to bodily integrity and the capacity to seek sexual satisfaction; the use of one's imagination and free expression; the capacity to have emotional attachments to others; engagement in practical reason and the formulation of a conception of the good life; the capacity to affiliate with others; the capacity to appreciate the non-human world; being able to engage in play and recreation; and the capacity to control one's environment—including the right to effective democratic participation, and the right to hold property and to enter contracts.

[38] Sen, A. (1999) 'Democracy as a Universal Value', *Journal of Democracy*, 10 (3): 3–17.

constructed categories. Starting with the comprehensive approaches of Rawls, Dworkin, and Cohen and moving on to the political liberalism of the later Rawls, Sen, and Nussbaum, the following sections offer a Foucauldian and postmodern liberal critique of the potential *illiberalism* of egalitarian welfare rights discourse on these lines.

Impartial reason as totalising reason

In contemporary philosophical discourse the principles advanced by Rawls, Dworkin, and Cohen operate at the level of 'ideal theory',—as 'guiding stars' against which 'non-ideal' arrangements can be judged, ranked, and potentially reformed to better approximate the relevant ethical standards. From a Foucauldian perspective, however, it is precisely the desire to find such *universal* principles by which entire societies should be 'ordered' that may threaten freedom. The assumption that there is *an* impartial ideal of justice or *a* specific pattern of resource allocation that maximises freedom is deeply problematic. What may be useful practices of freedom at a localised level may become dangerous and normalising *dispositifs* if they colonise an entire society. Instead of seeing their ideals as standards that may operate in different contexts or as potential *micro-level* practices of freedom, liberal egalitarian discourses seek instead to find and to implement *macro-ordering or totalising principles* that may close down the very processes of ethical contestation and reflexivity central to freedom, properly understood.

This propensity to close down, to narrow options, and to speak 'for or above others' with respect to the requirements of their freedom, or the 'worth of their freedom', reflects modernist and rationalist thought experiments that centre the philosophers' views. Just as neo-classical economics models 'rational choice' such that people do not choose but react robotically to background 'data' so the 'agents' in Rawls's original position are modelled as having fully formulated and rational life plans; of being able to accurately identify and to rank their desires, needs and preferences; of accurately anticipating what these will be in the future; and of having no contact with other actors who may influence their process of reasoning. It is these imaginary 'rational agents' who mechanically 'compute' a *singular* or *unanimous* understanding of justice.[39] Yet from a Foucauldian or postmodern liberal perspective, if one adopts a more creative, decentred, and reflexive notion of rationality, where the subjectivity of agents is criss-crossed by interactions with agents subscribing to different and perhaps contradictory evaluative standards; where these interactions may prompt unexpected changes

[39] Rawls, *A Theory of Justice*, 131.

in subjects' understandings of themselves and their choice situations; and where there is no endpoint to this process of individual and social reflexivity; then there will never be a complete or consistent ethical ranking of different states of the world, and such indeterminacy is as likely to prevail *within* subjects as well as across subjects. It is, therefore, to adopt an unduly disciplinary or normalising posture to suggest that people should opt into the ethical straitjacket designed for them by Rawls.

Now, one response here might be to suggest that rather that suppressing perspectival differences what Rawls offers with the device of the original position is not an omniscient view from 'nowhere' but a *symbolic* attempt to represent a view from 'everywhere'—a process wherein people are encouraged to think in a way that takes into account multiple perspectives and that represents their willingness to listen to and be moved by very different points of view.[40] The problem with this move, however, is that it is a rationalistic conceit to presuppose that the epistemic capacity exists *anywhere* to integrate all the relevant perspectives into a sovereign evaluative standpoint. There is no more reason to suppose that the implications of multiple ethical standpoints can be integrated into a sovereign conception of justice than there is to suppose that a central planner can comprehend all the factors that contribute to the content of prices in a market. If freedom requires maintaining a pluralism of rationalities, then this implies the need for institutional arrangements where a variety of evaluative standards can coexist, where there are at most temporary and localised overlaps between these plural perspectives, and where there is no attempt to order society according to a *singular* distributive pattern such as the difference principle.

Neither are there compelling reasons for 'fair equality of opportunity' or 'equality of resources' to be considered uniquely impartial or rational. One reason for this is that the pursuit of such equality may conflict with other values. Educational excellence may, for example, conflict with attempts to compensate those who may lack various abilities whether for genetic or cultural reasons, because the compensation required may be of such a magnitude that it may leave insufficient resources to develop the aptitudes of those with greater abilities. Dworkin concedes this very point when suggesting that positive rights should focus on 'adequate opportunities' for the disadvantaged rather than equal opportunities to avoid a 'slavery of the talented'—or the 'cultured'.[41]

Second, it is by observing *differences* in opportunities arising from a plurality of contradictory disciplines, traditions, and discourses that people may learn which opportunities they do or do not value, and where there may be no

[40] On this defence/interpretation of Rawls, see, e.g., Moller Okin, *Justice, Gender, and the Family*, 100–1.

[41] Dworkin, 'Equality of Resources', 322.

agreement on the opportunities to be equalised. What counts as an opportunity in a culture emphasising material progress may, for example, differ from what is valued in a culture that prioritises the sanctity of the earth.

Third, though the abilities egalitarians want to compensate for may be partly genetic, it is only through their interaction with *different* cultures, parenting styles, and educational models that the relevant abilities may be 'produced', and it is the inequalities in opportunity emergent from these different forms of 'cultural production' that may prompt a process of reflexivity across practices. Without such inequality reflexivity would be stifled and cultural difference suppressed.

Fourth and relatedly, if positive freedom requires access to more and possibly better opportunities, then equality of opportunity may conflict with this very goal. A rich lesbian may, for example, have the wherewithal necessary to challenge or resist heteronormative social pressure and to campaign for recognition of her sexual identity that may not be available to a poor lesbian—or even to a group of poor lesbians who pool their resources for the same purpose. Such inequality of opportunity to influence social attitudes today may, however, lower costs for those with fewer resources to freely express a lesbian identity in the future. Experimentation by those with more resources may generate opportunities for those with fewer resources by lowering the cost of future availability.[42] If no one can access an opportunity until all may do so, then the total number and quality of opportunities may decline.[43]

Unsurprisingly perhaps, there are similar grounds to question Cohen's universalising claims. The error that Cohen makes is to take what may be valuable micro-level practices of self-governance and to infer that these should be scaled up to judge distributive principles at the societal or global level. It is, however, no more impartial to say that 'camping trip ethics' represent the 'fullest realisation of our natures' because the experience of camping may deteriorate if people start behaving as selfish individualists, than it would be to say that the practices of a community of boxers should be universalised because the experience of boxing might deteriorate if the members of this community start behaving like Cohenite campers. The values reflected in the ideal boxing community might be ones of resilience in the face of adversity, where individuals have an experience of being pushed to their physical and mental limits, and where the possibility of personal loss or injury is part of the thrill of the fight. Such a community would be damaged if some of its members refused to capitalise when their opponents are pinned on the ropes or limited themselves to throwing only soft punches. Removing the possibility of losing or winning, or of 'coming back'

[42] For a more detailed discussion see Pennington, M. (2014) 'Against Democratic Education', *Social Philosophy and Policy*, 31 (2): 1–35.
[43] Hayek, F. A. (1960) *The Constitution of Liberty*, London: Routledge, 42–6.

from a defeat, would destroy the entire experience. The totalising error Cohen makes is to ignore that there may be *different* perspectives on realising the 'fullest potential of our natures' and that ongoing ethical reflection requires a setting where people can interact and learn from those attempting to create their own 'natures' in varied and changing ways. Foucault may concur with Cohen that the behavioural standards in capitalist societies are social constructs arising from prevailing discourses within those societies, but it does not follow that they should be replaced with a totalising egalitarian construct. If human subjectivity is a work of art, then people must have scope to *create themselves*, combining and recombining *different* practices of freedom in a kaleidoscope of forms—and not to judge or be judged against a one-dimensional perspective.

From a Foucauldian standpoint, there is no such thing as a neutral or power free form of reasoning from which to judge distributive norms separate from the multiple and often contradictory social practices or 'technologies of government' that *produce* a pluralism of rationalities—including the ethical power/knowledge claims of academic philosophers. As numerous critics have pointed out, Rawls constructs the original position in a way *biased* towards a highly risk-averse stance that stigmatises entrepreneurial action outside of a tightly bounded range, and that justifies subjecting wealth creation to a sort of 'sin tax' by privileging a particular perspective towards relative success.[44]

In Dworkin's case the bias is not one of risk aversion but towards marketised and materialistic values. Equality of resources requires that whatever physical, genetic, or cultural resources people possess are assigned a market price so they can be equalised against a universal measuring rod. As such, this principle marginalises subjects who believe that assets such as land, cultural heritage, or the provision of care should not be valued in monetary terms. Similarly, the argument for genetic compensation exhibits a cultural bias towards 'productivist' values because subjects who do not value high material rewards but benefit from the genetic or cultural lottery must work to pay off the high insurance premiums reflecting the value others place on their talents. Those less fortunate in the genetic and cultural lottery, however, and who place a similarly low value on material wealth, would not be required to pay such a tax or premium.

Cohen's radical egalitarianism exhibits a still different bias. Inequalities in ownership of capital or investment goods are tolerated in his egalitarian utopia because these may reflect differential abilities to run enterprises and to spot opportunities that may increase the wealth/positive freedom of others.[45] Inequalities in consumption income are, however, not to be tolerated because those who use their undeserved abilities to increase the social product should

[44] See, e.g., Kekes, J. (2003) *The Illusions of Egalitarianism*, Ithaca, NY: Cornell University Press.
[45] Cohen, *Rescuing Justice and Equality*.

not expect a higher consumption income. Nonetheless, Cohen does not require that those with more valued talents take up occupations that would maximise the social product because for him freedom of occupation is essential to the pursuit of one's 'self-realisation'.[46] Yet if it is legitimate to put the 'selfish' pursuit of *non-material* values above the general welfare, then Cohen fails to explain why it is not equally legitimate for people to put the pursuit of material values above the general welfare. Cohen's egalitarian gaze marginalises subjects who may 'realise themselves' through the thrill of risking, making, and spending money, as well as those who may not be aware that they have a particular 'self' to be realised, and who may want to hedge their bets, accumulating resources that might allow experimentation with different forms of self-creation through their consumption decisions.[47]

Positive rights and pastoral power

The problem with the philosophical 'modernism' of Rawls, Dworkin, and Cohen then is that they propose models of positive rights that are unduly totalising. If people institute the difference principle; equality of resources; a socialist conception of community; or some other principle of distribution in particular families, schools, leisure activities, religious associations, or enterprises; then they can contribute to a broader process of individual and social reflexivity where people create and recreate themselves through exposure to different standards and techniques of government. If, however, they function as regulative ideals for an entire society and if attempts are made to align the decentred practice of such ideals and techniques with sovereign state power, their pursuit may lead to a form of moral tyranny over individuals and communities alike—what the classical liberal philosopher Gerald Gaus refers to as the 'Tyranny of the Ideal'.[48]

From a Foucauldian perspective a political rationality interpreting ethical truth from a global or totalising standpoint must, of necessity, treat individuals as cogs in a machine—objects to be observed, classified, and manipulated into conformity with its own gaze. Instead of protecting a realm where individuals have the space to engage in ethical reflection and self-government to define and pursue their own goals, discourses of positive rights give rise to a managerialist state informed by a secular incarnation of a 'pastoral power' that monitors both individuals and statistical populations for pattern anomalies or inequalities and

[46] Ibid.
[47] On this, see Kukathas, C. 'The Labour Theory of Justice', in Kaufman, A., ed. (2014) *Distributive Justice and Access to Advantage: G.A. Cohen's Egalitarianism*, Cambridge: Cambridge University Press.
[48] Gaus, G. (2016) *The Tyranny of the Ideal*, Princeton, NJ: Princeton University Press.

that *overrides* the decisions of subjects in the name of securing or administering 'their freedom'.[49] As Foucault puts it, such power creates 'an entire economy and technique of the circulation, transfer and reversal of merits (and faults)' and establishes 'a kind of exhaustive, total, and permanent relationship of individual obedience'. It also instigates techniques 'of investigation, self-examination, and the examination by others . . . through which the pastor's power is exercised'.[50]

Crucially, since 'conducting the conduct' of individuals (discipline) and of populations (bio-power) cannot be achieved by legal edict or sovereign power alone, this pastoral state must enlist multiple public agencies, civil associations, and private companies to engage in acts of *decentralised* governance that penetrate deep into subjects lives—their incomes, employment and housing conditions, dietary and consumption patterns, parenting methods, family history, health and mental health status, to name but a few. The discourse of positive rights working in the 'shadow of the law' will 'govern at a distance',[51] stimulating a proliferation of regulatory or administrative techniques such as the production of statistical classifications, reporting, as well as data-collection requirements, 'social audits', and targets for public and private organisations which seek to mould subjects into conformity with officially approved behaviours.[52] These techniques may also work 'from below', stimulating the demand for more laws, as those concerned identify and push for the closure of gaps in the legal-regulatory nexus—with various actors engaging in 'cynicisms of power' seeking economic or political advantage over others through the adoption of such measures.

In this sense Foucault's concerns about the 'demonic' qualities of a disciplinary and bio-political state[53] echo Tocqueville's worry about the rise of administrative despotism and an 'immense tutelary power' that treats its citizens like sheep in constant need of shepherding.[54] They also reinforce Nozick's worry that since 'liberty upsets patterns', adherence to 'patterned principles of justice' requires constant interference in people's lives.[55] Significantly, however, Foucault's perspective strengthens the Nozickian argument by emphasising that this interference will not be confined to the realm of taxation or what Rawls calls the 'basic structure of society' but will generate multiple forms of classification,

[49] MF (1977/2007) *Security, Territory and Population*, New York: Palgrave Macmillan, 181.
[50] Ibid., 183.
[51] This term was popularised by Miller and Rose—see, e.g., Miller, P., and Rose, N. 'Governing Advanced Liberal Democracies', in Barry, A., and Osborne, T., eds. (1996) *Foucault and Political Reason: Liberalism, Neo-Liberalism and Rationalities of Government*, London: University College of London Press.
[52] For a discussion in the context of international human rights law see McGrogan, D. (2020) *Critical Theory and International Human Rights*, Manchester: Manchester University Press.
[53] MF 'Lemon and Milk', in Faubion, J., ed. (2001) *Power: The Essential Works of Foucault*, vol. 3: *1954–1984*, London: Allen Lane, 436.
[54] Tocqueville, A. (1835–40/2003) *Democracy in America*, vol. 2, London: Penguin, chap. 6.
[55] Nozick, R. (1974) *Anarchy, State and Utopia*, New York: Basic Books.

surveillance, and reporting *outside* the realm of formal 'government' that may impact people's subjectivity. Those 'caught within the threads of this capillary power' may come to see themselves as those who exercise discipline or bio-power over others or those who must be subject to such discipline or bio-power.[56] The crucial point here is not that there is an 'interference free' position outside of such actions but that *relative to regimes that do not seek to maintain a particular pattern* those interpreting freedom in positive rights or patterned terms will produce a form of 'governmentality' that *proliferates* multiple interferences and techniques of administration and surveillance that deeply penetrate private and community life.

Consider the implicit role that surveillance mechanisms play in Rawlsian welfare liberalism. Rawls suggests that those raised in a society conforming to 'justice as fairness' will undergo a 'psychological change' in their attitudes towards others, reflecting a new 'sense of justice' and producing a 'well-ordered society' where subjects *conform* in their personal behaviours and the policies they support to a stabilised set of normative practices.[57] Bringing about such psychological conformity, however, where people do not already embrace Rawlsian justice would require extensive use of disciplinary and bio-political techniques where subjects are watched or internalise the feeling of being so watched.

Now, many Rawlsians may reject this contention, maintaining that the target of justice is confined to the macro-level laws of the 'basic structure' such as taxes and public financing of education, which do not require the intrusive monitoring and manipulation of people's behaviour at the micro-scale. In Foucauldian terms, Rawlsian justice is 'bio-political' rather than 'disciplinary'—it works on the environmental background within which large numbers of individuals act rather than targeting specific individuals or groups as would be required in a more disciplinary regime. Others, however, fully recognise that such a distinction is untenable with a Rawlsian society requiring governance mechanisms that will *align* private behaviours with the 'basic structure' in ways that penetrate the minutiae of civil society and family life. O'Neill and Williamson, for example, argue for extensive 'pre-distributive' or 'pre-tax' interventions to reduce the inequalities that might otherwise be generated by the decisions of families and communities *prior* to the application of the difference principle.[58] Such measures presuppose a power/knowledge apparatus of surveillance and statistical classification to determine which families or subpopulations should be subjected to the relevant interventions and criteria for their success—measures that may impact their subjectivity as parents. In education, meanwhile, 'fair equality of

[56] MF (1976/2004) *Society Must Be Defended*, London: Penguin, 27–9.

[57] Rawls, *A Theory of Justice*.

[58] O'Neill, M., and Williamson, T., eds. (2012) *Property Owning Democracy: Rawls and Beyond*, New York: Wiley/Blackwell.

opportunity' may require not only public financing but also careful monitoring or policing of what is taught in schools to ensure a sufficiently standardised set of opportunities.

Beyond such controls, Brighouse and Swift suggest that while parents might be allowed to read bedtime stories to their children to satisfy the value of 'parental intimacy'—even if this 'unfairly' advantages the cognitive development of children in middle-class homes—in no circumstances should parents spend more of their *post-tax* income on their children's education lest this violates justice as fairness.[59] Presumably, therefore in 'non-ideal' settings where some parents weigh the value of education more highly than a publicly financed egalitarian standard, they would need to be monitored by their friends and neighbours as well as by public authorities to ensure that they do not smuggle private tutors into their homes; that they do not buy more expensive computers for their children; and that they avoid buying books beyond those deemed 'appropriate' for bedtime reading—or that they feel an 'inner sense' of guilt and shame exerted by the Rawlsian gaze whenever doing any of the aforementioned things. Such power is equivalent to the 'economy of faults and merits' observed historically by a Christian pastorate whose subjects had to recognise not only that they were 'sinners' but that to exercise any 'will of their own' was evidence of their inherent 'badness' as well.[60]

Cohen's radical egalitarianism implies still greater levels of social discipline. He rejects the Rawlsian separation between the private realm, where the pursuit of self-interest and private values is deemed legitimate, and those of the 'basic structure' which 'corrects' outcomes in line with 'justice as fairness'. In Cohen's ideal world there would be no need to enforce the relevant ethical standards through a legalistic tax and regulatory regime, because subjects would *internalise* socialist equality of opportunity and socialist community *in their private lives and selfhood* to such an extent that they no longer conceive of thinking and acting in ways that depart from these principles.[61] In Foucauldian terms Cohen's ideal is the instantiation of a 'carceral archipelago' where people are so disciplined as to 'economise' on the very need for a state apparatus to enforce egalitarian ethics. To move towards this 'fully disciplined' state in the 'non-ideal' conditions of contemporary capitalist societies, however, Cohen advocates a 100 percent tax on 'excess consumption incomes' to signal the importance of a socialist conception of community, as well as to orientate subjects (read discipline them) towards the 'fullest realisation of their natures'. Faced with such a tax, however, it is likely that

[59] Brighouse, H., and Swift, A. (2009) 'Legitimate Parental Partiality', *Philosophy and Public Affairs*, 37 (1): 43–80; Brighouse, H., and Swift, A. (2009) 'Educational Equality Versus Educational Adequacy: A Critique of Anderson and Satz', *Journal of Applied Philosophy*, 26 (2): 117–28.
[60] MF, *Security, Territory and Population*, 180.
[61] Cohen, *Rescuing Justice and Equality*.

subjects wanting to pursue their self-realisation in ways Cohen disapproves of would hide their income and expenditure by working on a cash-only basis or trading in underground currencies. Given the difficulties that would face public agencies in monitoring such conduct moving towards Cohen's ideal would thus require precisely the kind of decentralised surveillance experienced in countries such as the former Soviet Union, East Germany, Maoist China, and in contemporary Cuba and North Korea, where a capillary network of community-based informers were/are recruited by the state to use social sanctions or formal reporting to shame and discipline the recalcitrant. Such regimes were tellingly described by Foucault as systems of 'generalised obedience'.[62]

None of the above implies that societies with positive rights commitments—such as contemporary capitalist welfare states—are 'fully normalised societies'. Rather, the suggestion here is that to the extent such societies allow space for freedom as self-creation, it is because they *do not* attempt to live up to the ideals of modernist egalitarians such as Rawls, Dworkin, and Cohen—all of whom regularly condemn them as 'unjust' and 'unfree'. Were such societies to use these ideals as 'guiding stars' or 'targets', they would be moving towards *a disciplinary and bio-political state* that blocks the ethical creativity of its subjects and that requires mechanisms that seek to dramatically narrow the scope of people to think or to act differently.

First, the pursuit of such ideals would continually confront subjects with the dilemmas routinely faced in the formerly planned economies—of either subordinating themselves to egalitarian standards or acting in accordance with their own standards, 'gaming the system' and potentially internalising labels of moral 'deviancy'. The latter would not itself endanger freedom, and indeed on a Foucauldian view ethical transgression may be required for creative freedom to be exercised. The threat to freedom arises not from the risk that one may be criticised or shunned by neighbours, colleagues, or employers but rather from the *alignment* of these private and decentred forms of judgement with a formal system of public justice and punishment.

Second and relatedly, to avoid detection and punishment those wishing to resist egalitarian ethics would be forced 'underground', severely diminishing the processes of ethical reflexivity that occur whenever acts of resistance against dominant social norms—including distributional norms are hidden from public view.

Third, there may be an agency-diminishing effect not only on the targets of the relevant discipline but also on its supposed beneficiaries. If they are not to be nakedly authoritarian, the adoption of egalitarian measures will depend on their alignment with a dominant discourse elsewhere in society. Yet, wherever a

[62] *Security, Territory and Population*, 207.

dominant discursive formation across state and society constructs the 'less advantaged' as being 'unfree', 'less free', or 'lacking in opportunity', such a formation may 'produce the object of which it speaks'. If people are routinely described in ways portraying their freedom as 'worth less' than that of others because they are comparatively lacking in resources or opportunities, they may internalise these labels in their subjectivity and cease to exercise their freedom. Instead of seeing themselves as potential *creators* of wealth or opportunity, people may be habituated to see themselves as the passive recipients of administrative decisions. When resources are concentrated in public bodies and outcomes are perceived to be determined by such bodies, then a state of passivity may ensue, with any spirit of independent creativity or enterprise thwarted.[63] This is not to imply that the relatively disadvantaged are responsible for their fate or that they can transform *any* state of disadvantage through Nietzschean 'acts of will' or the power of 'positive thinking', but it does maintain that their capacities to exercise creative powers may be *deactivated* wherever the dominant discourse itself *devalues* their liberty. The freedom of the less advantaged may be compromised as much by a dominant egalitarian narrative as it may by a dominant discourse which describes the less advantaged as deserving of their fate.[64]

In the Foucauldian/Nietzschean sense, freedom as self-creation requires that people transcend the binary categories of a 'master morality' that valorises strength and independence and exerts power over the weak and a 'slave morality' that exerts power over the more advantaged by portraying the disadvantaged as in a permanent state of need or care.[65] Foucauldian freedom requires that subjects create themselves and their ethics by *refusing* such categorisations as 'the advantaged' and 'the disadvantaged', the 'compensators' and the 'compensated'. In contrast to a totalising egalitarianism, it would draw on diverse practices in multiple settings that may variously combine an ethic of achievement, personal independence, and rising above the crowd with one of fellowship, community, and support for others. It would allow subjects to be entrepreneurial innovators on some margins, conservative conventionalists on others, and egalitarians on still others—and not to be trapped in the totalising notion that they are 'runners' who should rank themselves or be ranked in terms of their position within a singular social 'race'. Indeed, it would refuse the entire egalitarian construction of a society where people must be categorised and equalised at a 'starting line' in favour of something closer to a Dionysian drama where the interaction of

[63] Hayek, F. A. (1944) *The Road to Serfdom*, London: Routledge.

[64] Consider here Eberstadt's discussion of unemployed males in the United States—where despite labour shortages large numbers of young males have opted out of the workforce, many of whom live sedentary and drug-dependent lives. See Eberstadt, N. (2016) *Men Without Work*, West Conshohocken, PA: Templeton Press.

[65] Nietzsche makes the distinction between master and slave morality in Nietzsche, F. (1887/1967) *On the Genealogy of Morals*, New York: Vintage.

subjects with varied and often incommensurable histories, talents, and values generates an intoxicating kaleidoscope of possibility, and where acts of creativity large and small continually transform self and society alike.

The over-governed subject and egalitarian liberalism II: Political liberalism and the democratic gaze

With its commitment to a more pluralistic understanding of freedom and an emphasis on democratic deliberation the political liberalism of the later Rawls and the capabilities approach of Sen and Nussbaum might be considered less susceptible to the foregoing critique. Yet, on the view advanced here there remain important reasons why from a Foucauldian perspective these seemingly more pluralistic approaches might themselves be considered as *insufficiently liberal.*

Public reason and the democratic gaze

The first and perhaps most important of these follows from the conception of the person central to the public reason tradition. At the core of political liberalism is a *democratic* conception of the subject—where people both exercise their freedom and discover what contributes to their substantive freedoms through public deliberation and debate. This view infuses the wider commitment by egalitarian political liberals to democratisation in spheres *outside* the realm of formal politics—notably in the home with respect to gender relations and in the workplace.

From a Foucauldian and postmodern liberal standpoint, however, the problem here is not with public reasoning or social reflexivity per se but with a specifically democratic conception of such reasoning. The commitment to democratic deliberation as the procedure through which the multiple factors that may affect people's freedom should be considered does not represent a 'power-free' position. First, because it already presupposes a conception of the subject trained, disciplined, and governed by democratic procedures. Rawls wants to avoid ontological disputes in political philosophy because the achievement of a stable conception of justice is thought to depend on citizens reaching an overlapping consensus and that such a consensus can be stable only when it is consistent with multiple views on human nature.[66] From a Foucauldian or postmodern liberal perspective, however, this approach tacitly assumes a kind of

[66] Rawls, J. 'Justice as Fairness: A Restatement', in Kelly, E., ed. (2001) *Justice as Fairness: A Restatement,* Cambridge, MA: Belknap Press of Harvard University Press.

naturalistic preference for stability when such preferences may be a 'power effect' of discursive and non-discursive practices that have 'disciplined' subjects into a set of attitudes and practices favourable to a 'stable and well-ordered society'.[67] While not necessarily 'wrong' this preference for stability hardly embodies a Foucauldian spirit of resistance or critique and is deeply at odds with the vision of a radically open society that allows for virtues, practices, and dispositions that *challenge* established norms. Rawlsian political liberalism thus marginalises a whole range of actual or potential subjectivities that it sees as threats to the discursive peace.

Second, the very process of requiring that people justify their beliefs, values, and practices in a public forum may have power effects on minority subject positions. Though the development of a democratic sensibility may be a manifestation of freedom, so too may be the desire for people to craft their subjectivity by leading largely private lives and for those who feel that the best way to develop a sense of self-mastery or self-government is by *withdrawing* from the public or democratic gaze—as far as may be possible. Minorities and especially those holding to unpopular beliefs or practices are likely to experience marginalisation in the economy and civil society come what may—but such marginalisation may be intensified wherever the relevant judgements are formally legitimated by democratic procedures enforced by law. In these circumstances there will be pressure for minority individuals or groups to identify with or to subordinate themselves to whatever democratic decisions are reached or to persist in resisting such decisions in highly public settings that will continually expose them to examination, judgement, and potential censure.

Third and most important, by restricting the expression of resistance to public argument and debate, what democratic deliberation gives to minorities in terms of rights to participate in decisions that shape their freedoms, so its preference for enforceable collective decisions takes away the capacity for all individuals and groups to *lead by example*. When people resist the gaze of dominant norms and standards by 'exiting' from relationships with others or even deliberately separating themselves from the wider society, this need not imply a solipsistic isolation from the public sphere per se. So long as others remain aware of their existence they can act as Foucauldian heterotopias—role models or anti-models that can be emulated or avoided. Yet for these social transmission effects to occur, people must not have their subjectivity overly 'disciplined' because this may prevent them from demonstrating the potential merits of their practices of freedom through their actions and results. In education, for example, whether resistance is targeted at traditional gender norms or at a society where adherence

[67] Rosenthal, I. (2019) 'Ontology and Political Theory: A Critical Encounter Between Rawls and Foucault', *European Journal of Political Theory*, 18 (2): 238–8.

to such norms is associated with low-status positions, allowing those in more 'radical' and more 'conservative' minorities to educate their children according to their respective values is more likely to reflect a pluralism of rationalities than one where all children are educated in accordance with whatever is approved by an overarching majority. If resistance against dominant social norms is confined to verbal argument, and people do not have the private space to *practice* their values, then the capacity to critique and to potentially transform existing societal norms by *acting* differently will be stifled as the relevant comportments will be suppressed or hidden from view.

Related arguments apply to the liberal egalitarian case for the extension of democracy in the workplace. Anderson and Herzog, for example, favour the extension of collective, democratic rights such as compulsory worker participation.[68] This argument is targeted at the ability of employers to internalise a state of subordinate passivity in their employees—an argument overlapping with Foucauldian concerns about the potential effects of disciplinary power. Since workers spend much of their time in corporate workplaces, the hierarchical norms often present in such settings may become internalised such that workers may fail to explore other opportunities and may adopt a wider attitude of civic subordination. Anderson goes so far as to liken corporate employment practices to 'communist dictatorships within our midst', while Herzog claims that corporations suppress the critical spirit of those they employ.

The problem here is that so long as those subject to disciplinary techniques can negotiate and engage with them, their existence need not indicate a state of unfreedom or domination. One reason for this is that the disciplines in question may be invoked to protect workers from majoritarian interference by *other workers*, as well as the possibility that they might raise productivity and wages relative to an environment where the division of labour must be approved by a complex network of deliberative committees. Second, unless workers cease to have access to the media and to have contact with those outside their workplace, including those working for other corporations, cooperatives, and the self-employed, then it is implausible to suggest that they will passively accept their lot. While a state of passivity might arise in a monopsony setting such as that of a 'company town', few if any labour markets come anywhere near the monopsony model, with multiple competitors reported in most markets.[69] Insofar as awareness of these alternatives exists, then the ability for workers to exit forms of workplace governance that constrain their agency and to enter those they

[68] Herzog, L. (2020) 'Citizen's Autonomy and Corporate Cultural Power', *Journal of Social Philosophy*, 51 (2): 205–30; Anderson, E. (2017) *Private Government*, Princeton, NJ: Princeton University Press.

[69] For a review of monopsony in labour markets see, e.g., Boal, W., and Ransom, M. (1997) 'Monopsony in the Labour Market', *Journal of Economic Literature*, 35(1): 86–112.

consider less constraining will give them scope to reshape their terms of employment. Third and most important, the extension of workplace democracy will do little to increase the capacity of individual workers to shape how their work is governed especially in large organisations—and indeed it may *reduce the range of options they face*. The extension of majority rule will limit the capacity of business leaders to exercise independent entrepreneurial judgement and to engage in 'permissionless innovation' or Schumpeterian 'creative destruction', and over time this may reduce the diversity of business and employment practices in the wider society to which employees in general might be exposed. Such conclusions do not depend on the notion of a frictionless or perfectly competitive market but on the suggestion that privileging collective bargaining and worker participation is likely to *reduce* the extent of competition and the scope for workers to be exposed to different modes of governance. Extending deliberative democratic control will constrain the scope for entrepreneurial initiative, instituting a kind of 'permission society' where more and more decisions are subject to a democratic gaze, and where the scope for subjects to make independent investments is constantly limited by the need to seek majority approval.

Instead of public reason taking place within a singular 'public sphere', the Foucauldian and postmodern liberal perspective thus points towards a more 'anarchic' process of social reflexivity across multiple, decentred, though partially overlapping 'public spheres', which need not be governed on a majoritarian basis or in accordance with an overarching sovereign purpose. It is precisely because there are so many ways for people to live creative and fulfilling lives and because people may be conflicted within themselves as well as in their relations to others by a diversity of perhaps incommensurable evaluative standpoints that the extension of democratic power may constitute a threat to freedom. While some level of 'Apollonian' order or stability is required for society to function, far from the Rawlsian ideal of a 'well-ordered society', Foucauldian freedom points towards a more 'Dionysian' process of ethical and cultural 'creative destruction'. The latter view does not imply an anarchic world of cultural warfare but emphasises instead an openness to innovation, dynamism, and processes of individual and societal reflexivity that may be hemmed in by a political project that prioritises 'stability'.

Capabilities and pastoral power

Sen's and Nussbaum's perspectives seem less problematic precisely because they do not benchmark any one distributive criterion or offer a single scale of weightings against which freedoms and capacities can be ranked. Nonetheless, they too favour deliberative democratic processes as the primary procedure through which the relevant mix of capacities and freedoms should be determined. Given the complex, varied, and highly contextual factors contributing to relative states of freedom it is, however, far from clear why democratic deliberation should be uniquely well placed to track this complexity.

Now, supporters of the capabilities approach may respond that the more anarchic conception of public reason advanced here implies a laissez-faire attitude that places insufficient bounds on what are considered legitimate cultural practices. Nussbaum and Sen are, for example, highly critical of traditional gender roles which they suggest are incompatible with women's capacity to create and to shape their own lives and with the basic notions of equal respect necessary for people to freely develop their capacities. Though emphasising that her threshold of minimal capability freedom is necessarily vague, Nussbaum argues that traditional/religious attitudes towards women's roles are often incompatible with meeting this threshold.[70] While Sen does not specify a threshold, he too singles out unequal gender roles as one of the most important limitations on women's capabilities.[71]

From a Foucauldian perspective, however, extending public law to regulate gender and other decentred power relations may significantly expand the scope for acts of cultural misrecognition or even domination by empowering some actors to speak 'for or above others'. The Sen-Nussbaum perspective assumes a democratically 'power-free' position against which the requirements of freedom or equal respect can be judged. Yet, even when there is agreement on values such as autonomy and equal respect, there are likely to be different perspectives on which cultural practices properly reflect these values. In the context of contemporary liberal commercial societies, for example, many traditional religious groupings, such as the Amish, do not try to isolate their children from the wider society to stifle their capacity for choice but because from their perspective the objectivating practices of what they see as the surrounding materialist/permissive culture are antagonistic to that choice—*properly understood*. Similarly, as al-Gharbi has noted, many non-Western cultures do not consider that respect for women requires that they are treated as equal or interchangeable with men in the home and workplace—but that they are treated as being *different* from men and that traditional gender roles properly honour these differences.[72]

Just as it is a power-laden social construct to suggest that there are differences between the sexes that should be reflected in gender roles, so too it is a social construction to maintain that there are no such differences. The values represented

[70] Nussbaum, M. (2000) *Sex and Social Justice*, Oxford: Oxford University Press, 29–54.

[71] Sen, A. 'Gender Inequality and Theories of Justice', in Nussbaum, N., and Glover, J. (1995) *Women, Culture and Development*, Oxford: Clarendon Press.

[72] Gharbi, M. al- (2016) 'From Political Liberalism to Para-Liberalism', *Comparative Philosophy*, 7 (2): 1–25.

by secular feminisms or various religious traditions should *all* be seen as discursive objectivations that produce different subject positions *none* of which are 'power free'. As one Foucauldian observer puts it:

> No individual woman harbours the variety of modes of subjection, power, desire, danger, and resourcefulness experienced by women living inside particular skins, classes, epochs or cultures. All that is solid melts into air—the sanguine 'we' uttered in feminist theory and practice only two decades ago is gone for good.[73]

Provided they do not monopolise decision-making or use violence against others, therefore, even choice- or autonomy-denying perspectives should not be precluded from processes of social contestation. So long as there is the potential for critical interchange between discursive positions though asymmetric power relations may be present within and across these discourses, *pace* Foucault, they should *not* be confused with domination or unfreedom.

In these circumstances, legislating for 'women's interests' may curtail a pluralism of rationalities and competition between different 'practices of freedom'. Wherever the majority perspective favours traditional gender norms, the Sen-Nussbaum approach would require intrusive and paternalistic policies that could only be advanced through recourse to authoritarian measures driven by a 'vanguard party' or equivalent. In a majority secular setting, meanwhile, so long as the women concerned can witness alternative possibilities and ways of living in the surrounding secular culture that might prompt them to resist or to challenge some of their own practices, it is far from clear what the freedom-based case for intervening in the practices of religious minorities would be. Sen's and Nussbaum's endorsement of the state's authority to intervene in how minority religious parents educate women and girls may privilege the majority concerned and constrain communication across different discursive traditions. It may also work 'outside of the law' to reinforce the normalising assumptions of the majority in a manner that itself constitutes a potentially oppressive subjectivation by rendering religious women open to decentred modes of public monitoring and censure.[74] Elsewhere, Nussbaum recognises this possibility in noting that the public position of a government in expressing an opinion is often fundamentally different in its power effects from those generated by private citizens or organisations. When public officials endorse a particular ethical stance, they have a greater capacity to affect how a subject feels about their place in society, or how others feel about particular individuals and groups than do most private

[73] Brown, W. (1995) *States of Injury*, Princeton, NJ: Princeton University Press.
[74] Valdez, 'Non-Domination or Practices of Freedom?'.

agents.[75] It is not clear therefore why Nussbaum endorses the authority of public agents to exercise this discursive power over minority perspectives when it comes to cultural mores surrounding sex and gender relations.[76]

The tendency to speak 'for or above others' in the capabilities approach follows from a perspective which assumes that if certain capabilities are required for people to lead creative and fulfilling lives, then these must be politically secured or guaranteed. By assuming that the relevant responsibility lies with the state and its agencies, however, were it to be institutionalised across society this very discourse may *deactivate* the creative potential for agents to secure or produce the relevant capacities themselves—either individually or working with others through bottom-up social movements or mutual aid. Where, for example, women are subject to unequal power relations, this does not mean that they are unable to engage in techniques of re-subjectification or to shift their terms of engagement with men by drawing creatively on the particularities of their cultural context. The recent social movements organised by women in Iran against theocratic rule illustrate this potential for bottom-up agency while showing how it may be closed down by organised state violence. The point here is not that such movements will necessarily be successful but that if groups such as women are depicted as *uniquely* vulnerable, those concerned may come to see themselves as being unable to change their situation without external intervention.[77]

Relatedly, if people do not choose to exercise a particular capacity, then it is hard to say whether they have reason to value such a capacity in the first place. Nussbaum and Sen claim only to favour providing people with opportunities to exercise their capacities rather than disciplining them to act in accordance with specific values. Yet, those initiating a capability-enhancing intervention have no means of evaluating the success of the intervention outside of witnessing a change in the behaviour or revealed preferences of those subject to it. If such changes are not forthcoming or not in 'sufficient quantities', there may be a tendency to pursue further interventions until the behaviours concerned comport with the evaluative judgements of the intervener. Suppose, for example, that consumers newly educated about the health risks of fatty or sugary foods continue to choose them over more nutritious options, then the response may be to seek still further educational measures or those that stigmatise certain foods (through advertising bans, for example) and the people who produce or consume them. Similarly, if women educated to an equivalent level as men in their

[75] Nussbaum, M. (2013) *The New Religious Intolerance: Overcoming the Politics of Fear in an Anxious Age*, Cambridge, MA: Belknap Press.

[76] al-Gharbi, 'From Political Liberalism to Para-Liberalism'.

[77] For a feminist-classical liberal critique of egalitarian feminism on these lines, see, e.g., McKitrick, J. 'Liberty, Gender, and the Family', in Machan, T., ed. (2006) *Liberty and Justice*, Stanford: Hoover Institution Press.

society continue to favour traditional gender roles, then this may be met with demands for further intervention in the home, in schools, and in the workplace to bring about the desired outcome. It this 'pastoral' or 'parental' attitude that raises the suspicion that subjects will only be allowed to use their freedom when their 'pastor' or 'parent' has decided they have the capacity to use it in the 'right way'. It was of course precisely this style of reasoning that some liberals used to justify the powers exercised by colonial authorities over Indigenous peoples—powers that would be kept in place until such people were judged by their masters' as capable of properly exercising freedom.[78]

Note, this argument should not be confused with the 'slippery slope' suggestion that *any* public intervention begets still further and ever-more totalising controls. Though it cannot suspend all evaluative judgements, the provision of a welfare safety net to ameliorate the most severe forms of poverty as well as the protection of women, LGBT people, and various minorities from physical violence need not be tied very closely to any judgements about specific behaviours. Rather, the suggestion here is that *relative to such minimalist measures* the Sen-Nussbaum focus on achieving specific capacities has a much greater propensity to invoke a normalising or disciplinary logic. From a Foucauldian perspective, it is precisely because there are so many capacities that might be considered as targets for surveillance and 'corrective' intervention that there will be a tendency for this discourse to create and to empower paternalistic actors.

The social construction of the egalitarian state: Dividing practices and egalitarian justice

The propensity to institutionalise the power to speak 'for or above others' is part of a wider tendency in egalitarian liberalism whether in its 'comprehensive' or in its 'political' manifestation to deploy what Foucault understands as discursive 'dividing practices'. Though professing to be egalitarian, these discourses systematically *minorize* and in some cases *demonise* private and civil actors in relation to public agents.

In Rawlsian discourse, for example, *only* public agents employed in the regulation, stabilisation, and distributive branches of a welfare liberal state are assumed to have the coordinative capacity to oversee the different elements comprising the 'basic structure' to ensure that the 'fair value of peoples' liberty is respected. Similarly, *only* public agents have the appropriate motivation to

[78] Notably the views of Locke and Mill—see Parekh, B. 'Liberalism and Colonialism: A Critique of Locke and Mill', in Pieterse, J., and Parekh, B., eds. (1995) *The Decolonisation of Imagination: Culture, Knowledge and Power*, London: Zed Books.

ensure that the freedoms of all are maintained because without state enforcement, even with 'full motivational compliance', the more advantaged might 'free-ride', exiting their obligations to the less advantaged or providing support in a manner demeaning their social status as free and equal citizens. That state agents may themselves act in a way that disempowers the disadvantaged is only ever attributable to the *corrupting* role of private agents in using their wealth or cultural prejudices to prevent civil servants from acting in their 'corrective' capacity. That state institutions may be an endogenous source of prejudice and disadvantage or that markets might be an arena for other-regarding as well as 'self-interested' conduct is scarcely countenanced.[79]

From a Foucauldian and postmodern liberal viewpoint, however, such analyses rely on excessively sovereign understandings of political authority that unduly privilege public agents. While liberal egalitarian discourses recognise that citizens cannot be expected to know how their decisions contribute to overall freedom, they position the experts 'in charge' of the 'basic structure' as capable of knowing how to manipulate the background conditions within which decisions in markets and civil society occur.[80] The latter, however, presupposes a scientistic 'predict and control' capacity to understand and to manipulate complex socio-economic orders that there is little reason to suppose that public agents, or indeed *anybody* in society, may have.[81] Just as the statistical categories deployed by utilitarian economic planners rarely comport with the evolving circumstances of time and place facing individual enterprises, workers, or consumers, so too the classifications of different income groups, distributive or capability categories will rarely reflect the subjective experience of those classified in such a way. While state agencies can pass binding laws and regulations and raise taxes that no individual or group has the power to do, this does not imply a synoptic capacity to coordinate such laws, regulations, and taxes to deliver justice or freedom—even assuming agreement on what such justice or freedom entails. Public officials may not know how to manipulate relationships between income levels, taxation, and welfare provision to produce a specific set of opportunities because there are so many contingent and context-specific cultural and environmental factors in play. Thus, countries with similar levels of income redistribution often exhibit different levels of inequality, social mobility, and health outcomes.[82] Though there is no clear evidence that they 'work' to

[79] For a comprehensive account of these tendencies in Rawlsian discourse see, e.g., Freiman, C. (2017) *Unequivocal Justice*, London: Routledge.

[80] Rawls, *Political Liberalism*. See also, Valentini, L. (2021) 'The Natural Duty of Justice in Non-Ideal Circumstances: On the Moral Demands of Institution Building and Reform', *European Journal of Political Theory*, 20 (1): 45–66.

[81] For a discussion see Gaus, G. (2021) *The Open Society and Its Complexities*, Oxford: Oxford University Press, esp. part 3.

[82] For a discussion see Gilbert, N. (2017) *Never Enough*, Oxford: Oxford University Press; Corak, M., Lindquist, M., and Mazumder, B. (2014) 'A Comparison of Upward and Downward

deliver justice or freedom in the above sense, discourses emphasising the importance of the welfare state's 'pastoral power' in shaping people's opportunities may nonetheless exercise profound 'power effects' on subjects who may become entangled in a complex of taxing, spending, and regulatory powers, and who may become routinised into seeing their fortunes as dependent on those 'in charge' of the basic structure.

Neither are there compelling reasons to believe that public agents are less likely to face collective action problems or to behave in ways generating or perpetuating inequalities of cultural status. If they are motivated to consider 'free-riding', people in *both* the private sector/civil society *and* in public agencies may find that their contribution to the provision of a good makes no difference to whether it is secured. Similarly, given the unique powers of compulsion that state agencies possess and their capacity to threaten others, those working for these agencies may be as likely to abuse positions of authority as any private individual, organisation, or group. Indeed, states may be more likely to act in ways that *reinforce* decentred power relations because of the coercive powers at their disposal. Thus, while many states have recently legislated to protect the freedoms of LGBT people, it was also legislative action by such states that in living memory *exacerbated* decentred cultural prejudices by *criminalising* homosexuality and subjecting those found 'guilty' to 'treatments' including chemical castration and electric shock therapy. Likewise, while many states now present themselves as champions of female equality, such states were historically responsible for *reinforcing* gendered divisions of labour by for example, forbidding women's employment in occupations such as mining—often under pressure from organised male labour—a process that reinforced the decentred power exercised by men in the home.[83] Finally, segregationist practices such as Jim Crow laws or those of apartheid South Africa could not have been enforced without widespread public interferences with freedom of contract—again restrictions often demanded by organised labour and organised capital to sustain decentred divisions that were threatened by competitive market forces.[84]

None of this implies that state action can *never* do any good from the point of encouraging greater fluidity in power relations. Rather, the suggestion here is that there are no *systemic reasons* to believe that state action is likely to have such effects relative to more 'bottom-up' forms of resistance operating in markets,

Intergenerational Mobility in Canada, Sweden and the United States', *Labour Economics*, 30: 185–200.

[83] Coonz, S. (1992) *The Way We Never Were*, New York: Basic Books; Goldin, C. (1991) *Understanding the Gender Gap: An Economic History of American Women*, New York: Oxford University Press.

[84] Roback, J. (1986) 'The Political Economy of Segregation: The Political Economy of Segregated Street Cars', *Journal of Economic History*, 46: 893–919.

civil society, and through social movements. Opportunities to explore such alternatives may, however, be suppressed in any discursive setting privileging state actors in the way that egalitarian liberals routinely do.

Postmodern liberalism on freedom, negative rights, and entangled political economies

If discourses of positive freedom threaten liberty because of their propensity to speak for or above others, then a regime of largely, though not exclusively, negative rights protections might be favoured because such rights may reduce the likelihood that power will be institutionalised or aligned in accordance with a single normalising code. Rights to person and property, freedom of contract, freedom of speech, freedom of association and disassociation, and freedom of religion may operate as a *moral minimum*, allowing people with plural rationalities to coexist without a state of permanent and potentially violent conflict.

From the evolutionist and post-foundationalist account offered by a 'postmodern' liberalism, such rights are not derivative moral requirements of an underlying and identifiable human nature or rationality as emphasised by deontological classical liberals in the Lockean tradition.[85] Neither do they reflect a strongly utilitarian focus on maximising the greatest good of the greatest number—an ethical framework which presupposes that the knowledge required to deliver such a standard is available to moral or social scientific experts. Rather, negative rights are understood as evolved rules or Humean *artifices*, which historical experience suggests enable subjects who disagree about values to coexist. Understanding these rules as emergent properties from complex historical processes, postmodern liberalism thus decentres the philosophers' views. Negative rights are not an invention or projection from a moral expert's mind but are the outcome of the practical experiences of multiple actors as they go about their business and come into conflict with others doing likewise. While philosophers may understand the evolutionary process through which these rules emerge and the functions they perform, just as economists may understand how prices emerge in a market and their coordinative properties, they are no better placed to specify the appropriate content of the rules in particular cases than are economists to specify which prices should prevail in any given market. This understanding is, thus, compatible with a 'weak' or 'rule utilitarianism' which recognises that there may be generalised benefits from limiting the powers granted to those who claim moral or social scientific expertise.

[85] For example, Nozick, *Anarchy, State and Utopia.*

Negative rights are not directed towards a totalising ethical purpose, because people's evaluative standards reflect the diverse experiences, practices, and traditions from which their rationality emerges. Subjects identify with conventions of property and contract, but the conventions themselves are not directed towards a specific goal. Where positive rights or patterned conceptions of justice presuppose a social purpose requiring the state to act as what Oakeshott refers to as an enterprise association, or *universitas*, and Hayek describes as a *taxis,* directing or moulding society according to its ends, negative rights are oriented towards the maintenance of a largely purposeless 'civil association' or 'catallaxy'. While such associational forms may contain normalising projects at the *micro-level*, they lack any overarching social goal or normalising purpose at the *macro-level*. As Oakeshott explains,

> Civil freedom is not choice to be and remain associated in terms of a common purpose; it is neither more nor less than the absence of such a purpose or choice.[86]

Where the maintenance of civil freedom is concerned the primary role of political authority is to supervise the rules of the game rather than judge the results of the relevant game or games against a universal standard.[87] This 'amoral' or 'indifferent' stance seeks to drain formal law of moral or ethical content and aligns with the Foucauldian concern not to work with an overly normative conception of rights.

While negative rights presuppose a certain level of disciplined conduct, they are less reliant on the micro-controls that occupy Foucault's critique of normalising regimes. What Hayek refers to as the 'discipline of civilisation' pertains to a thin set of 'rules of just conduct', including respect for property, contracts, and norms of promise keeping not dissimilar to the 'few binding rules' that as Foucault saw it allowed for a creative individualism to unfold in the Greek city-state.

Though enforcement of these rules may require some degree of classification and categorisation to mediate disputes and to rectify transgressions, the informational requirements and power/knowledge claims necessary to adjudicate these negative rules pale in comparison to the pastoral apparatuses favoured by egalitarian liberals and utilitarians alike. Stability on a 'thin' set of 'Apollonian' rules may enable 'Dionysian' creativity to proceed on multiple other margins without endangering the minimal social order on which such experimentation

[86] Oakeshott, M. (1975/1990) *On Human Conduct*, Oxford: Clarendon Press, 158.

[87] Ibid. See also, Kukathas, C. (2003) *The Liberal Archipelago: A Theory of Diversity and Freedom*, Oxford: Oxford University Press.

depends. This dynamism generates wealth and expands positive freedom *indirectly* through the opportunities it brings. Though it may generate substantial differentials in wealth, the coordination, dynamism, and growth afforded by a market-based 'spontaneous order' is a positive-sum game that generates multiple opportunities for people to create and to recreate themselves, and such opportunities simultaneously generate dynamism and growth.

Crucially, this philosophical stance does not claim that negative rights emanate from a 'power-free' position. Postmodern liberalism recognises that no set of legally enforced rules and institutions can be *entirely* neutral or unbounded in the values it supports. This form of government does not, for example, tolerate violent practices to force others into a particular set of cultural norms or as a way of resolving disputes. It maintains, however, that *relative to any historically practiced alternatives*, negative rights may increase the scope for the coexistence of rival cultural or evaluative standards and the possibility of reflexivity or interchange between these standards. Such restrictions *expand* the ability of subjects to pursue creative acts compared to a scenario without boundary rules, where no one knows who has the right to take decisions in a particular domain and in comparison to those where some are empowered to speak for and above others.

Neither is there any suggestion that the operation of negative rights regimes will be immune to power imbalances. Historical experience shows that protections of this kind have been unequally enforced on grounds of class, sex, sexuality, race, or religious identification, and it is owing to the inevitability of such imbalances that postmodern liberalism favours a fracturing of sovereign power such that those responsible for enforcing these rights remain open to contestation and challenge. So long as critique is immanent rather than reflecting a totalising or 'constructivist rationalism' that seeks to challenge all rules and practices at once, then on a postmodern liberal view, no set of rules should be immune to challenge and no agency should be entrusted with a monopoly of rule experimentation in the social order.[88] Power relations are omnipresent so subjects cannot question all aspects of their cultural situation simultaneously. Nonetheless, having the scope to engage in localised and entrepreneurial challenges to specific manifestations of power is what makes a social order 'liberal'. The historical record suggests that conditions of relative political 'anarchy' where authority has been divided between different states and jurisdictions though never 'power free' may be less likely to reproduce power imbalances. In the context of Western European history, for example, notwithstanding massive background inequalities in wealth and political power, competitive dynamics appear to have pushed elites towards less predatory and more inclusive

[88] Hayek, F. A. 'The Errors of Constructivism', in Hayek (1978) *New Studies in Philosophy, Economics and the History of Ideas*, London: Routledge.

governance regimes compared to those in more centralised jurisdictions such as those that prevailed in Russia and China.[89]

Similarly, this position understands that non-interference rights will never be neutral with respect to their Foucauldian 'power effects'. Wherever minority religious practices, gender norms, or sexualities are viewed with suspicion or disgust by the majority, this may seriously impact the subjective experience of those in the minority position even if their negative rights are formally protected. Though the decentred tyranny of other people's opinions can never be escaped, what the postmodern liberal view maintains is that *relative* to a situation where the ethics of either the majority or the minority are publicly endorsed or enforced by law, a regime focussed on largely negative rights protections *increases* the scope for both minorities and majorities to practice their values and standards, allowing for a process of reflexive, though asymmetric, contestation.

Entrepreneurship requires that subjects put their money, property, and their identity on the line. In the case of norm or cultural entrepreneurs this may require facing the social opprobrium directed against those seeking to disrupt established practices such that new norms and practices might be created—with negative rights providing *the minimal protected domain* necessary for such challenges to proceed.[90] This is why postmodern liberalism favours restricting legalistic regulation to predominantly negative functions and relying instead on the 'decentred' forms of governance provided by informal norms. The governance of religious practice, gender, sexuality, or commercial interaction through such norms may allow for Foucault's 'games of power and truth to be played with a minimum of domination' because rules of this type may be easier to avoid, resist, or change than formal legislation. It may, for example, be easier for LGBT individuals to escape decentred oppressions by moving to the relative anonymity of a city, or to a jurisdiction more tolerant in its attitudes, than to have to wait to persuade a national majority of the case for cultural change before expressing their sexuality or gender identification. Similarly, in commercial markets there are usually gaps or unexploited possibilities that allow those with relatively little to rise by acting on alertness to open niches, price discrepancies, or arbitrage opportunities, which may prove a speedier route to absolute and relative advancement than waiting on legislated income transfers.

On this view, it is precisely the complexity of the factors contributing to people's freedom and their capacity to identify and to achieve different objectives

89 Salter, A. (2015) 'Rights to the Realm: Reconsidering Western Political Development', *American Political Science Review*, 109 (4): 725–34; Lemke, J. (2016) 'Interjurisdictional Competition and Married Women's Property Acts', *Public Choice*, 166: 292–313; Somin, I. (2011) 'Foot Voting, Political Ignorance and Constitutional Design', *Social Philosophy and Policy*, 28 (1): 202–27; Ogilvie, S. (2003) *A Bitter Living: Women, Guilds and Social Capital in Early Modern Germany*, Oxford: Oxford University Press.

90 Hayek, *The Constitution of Liberty*, 63.

that require a reliance on simple and largely negative rules. Negative rights enable an intricate ecology of individuals and organisations to exercise creativity in responding to the cultural-economic power relations within which they are embedded and for the results of this creativity to be communicated to others through demonstration effects. While these rights do not protect subjects from non-violent forms of 'interference', they may be less dangerous to freedom than processes that seek to 'protect' them from cultural interference. Though he errs when associating the Foucauldian position with a search for 'authenticity' or 'purity', Rorty articulates this stance effectively when suggesting a strategy that seeks to

> privatise the Nietzschean-Sartrean-Foucauldian attempt at authenticity and purity, in order to prevent yourself from slipping into a political attitude which will lead you to think that there is some social goal more important than avoiding cruelty.[91]

Or as Foucault once put it, 'the guarantee of freedom, is freedom'.[92]

It must be remembered, however, that there has never been a society governed solely by negative rights. In most societies these rights have co-evolved with at least some positive welfare commitments that go beyond dispute resolution. One reason for this is that though negative rights are largely purposeless, they are not *entirely* so. If allowing subjects to pursue their separate and incommensurable purposes requires protecting them from violence, then negative rights may be compatible with *purposeful* or *instrumental* attempts to sustain the conditions that reduce violence against person and property—and these efforts may involve some positive rights claims. Such claims are not *necessarily* in tension with negative rights and freedoms—transfer payments such as basic social security systems or a basic income guarantee may, for example, work to protect these freedoms in contexts where the relief of extreme poverty may reduce crimes against person and property. They may also enable people to defend their negative rights against external attack; and by providing a minimum of sustenance, they may give subjects the confidence to exercise resistance through their freedom of speech.

Nonetheless, while the attainment of entirely purposeless social rules is chimerical, postmodern liberalism maintains that purposive 'social action' must remain limited if freedom is to be preserved. First, because it must avoid institutionalising discursive objectivations that may rob subjects of their capacities for self-creation. Second, because wherever sovereign or state law

91 Rorty, R. (1989) *Contingency, Irony and Solidarity*, Cambridge: Cambridge University Press, 65.
92 MF 'Space, Knowledge, Power', in Rabinow, *The Foucault Reader*, 245.

operates it has the potential to morph into an increasingly goal-oriented stance proliferating both sovereign and decentred attempts to govern subjects rather than maintaining the space within which they might govern themselves. Even laws focussed on negative rights may have this tendency. Indeed, this point is central to 'Left-Foucauldian' analyses which maintain that 'neo-liberal' discourses of 'non-interference' and 'self-governance' are nothing more than a managerial/capitalist tool 'governing at a distance', by *indirectly* moulding subjectivities to align with the goal of market-oriented growth.[93]

While such power effects are conceivable, there are several reasons not to overstate them or to understand them as a manifestation of 'neo-liberal governmentality'. First, while negative rights may be used as an indirect tool to promote markets and growth, they also afford significant scope for subjects to *refuse* growth-promoting transactions, to *resist* consumerism, and to avoid becoming overly entangled in commerce—especially if complemented with a minimal form of security provided outside of the market. Negative rights facilitate markets but do not require that people associate through markets in all aspects of their lives. Though creative destruction is facilitated by a market order, a regime of negative rights also allows scope for those who seek to resist any normative pressure to permanently innovate to engage in strategies of conservative resistance against such imperatives.

Second, 'governing at a distance' should not be seen as a uniquely 'neo-liberal' strategy of power because *no remotely complex society can be governed entirely through direct commands.*[94] Even the formerly 'planned economies' had to devolve responsibility down to individual enterprises or groupings of enterprises in order that they might function at all. Governing at a distance under socialism involved selective tolerance of informal markets,[95] alongside the assignment of multiple responsibilities for public enterprise managers to meet planning targets, to produce data and statistical reports, and to be ready for audit and inspection.[96] It is precisely these managerial techniques that have proliferated in the public sectors of many liberal, mixed or entangled political economies and that have increasingly encompassed private sector organisations and civil society groups that have been 'contracted' or 'recruited' by states as decentralised 'partners' in the process of 'governing'. What has been referred to as the creation of a 'privatised state'[97] might better be described in Foucauldian terms as

[93] See, e.g., Brown, W. (2015) *Undoing the Demos*, New York: Zone Books.
[94] Miller and Rose, 'Governing Advanced Liberal Democracies'.
[95] Private plots in Soviet Russia, although representing only 3% of the cultivated land area in the 1960s, accounted for 66% of eggs, 64% of potatoes, 43% of vegetables, 40% of meat, and 39% of milk produced. See de Pauw, J. (1969) 'The Private Sector in Soviet Agriculture', *Slavic Studies*, 28 (1): 63–71.
[96] On this see Roberts, P. (1971) *Alienation and the Soviet Economy*, Albuquerque: University of New Mexico Press.
[97] Cordelli, C. (2020) *The Privatized State*, Princeton, NJ: Princeton University Press.

the 'governmentalisation of the private and civil sectors'. This process should not be understood as reflecting the power of 'neo-liberal' discourses but as a pragmatic response to the massive coordination problems that face contemporary administrative-welfare states in the face of their ever-expanding positive rights commitments.[98] Reliance on this 'decentred managerialism' is analogous to a form of cultural 'market socialism' and reflects both the cognitive overload generated by attempts to centrally manage positive freedom objectives and the unwillingness of states and many of their citizens to allow a realm of relatively purposeless markets and civil association to operate in the absence of pastoral/managerial control.

Finally, while regimes favouring negative rights may not entirely avoid an alignment with managerialist goals, they may be less likely to morph in this way than those with expansive positive freedom objectives. Markets are favoured because relative to historically experienced alternatives, they allow greater scope for subjects to 'speak for themselves'. Moreover, when markets play a significant coordinative role, spaces may open that tend away from what Foucault refers to as a 'normalising society'. The tendency in markets will be towards a 'catallactic order'[99] that both produces and tolerates multiple individuals and practices and that facilitates an interplay between and across differences as people who value the same things *differently* find grounds for cooperation.[100] It is because relationships in commerce are 'weak' and do not depend on agreement over ethical, religious, or other norms beyond a willingness to respect property and to observe contracts, that people in search of a 'better deal' may be more likely to tolerate differently situated others and may be less likely to 'police' their conduct in multiple domains. Conversely, by conceptualising society as a collectively manageable and statistically 'knowable' whole and by equating freedom with specific patterns or outcomes, positive rights regimes and their supporting discourses

[98] On this expansion see Lindert, P. (2023) 'Social Spending and the Welfare State', chap. 4 in OECD I Library (2023) *How Was Life: New Perspectives on Wellbeing and Inequality Since 1820*, OECD. For middle-income countries see Dorlach, T. (2021) 'The Causes of Welfare State Expansion in Democratic Middle-Income Countries: A Literature Review', *Social Policy and Administration*, 55 (5): 767–83.

[99] Hayek, F. A. (1982) *Law, Legislation and Liberty*, vol. 2, London: Routledge, 108–9; Hayek (1988) *The Fatal Conceit*, London: Routledge, 112.

[100] In the *Birth of BioPolitics* (1978/2008), London: Palgrave, Foucault explicitly recognises this argument—though in connection with the Chicago school economics of Gary Becker rather than the post-foundational/Austrian tradition represented here. As Foucault understands him, Becker is presenting a view of society 'in which there is an optimisation of systems of difference, in which the field is left open to fluctuating processes, in which minority individuals and practices are tolerated, in which action is brought to bear on the rules of the game rather than on the players, and finally in which there is an environmental type of intervention instead of the internal subjugation of individuals', 259–60.

Though differing markedly on the social scientific method and on the extent to which markets 'optimise' (see the discussion in chapter 3), in their analysis of the social relations engendered by market arrangements, the positions of the Austrian and Chicago schools are closely aligned.

cannot help but instigate a form of 'pastoral power' or 'governmentality' that both sees subjects as manageable objects and that produces subjects who see themselves as the legitimate targets of a permanent 'shepherding' by organised expertise. In contrast, the Foucauldian/postmodern liberal case for negative rights problematises the very concept of self and society as 'knowable' objects in this sense.

Conclusion

Just as freedom may be threatened by scientistic and utilitarian expertise that attempts to manage socio-economic life according to a predict and control model, so too discourses of positive rights may similarly narrow the scope for people to exercise their freedom by institutionalising the power of some to speak for or above others. In practice contemporary liberal political economies are not governed entirely either by a socio-economic scientism or by positive rights commitments but are entangled mixes where historically evolved negative freedoms exist in tension with these rationalist and modernist discourses and practices of government. As such, there remain significant gaps within these societies, allowing subjects to exercise their creative freedom and especially so when compared with the historic example of fascist states, socialist states, and theocratic regimes. Nonetheless, this freedom may be highly fragile, with the entanglements between state and society prone to morph in ways narrowing the scope to exercise creative freedom on multiple dimensions. Part II of this book will thus present a critical political economy on four distinct though interlocking *dispositifs* in contemporary liberal societies, focussed on 'social justice', 'public health', 'sustainability', and 'law and order'—all of which have the potential to institutionalise a correctional or pastoral impulse that threatens to transform 'constitutions of liberty' into 'constitutions of control'.

PART II
FOUCAULDIAN LIBERALISM AND SOCIAL CRITIQUE

5

Bio-Power and the Political Economy of Inequality

The Social Justice *Dispositif*

Introduction

Part I of this book set out a dialogue between the Foucauldian and postmodern liberal perspectives. What emerged from that dialogue was an understanding of threats to freedom arising from bio-political or pastoral discourses that align state power with more decentred forms of power and that conceive of individuals and populations as knowable, and manageable objects. Part II now applies this framework offering a critique of some of the most important and often overlapping manifestations of these pastoral *dispositifs.*

Critique, in the Foucauldian sense,

> is not a matter of saying things are not right as they are. It is a matter of pointing out on what kinds of assumptions, what kinds of familiar, unchallenged, unconsidered modes of thought the practices we accept rest.[1]

The chapters that follow thus seek to problematise the common assumptions and understandings that characterise some of the most significant *dispositifs* in contemporary liberal political economies. The aim of these analyses is not to offer exhaustive accounts of the practices that govern these societies or to offer detailed histories of their emergence; rather, they aim to highlight some common discursive and governmental trends that should be recognisable to readers across a range of countries and policy settings. The expectation is that by illustrating the potential value of Foucauldian or postmodern liberal critiques of these trends, the analyses may inspire future, more detailed empirical and philosophical work in this regard.

[1] Foucault, M. (hereafter MF) 'Practising Criticism or Is It Really Important to Think, Interview by Eribon, D. May 30–31', in Kritzman, L., ed. (1988) *Politics, Philosophy, Culture: Interviews and Other Writings 1977–1984*, London: Routledge.

Foucault and Liberal Political Economy. Mark Pennington, Oxford University Press. © Mark Pennington 2025.
DOI: 10.1093/9780197690550.003.0005

The present chapter sets in motion the critical analysis focussing on the social justice *dispositif.* Contemporary liberal societies are increasingly colonised by bio-political discourses that see the freedom of subjects as inhibited by the failure to achieve a particular set of patterned outcomes. Traditionally such 'end-state' theories focussed on the distribution of income and wealth and were critical in justifying the expansion of the welfare state, but they have now been joined and, in some cases, superseded by discourses that understand unfreedom in terms of multiple inequalities of cultural status. The exposure by the civil rights, feminist, and LGBT movements of the most severe forms of unfreedom in this regard encouraged many analysts to favour a form of 'group differentiated' or 'intersectional' democracy to reallocate resources and social status towards historically disadvantaged groups.

The Foucauldian or postmodern liberal perspective offered here, though recognising the contributions of these movements to enhancing the freedom of the marginalised, argues that the discourses underlying them and their alignment with public authority may now constitute a significant threat to freedom. This arises from the dominance of interpretive frames which assume that complex power relations, whether cultural or material, are knowable and subject to bureaucratic administration and from techniques of government that may instantiate processes of 'cultural cartelisation' both within and across groups. Having outlined the discursive and philosophical currents reflected in the social justice *dispositif*, the analysis sets out the terms of this critique first in the context of race, gender, and sexuality, and second in the context of social class. It concludes by highlighting some possible lines of resistance that may address discourses of social justice without reproducing the very categories they seek to destabilise.

Discourses of social justice

Though there have been brief periods of retrenchment following financial crises, recent decades have witnessed a more or less consistent shift from a minimal or safety net conception of the welfare state to a more expansive set of social welfare commitments. While most liberal political economies retain a place for negative rights, these principles are increasingly compromised by an expanding range of positive rights obligations. Total government spending across the industrialised world increased from less than 10% of economic output in the early twentieth century to over 50% in many European countries and close to 45% in the United States by the early 2020s. The share of this enlarged expenditure devoted specifically to social spending has also increased significantly across the wealthier democracies, with much of this accounted for by transfer payments or subsidies and spending on education and health. Even during the era of 'neo-liberalism' that some have described as 'dismantling the welfare state',[2] excepting the case of Sweden, social spending has increased moderately or significantly as a share of an expanding economic output across *all* the wealthier economies—and even in Sweden the small relative decline was from a historic and internationally comparative high.[3] Similar increases have been evident across all middle-income democratic countries as well.[4]

In addition, there have also been marked increases in the regulatory remit of democratic nation-states. In the United States, for example, between 1960 and 2016 the US Federal Code of Regulations increased from a page count of just under 23,000 to 178,000, and between 1993 and 2013 the ratio of new federal regulations to congressionally enacted statutes was 223:1.[5] The latter expansion has been justified partly through the macro- and microeconomic efficiency discourses examined in chapter 3. Regulatory activism is, however, also increasingly framed in terms of governments exercising a 'power of care' over their subjects. These narratives are prominent in contexts such as public health and environmental protection and will be considered in chapters 6 and 7 respectively. Of particular interest in this chapter, however, is the proliferation of regulations focussed on cultural recognition as well as the more traditional economic concerns of the welfare/regulatory state. In the United States, for example, in addition to the agencies of the federal government, all major corporations are required to produce statistics on the race and gender composition of their workforce, and all contractors with the US government must engage in measures that promote the representation of minority groups, requirements regulated by agencies such as the Department of Labor.[6] Elsewhere, private enterprises that do not contract with the federal government are subject to the 'Disparate Impact' doctrine overseen by the Equal Employment Opportunity Commission, where practices leading to an underrepresentation of minority groups are potentially subject to legal challenge.[7] In the United Kingdom, meanwhile, the Equality Act of 2010 places obligations on all public sector employers to promote the representation of groups identified to have 'protected characteristics'—and those

[2] See, e.g., Brown, W. (2015) *Undoing the Demos*, New York: Zone Books.

[3] Lindert, P. 'Social Spending and the Welfare State', chap. 4 in OECD I Library (2023) *How Was Life: New Perspectives on Wellbeing and Inequality Since 1820*, OECD.

[4] Dorlach, T. (2021) 'The Causes of Welfare State Expansion in Democratic Middle-Income Countries: A Literature Review', *Social Policy and Administration*, 55 (5): 767–83.

[5] Friedman, J. (2019) *Power Without Knowledge*, New York: Oxford University Press, 6.

[6] These measures do not include the use of race or gender 'quotas' but require that contractors set themselves goals to improve representation of underrepresented groups and indicate the actions taken to deliver on these goals. Requirements for contractors in this regard came about through executive orders—notably E011246 (contracting) and E011478 (federal government)—initially confined to race and gender; they have since been extended to include sexual orientation and gender identity.

[7] This principle became established through the Title VII provisions of the Civil Rights Act of 1964 and in subsequent legislation, such as the Equal Employment Opportunity Act of 1972 and the Civil Rights Act of 1991.

bodies that contract with or regulate private enterprises may use these powers to influence these actors accordingly.

Though no single discourse underlies these trends, it is possible to identify three framings that circulate widely in the public realm through academia, social movements, public agencies, and increasingly charities and private sector organisations, all of which overlap to constitute the social justice *dispositif*.

Discourses of liberal equality

Coming to prominence at the end of the nineteenth century with the rise of the Progressive movement in the United States and the 'new liberalism' of Hobhouse and Keynes in the United Kingdom, the most long-standing and until recently most influential discourse of social justice has been associated with liberal equality.[8] Arising in part from philanthropy and academia these discursive currents also drew extensively on the representations and actions of the trade union and labour movements[9] and reflected trends in non-Anglophone societies, notably the emergence of the Bismarckian social insurance state in Germany. Common to the alliances culminating in the US New Deal and the founding of the postwar British welfare state was a discourse of positive freedom. In this perspective, unless people have sufficient resources to achieve their objectives, their freedom may be worth very little. The freedom of the less advantaged requires unemployment insurance, social security systems, public pensions, and extensive government financing of education so that access to socio-economic opportunities is decoupled from wealth.

This narrative was prevalent throughout most of the postwar period and paralleled the discourses of Keynesian macroeconomic managerialism that also dominated this era with public agencies framed as balancing the demands of wealth creation with the fairer distribution of opportunity. Philosophically, it was reinforced in the Anglophone world by the dominant influence achieved by Rawlsian welfare liberalism, and its conceptualisation of technocratic experts impartially supervising the stabilisation, regulatory, and distributive branches of the welfare state.

In the wake of the civil rights movement, second-wave feminism, and the rise of LGBT rights movements, these discourses widened their reach to incorporate cultural inequalities associated with dimensions of race, gender, and sexuality. In part this reflected longer standing liberal support for anti-discrimination

[8] Hobhouse, L. (1911) *Liberalism*, London: Williams and Norgate; Keynes, J. M., 'The End of Laissez Faire', in Keynes, J. M. (1931) *Essays in Persuasion*, London: Macmillan.

[9] Roberts, B. (1956) 'Trade Unions in the Welfare State', *The Political Quarterly*, 27 (1): 6–18.

laws placing limits on freedom of contract. It was, however, also a response to bottom-up campaigns by social movements to remove discriminatory distinctions in public institutions—the most recent manifestation of which was the extension of marriage rights to include same-sex couples and allowing gay, lesbian, and trans individuals to join military establishments. This pivot towards cultural inequalities has also been reflected in efforts to challenge less overt discrimination, most notably stereotyping in school curricula and public fora that reproduces hierarchies between men and women and between majority and minority ethnic groups and sexualities. In tandem with this approach has been a concern for public, private, and civil agencies to collate and to publish data on the representation of different groups in employment and for the publication of data on relative rates of pay between different categories of actors to highlight disparities and potential discrimination.[10]

Discourses of stakeholder democracy

Overlapping these narratives are 'stakeholder' models of democratic participation that while drawing on liberal themes also exhibit communitarian and social democratic inflexions. On this view business corporations should not simply act within the law to make decisions according to what secures profits for their shareholders, and neither should consumers simply choose what maximises their personal preferences and interests. Rather, the direct and indirect consequences for multiple internal and external stakeholders—whether employees, neighbourhood groups, or the members of various marginalised communities should all be considered.

In its liberal register this discourse maintains that equality will not be achieved without democratic supervision of resource allocation and distribution. Where market processes and those based on political bargaining may reproduce prevailing patterns of inequality, requirements for all actors to justify their decisions in public fora may bring unjustifiable inequalities to public attention leading to demands for their correction.[11] Traditional welfare liberal discourse conceives of policy experts manipulating the 'basic structure' to produce desired outcomes, but stakeholder narratives suggest that democratic procedures are better placed to avoid the potential for technocratic error and misrecognition by drawing on a wider pool of perspectives from those who experience inequalities of income

[10] In the United Kingdom, this approach is evident in the campaigns of, e.g., the Fawcett Society, see https://www.fawcettsociety.org.uk/.

[11] For example, Guttman, A., and Thompson, D. (2004) *Why Deliberative Democracy?*, Princeton, NJ: Princeton University Press; see also Rawls, J. (1993) *Political Liberalism*, New York: Columbia University Press.

and wealth or those relating to race, ethnicity, gender, or sexual orientation. The outcomes required by liberal equality will not be achieved without participatory democracy. Neither, however, will the latter achieve its egalitarian potential without the conditions of fair equality of opportunity the welfare state grants to the less advantaged to participate effectively in democratic processes.[12]

In its communitarian register stakeholderism moves beyond what it sees as the largely 'aggregative' conception of democracy in liberal egalitarian discourse. Where the latter understands democratic participation as a tool for actors to have their preferences better reflected, communitarian stakeholderism emphasises the value of collective, democratic decision-making in questioning the values and preferences that people have and their effects on other actors.[13] It favours a reflexive democracy where people attempt to persuade others through arguments to arrive at consensus positions embodying the collective will—a process with the potential to transform the preferences, values, and stereotypes of those concerned in a way that reduces inequalities between groups. Subjects should thus be represented as members of stakeholder groups or communities such as workers, women, gays, or lesbians, or as members of ethnic, racial, or religious minorities if this process is to unfold.[14]

Where the import of liberal equality is reflected in at least some of the core institutions of contemporary welfare state capitalism, the influence of stakeholderism is more diffuse. Some broadly liberal political economies do exhibit elements of stakeholderism—as in the requirements for worker representation on company boards found in Germany or the corporatist arrangements between labour, business, and the state in parts of Scandinavia—though these arrangements come nowhere near the more radical aspirations for the mass extension of worker-owned enterprises or cooperatives favoured by many academic supporters of participatory democracy. Elsewhere, stakeholder discourses appear most influential in contexts such as urban and land-use planning and in decisions surrounding the location and construction of transport facilities, where those bringing forward proposals for new housing, roads, airports, and other infrastructure require engagement with extensive processes of public consultation—procedures justified in terms of their capacity to alert those concerned to positive and negative impacts on multiple constituencies.

Stakeholder discourse has also become increasingly evident in the marketing, public relations, and governance practices of large businesses that frequently make public reports on multiple dimensions of their 'corporate social

[12] Guttman and Thompson, *Why Deliberative Democracy*; Rawls, *Political Liberalism*.

[13] Following Habermas, J. (1984) *The Theory of Communicative Action*, vol 1: *Reason and the Rationalisation of Society*, Boston: Beacon Press.

[14] Young, I. M. (1990) *Justice and the Politics of Difference*, Princeton, NJ: Princeton University Press.

responsibility' and, more recently, their environmental and social governance, or ESG, practices. In part, these trends may reflect attempts to build reputational capital with social movements, consumers, and investors—the campaigns of which have fuelled the narrative of stakeholderism, and which extend beyond the narrow realm of academic and philosophical discourse. Equally, however, corporate efforts to accommodate these demands may be adopted to satisfy regulatory agencies or to *pre-empt* direct regulatory or legal intervention pertaining to allegations of discrimination in their business practices.

Discourses of intersectional equity

That people should be represented according to group-based identities is also central to discourses of intersectional equity. Though overlapping with liberal and stakeholder narratives, what distinguishes these perspectives is a commitment to 'standpoint' epistemologies.[15] Where the liberal and stakeholder frames emphasise the value of democratic processes in aggregating or communicating preferences, standpoint theories focus on how the uniqueness of people's cultural experience may mean that their knowledge *cannot* easily be shared or accessed by others. Knowledge is so heavily contextualised by ones' identity as part of socially situated groups that it may not be possible for those in differently positioned groups to acquire it. Those historically marginalised by prevailing cultural practices may experience the world in ways inaccessible to the powerful or advantaged. Women may have to adopt 'masculine behaviours' or put up with sexually coloured remarks in the workplace, LGBT people may have to submit to heteronormative expectations if they are to be accepted, and people of colour may have to submit to racialised standards. In all such cases those benefitting from the relevant power differentials may act to perpetuate them without recognising their normative content and potentially oppressive effects.[16]

Intersectional discourses also recognise the Foucauldian point that people are not singular selves but are criss-crossed by a plethora of partial and often contradictory identifications, and it is the varied combination of these 'intersections' that may generate unique standpoints, perspectives, and experiences of inequality that elude practices that fail to see issues of inequality and difference in intersectional terms. Thus, anti-discrimination legislation historically failed to

[15] For example, Code, I. (1981) 'Is the Sex of the Knower Epistemologically Significant', *Metaphilosophy*, 12: 267–76; Harding, S. (1982) 'Is Gender a Variable in Conceptions of Rationality? A Survey of Issues', *Dialectica* 36 (2–3): 225–42; Harding, S. (1991) *Whose Science? Whose Knowledge?*, Ithaca, NY: Cornell University Press.

[16] For a summary see Medina, J. (2013) *The Epistemology of Resistance: Gender and Racial Oppression*, New York: Oxford University Press.

recognise that a female and black subject may experience different forms of inequality from those situated as female and white or male and black.[17] Similarly, black working-class subjects may have different experiences from those who are white and working class, or black and middle class, and those who are gay and black may have different experiences from those who are gay and white or straight and black. These differences are not simply additive but interact in complex ways generating unique forms of socio-cultural experience, including ones of oppression and unfreedom.[18]

In its diagnostic mode intersectional equity considers injustice to include all instances where access to goods and social status is affected by the existence of systemic power relations that advantage certain actors over others. Concepts such as epistemic violence and epistemic injustice are invoked to explain how the knowledge, standards, and values of marginalised groups or of specific intersections between such groups are not recognised by dominant cultural norms that present themselves as normal, neutral, or unbiased.[19]

Inspired by the campaigns of social movements in its prescriptive mode, intersectionality advocates solutions to structural or systemic inequalities that centre the experience of marginalised subjects via a form of group differentiated democracy. Central to this is a 'strategic essentialism' that celebrates the group identity of marginalised people.[20] While it recognises that identities are socially constructed, it seeks to use the relevant identities as a resource to secure greater status in relation to more advantaged or privileged groups. This framing overlaps closely with communitarian stakeholder models, requiring that subjects participate in decision-making as members of distinct social groups or intersections.

Rejecting 'merit-based' approaches to equality and opportunity, intersectional equity requires instead that subjects are treated *differently* by democratic and other institutions in accordance with their positionality as members of advantaged or disadvantaged groups.[21] English-language requirements emphasising standard grammar may, for example, reproduce advantages for white, middle-class students compared to those from black working-class homes who may

[17] Crenshaw, K. (1991) 'Mapping the Margins: Intersectionality, Identity, Politics and Violence Against Women of Colour', *Stanford Law Review*, 43 (6): 1241–99; Collins, P. H. (1993) 'Towards a New Vision of Race, Class and Gender as Categories of Analysis and Connection', *Race, Sex and Class* 1 (1): 25–45; Collins, P. H., and Bilge, S. (2016) *Intersectionality*, Cambridge: Polity Press.

[18] Crenshaw, 'Mapping the Margins'; Collins, 'Towards a New Vision of Race, Class and Gender'.

[19] On epistemic violence, see, e.g., Dotson, K. (2011) 'Tracking Epistemic Violence: Tracking Practices of Silencing', *Hypatia*, 26 (2): 236–5; On epistemic injustice see, e.g., Fricker, M. (2007) *Epistemic Injustice Power and the Ethics of Knowing*, Oxford: Oxford University Press.

[20] Spivak, G. C. 'Can the Sub-Altern Speak?', in Nelson, C., and Grossberg, L. (1988) eds. *Marxism and the Interpretation of Culture*, Chicago: University of Illinois Press.

[21] Young, *Justice and the Politics of Difference*.

communicate via non-standard English and who may experience the requirement to speak and write in approved English as a form of minorising oppression. Addressing these group-based differentials may require treating the members of different social groups differently by, for example, holding them to alternative educational standards or providing additional resources to compensate for disadvantage, as well as positive discrimination.

Intersectional equity also extends the concept of 'harm' to include all direct and indirect consequences for subjects' experience of their identities that result from decentred actions in the economy and civil society. If unequal power relations are generated and sustained through multiple discursive and non-discursive acts, then it is these 'micro-aggressions' by the members of more advantaged groups that must become the focus of regulatory attention. This means moving beyond direct discrimination to a view that sees discriminatory practice as the failure to address language, norms, and standards that work indirectly to reproduce group-based differentials.

Given the overlaps between this discourse and those of liberal equality and stakeholder democracy, it is hard to discern its specific influence on public and private decision-making practice. Early US civil rights legislation that allowed for positive discrimination and that considered hiring practices that might have 'disparate impact' on marginalised groups as indirectly discriminatory was initially influenced by liberal egalitarian discourse but is increasingly interpreted through an intersectional equity lens. More recently, legislation to protect people of colour, LGBT people, women and ethnic and religious minorities from harassment or hate speech and the designation of such groups as having 'protected characteristics' as in UK equalities law might be considered to reflect this grid. Both US and UK legislation has also facilitated the spread of diversity, equity, and inclusion (DEI) practices through multiple forms of public guidance, partnership agreements, and contracting processes where governmental bodies seek to influence the behaviour of other public agencies, charities, private corporations, and individual citizens, moulding them to embed group-based representation at multiple levels. The result of these developments has been an explosion in the size and scope of human resources (HR) departments and other forms of regulatory compliance within the private sector. In the United States the proportion of those employed in HR management has doubled in the last twenty years,[22] and in the UK the HR sector has grown by over 40% in the last decade—a rate four times the growth in the wider workforce.[23]

[22] On this see Hanania, R. (2023) *The Origins of Woke*, New York: Broadside/Harper Collins, 66–7.
[23] 'HR Profession Grows Four Times Faster Than the UK Workforce in the Past Decade', 14 October 2022, *HR Magazine*.

The social justice *dispositif*

In Foucauldian terms the overlapping discursive and non-discursive practices constituting the social justice *dispositif* are 'bio-political' or 'pastoral' governmentalities that construct or make visible population anomalies and target them for different forms of intervention and regulation. What is common to the different elements of the *dispositif* is the belief that inequalities in economic and socio-cultural status can and should be brought under collective control through a 'governmentalisation of power' so that states of injustice or unfreedom can be replaced with those where injustice is lessened and freedom enhanced.

The import of these ideas derives from a complex of entanglements between public law and more decentred socio-economic processes. The US Civil Rights Act of 1964, as well as its subsequent amendments, for example, though having significant public support, operates in largely 'top-down' or sovereign form to directly outlaw discrimination against protected groups such as African Americans and women. Similarly, the UK Equality Act 2010 requires all public sector bodies to promote equality of opportunity for groups classified as 'protected'.

On the other hand, most cultural legislation and regulation is not prescriptive. In both the US and British contexts, the social justice *dispositif* 'governs at a distance' by encouraging or 'incentivising' multiple public, private, and civil organisations to change their behaviour through contracting requirements, setting targets, and various audits which leave discretion to those concerned to decide how they are to demonstrate progress in achieving the relevant outcomes. Ambiguity over concepts such as disparate impact, indirect discrimination, systemic inequality, and equality of opportunity also leaves scope for multiple interest groups, HR departments, lawyers, and civil servants to engage in bargaining processes that determine how regulatory requirements are interpreted in specific instances. Though sovereign law sets the parameters within which this bargaining takes place, the specific outcomes generated within these parameters emerge as the intended and unintended consequences of strategising and bargaining by multiple individuals and organisations who deploy discursive constructs from within the *dispositif* to secure resources, power, and positionality.[24]

[24] For a discussion exploring this process in the US specifically see, e.g., Dobbin, F., and Sutton, J. (1998) 'The Strength of a Weak State: The Rights Revolution and the Rise of Human Resources Management Divisions', *American Journal of Sociology* 104 (2): 441–76.

Problematising the social justice *dispositif* I: Race, gender, and sexuality

Chapter 4 questioned discourses of freedom and rights which justify a 'pastoral power' that overrides or administers the decisions of subjects in the name of protecting their freedom. The pages that follow apply this theoretical lens to critique specific manifestations of this 'correctional' power in the social justice *dispositif*. The analysis builds on a Foucauldian liberal variant of intersectionality and standpoint theory to problematise the suggestion that complex power relations can be brought under 'conscious control' and to explore the potentially *illiberal* 'power effects' from seeking to exercise such control either directly or by 'governing at a distance'.

Before commencing this critique, it is important to state that the perspective set out here acknowledges the achievements of social justice movements. The campaigns of civil rights activists and those for female and LGBT equality have played a fundamental role in challenging the alliances between private and state-supported violence that have historically subjugated or marginalised large groups of people whether in the form of imperialism, the denial of rights to own property in different forms, or to find sexual satisfaction or love without fear of persecution. Correspondingly, it recognises that the legacy of such violence and exclusion continues to be felt by many people in their daily lives. What it questions, however, is whether these experiences are best addressed through the discursive and governmental practices centred by the social justice *dispositif*. There are two aspects to this critical stance: the first questions whether attempts to correct or to avoid pattern anomalies across socio-cultural groups are compatible with a recognition of the complex and dynamic quality of intersectional power relations; the second questions whether group-based forms of representation enhance or constrain the scope for subjects to escape from socially constructed categorisations and to engage in positive-sum forms of cultural-economic interchange. This section presents the elements of this critical political economy in the context of race, gender, and sexuality, while the subsequent section turns to issues of social class.

Power relations as complex phenomena: Assuming the capacity to control

Though differing in some respects, the constituent discourses of the social justice *dispositif* view cultural inequalities of race, ethnicity, gender, and sexuality as *systemic*. By that they mean that the practices generating relative advantage for some subjects and relative disadvantage for others cannot be attributed to the actions of specific persons who may be held responsible for the outcomes. Systemic inequalities are 'interactional', 'emergent', or 'spontaneous order' phenomena and are thus *beyond* any individual's or group's capacity to direct or control. While liberal political economy emphasises the freedom-enhancing quality of market-based spontaneous order, Foucauldian or postmodern liberalism also recognises that the entanglement of markets with cultural and political spontaneous orders may generate practices that constrain agency. Just as no individual or group is responsible for generating a spontaneous order that may enhance the capacity for people to secure their ends, so no individual can be held responsible either for the norms, discourses, and linguistic practices generating experiences of exclusion and oppression or for undermining such practices.

The discourse coalitions now framing discussions of social justice maintain that while there may be no agent responsible for systemic inequality there is *a collective responsibility* to institute and support laws and modes of social interaction that can *consciously dismantle* the relevant power relations. Where the Marxist tradition sought to replace the 'anarchy of capitalist production' with a system of 'conscious control', the contemporary social justice *dispositif* either explicitly or implicitly seeks to replace the 'anarchy of cultural production' with one of 'conscious cultural control'. From a Foucauldian or postmodern liberal perspective, however, this analysis needs to be problematised.

The first critical issue here is that if systemic power relations are examples of what Foucault and Hayek understand as 'complex phenomena', then it is precisely the complexity and often opacity of these interacting 'spontaneous orders' that may *preclude* any synoptic or collective point from which their operation can be viewed, understood, and undermined. Overt forms of discrimination, violence, or bullying may partially be addressed through organised collective action and changes in the law, but this is unlikely to be so for the more subtle and decentred forms of exclusion motivating concerns about systemic inequality. While it may be possible to comprehend the general character of the processes through which power relations operate, it may not be possible to determine the consequences arising from specific attempts to manipulate or alter such relations. In any complex strategic situation of power, no collective sovereign may anticipate the creative and strategic moves that will be made in response to the intended and unintended consequences of multiple private or public acts and how these may strengthen or weaken different subject positions. *Every* decision to buy or sell, to invest or divest, to favour one policy or another, to adopt or reject a particular cultural practice or mode of speech will both affect the 'systemic conditions' that face other agents and will be simultaneously affected by those conditions. Quite apart from the level of intrusion and surveillance required to track power as it flows through multiple homes, schools, workplaces, and consumption points, it is the inability to know how any act or acts within 'the system' interact with all the other decisions that may preclude any synoptic or sovereign attempt to 'control' systemic power *either* individually *or* collectively.

Consider in this context the problem of racialised inequality in the United States. The implicit or explicit attitudes and stereotypes that have contributed to racial disparities in that country may best be understood as an emergent property that has both produced and has been produced by the complex entanglement of multiple discursive and non-discursive practices. These include a history of public and private violence in the form of racialised slavery and its cultural legacy;[25] the legacy of enforced segregation through Jim Crow laws;[26] zoning regulations and urban renewal policies that, intentionally or not, have blocked or segregated minority/low-income housing development;[27] anti-drug laws that intentionally or otherwise have disproportionately affected minority communities;[28] employment regulations such as minimum wage laws that, intentionally or not, may have hampered the employment prospects of minorities lacking education and skills;[29] and multiple locational, employment, and consumption choices, informed or not, by racist assumptions and stereotypes or by knowledge of others assumptions and stereotypes.[30]

What matters is that while some of these contributors to inequality have been driven by overt racism others may have reflected very different motivations. In the case of minimum wage laws for example, these have often been driven by a 'colour blind' concern to help low-income people, *irrespective* of their race, but insofar as they may have reduced the number of low-skilled positions and raised the costs of starting small enterprises, these costs have often fallen disproportionately on African Americans who already suffer historical disadvantage in the form of lower skill levels and education.[31] Similarly, zoning or land-use regulations may be introduced with the 'colour blind' intent of preserving open space and limiting urban sprawl, but insofar as these policies reduce the supply of new housing and raise its price, they may disproportionately disadvantage minority groups. Problems of this kind are especially challenging because policies such as zoning laws may enable people to achieve objectives such as aesthetically pleasing environments that might not otherwise be achievable. Equally, however, the very same governmental practices may be taken up and disseminated in Foucauldian 'cynicisms of power' by those seeking to preserve patterns of racial

[25] Higgs, R. (1977) *Competition and Coercion*, Cambridge: Cambridge University Press.

[26] Ibid. See also Roback, J. (1986) 'The Political Economy of Segregation: The Case of Segregated Streetcars', *Journal of Economic History*, 56 (4): 893–917.

[27] Anderson, M. (1964) *The Federal Bulldozer*, Cambridge, MA: MIT Press.

[28] Forman, J. (2017) *Locking Up Our Own*, New York: Farrar, Straus, and Giroux.

[29] Higgs, *Competition and Coercion*; Moreno, P. (2008) *Black Americans and Organised Labour*, Baton Rouge: Louisiana State University Press.

[30] Schelling, T. (1978) *Micro-motives and Macro-behaviour*, New York: W. W. Norton.

[31] For a discussion of these interaction effects see Ferguson, R., and Witcher, M. (2021) *Black Liberation Through the Marketplace*, New York: Post Hill Press/Emancipation Books.

segregation and unequal access to various goods. It is, however, the incapacity for any sovereign site to know how the practices in question will be used and how they will interact with other dimensions of inequality that may preclude the effectiveness of any 'systemic' attempt to consciously 'dismantle' racialised power.

These problems multiply once it is recognised that not all inequalities of representation or of experience need necessarily be linked to direct or indirect discrimination, injustice, or unfreedom. In any pluralistic society, whenever subjects with different histories, cultures, dispositions, and value orientations interact, there is no reason to suppose that at any point in time they either will or should be equally represented across occupations or experience the same rates of remuneration. This is most apparent with immigration where new arrivals in a country may have educational backgrounds or linguistic skills that limit their opportunities compared to those historically more established. Since widely shared linguistic norms may have network effects reducing the transaction costs of association and expanding the scope for cooperation between otherwise diverse actors, those new to such norms may not be equally positioned, and it may take time for them to overcome the resulting disadvantage—even if their absolute position may be better than in the society from whence they came.

Given their specific histories subjects may also have cultural dispositions, preferences, or comparative advantages leading them towards certain fields and occupations and away from others. Islamic subjects who view female participation in the workforce differently from Westernised subjects and who are sceptical of secular lending practices may, for example, be less attracted to certain sectors such as banking and financial services. Similarly, people embedded in cultures emphasising team spirit or hierarchy over individual flair may be attracted to organisations and sectors that value these traits. Though there are important differences within these traditions, Japanese culture has, for example, often been more favourable to collective and hierarchical forms of enterprise, whereas an important strand in Chinese culture has tended towards smaller enterprises based on a sole proprietor model.[32]

Elsewhere, any understanding of social difference granting scope for reflexivity across cultural practices must recognise that some such practices may prove more conducive to socio-economic success than others. If, for example, organisations challenging traditional gender norms and encouraging a diverse workforce prove more adaptive and profitable than those with more conservative norms, the inequality between these groupings may operate as a signal for the latter to adapt accordingly or to persist in recognition of the trade-off between conservativism and relative economic success. Neither need such trade-offs be static, with different norms, standards, and practices proving more successful

[32] Lavoie, D., and Chamlee-Wright, E. (2001) *Culture and Enterprise*, London: Routledge.

across different time periods. Historically, Islamic and East Asian cultures experienced levels of economic development far surpassing those in Western Europe, but this pattern was later reversed. Though such differences may be long lasting, they may also be subject to rapid change or rupture. As little as fifty years ago Western development 'experts' maintained that East Asian cultures were stuck in a 'low growth equilibrium' or 'poverty trap' from which they could not escape without massive developmental assistance; but in subsequent years these regions, which received little in the way of such assistance, far outstripped the economic performance of Western economies, reducing cross-country inequality and in some cases overtaking Western states.[33]

Once the complexity and fluidity of the circumstances contributing to the experience of diverse subjects is so recognised, then not only is it questionable whether equality of opportunity or of outcomes is compatible with cultural or evaluative pluralism, but it also may not be possible to discern which cultural practices or policies should be preserved, modified, or jettisoned to secure a more equitable outcome—or indeed any other outcome. An intersectional perspective requires that multiple lines of difference are accounted for but there is no sovereign or synoptic point from which all the relevant intersections can be surveyed or how changes on one margin of inequality may intersect with changes on others. The notion of 'correcting' various pay and representation 'gaps' centred in the social justice *dispositif* may thus fail to capture what standpoint theorists refer to as the 'lived experience' of differently situated agents and what the Hayekian tradition describes as the 'circumstances of time and place', which are often obscured or erased by aggregate classifications.

In the context of sex and gender inequality, for example, the identification of injustice with statistical 'pay gaps' frequently fails to disaggregate between the different types of work that men and women do. Men may work longer hours, they may engage in riskier forms of employment, and they may be more likely to work in the private sector where rates of pay are frequently more varied than in the state sector.[34] The response of the social justice *dispostif* to this diversity has typically been to introduce notions such as the doctrine of 'comparative worth' for different roles and positions to generate a disciplinary norm or benchmark against which rates of pay across the sexes might be compared. The problem here, however, is that the notion of comparative worth presupposes in an almost Marxist vein that the 'worth' of different jobs or roles can be attributed to 'objective' parameters such as the number of labour or training hours involved rather than the temporary, subjective, and often contradictory evaluations of

[33] For a discussion see Easterly, W. (2014) *The Tyranny of Experts*, New York: Basic Books.

[34] Polachek, S. (1981) 'Occupational Self Selection: A Human Capital Approach to Sex Differences in Occupational Structure', *Review of Economics and Statistics*, 63 (1): 60–69; Goldin, C. (2014) 'A Grand Gender Convergence: Its Last Chapter', *American Economic Review*, 104 (4): 1091–119.

multiple businesses, workers, and consumers that generate shifting patterns of demand and supply. In these circumstances, the Foucauldian 'power effect' of the comparative worth doctrine may be to privilege a bureaucratically imposed construct of what specific jobs are 'worth' with significant scope for disciplinary misrecognition. As one Foucauldian and feminist observer puts it:

> Comparable worth policy . . . involves extraordinary levels of rationalisation of labour and the workplace: the techniques and instruments of job measurement, classification, and job descriptions required for its implementation, make Taylorism look like child's play.[35]

Of course, the fact that men and women make different choices *is* likely to reflect systemic gender stereotyping and power relations that produce different orientations or path dependencies in employment choices and other behaviours. Nevertheless, actions designed to address these very differences—such as banning all gender-related discrimination in contractual relationships—may in some cases worsen the position of those produced by these power relations. There is no 'stereotype free' understanding of sex and gender, and attempting to restrict interactions involving such stereotypes may block processes that may undermine the relevant stereotypes. Thus, if women are perceived as less capable of doing jobs requiring physical strength, a rule prohibiting sex-based pay differentials may discourage employers from taking on women and may thus remove the potential for those concerned to disrupt this stereotype and to demonstrate their capability.[36] Likewise, a quota-based regime may discourage employers who perceive gender balance as threatening their profitability from making investments *at all* or substituting capital for labour to achieve their desired margins. Alternatively, anti-discrimination rules may prevent women from taking advantage of stereotypes working in their favour. In the European Union for example, insurance companies are now prevented from marketing cheaper car insurance to women, who on average are less likely to make accident claims, on the grounds that this is unduly discriminatory.[37]

Crucially, the governance of inequalities through statistics and bureaucratic classifications may also ignore the significance of differences *within* the groups they target and how these intersect with other disparities. Historically, for example, data suggest that gay men have earned less than heterosexual men with

[35] Brown, W. (1995) *States of Injury*, Princeton, NJ: Princeton University Press, 171.
[36] Epstein, R. (1992) *Forbidden Grounds: The Case Against Employment Discrimination Laws*, Cambridge, MA: Harvard University Press.
[37] Insley, J. 'Sheilas' Wheels Promises Few Price Changes for Existing Customers', *The Guardian*, 2 October 2012, https://www.theguardian.com/money/2012/oct/10/sheilas-wheels-car-insurance.

equivalent qualifications,[38] but lesbian women have earned more relative to heterosexual women such that improvements in the relative pay or representation of gay men may have had little relevance to the statistical gender pay gap. More recent evidence, however, suggests that gay men in the United States may now enjoy a significant pay premium over straight men,[39] so depending on the size of the gay population, efforts to promote gay men now have the potential to increase these statistical 'gaps'. One reason for these premiums may be the generally lower childcare commitments for gays and lesbians, which raises the possibility that this difference may now function to indirectly advantage them in the way that traditional gender norms have often advantaged straight men. Any reduction of this 'sexuality premium', however, might be to ignore how this inequality intersects with experiences based on age. With fewer family support networks producing disproportionate levels of isolation and loneliness for elderly LGBT people, what advantages gays and lesbians in their working lives may disadvantage them in later life.[40]

Elsewhere, providing greater public or private childcare to encourage women into higher paying professions or engaging in acts of affirmative action may contribute to disparities on other dimensions *within* the female category. Thus, in contexts where non-white women are disproportionately situated in religious or cultural traditions placing an emphasis on domestic childcare, and that oppose state-sponsored provision or private commodification of care, then secular white women may be more likely to benefit from these opportunities—opportunities that may work to increase ethnic or racial pay gaps. Correspondingly, actions reducing racial and ethnic pay or representation gaps may increase gender disparities if those recruited or better remunerated are drawn disproportionately from groups favouring traditional gender divisions of labour.

Similar problems arise not just in terms of pay or representation but also through changes in the experiences of subjects from attempts to design culturally inclusive environments. Consider, the proliferation of DEI initiatives across public and private sector organisations that now encourage employees to 'bring their whole selves' to the workplace.[41] While an initiative encouraging subjects to speak freely about their sexuality in the workplace may enhance the lived experience of some LGBT people, it may at the same time make those whose

[38] Arabsheibani, R., Marin, A., and Wadsworth, J. (2005) 'Gay Pay in the UK', *Economica*, 72 (286): 333–47—for a meta-analysis of some recent historical trends, see Drydakis, N. (2022) 'Sexual Orientation and Earnings: A Meta-Analysis 2012–2020', *Journal of Population Economics*, 35: 409–40.

[39] Carpenter, C., and Eppink, S. (2017) 'Does It Get Better? Recent Estimates of Sexual Orientation and Earnings in the United States', *Southern Economic Journal*, 84 (2): 426–41.

[40] Espinoza, R. (2011) 'The Diverse Elders Coalition and LGBT Aging: Connecting Communities, Issues and Resources in a Historic Moment', *Public Policy and Aging Report*, 21 (3): 8–12.

[41] These are now widespread in corporate and educational settings. See, e.g., this author's employer—https://www.kcl.ac.uk/jobs/our-culture/equality-diversity-inclusion.

religious beliefs may be pathologised as 'homophobic' in such a setting less comfortable in expressing their beliefs. The dimension of religious or philosophical belief in this context may intersect with other markers of identity such as race and ethnicity. There is, for example, evidence that people of colour in the United States are more likely to espouse traditional or conservative beliefs than white people,[42] such that the cultural dominance of the latter's values in settings such as universities and large corporations may be one of the factors discouraging non-white subjects from seeking to participate in these organisational structures, and for those that do, not to be representative of the communities from which they are drawn.[43] For LGBT subjects meanwhile, there may be significant differences in experience arising from work environments that are more, or less, culturally inclusive. Gay Muslims, for example, may wish to stay in the closet at work if that environment has a representative share of other Muslim employees even if the latter do not speak openly about their views on same-sex love. Rather than improving their experience, the presence of other Muslims who take a negative view of homosexuality may make gay Muslims fearful of being reported to *external* community members and ostracised by family and friends.[44] For a gay Muslim to 'bring his whole self to work' may require not only that other Muslims do not bring their 'whole selves' to work—but also that such Muslims do not bring themselves to his workplace at all. Even the exhortation for a gay Muslim subject to bring the whole of *himself* to work may further stoke an agonistic and perhaps unresolvable tension between his 'gay self' and his 'Islamic self' where the expression of one part of the subjects' identity may involve renouncing or suppressing another part of that identity.

None of this implies that acts taken by legislators, individuals, or organisations, in the name of reducing inequalities, are necessarily 'wrong'. A free, open, and pluralistic society provides space for multiple agents to pursue their understanding of what inclusion or social justice requires, and within specific businesses, universities, or civil associations these may include pay audits, positive discrimination, and DEI initiatives. Rather, what is problematised here is the institutionalisation or 'governmentalisation' of a discursive formation that homogenises cultural regulation and routinises subjects into believing that certain acts are *morally required* because of their predictable effects on different individuals and groups, *irrespective of whether any such effects are present*. Though it cannot rule out the possibility that conscious efforts to

[42] Gay, C. (2014) 'Knowledge Matters: Policy Cross-Pressures and Black Partisanship', *Political Behaviour*, 36: 99–124.

[43] Gharbi, M., -al (2019) 'Viewpoint: Diversity Is About Much More Than Politics', Heterodox Academy, 29 April.

[44] Jaspal, R., and Siraj, A. (2011) 'Perceptions of Coming Out Among British Muslim Gay Men', *Psychology and Sexuality*, 2 (3): 183–97.

reduce inequality or unfreedom may somehow align successfully on all relevant margins, an approach recognising the complexity of intersectional power maintains that such efforts may be as likely to increase inequality or unfreedom as to result in any global increase in equality or freedom.

Cultural justice, social action, and police power

A Foucauldian or postmodern liberal perspective also recognises threats to pluralism from power effects generated by a *dispositif* that erases this intersectional complexity and that privileges the role of directional intelligence in the pursuit of freedom and justice. Two such effects should be highlighted in this regard.

First, the notion that complex power relations are subject to conscious egalitarian 'correction' may divert attention from the less visible ways that power relations may be destabilised through non-directional spontaneous ordering processes in markets and civil society. In the social justice *dispositif* it is not enough to 'mind one's own business' or to concentrate on offering products and services that others are willing to buy—unless it can also be demonstrated how these actions contribute to a wider 'social purpose' such that many private enterprises as well as public sector bodies increasingly seek to position themselves as quasi-missionary organisations. In such a discursive climate the words and actions of those adopting the mantle of social justice are granted a kind of moral superiority by the *dispositif* and the ability to exercise power over those making no such claims when justifying their decisions—even when there may be no demonstrable difference in their contribution to whatever outcomes emerge. There is, for example, little evidence that equalities legislation is responsible for shifts in gender, race, and ethnic representation or for reductions in various pay gaps with these declining prior to legislative action.[45] In the context of racial inequality specifically, the gap between people of colour and white people in the United States declined significantly prior to the widespread adoption of equalities legislation—and even during the pre-civil rights era when overtly racist language and discrimination was commonplace, this trend was established.[46] More recently, there is minimal evidence that workplaces adopting DEI initiatives, such as unconscious bias training, are any more successful in promoting positive work relations relative to those organisations that avoid such measures. In some cases the actions that appear to do most to enhance workplace diversity

[45] For a summary of evidence on gender pay gaps see Polachek, S. (2019) *Equal Pay Legislation and the Gender Wage Gap*, IZA: World of Labour.

[46] Higgs, *Competition and Coercion.*

were not adopted for that purpose.[47] Elsewhere, profit-driven investments in fields such as the garment industry may have done as much if not more to disrupt hierarchical gender relations and to improve female access to education in poor and traditional societies than deliberate efforts by governments and international social justice NGOs to promote female empowerment[48]—and in some cases the 'social actions' of such NGOs may have reduced these opportunities.[49] Or, consider how technological developments such as generative AI may reduce the disadvantages facing non-native speakers in employments requiring written communications—and how these same developments may 'dismantle' the power of professions that distinguish themselves through the power of the written word. In each of these examples, however, the *dispositif* tends to ignore or treat with ambivalence activities and processes that have the potential to undermine established power relations, while actions directly justified in the name of promoting equality are held to be essential *irrespective* of any effect they may or may not exercise. The dominant social construction of a pastorally guided society thus grants authority to 'positive actions' not because of their actual effects but in terms of their symbolic association with 'social improvement' through the application of conscious reason or directional intelligence.

Second, the discursive power granted to those claiming the capacity to promote social justice may facilitate the creation and empowerment of ethical 'policing mechanisms' that extend their reach deep into private and civil life. These disciplinary powers may 'govern at a distance' through a capillary network of agents 'installed' or 'embedded' by the *dispositif* in multiple private, public, and civil organisations and empowered by equalities legislation to conduct the terms of social interaction in decentred vein. Though power is diffused through society like a dye, the elements of the relevant dispersal may still be 'injected' into the social order through acts that stimulate or draw on the wills to power of multiple other agents eager to exert various forms of positionality over others. Consider here the Biden administration's 'whole of government equity agenda' in the United States which institutionalises DEI procedures right across the federal government and its numerous subsidiaries.[50] Where government expenditure now

[47] Paluck, E. Green, D. (2009) 'Prejudice Reduction: What Works? A Review and Assessment of Research and Practice', *Annual Review of Psychology*, 60: 339–67, https://hbr.org/2016/07/why-diversity-programs-fail.

[48] On this see, e.g., Heath, R., and Mobarak, A. (2015) 'Manufacturing Growth and the Lives of Bangladeshi Women', *Journal of Development Economics*, 115: 1–15.

[49] For example, Grier, K., Mahmood, T., and Powell, B. (2023) 'Anti-Sweatshop Activism and the Safety-Employment Trade-Off: Evidence from Bangladesh's Rana Plaza Disaster', *Journal of Economic Behaviour and Organisation*, 208: 174–190.

[50] Whitehouse Executive Order on Diversity, Equity and Inclusion and Accessibility in the Federal Workforce, Washington DC, https://www.whitehouse.gov/briefing-room/presidential-actions/2021/06/25/executive-order-on-diversity-equity-inclusion-and-accessibility-in-the-federal-workforce/.

constitutes a large and growing share of output and where the state is increasingly engaged in industrial policies that seek to 'partner' government agencies with private corporations, such regulation is likely to stimulate the demand for a new layer of bureaucratic actors to promote, enforce, and to document the relevant actions right across the public and private domains. Public agencies working 'in the shadow' of such legislation may also use their position to enforce these requirements on those they regulate irrespective of whether the latter are in receipt of government funds or contracts. In the United Kingdom, for example, the Bank of England and the Financial Conduct Authority are proposing that all the financial institutions they regulate engage in DEI initiatives.[51] Away from this, in a discursive setting that institutionalises the pursuit of social justice, many businesses and organisations not formally required to initiate the techniques propagated by the *dispositif* may adopt them regardless to minimise the perceived threat of negative publicity, legal action, or the possibility of future regulatory disadvantage.

This penetration of discursive categories and governance techniques into multiple organisational cultures may also contribute to the generation of new subjectivities who fill or who are 'scripted into' the respective 'policing' and 'policed' roles. Large numbers of subjects may come to see their actions through a form of 'government by audit' enforcing the categories of the *dispositif* on themselves and on others through their hiring decisions, the proliferation of allyship schemes and speech codes, and the adoption of pastoral symbols such as lanyards and badges to signal the subjects policing role and to generate evidence of positive 'social action'. Similarly, the exercise of pastoral power within these organisational cultures may institute 'confessional' techniques and rituals reminiscent of medieval Christian practices with employees encouraged to 'search their souls' to reveal 'the truth' about their inner racism, homophobia, or misogyny and to 'work' on themselves accordingly. Those sceptical of whether such initiatives do in fact promote DEI, meanwhile, may be forced to choose between submitting to these micro-disciplinary regulations or expose themselves to censure. Though it 'governs at a distance', this type of power may also generate relationships of dependence between those it purports to protect and the state and its subsidiaries. It may do so by relentlessly categorising subjects into identity groups that require different levels of 'protection'—protection that cannot be negotiated by the subjects themselves but that must be delivered to them by the relevant pastorate or its representatives.

Once again, the threat to freedom and pluralism arising from these potential 'power effects' comes not from the existence of pay audits and DEI policies

[51] Financial Conduct Authority, London, https://www.fca.org.uk/publication/consultation/cp23-20.pdf.

per se; rather, it comes from a Foucauldian 'governmentalisation of power' that aligns or codifies legislative or sovereign power with the decentred forms of administrative and managerial power exercised within multiple organisations such that options for subjects to be governed, to think, and even to speak differently are progressively narrowed. It is this narrowing of the 'strategic field' within which power is exercised and resisted that may best account for the significant reported fall in those expressing confidence in their scope to exercise freedom of expression, and especially so in Anglophone societies where these strategic alignments or codifications between sovereign power and decentred power have become increasingly pronounced.[52]

Strategic essentialism, group differentiated discipline and cultural cartelisation

Just as the social justice *dispositif* privileges conscious reason and grants disciplinary power to those claiming to exercise this reason to advance justice, so too it privileges a form of group-centred action that may narrow the scope for subjects to engage in processes of self-governance and re-subjectification. The discourse coalitions of stakeholder theory and intersectional equity emphasise a strategic essentialism where subjects participate whether at work, in civil society, or in politics as the members of specific identity groups and where collective action is considered better placed than individual action to destabilise systemic power relations. The Foucauldian or postmodern liberal view advanced here recognises the potential for this strategic essentialism to operate as a tool of freedom, but it maintains nonetheless that privileging and institutionalising a group differentiated model opens the way for people to be subject to both *internal and external* disciplinary powers that may narrow the scope for the expression of difference *within* the groups concerned.

Problematising collective representation in this way does not deny that subjects positioned within racial, ethnic, gendered, or sexual identities may have common forms of experience that cannot easily be shared. Foucauldian or postmodern liberalism is at one with standpoint theories in recognising that while the concepts of systemic inequality or exclusion may be communicable to other actors in general or propositional form, their specific manifestations may not be. The experience of being a black man repeatedly subject to stop and search,[53] of

[52] See, e.g., https://www.nytimes.com/2022/03/18/opinion/cancel-culture-free-speech-poll.html; Hope, C. Freedom of Speech in UK 'under threat' say half of Britons in cancel culture poll, *The Telegraph*, 13 February 2021, https://www.telegraph.co.uk/politics/2021/02/13/freedom-speech-uk-threat-say-half-britons-cancel-culture-poll/

[53] On this, see, e.g., Bowling, B., and Phillips, C. (2007) 'Disproportionate and Discriminatory: Reviewing the Evidence on Police Stop and Search', *The Modern Law Review*, 70 (6): 93–61.

a woman walking home late at night in fear of sexual assault,[54] or of a boxer who 'passes as straight' hearing locker room stereotypes about 'gays who can't fight'[55] may not be readily understood or appreciated by those who have never been subjected to these experiences. Indeed, there is an important complementarity here between the postmodern liberal critique of socio-economic planning and standpoint theory. For the former, it is the inability of planners to access and comprehend the experiential knowledge embedded in the dispersed routines and practices of multiple entrepreneurs, workers, and consumers immersed in a particular business or line of trade that prevents socio-economic planning from drawing on an equivalent pool of knowledge as decentralised markets. For standpoint theory meanwhile, it is the inability for more advantaged cultural groups to appreciate the lived experience of those who face social exclusions, which means that cultural innovations attentive to these problems are more likely to arise from those who have been subject to them.[56] Emphasising the difficulties of transferring such knowledge does not of course imply that there is no scope for reflexivity. Both standpoint theory and postmodern liberalism recognise that so long as people can signal aspects of their situation to others, then adjustments or bridges across positionalities may arise *without* those concerned needing to know why the adjustment is necessary. In commercial settings for example, entrepreneurs need not understand why women might feel physically safer when walking with a personal alarm system or why women of colour who have spent years being excluded by the cosmetics industry may feel empowered by the availability of makeup suited to darker skin to respond to profit signals reflecting the demand for such products.

Though at one with standpoint theories in these respects, the Foucauldian or postmodern liberal stance questions the institutionalisation of group differentiated decision-making as the appropriate tool for addressing exclusion and epistemic disadvantage without rejecting group-based/collective action per se. Securing basic rights such as protections of bodily integrity against assault, ownership of property, the right to make contracts, and voting rights are obvious candidates where there is likely to be close agreement between those affected by social exclusion and where collective mobilisations—such as the civil rights, women's rights, and LGBT rights movements—may have a comparative advantage in exerting pressure for change over smaller scale or individual initiatives. If there are frequently advantages from organising production and division of labour through the hierarchical structures of business firms rather

[54] Keane, C. (1998) 'Evaluating the Influence of Fear of Crime as an Environmental Mobility Restrictor on Women's Routine Activities', *Environment and Behaviour*, 30 (1): 60–74.

[55] Matthews, C. (2016) 'The Tyranny of the Male Preserve', *Gender and Society*, 30 (2): 312–33.

[56] Pils, R., and Schoenegger, P. (2021) 'On the Epistemological Similarities of Market Liberalism and Standpoint Theory', *Episteme*, online, https://doi.org/10.1017/epi.2021.13.

than via individualised spot contracts, then so too resistance against cultural oppression may be more effective in the context of an organised social movement representing large numbers of actors that can alert similarly large numbers to demands for cultural or legislative change.[57]

Nevertheless, once the struggle moves from basic rights to more subtle and decentred exercises of power, it is unlikely that those sharing a social location will agree on what their interests may be or how best to advance them. One reason for this follows from a recognition of intersectionality, where subjects sharing a socially constructed attribute such as race may differ from others in terms of their gender, sexuality, religion, or income such that there is no unity of experience or perspective *within* the relevant category. More important, however, even when there *is* commonality of experience that marks individuals out in terms of a specific identity or intersection, it does not follow that there will be agreement on the interests generated or produced by that identity and on the appropriate strategies to advance it. Business entrepreneurs may share a common experience and identity derived from their unique position running enterprises, and they may agree that protecting private property rights and making profits are central to their interests—but beyond this there may be little agreement on the specific business or political strategies commensurate with these objectives, and these differences may be as pronounced *within* sectors (finance, retail, manufacturing, services etc.) as they are between sectors. Likewise, women may share a common experience of gendered stereotyping, and black women may share the intersectional experience of racialised and gendered stereotyping, but it does not follow that they will share a common view on the strategies best placed to advance their interests in such conditions.

Consider here different attitudes towards the practice of code-meshing where African American students are encouraged to use non-standard forms of spoken and written English in fields such as literary composition, which has become the hallmark of anti-racist pedagogy in the United States. Some African Americans view these techniques as essential if students of colour are not to experience feelings of exclusion or minorisation.[58] Others within this group, however, see acquiring and practising standard English as an effective tool that can challenge racist stereotypes and provide the best route towards well-paid employment. Where the former perspective sees learning and practising standard English as a negation of black identity incompatible with a strategic essentialism that challenges white norms, for the latter perspective practising standard English

[57] Novak, M. (2021) *Freedom in Contention: Social Movements and Liberal Political Economy*, London: Rowman and Littlefield.

[58] Young, V., and Young-Rivera, Y. (2013) 'It Ain't What It Is: Code-Switching and White American Celebrationists', *JAC*, 33 (1/2): 39–401.

and doing so as well, if not better, than 'white speakers' is a strategic move to destabilise racial stereotypes and to positively affirm a different type of black identity.[59]

Similar strategic disagreements are commonplace across other historically disadvantaged groups. Feminist campaigners have often been at the forefront of anti-pornography and anti-prostitution activism, maintaining that such practices perpetuate masculinist norms that allow the sexually dominant to exploit and demean the sexually vulnerable.[60] For other feminists, however, participation in pornography and prostitution—including demands for access to male pornography and prostitution—may be seen as a positive affirmation of a more robust and confident female sexuality, and one that offers new possibilities and freedoms to men as well.[61] In the case of LGBT subjects meanwhile, where many in the freedom movement were sceptical of the campaign for gay marriage because it retrofitted gayness into a heteronormative straitjacket, other gays and lesbians embraced the campaign for marriage equality as a strategy to affirm their identity and to disrupt heterosexual stereotyping. Elsewhere, even the act of 'coming out' has not been without controversy. While for many the freedom to come out as gay or lesbian without the fear of verbal or physical aggression is a fundamental achievement of the LGBT movement, for others the pressure to define oneself as 'gay' or 'lesbian' is to expose oneself to a classificatory gaze eager to essentialise what it means to engage in homosexual acts.[62]

In all these cases and many others there is no agreement about the most effective strategy to advance the relevant identity, in choosing which social practices to challenge, and how best to challenge them. The strategic deployment of identity is, in other words, open to entrepreneurial judgement with no sovereign view or meta-interpretation over how this judgement should be exercised. Codifying group differentiated perspectives into law either directly or 'governing at a distance' by 'installing' group-based representation in multiple organisational sites may thus empower certain factions within the relevant identity sets who secure positions of authority in bureaucratic structures to speak 'for and above' others, reducing experimentation and the expression of *intra-group* pluralism.

While the empowerment of organised groups does not preclude those who disagree from pursuing more localised or individualised strategies, the legally

[59] For a discussion see Smith, E. (2020) *A Critique of Anti-Racism in Rhetoric and Composition*, London: Rowman and Littlefield.

[60] For example, Mackinnon, C. (1989) *Towards a Feminist Theory of the State*, Cambridge, MA: Harvard University Press.

[61] For example, Strossen, N. (1995/2024) *Defending Pornography: Free Speech, Sex and the Fight for Women's Rights*, New York: New York University Press.

[62] Kopelson, K. (2002) 'Dis/integrating the Gay/Queer Binary: Reconstructed Identity Politics for a Performative Pedagogy', *College English*, 65 (1): 17–35.

codified and formal or semi-formal recognition of group identity in public and private structures privileges group-centred modes of representation in much the same way that corporatist economic structures and closed shop/union shop arrangements privilege centralised or cartelised economic decision-making over more entrepreneurial or decentralised modes. As organised group power becomes institutionalised, it may then operate as a selective magnet for those keen to exercise it, and more specifically for those who in the absence of any coherent or sovereign perspective within the group are willing to impose such a view. When political authority depends on projecting a coherence of opinion that does not exist, then there may be an imperative for those in authority to exercise disciplinary power over others enunciating what counts as the 'black', 'female', or 'LGBT' strategic interest, policing and marginalising those who fail to conform with the approved or 'correct' stance. A corresponding power effect of this 'cultural cartelisation' may be the erasure of intra-group difference in the eyes of actors *external* to the identity set with the majority of non-white, female, and LGBT subjects who do not participate in organised group action defined in terms of the projections circulated by those who do. When there is a legally backed primacy of group strategy over more individualised strategy, many of those concerned may then experience a form of social expectation to 'perform' a particular kind of 'blackness', 'femaleness', or 'gayness' that they experience as a form of misrecognition.[63]

If institutionalising group difference narrows the scope for subjects to advance their interests in different ways, so too it may freeze people into a particular understanding of their subjectivity and block the interactive, reflexive processes through which new identities and standpoints that cross classificatory boundaries might be forged. The freedom of subjects historically denied basic freedoms requires that those freedoms are secured, but it does not follow that *additional* formal protections against conducts or expressions that might be experienced as oppressive *in the absence of basic rights* are also required. Rather, special protections such as speech codes or restrictions on freedom of contract for those defined as 'at-risk' or 'vulnerable' groups may simply reinforce rather than destabilise the disciplinary categories that have historically marked them out as specific 'types' of individuals. That historically people of colour have often experienced hearing authoritative voices in educational settings as an echo of white overlordship does not mean that hearing such educational expressions today, whether from white people or from other persons of colour, is a signifier of ongoing racial subordination or acquiescence with white supremacist norms. Similarly, that the existence of pornography and prostitution may have been

[63] For example, Royster, J. (1996) 'When the First Voice You Hear Is Not Your Own', *College Composition and Communication*, 47 (1): 29–40.

historical signifiers of women's subjection does not preclude these practices from being *re-signified* today as creative tools of sexual freedom and exploration for women and for men alike. And that LGBT subjects may have had to sit in silence when hearing verbal slights about their sexuality or gender identity when their expression was publicly prohibited does not mean that such subjects should be prevented from hearing opinions critical or even scornful of homosexuality or transgenderism in contexts where LGBT people can be more open and engage their freedom of speech to challenge such viewpoints.

All such interactions will take place under asymmetries of power and involve psychological discomfort and risk, but on a Foucauldian view it is through the exercise of creative agency in the face of such power that those asymmetries may be challenged, transgressed, and reconfigured rather than essentialised or codified in the meanings of specific actions and words. Yet, by construing freedom from violence and its incitement, freedom of speech, and freedom of contract as inadequate freedoms in this regard, the social justice *dispositif* may push subjects to enforce on themselves and on others a regime that *intensifies* the regulation and discipline of race, gender, and sexuality in precisely these terms. If subjects can gain access to promotions or contracts over others because of a specific dimension of their identity, then they may be encouraged to emphasise or accentuate that aspect of themselves to the neglect of other elements of their identity or the cultivation of new identifications. Relatedly, when members of marginalised groups can invoke disciplinary powers to block the speech of others, not only do they restrain the freedoms of the relevant speakers, but they also restrict the freedom of other marginalised subjects to hear the words at issue and, for those who are able, to respond creatively to them in ways that may change their self-understanding and that of their would-be oppressors. In this way the language of visibility and acceptance centred in the social justice *dispositif* may morph into a carceral archipelago of discursive unfreedom. As one Foucauldian observer puts it:

> Contemporary politicised identity is also potentially re-iterative of regulatory/disciplinary society in its configuration of a disciplinary subject. It is both produced by and potentially accelerates the production of that aspect of disciplinary society that 'ceaselessly characterises, classifies, and specialises'—which works through 'surveillance, continuous registration, perpetual assessment and classification', through a social machinery that is both 'immense and minute'.[64]

The irony here is that many of the social movements that have been responsible for challenging naturalist, essentialist, positivist understandings of

[64] Brown, *States of Injury*, 65.

identity which depict the social world in law-like or mechanical terms are now subscribing to a managerialist narrative where particular categories of subject are depicted in terms of predictable psychological responses to the expression of specific words, phrases, and bodily 'micro-aggressions'. Far from reflecting Foucault's project of problematising 'the type of individuality linked to the state' and its governing techniques,[65] these methods may freeze people into these very classificatory grids.

There are also significant parallels here between the potential 'power effects' from institutionalising protectionist cultural justice narratives and those associated with economic protectionism. 'Infant industry' or 'dependency' discourses presuppose that certain firms or countries must be protected from 'uneven playing fields', or conditions of 'unequal exchange', until some point when their position is judged to have been sufficiently 'equalised' with that of incumbents.[66] Analogously, the social justice *dispositif* treats historically marginalised subjects as in need of 'equalisation' *prior* to their being able to participate freely in the discursive/cultural realm. The danger is, however, that these narratives may 'produce the objects of which they speak'. In the case of economic protectionism, countries that have enforced on themselves a *dependencia* narrative, closing themselves to the inequalities of the global market and enmeshing their people and enterprises in a maze of regulatory 'protections', have remained mired in poverty.[67] By contrast, countries that have taken opportunities to engage relatively freely in 'unequal exchange' have not only prospered but in some instances have also overtaken previously more 'advanced' societies and have transformed how they are perceived by the external world.[68] Similarly, where the historically marginalised are described as subject to permanent injury by expressions that may cause them discomfort, such an environment may be responsible for *producing* a heightened sense of vulnerability and encasement in a 'plastic cage' of discursive control.[69] Thus, even in contexts where they have unprecedented freedoms and opportunities, many LGTB youth continue to express fears about revealing their orientation to family and friends.[70] Some of this reluctance surely reflects their experience of the routinised stereotyping that persists in contemporary societies. Equally, however, these vulnerabilities and anxieties may reflect that LGBT youth are repeatedly told by the dominant 'cultural safetyist'

65 MF (1982) 'The Subject and Power', *Critical Inquiry*, 8 (4): 777–95, quote at 785.

66 Frank, A. G. (1967) *Capitalism and Underdevelopment in Latin America*, New York: Monthly Review.

67 Lal, D. (2006) *Reviving the Invisible Hand*, Princeton, NJ: Princeton University Press.

68 Easterly, *The Tyranny of Experts.*

69 Brown, *States of Injury.*

70 Banfield-Nwachi, M. Half of lgbt young adults are estranged from a relative, survery finds, *The Guardian*, 19 April 2023, https://www.theguardian.com/world/2023/apr/19/half-of-lgbt-young-adults-in-uk-are-estranged-from-a-relative-survey-finds.

discourse that they may face psychological devastation if they hear anything that might be construed as injurious to their sexual identity.

Relatedly, by depicting empowerment as a state that must be achieved at the expense of others, there is a pronounced risk that cultural justice narratives may reinscribe a zero-sum model of cultural 'warfare' rather than a more positive sum or transactional understanding. If intersectionality is depicted as a 'pyramid of oppression' where, for example, people of colour cannot incorporate elements of what have previously been coded 'white' practices without this being a sign of continued subordination and where white subjects cannot incorporate elements of 'blackness' without this being signified as a form of cultural disrespect this is likely to thwart the possibility for the Foucauldian 'limit experiences' that challenge and transgress cultural boundaries.[71] Just as discourses depicting trade in zero- or negative-sum terms stifle the emergence of new production and consumption possibilities, so narratives depicting cultural interaction as akin to a form of warfare and that deploy practices often associated with states of war, such as the routinised surveillance of speech, may block the emergence of new subjectivities that transcend existing binaries. These processes may be an important factor in the increasing levels of polarisation reported in many liberal societies—a polarisation that appears to have intensified during a period in which a redistributive and 'equity' based rather than a transactional or positive-sum understanding of intersectionality has taken root.[72]

Problematising the social justice *dispositif* II: Social class

The discussion so far has focussed on a *dispositif* that frames inequalities of cultural status as subject to egalitarian correction. The analysis has questioned whether the distribution of cultural status can be subject to such 'conscious collective control' while also drawing out the potential Foucauldian 'power effects' associated with institutionalising the relevant techniques of government at multiple levels. These processes, through which the 'strategic fields' where subjects exercise their freedom may be narrowed, may also be evident in the context of more long-standing pastoral efforts to reduce class-based inequalities of income, wealth, and status that cut across the intersections of race, ethnicity, gender, and sexuality. On the one hand, the efficacy of such measures in a context of socio-economic complexity is highly questionable, while on the other, the discursive and non-discursive practices that have sustained the more, or less continuous

[71] On this, see, e.g., Smith, *A Critique of Anti-Racism in Rhetoric and Composition.*
[72] For a discussion see Mounk, J. (2023) *The Identity Trap*, London: Allen Lane.

expansion of the social welfare/regulatory state may conceal their own power effects.

Income and wealth inequality: Pastoral power and the welfare-regulatory state as its own cause

The overlapping discourses of the contemporary welfare/regulatory state assume that socio-economic outcomes are largely exogenous to public policy with patterns of inequality reflecting processes operative in markets and civil society. In highly complex societies, however, where social outcomes are the emergent property of multiple and overlapping discursive and non-discursive practices far from exogenous to state action, many inequalities may be *endogenous* to previous rounds of governmental regulation or expenditure. This means that a large proportion of the inequality that the welfare/regulatory state targets may be an example of *policy as its own cause*.[73] In these circumstances the deployment of pastoral power by states may be as likely to increase the relevant inequalities as to decrease them.

Consider in this context debates about wealth inequality. Public discourse has recently focussed on alleged increases in the share of wealth found in the upper 10% or 1% of the population. The process of wealth concentration has been depicted as a law-like relationship where absent 'corrective' intervention returns to capital will continually outstrip wage growth such that the distribution of economic opportunity will become increasingly class based.[74] Data on wealth inequality that sparked these debates have since been widely questioned.[75] Moreover, the suggestion that returns to capital are quasi-automatic is deeply problematic from a theoretical standpoint. In a world characterised by radical uncertainty, it is unlikely that returns to capital can be guaranteed—with some entrepreneurs achieving returns that far outstrip the average rate while others underperform or make substantial losses. In such a world the idea of a 'representative return to capital' may be little more than a statistical artefact with

[73] I borrow this phrase from Wildvasky, A. (1987) 'Policy as Its Own Cause', reprinted in Wildavsky, A. (1987/2017) *Speaking Truth to Power*, Brunswick, NJ, and London: Routledge.

[74] This debate was partially informed by Piketty, T. (2014) *Capital in the 21st Century*, Cambridge, MA: Belknap Press.

[75] For example, Magness, P. (2019) 'Detecting Historical Inequality Patterns: A Replication of Thomas Piketty's Wealth Concentration Estimates for the United Kingdom', *Social Science Quarterly*, 100 (5): 1566–76; Geloso, V., Magness, P., and Moore, J. (2022) 'How Pronounced Is the U-Curve: Revisiting Income Inequality in the United States, 1917–60', *The Economic Journal*, 132 (647): 2366–91; Auten, G., and Splinter, G. (2024) 'Income Inequality in the United States: Using Tax Data to Measure Long-Term Trends', *Journal of Political Economy*, 132 (7): 2179–530. The latter also shows evidence of substantial income gains right across the distribution during the past forty years in contradiction to the thesis which suggests that gains have been concentrated in the upper quartile.

no real counterpart in the lived experience of actual entrepreneurial actors.[76] Much of the contemporary discussion on economic inequality may thus reflect the discursive dominance of a modernist narrative that constructs economic relationships as mechanical interactions between abstract statistical categories, erasing the divergent interpretations and experiences of the actors making up the relevant aggregates.[77]

What matters for present purposes, however, is that insofar as there have been increases in wealth inequality, these may not arise from quasi-mechanistic forces within market economies but may reflect past and present policy measures that sought to guide markets in a particular direction. The substantial growth in real estate and asset values may, for example, have been one of the most significant contributors to any increase in wealth inequality,[78] but much of this may have been policy induced, notably in countries such as the UK and US by the massive growth in land-use regulation. The mushrooming of land-use controls has significantly reduced the level of new housing over a sustained period, a reduction that may have disproportionately raised the capital returns to incumbent property owners.[79] These measures were initially introduced with the intent of protecting environmental amenities such as open spaces and not of raising property values per se, but over time they have become subject to multiple 'cynicisms of power' with incumbent property owners appropriating discourses of environmental protection and working in 'stakeholder coalitions' with expanding land-use bureaucracies to block new housing supply. These coalitions may also have contributed to significant reductions in competition in the housebuilding sector, an effect that has been particularly pronounced in the UK where the structure of the regulatory regime disproportionately raises costs for smaller scale developers.[80]

Significantly, the resulting unaffordability of housing may also have contributed to a further set of pastoral measures that may have exacerbated wealth inequality. 'Cheap money' policies pursued by central banks for the

[76] Of the ten richest people in the world in 1987 all had seen their fortunes fall relative to the growth rate of the economy by 2014—on this see Rallo, J. 'Where Are the Super Rich of 1987?', in Delsol, J., Lecaussin, N., and Martin, E., eds. (2017) *Anti-Piketty*, Washington, DC: Cato Institute.

[77] McCloskey, D. (2014) 'Measured, Unmeasured, Mismeasured, and Unjustified Pessimism: A Review Essay of Thomas Piketty's *Capital in the 21st Century*', *Erasmus Journal for Philosophy and Economics*, 7 (2): 73–115.

[78] Rognlie, M. (2015) 'Deciphering the Fall and Rise in Net Capital Share: Accumulation or Scarcity?', Brookings Papers on Economic Activity, Spring 2015, Washington, DC: Brookings Institution.

[79] For the US, see Glaeser, E., Gyourko, J., and Saks, R. (2005) 'Why Is Manhattan So Expensive: Regulation and the Rise in Housing Prices', *Journal of Law and Economics*, 48 (2): 331–69; for the UK, see Pennington, M. (2000) *Planning and the Political Market*, London: Athlone/Continuum.

[80] Pennington, *Planning and the Political Market*. See also Ball, M. (2013) 'Spatial Regulation and International Differences in the House Building Industries', *Journal of Property Research*, 30 (3): 189–204.

last quarter century have been driven in part by a concern to improve access to home ownership in the face of spiralling real estate values. In the US these policies were also accompanied by regulatory mandates that lowered the terms of mortgage access for low income and marginalised groups.[81] The combination of these measures alongside other regulatory controls in the banking industry that encouraged firms towards higher risk investment portfolios were arguably a critical factor in the 'perfect storm' of events precipitating the financial crisis of 2008.[82] The subsequent governmental response to the potential collapse of major financial institutions during that crisis may itself have contributed to inequality—in part by protecting many of those who had invested badly from the full scale of capital losses that they might otherwise have incurred, and in part through the continuation of quantitative easing measures that have seen significant injections of money into property and asset markets.[83]

There are multiple other areas where states are similarly entangled with markets in ways that may generate or increase inequalities. One such field is occupational licensure, the scope of which has grown significantly in the United States with around 25% of occupations now requiring a license compared to only 5% in the late 1940s—a trend replicated in many European societies.[84] Regulatory 'dividing practices' of this kind may generate higher incomes for those inside the licensed trades as fewer workers are allowed to enter them—thus raising the gap between the wages of those protected from competition and those not so protected.[85] Correspondingly, the increase in prices for products and services in the protected sectors may redistribute income away from the consumers of those services and towards those who provide them. In the case of childcare, specifically, increasing professionalisation combined with occupational licensure and health and safety regulations may be a factor behind soaring costs—costs which may themselves contribute to inequality by reducing the scope for low-income parents to become dual-earner households relative to parents in higher income groups. Theoretically, occupational licensure is a form of quality control in contexts plagued by information asymmetries which make it difficult for consumers to evaluate the products or personal services they seek to purchase. In practice, however, comparisons of satisfaction between licensed an

[81] See, e.g., Friedman, J., and Krauss, W. (2011) *Engineering the Financial Crisis*, Philadelphia: University of Pennsylvania Press.

[82] Ibid.

[83] See, e.g., Adkins, L., Cooper, M., and Konings, M. (2021) 'Class in the 21st Century: Asset Inflation and the New Logic of Inequality', *Environment and Planning A*, 53 (3): 548–72.

[84] Kleiner, M. (2017) 'The Influence of Occupational Licensing and Regulation', *IZA World of Labour*, 392.

[85] For example, Dodini, S. (2023) 'The Spillover Effects of Labour Market Regulation on the Structure of Earnings and Employment: Evidence from Occupational Licensing', *Journal of Public Economics*, 225: 104947.

unlicensed trades and professions often show little in the way of difference, so at the very least there is uncertainty over the extent to which regulatory restrictions of this kind may be worth their costs.[86]

Even direct efforts to alter the distribution of income and wealth in an egalitarian direction may themselves contribute to changes in behaviour that counteract egalitarian intentions. In the Scandinavian social democracies for example, high levels of taxation, combined with high levels of public sector employment and, in some cases, corporatist bargaining arrangements between labour unions and employers appear to have contributed significantly to reductions in *income* inequality, suppressing the wage gap between lower skilled and higher skilled labour. Thus, Denmark, Norway, and Sweden consistently report some of the lowest levels of income inequality in Europe. The very same policies in this group of countries may, however, also be a contributory factor in their reporting some of the highest levels of *wealth* inequality. In contexts where states assume a significant responsibility for social services and old-age provision, then not only may people be taxed at a level depriving them of the wherewithal to build private savings, but also, even where they do have the capacity to save, when most of the relevant needs are provided by the state, they may be more likely to consume any surplus rather than to invest it. Large numbers of lower and middle-income households in Scandinavia thus have relatively little in the way of private savings such that the accumulation of capital is concentrated in the upper echelons of the wealth distribution.

The Scandinavian countries are a particularly interesting case since they are held by the constituent discourses of the *dispositif* to be exemplars of pastoral state power, successfully combining the dynamic wealth-generating properties of a predominantly market-based political economy with a model where wealth and opportunity are more equally distributed and where mobility between income groups is higher than in societies with less well-developed welfare systems. Yet, notwithstanding the frequency of these claims, there is little in the way of systematic evidence to support this narrative with no clear association between the extent to which societies engage in redistributive measures and indicators of socio-economic mobility.[87] Neither does the historical trajectory of these societies support the social justice narrative. To take one pertinent example, while the Swedish welfare state is seen by many as a role model that has equalised opportunities by suppressing income differentials, recent historical research suggests that while income inequality in Sweden was much higher in the decades *prior* to the creation of its welfare state, those decades also reported *higher levels of social mobility than has prevailed in Sweden since the inception of its welfare*

86 Kleiner, 'The Influence of Occupational Licensing and Regulation'.
87 For example, Gilbert, N. (2017) *Never Enough*, Oxford: Oxford University Press.

state. Social mobility in Sweden appears also to have been higher prior to the creation of its welfare state than it was in neighbouring Norway and in both the US and UK after the creation of their respective welfare regimes.[88]

To make these points is not to suggest that the relevant regulatory/welfare measures can be said definitively to have increased rather than to have decreased inequality. The complex and shifting character of the entanglements among market processes, societal norms, and public policy makes it hard to discern the extent to which any given policy affects the trajectory of resource distribution that would have transpired in its absence. The data in this regard, including that cited here, are often sketchy and open to divergent interpretations. More important, as the post-foundational critique of positivist philosophy of science in chapter 3 suggested, it is precisely the magnitude and complexity of the relevant interaction effects that cast doubt on the value of a predictive 'stimulus-response' or 'scientistic' model of socio-economic causation. Put simply, the causes of any given level of inequality, as with the cultural inequalities discussed earlier, may not be measurable or even knowable, and they may not be readily subject to a form of quasi-scientific 'management'. Rather, the aim here has been to draw attention to alternative narratives that indicate the various ways that public policy might plausibly be considered as an endogenous generator of inequality but which are rarely considered let alone centred by dominant discourses. Within this context, there are three interrelated ways the social justice *dispositif* may conceal its own power effects.

First, wherever it is assumed by dominant discourse coalitions that the role of public policy is to identify and correct imbalances or inequalities in markets and civil society, then the likelihood is that attention will focus on the alleged deficiencies of the civilian sheep who are to be herded and not those of the public shepherds. In a pastoral discursive formation, the response of the networks of actors within the state apparatus and its entanglements with agents in the private sector, charities, and in the media may disproportionately favour an expansion of regulation or expenditure rather than seek potential remedies that involve reductions in regulation and expenditure.

Second, and relatedly, a discursive formation attributing pastoral powers to public authorities may produce a class of bureaucratic actors with an interest in expanding the apparatus of public pastorship. While the latter may not originate through such motivations, once established those deriving power and positionality from exercising such powers may be reluctant to relinquish them or they may come to associate their interests with their continual expansion. They may also use their position as a focal point for public discussion to project the

[88] Berger, T., Engzell, P., Eriksson, B., and Molinder, J. (2023) 'Social Mobility in Sweden Before the Welfare State', *Journal of Economic History*, 83 (2): 431–63.

most readily visible and positive primary effects of regulatory or expenditure decisions on inequality while downplaying or marginalising the less readily visible secondary effects or unintended consequences of these decisions that may increase inequality.

Third and finally, the interventions engaged in by the pastoral apparatuses of the contemporary welfare/regulatory state are of such scale and scope that it may become increasingly difficult for those living under them to conceive of the patterns of resource allocation that might unfold in their absence. The power effects of the welfare-regulatory state may thus mirror those of the macroeconomic *dispositif* examined in chapter 3 where the territorial monopoly of fiscal and monetary activism was argued to limit or block the capacity for subjects to be exposed to counterfactuals. Though this problem may be lessened in more decentralised or polycentric political systems, the prevalence of social justice narratives has gone hand in hand with a tendency towards political centralisation—with decentralisation itself seen as a source of 'unjust' or 'arbitrary' differences in outcome that require 'corrective' pastoral action. As the scale over which policy interventions takes place increases, then so too the scope for these interventions to generate unintended consequences may proliferate. Policy interventions may thus become growth industries as interventions in one sector or another generate demands for intervention in interconnected sectors.[89] Correspondingly, as intervention and regulation swarm out into multiple fields, it may become harder for citizens to discern which of the multiple entanglements is responsible for the effects to which the *dispositif* demands a 'corrective' response.

Status inequality: Pastoral power, and the welfare/regulatory state as its own cause

The preceding analysis focussed on the panoply of regulatory controls and expenditures targeting material differences between groups. A further and overlapping way that class-based inequalities may be produced by public policy relates to questions of social status and positionality.

The constituent discourses of the social justice *dispositif* understand inequalities of outcome as undeserved 'privileges' when these reflect unequal starting points based on income/wealth/family background or inequalities of cultural status that make it harder for some subjects to progress than for others. Central to this narrative is an expansion in the role of the educational sector with

[89] Wildavsky, 'Policy as Its Own Cause'.

access to publicly provided or publicly subsidised education through primary, secondary, and higher levels seen as critical to the equalisation of life chances.

Though it does not necessarily reject a role for public provision or funding to provide a basic level of educational opportunity for all, the Foucauldian or postmodern liberal position is sceptical of the egalitarian claims made on behalf of the educational sector. The first problem here is that while the social justice *dispositif* constructs educational expenditures as central to a programme of increasing social mobility, there is no strong or consistent evidence to support any such connection. In the United States for example, real terms per capita spending on secondary education has tripled since the 1960s,[90] but this has not translated into higher rates of social mobility. In most liberal democracies decades of increased spending on education at all levels has been accompanied by little or no change in rates of social mobility where the latter is taken to reflect changes in the class position or income group of children compared to their parents.[91] One reason for this may be that any reduction of the opportunity gap arising from increases in state financing, absent a proportionate increase in the absolute availability of high-paying or high-status positions, may be counteracted by the actions of higher status/higher income groups who may increase their efforts to provide advantages to their offspring either by spending more on education or by using their socio-cultural resources to access opportunities in their stead. Relatedly, if educational qualifications act as a form of accreditation to employers about the characteristics of potential employees, then as higher shares of the population attain similar levels of qualification, the signalling value of any given level of qualifications may diminish, leading employers to demand additional levels of accreditation. While such processes are not necessary or mechanical effects of increased spending where they operate, they may generate an 'accreditation spiral' with higher levels of qualification needed for subjects to access employments and remunerations than was previously the case.[92]

Combined with these possibilities, a secondary power effect of a discursive focus on education as an engine of mobility is that the channelling of funds towards the educational sector brings more and more people, and for longer periods of their lives, under the disciplinary gaze of approved educational institutions. Foucault's analyses in *The Birth of the Clinic* and the first volume of *The History of Sexuality* emphasise the role of the state in creating the power/

[90] National Center for Educational Statistics, Washington DC, https://nces.ed.gov/programs/digest/d19/tables/dt19_236.55.asp?current = yes

[91] For example, Budoki, E., and Goldthorpe, J. (2018) *Social Mobility and Education in Britain*, Cambridge: Cambridge University Press.

[92] On accreditation spirals see, e.g., Caplan, B. (2018) *The Case Against Education*, Princeton NJ: Princeton University Press.

knowledge complex of the medical establishment and its administrative powers over patients. The emphasis of contemporary social justice narratives on education may have a similar effect by intensifying the disciplinary power of educational institutions in the production of subjects and those who demand their services. The professional educational apparatus deploys disciplinary 'technologies of the self' through which educators may produce a particular species of governed subject that associates its worth and that of others with the passing of formal assessments, certification, and a rationalistic commitment to the power of accredited expertise. To invoke Foucault's words, modern credential-focussed educational processes are ones where

> the superimposition of power relations and knowledge relations assumes in the examination all its visible brilliance.[93]

Public funding may reinforce the power and positionality of this credentialed class and may produce subjects who, if not the 'docile bodies' depicted in *Discipline and Punish*, may be well suited to the increasingly rule-governed procedures characteristic of the modern bureaucratic state and the large corporate actors 'governed at a distance' by that state and its multiple satellites. Incumbent corporations and those who manage them may have little interest in maintaining a competitive, entrepreneurial environment, preferring instead the routinised world of regulated and quasi-cartelistic markets characteristic of 'stakeholder capitalism'.

The implicit alliances and overlapping worldviews of public bureaucrats, corporate managers, and members of the expert/regulatory class may thus work to marginalise entrepreneurial subjectivities that embrace uncertainty and a disruptive, less rule-bound approach. When the state subsidises education and in particular higher education to the point where a large share of the population attends credentialing institutions and where such attendance is described as reflecting the superior merits of those concerned, then lack of attendance at such institutions may be construed as evidence of meritocratic 'failure'. This analysis has distinct echoes of the processes depicted by Schumpeter with the creative destruction of capitalism progressively undermined by its sustenance of a managerialist or technocratic class that sees its interests if not in socialism, then in a highly regulated or cartelistic society that produces subjects disciplined into a credentialled notion of socioeconomic 'worth'.[94]

93 MF (1977) *Discipline and Punish*, London: Allen Lane, 185.
94 Schumpeter, J. (1942) *Capitalism, Socialism and Democracy*, New York: Harper.

Resisting the social justice *dispositif*

Whether its gaze focuses on markers of positionality such as race, gender and sexuality, or income, wealth, and social class, the social justice *dispositif* assumes that a state-supervised bio-power can reduce various inequalities and deliver greater levels of freedom and justice. The analysis put forward in this chapter has questioned the assumptions underlying this interpretive grid. It has argued that social outcomes in complex and entangled political economies may fall largely outside the scope of a directional intelligence. Nevertheless, attempts to exert such pastoral control may encase subjects in an expanding web of micro-regulations that limit their freedom to speak, to act, and to engage in processes of self-constitution. To the extent this is an accurate portrayal of processes operative in contemporary liberal societies, then the preservation of spaces where people may constitute themselves as self-governing agents may require resistance to the underlying assumptions of this governing order.

One element of this resistance might focus on the dominance of a desert-based or meritocratic understanding of inequality. Though differing in how to 'correct' what they see as 'unearned privileges' of wealth or cultural status, dominant discourses are united in a 'compensatory ethic' that seeks to 'level' positions so that whatever differences remain between individuals and groups are considered as 'deserved' or 'fair'. Increasing the scope for subjects to constitute themselves as self-governing agents may, however, require the refusal of *any* approach that seeks to 'equalise people' at a 'starting line' from which their share of wealth or cultural status can be judged as being more, or less, meritorious. To presume that merit should be used to evaluate the positions subjects find themselves in is to presume that they are 'knowable' entities. Yet, when people are situated in very different histories, traditions, and value orientations; and where they may choose between different investments, career paths, and rates of remuneration; neither the categoriser nor the categorised may know what is attributable to the subject's efforts and choices, the history of their family and community, their genetics, or to other forms of caprice. The attempt to 'equalise people' against a 'starting line' may thus secure neither equality nor liberty because it requires that those who are to be equalised are first categorised and subjected to the power of those who do the relevant categorising.

Refusing this compensatory ethics would not abandon all evaluative judgements but would view interactions through a lens that sees people according to their potential to bring positive value to one's life or that of others. Such a stance hardly removes the need for judgement, but it would not be a judgement that relentlessly classifies people according to how 'deserving' or 'undeserving' they are of whatever attributes or qualities they bring to the table. In such a model subjects would also recognise that risk and misfortune cannot be avoided or compensated. Though not necessarily incompatible with a role for public insurance against catastrophic risk, self-government may require people to take responsibility for coping with uncertainty through the rules and disciplines they *give themselves* and the relationships they choose to form with others in families, clubs, mutual aid associations, and religious organisations. The free and self-constituting subject does not inhabit a world without economic and cultural constraint but has sufficient room to *choose* at least some of the constraints and disciplines under which they live. It is this breathing space that may be threatened by the penetration of the social justice *dispositif* into multiple public and private agencies, charities, schools, universities, and even into private homes as it seeks to achieve its pastoral goals by aligning state power with the more decentred powers dispersed elsewhere in society. These alignments may need to be resisted and perhaps even shattered if the scope for subjects to exercise their creative agency is to expand.

Second, and relatedly, resistance may entail refusing zero-sum understandings of social interaction that interpret differences in outcomes across identities as necessarily reflective of oppression. This resistance would not deny the historical reality of racism, sexism, and homophobia as oppressive systems. It would, however, refuse to see all interaction through a lens of 'cultural warfare' and a negative *ressentiment* that encourages the disadvantaged to better their position by tearing down the more advantaged—a process that may condemn all to a life of misery and frustration. Rather, it may embrace or celebrate a pragmatist and transactional approach to intersectionality which, instead of seeking to seize power from those more advantaged, would adopt strategies that illustrate the mutual gains from recognising the scope for cooperation. It would champion cultural exchange not merely in terms of the gains to be had for existing cultural identities but highlight the possibilities for new and unanticipated identities to be formed in the process. Refusing cultural warfare, it would adopt a more playful discursive stance, breaking from safetyism to champion freedom of expression and embracing a cultural voyage of exploration into the unknown.

This resistant discourse might also challenge a model that institutionalises a 'permission-oriented' society where subjects cannot do things with their property, their bodies, or their thoughts without receiving the consent of those deemed to be sufficiently 'expert' to judge the 'social consequences'. While it would not reject the notion of expertise per se, it would cultivate a radical scepticism of institutions that seek to enforce a monopoly of expertise and where a subject's position is determined by those who issue licenses to others, whether to build houses, to negotiate terms of employment, or to express their opinions.

If the social justice *dispositif* works through a relentless drive to label and to classify subjects, then an important element of any resistance to this pastoral apparatus may entail refusals to be identified with the categories it propagates and reproduces. A 'difference blind' or 'identity free' approach to social interaction is chimerical, but it does not follow that the differences in question need be rigidified in bureaucratic classifications in order that they might be subject to managerial control. A resistant ethos would thus seek to protect the spaces within which subjects define their own identities and negotiate for themselves across difference without supervision from the state or its pastoral subsidiaries. Though it would not prevent people from identifying in any way they choose, it may involve multiple refusals or acts of disobedience by people in educational settings, in the workplace, and in their engagement with public authorities by refusing to cooperate with bureaucratic and statistical categories that impose an externally scripted identity on them. Inspiration might be drawn here from a somewhat unlikely source. The former financial secretary of Hong Kong John Cowperthwaite famously abolished the collection of most economic statistics on the grounds that they obscured the entrepreneurial processes that generate wealth and worked as a pretext to justify bureaucratic regulation and control. A similar attitude might be mobilised today against the compilation of statistical identity categories by public and private agencies. Hong Kong was transformed from an economic backwater to a prosperity surpassing that of its colonial master by multiple small entrepreneurs and without extensive state control.[95] Resistance to the social justice *dispositif* might similarly be built on a playful refusal to cooperate with 'data gatherers' and a vision of cultural entrepreneurship that allows people to forge cooperation across differences in the absence of pastoral oversight. As Foucault once put it:

> Do not ask me who I am and do not ask me to remain the same: leave it to our bureaucrats and our police to see that our papers are in order.[96]

If an embrace of entrepreneurship is central to such a counter discourse, then a model of entrepreneurship may also be required to build new social movements to disrupt the categorisations propagated by the *dispositif*. Inspiration and imagery might be sought here from immigrant entrepreneurs, LGBT entrepreneurs, and increasingly religious conservative entrepreneurs who, in their different ways and contexts, though challenging dominant social norms also cooperate pragmatically with prevailing norms and take risks in situations by dealing with others with whom they feel uncomfortable to secure the chance of a better life. Though they face challenges and inequalities these entrepreneurs do not ask to be 'equalised' at some hypothetical starting line and do not see themselves as the

[95] See, e.g., Cheang, B. (2022) *Economic Liberalism and the Developmental State: Hong Kong and Singapore's Postwar Development*, London: Palgrave.
[96] MF (1972) Introduction, *The Archaeology of Knowledge*, New York: Harper and Row.

victims of oppression. They might thus be well placed to forge a more positive-sum and transactional intersectionality across many individuals and groups who refuse a model that promises freedom by protecting them from all possible forms of disadvantage, risk, or discomfort only to enforce a net of discursive and regulatory control.

Similar discourse coalitions might be forged by subjects keen to challenge other elements of the *dispositif*. In the wake of the mass school closures precipitated by the COVID-19 pandemic, parents who out of necessity had to homeschool their children may now be questioning whether taxpayer-funded state schools offer value for money and whether they reflect their values or those of a philosophically homogenous educational class. What has often been depicted as a fringe ideological movement is now mushrooming across a spectrum of identity groupings. In the United States, for example, increasing numbers of African American parents have joined the homeschool movement in opposition to what they perceive as a system that fails to place sufficient emphasis on black history while simultaneously projecting onto black students a narrative of low expectations which portrays them as permanent victims of white society.[97] Many such parents have a strong religious ethos and could build bridges with working-class white people and social conservatives who are sceptical of the cultural values of what many see as a progressive educational elite. A still more transgressive alliance would also include LGBT parents who for different reasons are dissatisfied with what they perceive as the unduly restrictive curriculum offered by most public schools. Inspiration might be drawn here from LGBT entrepreneurs elsewhere who have sought to diffuse tensions in cultural and artistic contexts, refusing public funding that may raise the ire of religious groupings and seeking voluntary contributions through methods such as crowdfunding.[98] Though they may be in tension with one another, what might unite these groupings is resistance to a model that privileges educational experts at the expense of parents and support for different models that allow parents greater freedom of action over the education of their children, breaking down disciplinary conceptions of who educates, what education should consist of, and where it takes place.

Elsewhere, cross-cultural and cross-class coalitions might be formed to resist the march of credentialism and the permission society. Though they would not

[97] Rascoe, A. Why more Black families are opting to home school their children, National Public Radio, 2 October 2022, https://www.npr.org/2022/10/02/1126453605/why-more-black-families-are-opting-to-homeschool-their-children; Parks, C. The Rise of Black Homeschooling, *The NewYorker*, 14 June 2021, https://www.newyorker.com/magazine/2021/06/21/the-rise-of-black-homeschooling#:~:text=For%20Black%20families%2C%20the%20growth,risen%20to%20sixteen%20per%20cent.

[98] Dalla Chiesa, C. 'Crowdfunding the Queer Museum: A Polycentric Identity Quarrel', in Dekker, E., and Kuchar, P., eds. (2022) *Governing Markets as Knowledge Commons*, Cambridge: Cambridge University Press.

challenge the value of higher education per se, such coalitions might question the egalitarian status of a model that produces subjects geared towards the credentialed environments of public sector organisations, the legal profession, large corporations, and the regulatory nexus between them. A counter-coalition of start-up entrepreneurs, tradespeople, small- and medium-size business owners, all of whom depend for their living on their responsiveness to changing market conditions, might question why the welfare state subsidises people to attend universities but does not countenance redirecting those subsidies towards young people to start them off as independent entrepreneurs or simply to spend as they choose.

In the wider economic sphere resistance might also be found in the actions of 'evasive entrepreneurs'[99] who use new technologies to challenge social and legal rules and who create new products and services outside the reach of regulatory authorities. What have been described by some as 'technologies of resistance' or 'technological civil disobedience', including smart phone apps, new social media platforms, alternative news, and education platforms, as well as cryptocurrencies and blockchain-supported services, are all forms of 'permissionless innovation' that provide spaces where subjects can engage in acts from financial transactions to learning about sex and sexuality, away from a regulatory gaze. Many of these ventures take place at the margins of the law, providing alternative governance structures that may have the effect of either delegitimising or making redundant existing legal and regulatory structures.

The purpose of such challenges might not be to 'overthrow' the ruling apparatus—when many subjectivities have been formed by and within pastoral structures such an approach would amount to a form of constructivist rationalism that may itself threaten freedom. Rather, what is envisaged here is a process where continuous entrepreneurial micro-revolutions or insurrections take place in multiple dispersed sites, offering the glimmer of an alternative where subjects can negotiate their cultural and economic interactions without pastoral control or at the very least where they have greater scope to choose their own pastor. Many such ventures will fail—and some may come with risks of their own—but the importance of taking risks to establish these heterotopias is profound. As the remaining chapters of this book will show, the discursive and non-discursive practices that narrow the scope for human agency in the name of social justice are but one manifestation of potentially totalising pastoral powers pregnant with threats to freedom.

[99] On this see Thierer, A. (2020) *Evasive Entrepreneurship and the Future of Governance*, Washington, DC: Cato Institute.

6
Bio-Power and the Political Economy of Life and Death
The Public Health *Dispositif*

Introduction

The discourses of social justice considered in the previous chapter represent one of the most significant sources of 'correctional' or 'pastoral' governance in contemporary liberal political economies. The practices of governance they have engendered, however, increasingly overlap with an array of public, private, and civil agencies sustaining discursive coalitions pursuant of still further forms of bio-political or pastoral control. One such coalition is organised around what will be referred to in this chapter as the 'public health *dispositif*. The coronavirus pandemic of 2020–2022 led many countries across the world to introduce unprecedented restrictions on personal liberty. Whether those restrictions were appropriate to the threat to life and health posed by the pandemic remains unclear. It will be the contention in what follows, however, that the approach adopted in many liberal political economies towards COVID-19 may have been symptomatic of a wider set of discursive and non-discursive practices that have the potential to undermine a liberal social order.

Though it does not reject a role for the state in public heath governance, the chapter argues that the social constructions engendered by overlapping forms of scientific rationalism and positive rights discourse empower certain actors to 'police the truth' in ways that are enmeshing increasingly large swathes of the population in a network of micro-regulatory controls, narrowing the scope for subjects to constitute themselves as self-governing agents. The focus will be on epidemiological and socio-economic discourses related to the governance of health and lifestyle including diet, smoking, and alcohol consumption and the similarities between the technologies of government deployed to manage these behaviours and those evident in the response to the COVID-19 pandemic. The critical political economy developed here suggests that the discursive and non-discursive practices constituting this *dispositif* work with an excessively scientistic and normalising approach which assumes the validity of a positivist, stimulus-response model

Foucault and Liberal Political Economy. Mark Pennington, Oxford University Press. © Mark Pennington 2025.
DOI: 10.1093/9780197690550.003.0006

that can engineer changes either in the social environment or in individual psychology/rationality to produce 'better' health outcomes. The discussion concludes with some suggestions about the possible strategies of resistance that may help to destabilise this *dispositif* and the threats to freedom and pluralism it represents.

Discourses of public health governance

Though it cannot be entirely disentangled from debates about the organisation of health services such as the mix between private and public forms of finance and supply, public health as understood here is concerned with the determinants of health, the anticipation of longer-term health risks, and is focussed on the prevention of ill health rather than on the provision of treatment and care.

A widely and long-established definition is as follows:

> Public health is the science and art of preventing disease, prolonging life and promoting physical health and efficiency through organised community efforts for the sanitation of the environment, the control of community infections, the education of the individual in principles of personal hygiene, the organisation of medical and nursing services for the early diagnosis and preventive treatment of disease and the development of social machinery which will ensure to every individual in the community a standard of living adequate for the maintenance of health.[1]

In Foucauldian terms this 'science and art of preventing disease, prolonging life, and promoting physical health' is a form of governmentality with disciplinary and bio-political elements. Several discourses that combine medical, social scientific, and philosophical reasoning have underpinned the emergence of this governmentality; and the intersection between these discourses and the actors who propagate them constitutes the public health *dispositif*. The disciplinary component of these modes of governance targets individuals, managing the behaviour of bodies in ways thought to improve their health on some dimension. A medical doctor may, for example, prescribe changes in diet to a patient to limit the risk of heart disease or stroke. Though this power works by trying to bring individual behaviour into line with a norm by regulating eating habits, it need not be justified in terms of wider population effects. Bio-power, on the other hand, is focussed explicitly on the population as a whole and is formulated and justified in terms of aggregate level rather than individual results. This form of governance may deploy disciplinary or normalising techniques to achieve aggregate

[1] Winslow, C. (1920) 'The Untilled Fields of Public Health', *Science*, 51: 23.

objectives, but it may also work by trying to alter the background conditions within which large numbers of people act in ways that do not focus directly on seeking to reform or to treat anomalous individuals.

Epidemiological discourse and public health governance

The first discourse to have played a significant role in the emergence of the public health *dispositif* originates in epidemiology where the human body is understood as a vector for contagion. Early variants were evident in eighteenth-century German states which supported a form of public health governance known as 'medical police'. This approach emerged from a confluence of theories that equated the power of the state with a large and healthy population and with efforts to develop better knowledge of populations through the collection and use of statistics.[2] In nineteenth-century Britain, meanwhile, the public health movement was heavily influenced by utilitarian political philosophy and its concerns with the improvement of public welfare.[3] The favoured solution to the incidence of disease was underground drainage to reduce the prevalence of 'bad air' or miasmas and to keep infectious particles away from human populations. In the latter half of the nineteenth century these theories were gradually superceded by the new science of bacteriology.[4] While this approach continued to emphasise public sanitation and clean water and the importance of investments in public sewerage systems, it also led to an appreciation of personal hygiene in limiting the spread of infection.[5] This was reflected in the growth of public education campaigns focused on the regulation of conduct in or around the home—including appropriate cooking methods, cleaning methods, and increasing concerns with sexual practices and morality. The emphasis on sanitation and personal hygiene also coincided with developments in the theory and practice of vaccination, with a series of legislative acts focussed on extending compulsory vaccination requirements, especially for children.[6]

The combination of improved understanding of disease transmission and investments in public sanitation, vaccination, and basic health education played

[2] Epitomised in the writings of Johann Peter Franck—see Franck, J. P. (1784) *System der vollstandigen medicinischen polizey*, Mannheim: C F Schwan.

[3] Notably Edwin Chadwick and his followers. See Chadwick, E. (1842) *Report on the Sanitary Condition of the Labouring Population of Great Britain*, House of Commons Sessional Paper, London: HOC.

[4] Associated primarily with Robert Koch and Louis Pasteur.

[5] For a discussion, Worboys, M. (2000) *Spreading Germs: Disease Theories and Medical Practice in Britain, 1865–1900*, Cambridge: Cambridge University Press. See also Duffy, J. (1990) *The Sanitarians: A History of American Public Health*, Urbana: University of Illinois Press.

[6] Berridge, V. (2016) *Public Health: A Very Short Introduction*, Oxford: Oxford University Press, 50–1.

a critical role in reducing the frequency and severity of infectious diseases such as cholera and typhus from the end of the nineteenth century to beyond the Second World War, a period that witnessed significant improvements in life expectancy across the industrialised world. The basic public health tools honed during this period and the discursive frames around them have remained ever since, though they have receded into the background owing to the declining frequency of the risks they addressed. What has changed in subsequent years has been the attempt to scientifically analyse the evolution of disease outbreaks with mathematical models and simulation techniques that are increasingly used to predict the longevity of outbreaks and the likely number of fatalities.[7] These statistical techniques were significant in driving policy response to the HIV/AIDS epidemic of the 1980s and 1990s and the 2003 SARS outbreak in East Asia. It was, however, in the response to the COVID-19 pandemic of 2020–2022 that epidemiological models assumed centre stage with predictions of mass fatalities and the possibility of health systems overwhelmed with patients suffering severe breathing difficulties, which influenced the adoption of 'lockdown' policies in many countries.

Aside from simulation modelling the major evolution in this discourse has been the transfer of epidemiological metaphors and models to the analysis of diseases associated with lifestyle and consumption—notably various cancers, conditions such as coronary heart disease, and the prevalence of bodily states such as obesity.[8] Metaphorically, the phenomena of people smoking, being above a certain weight, or consuming alcohol are now routinely described as 'epidemics' and/or contagions with the relevant bodies seen as vectors for 'harmful' behavioural practices and the potential for crisis or health emergencies arising from them.[9] Though in principle public health advice could be focussed on 'at-risk' individuals—for example, those who smoke forty cigarettes per day as opposed to those who smoke only four—lifestyle epidemiology favours instead a 'whole population' approach where policies are directed at reducing consumption practices at the societal level.[10]

Replacing the focus on the direct cause of infectious disease has been an emphasis on modelling multiple 'risk factors' linked to non-communicable diseases.[11] The discovery of a connection between smoking and lung

[7] Many of these models were first developed in the 1920s by Kermack and McKendrick—see, e.g., Kermack, W., and McKendrick, A. (1927) 'A Contribution to the Mathematical Theory of Epidemics', *Proceedings of the Royal Society*, A 115 (772): 700–21.

[8] Wain, H. (1970) *A History of Preventive Medicine*, Springfield, IL: Charles C Thomas.

[9] See, e.g., Cotter, C., Samos, D., and Swinglehurst, D. (2021) 'Framing Obesity in Public Discourse', *Journal of Pragmatics*, 174: 14–27; Mitchell, G., and McTigue, K. (2007) 'The US Obesity "Epidemic": Metaphor, Method, or Madness', *Social Epistemology*, 21 (4): 391–423.

[10] Rose, G. (1981) 'Strategy of Prevention: Lessons from Cardiovascular Disease', *British Medical Journal*, 282: 1847–51.

[11] Terris, M. (1992) 'Healthy Lifestyles: The Perspective of Epidemiology', *Journal of Public Health Policy*, 13 (2): 186–94.

cancer[12] was a critical juncture in this lifestyle epidemiology, with the older public health technique of campaigns around personal hygiene repurposed towards population-level reductions in smoking, alcohol consumption, and changes to diet. These newer epidemiological discourses have also linked ill health to characteristics of the socio-economic environment with the incidence of smoking, alcoholism, or obesity modelled in relation to other 'risk factors' such as poverty and income inequality. In the context of obesity, for example, the term 'obesenogenic environment' is now used to invoke the multiple factors held to increase the likelihood of obesity and the medical conditions associated with it—including income profile and socio-economic status, prevalence of sugary drinks and saturated facts in diets, the range and price offerings in supermarkets, the incidence of sedentary activities such as television watching and use of digital technologies, rates of walking, and use of private cars.[13] Attempts to quantify these risk factors and to predict future levels of obesity, alcohol dependence, and related health problems have corresponded with campaigns by public health professionals for the taxation of tobacco products, alcohol, and various foodstuffs; limits on advertising; and in some cases calls for outright bans on behaviours such as smoking.[14]

Discourses of social medicine and public health governance

With its focus on background environmental risks, the recent evolution of lifestyle epidemiology has significant overlaps with the longer established public health discourse of 'social medicine'. Philosophically, this discourse arose out of early twentieth-century socialist movements that questioned the value of educational campaigns focussed on personal behaviours and individual responsibility. Post-revolutionary Soviet public health doctrine saw socio-economic inequalities as the primary determinants of disease, and in the context of Cold War conflict, it challenged liberal conceptions of personal responsibility for health in a way that exercised considerable influence outside the Soviet bloc itself. In the United Kingdom, for example, the work of Titmuss and his colleagues drew connections between socio-economic conditions and health outcomes,

[12] Royal College of Physicians (1962) *Smoking and Health*, London: RCP; Royal College of Physicians (1971) *Smoking and Health Now*, London: RCP; US Surgeon General (1964) *Smoking and Health*, Washington, DC: US Department of Health, Education, and Welfare.

[13] Swinburn, B., Egger, G., and Raza, F. (1999) 'Dissecting Obesenogenic Environments: The Development and Application of a Framework for Identifying and Prioritizing Environmental Interventions for Obesity', *Preventive Medicine* 29 (6): 563–70; Nestle, M., and Jacobsen, M. (2001) 'Halting the Obesity Epidemic: A Public Health Policy Approach', *Public Health Reports*, 115: 12–25; Young, I., and Nestle, M. (2002) 'The Contribution of Expanding Portion Sizes to the US Obesity Epidemic', *American Journal of Public Health*, 92: 246–9.

[14] Hansen, E., and Easthope, G. (2007) *Lifestyle in Medicine*, New York: Routledge.

highlighting social class as one of the primary determinants of ill health.[15] Though not rejecting health education per se, social medicine maintains that an excessive focus on personal responsibility risks 'blaming the individual' and ignoring the socio-economic conditions that are the 'root causes' of behaviours that increase health risks. Where publicly organised collective action, such as provision of sewerage systems and compulsory vaccination, generated improvements in health that could not have been delivered by individual action alone, so further health improvements require large-scale income redistribution and structural reforms to capitalism to deliver greater equality—and better health.[16] As such, this discourse has many affinities with the philosophies of welfare state or egalitarian liberalism and related notions of positive rights. The Rawlsian concept of the 'basic structure' is, for example, highly amenable to a model where health outcomes and especially those of the least advantaged are not the direct responsibility of the members of that class but of the policy experts responsible for creating the background 'structural conditions' within which they develop their capacities.

The social medicine perspective remained a significant if minority discourse in liberal political economies throughout the postwar period, and the tradition of using statistical analysis to draw connections between inequalities and ill health continues to attract influential adherents.[17] Nonetheless, in a context where the relatively poor economic performance of 'planned economies' was laid bare, recent years have seen the practitioners of social medicine redeploy this discourse in more sector-specific health environments rather than critique 'capitalism' per se. Following the establishment of a clear link between smoking and lung cancer, for example, discourses of the 'new public health' emphasised the role of corporate businesses in generating unhealthy environments through their production and marketing decisions—and in their lobbying efforts to conceal or to deny their health consequences. On this framing, the key to improved health is structural reform of unhealthy consumption environments through more extensive government regulation of specific markets. In the case

[15] Titmuss, R. (1943) *Birth, Poverty and Wealth: A Study of Infant Mortality*, London: Hamish Hamilton.

[16] For example, Baum, F. (2003) *The New Public Health*, Singapore: Oxford University Press; Baum, F. Sanders, D. (2011) 'Ottawa 25 Years On: A More Radical Agenda for Health Equity Is Still Required', *Health Promotion International*, 26 (suppl. 2): ii253–7; Krieger, N. (2011) *Epidemiology and People's Health: Theory and Context*, New York: Oxford University Press; Marmot, M. (2010) *Fair Society, Healthy Lives*, London: Institute for Health Equity; Marmot, M. (1981) 'Social Class and Coronary Heart Disease', *British Medical Journal*, 45: 13–19; Rose, G. (2001) 'Reiteration: Sick Individuals and Sick Populations', *International Journal of Epidemiology*, 30: 427–32; Black, D. (1982) *The Black Report* London: Pelican; World Health Organisation (2008) *Commission on the Social Determinants of Health: A Report*, Geneva: WHO; World Health Organisation (1986) *Ottawa Charter for Health Promotion Social Determinants of Health*, Geneva: WHO.

[17] Wilkinson, R., and Pickett, K. (2010) *The Spirit Level: Why Equality Is Better for Everyone*, Harmondsworth: Penguin.

of 'obesenogenic environments', for example, this includes regulation of the fat and sugar content of marketed foods as well as controls on their advertising. On the demand side it involves a combination of better health education on diet and exercise—especially for those in low-income or socially disadvantaged groups—alongside the taxation of 'unhealthy' products. The latter is justified both as a revenue-raising device for funds that can be ploughed back into public health research and as a financial inducement to behavioural change for those who fail to be reached by educational campaigns.

Economic discourse and public health governance

The third set of discourses influential in the development of public health governance are associated with an economic approach rooted in modern neo-classical theory. With their focus on externalities and collective action problems, the welfare economic theories developed before and after World War II have a close affinity with epidemiological narratives. In the context of infectious diseases for example, individuals taking risks with their own health are understood to 'impose costs' analogous to a form of 'pollution' on innocent parties. While these costs might be internalised through private bargaining if rights to pollute or to be pollution free are assigned to an affected party, or by taxing the activities in question, the high transactions costs of such methods during a contagious disease outbreak may justify emergency 'command and control' methods such as quarantines. Relatedly, the notion that certain goods might be 'undersupplied' owing to problems of 'non-excludability' and 'free-riding' is evident in arguments for compulsory vaccination. When any single individual's contribution to slowing the spread of a contagion may be vanishingly small and where those at low risk may not sufficiently consider the costs of their failure to be vaccinated on those at greater risk an 'undersupply' of vaccination is likely. This framing is also apparent in rationales for the public supply and/or financing of sanitary infrastructures such as drainage and sewerage systems in contexts where private suppliers might be unable to organise or to recoup the costs of large-scale infrastructural investments.[18]

Though neo-classical theory was initially applied to these traditional public health concerns, as with the epidemiological and social medicine discourses, it has now been 'repurposed' and 'redeployed' in the context of 'lifestyle governance'. This conceptual mobility was given initial impetus in debates surrounding 'passive smoking', which suggested that as well as risking their own health

[18] A classic statement of welfare economics with applications to public health measures such as sanitation remains Pigou, A. (1920) *The Economics of Welfare*, London: Macmillan.

smokers were also subjecting those in their immediate environment to increased cancer risk. Smoking was thus reconceptualised as an 'externality generating' behaviour, and arguments were made for its regulation on standard welfare economic lines. More recently, the analysis of externality and collective action problems has been applied to socio-cultural norms where these are thought to 'lock in' unhealthy behaviours.[19] If challenging a social norm such as smoking in public is costly to those conducting the relevant challenges—for example in terms of losing friendships with those who smoke—then a case can be made for the state to restructure the social environment via regulatory mandates that limit smoking in public spaces.

Though neo-classical welfare concepts have played a significant role in public health discourse, the most significant application of economic reasoning to lifestyle has, however, emerged from a tradition that appears to question some of the core tenets of neo-classical analysis. Where welfare economics focuses on 'suboptimal' outcomes arising from individually rational decisions in settings where the 'private costs' of decisions are misaligned with their 'social costs', the discourse of behavioural economics emphasises failures of rationality at the individual level that produce suboptimal outcomes *for the individual*.[20] In neo-classical theory subjects are considered to act rationally when they have a clear and consistent set of preferences that they rank transitively; the choices they make reflect the true costs and benefits of the available options; and where in situations of imperfect information or uncertainty about costs and benefits, they update their beliefs on outcome probabilities in accordance with Bayesian reasoning as new information transpires.

In practice individuals are frequently thought to diverge from this model in multiple ways owing to what are referred to as cognitive biases or motivational failures. People regularly exhibit inconsistency of preferences, where their favoured choice is sensitive to framing effects; they exhibit time inconsistency, placing excessive weight on the present rather than on the future simply because it is the present—the latter reflecting 'status quo bias' and/or 'endowment effects' where agents demand higher payments for giving something up than they would to acquire the good in the first place; individuals are also unable to take decisions

[19] Anomaly, J. (2012) 'Is Obesity a Public Health Problem', *Public Health Ethics*, 5(3): 216–21.

[20] Representative works in this tradition include Camerer, C., Issacharoff, S., Loewenstein, G., and Donoghue, O. (2003) 'Regulation for Conservatives: Behavioural Economics and the Case for "Asymmetric Paternalism"', *University of Pennsylvania Law Review*, 151: 1211–54; Jolls, C., and Sunstein, C. (2006) 'De-Biasing Through Law,' *Journal of Legal Studies*, 35: 199–241; Le Grand, J., and New, B. (2015) *Government Paternalism, Nanny State or Helpful Friend?*, Princeton, NJ: Princeton University Press; Sunstein, C. (2016) *The Ethics of Influence*, Cambridge: Cambridge University Press; Sunstein, C., and Thaler, R. (2003) 'Libertarian Paternalism', *American Economic Review*, 93: 175–9; Sunstein, C., and Thaler, R. (2003) 'Libertarian Paternalism Is Not an Oxymoron', *University of Chicago Law Review*, 70 (4): 1159–1202; Sunstein, T., and Thaler, R. (2009) *Nudge: Improving Decisions About Health, Wealth and Happiness*, New York: Penguin Books.

in the present that they know will benefit them in the future owing to weakness of will; and finally, people often lack the skills to assess event probabilities being unduly influenced by how easily the memory of an event may be brought to mind. This may, for example, lead them to overestimate the likelihood of dying from cancer when they have recent experience of someone suffering from the disease while underestimating the risk when they have no such experience.

What matters is that these biases and failures prevent individuals from achieving their subjectively defined goals, and this opens a space for external intervention to improve individual welfare. Where paternalist arguments suggest that individuals have the 'wrong preferences', behavioural economics argues for interventions in 'choice architecture' so that people might be better placed to fulfil *their own true preferences and values*. Those who want to stop smoking, reduce alcohol consumption, or shift to a healthier diet are prevented from doing so by failures of reasoning or motivation and by actors in their environment such as profit-seeking businesses who take advantage of these failures through their advertising and marketing practices. The favoured changes to choice architecture thus include 'sin taxes' on alcohol, tobacco, and fatty foods to address problems of present bias and weakness of will; labelling requirements on products that provide written warnings to consumers so they might be better acquainted with the risks involved; use of graphic imagery such as images of organs affected by smoking or excess alcohol consumption; requirements for supermarkets to relocate 'tempting' foods with high fat or sugar content to less accessible or less visible parts of stores; and in extreme cases outright bans on products considered especially dangerous and/or prone to generate addictive behaviours.

Philosophically, behavioural economics draws support from liberal positive rights perspectives that value personal autonomy not by seeking to eliminate choice but by 'nudging' people in ways making it 'easier' for them to act in accordance with their own underlying values. It is also compatible with the traditional utilitarianism of economic theory with nudging justified as a route to promoting social as well as individual welfare. By rejecting approaches that 'blame the individual', focussing instead on biases or motivational failures exacerbated by 'choice architecture', behavioural economics also overlaps with social medicine and 'new public health' perspectives. It questions the classical liberal emphasis on negative rights and freedom as 'non-interference', suggesting that a refusal to interfere ignores how 'choice architecture' already 'interferes' with freedom by preventing individuals from achieving their capacities for autonomous action. As such, this discourse is also closely aligned with welfare liberal and capabilities discourses. It is 'libertarian' in the sense that it values autonomy and individual freedom while also being 'paternalistic' in suggesting that this freedom can be expanded via judicious public policy.

The public health *dispositif*

What is referred to here as the 'public health *dispositif*' is a decentred network connecting multiple agencies in the public and private sectors, academia, international organisations, civil society, and the media, all of whom deploy elements of the discourses sketched above to understand and to construct the notion of public health and to pursue individual and collective interests in a discursive-institutional context not of their own making. Though the multiple interests within this network sometimes conflict, the cumulative effect of discursive entrepreneurship by public health professionals and academics, activist groups, and media organisations pursuing localised goals within their own discursive frame and borrowing concepts from overlapping discourses to create alliances or coalitions with other actors appears to have led to the emergence of a discursive formation with several shared elements.

The first is a positivist focus on expert-led guidance where those with access to the appropriate models and statistical techniques identify causal connections between variables and design policy responses to achieve desired health outcomes. Second is an emphasis on collective action that invokes the power of public authority to achieve those outcomes or to do so by 'governing at a distance'—influencing or guiding private and civil actors. While individuals are assumed to have some capacity to exercise 'responsible choices', these choices must be shepherded by experts who manipulate choice architecture. Within this context, the 'social' component to health, whether understood in terms of contagion effects or externalities, leads to a rejection of approaches that grant 'too much' responsibility to individuals in managing the conditions of their health. Third, the focus on publicly organised collective action is justified in terms of securing desirable outcomes at both the individual and population levels. On this understanding, the autonomy of the individual and the general welfare can both be expanded in a context where public health experts are empowered to restructure aspects of the environment within which people make their decisions.

The specific constellation of discourses constituting the *dispositif* varies from country to country, but there has been a discernible trend across Western liberal democracies for governments to move well beyond the traditional concerns of public health, such as control of infectious diseases, to become progressively more concerned with 'correcting' the consumption practices of their citizens in the name of improving health and well-being. These 'pastoral' activities include direct government action or regulation such as restrictions on tobacco advertising and smoking in public spaces, minimum-unit alcohol pricing, and the introduction of 'sin taxes' on fatty or sugary foods. They also include various measures that 'govern at a distance' with a proliferation of officially approved guidance such as 'traffic light' warnings on foods or other products, designed to mould or to steer the production and marketing decisions of private companies and the purchasing decisions of consumers.

Problematising the public health *dispositif* I: Lifestyle epidemiology

In seeking to analyse and critique the impact of these discursive coalitions and their favoured modes of governance, it is important to note that the Foucauldian or postmodern liberal perspective does not deny a role for medical science in contributing to improvements in health and longevity. Epidemiological understandings of how infections spread and the development of vaccines have clearly played a significant role in this regard. It is also evident that behaviours such as smoking tobacco and extreme alcohol consumption or eating behaviours can have severe health consequences. The critical political economy offered here does not question this. Rather, it seeks to problematise applications of natural scientific and positivist reasoning in contexts that may not be amenable to a predict and control model and/or where the use of scientific knowledge to govern human health may come *at the expense of other values.* What Foucault refers to as the 'power over life and death' may be understood as a form of scientistic overreach that threatens freedom and pluralism by speaking 'over and above' subjects and limiting their capacity to develop themselves as self-constituting and self-governing agents. This section explores the character of these threats in the context of the new 'lifestyle epidemiology', while the subsequent section turns to the more traditional concerns of public health governance.

Erasing the complexity of health

The first set of threats to freedom and pluralism to be considered here follow from the discursive dominance of a positivistic, natural science model that identifies relationships between population-level outcomes and the presence of certain consumption practices, behaviours, or environmental conditions. Where 'germ theories' of communicable disease specify infection as the causal factor in ill health, discourses of 'lifestyle epidemiology' attribute predictive and explanatory power either to specific behaviours or to background socio-economic variables captured by statistical classifications. While this stimulus-response model has achieved some limited success, notably in identifying a clear link between smoking and the incidence of lung cancer, such successes may be the exception and not the rule. If health reflects a concatenation of environmental, genetic, cultural, and socio-economic conditions, and their interaction with human cognition and choice, and if these interaction effects are non-linear, then outcomes may not have a mechanistic explanation.[21] In Hayekian terms, should health outcomes at both the individual and at the population level be understood as 'complex' rather than as 'simple' phenomena, then it may not be possible for scientific observers to devise any clear-cut behavioural strategy either at the individual *or* at the societal level that will lead to predictable improvements in health and/or longevity.

The latter analysis may best account for why, outside of the connection between smoking and lung cancer, little if any progress appears to have been made in establishing any strong causal relationships between consumption/behavioural practices and the incidence of specific health conditions. Even in the case of passive smoking where it might be thought that conditions offer a close approximation to those generating the strong associational link between first-hand smoke and the incidence of respiratory ailments, the evidence remains far from clear-cut.[22] Elsewhere, while extreme levels of body mass are related to premature death, 'moderate' levels of being 'overweight' exhibit no such association and indeed have often been correlated with greater longevity[23] —though it is unclear if the greater propensity to ill health for the 'non-obese' reflects conditions that lead them to have a lower body mass index (BMI) or whether body mass itself plays any causal role in health conditions. Similarly, in the case of diet while it was once considered that high consumption of saturated fats led to significantly increased risks of heart disease, subsequent research has suggested little if any link with no clear association between fat-rich diets and the incidence of coronary conditions.[24] There is some association between raised cholesterol levels and coronary conditions, but very weak evidence on the relationship between diet and cholesterol levels in the body.

On a wider scale, understandings of why some cultural/ethnic groups live longer lives than others are limited. Those of East Asian ethnicity, for example, whether resident in East Asia or in the United States, exhibit greater longevity than those of 'Caucasian' ethnicity, but the balance among genetic factors,

[21] Farmer, R., and Lawrenson, R. (2004) *Lecture Notes: Epidemiology and Public Health*, 5th edn, Oxford: Oxford University Press; Hansen and Easthope, *Lifestyle in Medicine*; Krieger, N. (1994) 'Epidemiology and the Web of Causation: Has Anyone Seen the Spider?', *Social Science and Medicine*, 39 (7): 887–903.

[22] Ho., V., Ross, J., Steiner, C., Mandawat, A., Ku-Goto, H., and Krumholtz, H. (2016) 'A Nationwide Assessment of the Association of Smoking Bans and Cigarette Taxes with Hospitalisations for Acute Myo-Cardial Infraction, Heart Failure and Pneumonia', *Medical Care and Research Review*, 74 (6): 687–704; Peres, J. (2013) 'No Clear Link Between Passive Smoking and Lung Cancer', *Journal of the National Cancer Institute*, 105 (24): 1844–6.

[23] Gaesser, G. (2002) *Big Fat Lies: The Truth About Your Weight and Your Health*, Carlsbad, CA: Gurze.

[24] See, e.g., Chowdury, R., and Warnakula, S. (2014) 'Association of Dietary, Circulating and Supplementary Acids with Coronary Risk: A Systematic Review and Meta-Analysis', *Annals of Internal Medicine*, 18 March, https://doi.org/10.7326/M13-1788.

diet, and cultural norms and practices and the interaction between these in producing health outcomes is simply unknown.[25] Similar problems afflict attempts to attribute causality to socio-economic conditions such as relative levels of inequality and their relationship to the incidence of ill health. While there appears to be some connection between the alleviation of *absolute* poverty and health, with wealth enabling people to secure a level of nutrition that makes them more resilient to disease,[26] there is no such clarity with respect to the relationship between *relative* poverty and health. Practitioners of social medicine have produced superficial statistical associations claiming to establish a connection between inequality and health outcomes, but more detailed analyses show no relationship between economic inequality and longevity.[27] On the post-foundational view of science advocated in this book, even if more robust associations could be found, in the absence of anything resembling experimental conditions that could control for multiple background variables, the reliability of any causal inferences, let alone their stability over time, would remain in doubt.

All these complexities multiply when moving beyond the construction or understanding of health as a quasi-technological problem. The latter sees the goal of increasing longevity or the avoidance of specific health conditions as a *singular* concern, but if health is situated in the context of other potentially competing values, such as personal enjoyment or the preservation of valued traditions associated with various forms of consumption, then to avoid a one-dimensional and disciplinary 'healthism' or 'safetyism', some attempt must be made to assign relative weightings to these potentially conflicting and pluralistic goals. It is, however, unlikely that statistically modelled estimates of variables such as 'deaths averted' by specific behavioural changes (even assuming that such causal connections can be discerned) versus the prices people pay for various foods, beverages, or pastimes will comport with the complex and differentiated

[25] Acciai, F., Noah, A., and Firebaugh, G. (2015) 'Pinpointing the Sources of East Asian Mortality Advantage in the United States', *Journal of Epidemiology and Community Health*, 69 (10): 1006–11.

[26] McKeown, T. (1983) 'Food, Infection and Population', *Journal of Interdisciplinary History*, 14: 227–48—note McKeown's work in this connection questions the extent to which earlier public health campaigns for sanitary legislation were responsible for improvements in mortality, suggesting instead that better nutrition resulting from economic growth may have played a greater role in improving resilience against disease.

[27] Deaton, A. (2003) 'Health, Inequality and Economic Development', *Journal of Economic Literature*, 41 (1): 113–58; Deaton, A., and Lubotsky, D. (2003) 'Mortality, Inequality and Race in American Cities and States', *Social Science and Medicine*, 56 (6): 1139–53; Deaton, A., and Lubotksy, D. (2009) 'Income Inequality and Mortality in US Cities—Weighing the Evidence: A Response to Ash', *Social Science and Medicine*, 68: 1914–17; Leigh, A., and Jenks, C. (2007) 'Income Inequality and Mortality: Long Run Evidence from a Panel of Countries', *Journal of Health Economics*, 26 (1): 1–24. For a literature review and critique of links between inequality and ill health see Bergh, A., Nilsson, T., and Waldenstrom, D. (2016) *Sick of Inequality? An Introduction to the Relationship Between Inequality and Health*, Cheltenham: Edward Elgar.

trade-offs associated with lifestyle decisions as these are experienced by multiple heterogeneous agents.

In view of these uncertainties and possibilities for error or statistical misrecognition, it might be thought that caution would be exercised before restricting the options people face. In practice, however, while acknowledging that decisions are made with limited information, many of the professional associations active within the public health *dispositif* do not hesitate to make policy recommendations and campaign for them. Understood in Foucauldian terms, this tendency may reflect a series of 'power effects' arising from the prevailing discursive construction of public health expertise and the constellation of interests this construction works to produce and reproduce.

The first such effect may be that when the positionality and prestige of public health professionals depend on their perceived ability to identify scientific 'answers' to well-defined 'problems', there may be few professional rewards for practitioners who emphasise uncertainty and exhibit a reluctance to offer clearly defined 'solutions'. The interactions between public health officials and politicians eager to secure votes, as well as with media outlets who have commercial imperatives to cover news items that can be depicted in highly simplified or dramatised form, may frame an incentive structure or selection effect that favours those who downplay complexity and uncertainty.[28] Relatedly, wherever scientific discourses provide social status for public health practitioners, that status may be threatened or destabilised should 'too many' conflicting views be raised. If the public and media gaze is focused on the ability of professionals to determine clear scientific answers, then a perceived inability to provide such answers may generate scepticism of public health expertise in other domains. Professional bodies thus routinely limit diversity of opinion and seek to exert disciplinary power over dissenters for fear that the public appearance of 'too much' disagreement will undermine the credibility of the profession at large.[29]

Second, public health professionals may also have financial and or political interests in seeking to expand the reach of their power and influence. The discursive stimulation of a public interest in a specific behaviour or health problem may help secure additional funding for government departments, universities, and research institutes and the possibility of their supervising or informing additional regulatory powers. Public health research is often government funded or funded through partnerships between states and private businesses or research institutes and is thus prone to influence from those controlling access to these funds. Public health academics and researchers also operate in a professional

[28] Rydin, Y., and Pennington, M. (2001) 'The Discourses of the Prisoners Dilemma', *Environmental Politics*, 10 (3): 48–71; Yates, A., and Stroup, R. (2000) 'Media Coverage and EPA Pesticide Decisions', *Public Choice*, 102: 297–312.

[29] Koppl, R. (2018) *Expert Failure*, Cambridge: Cambridge University Press.

setting where there are rewards for publications that attract media attention, and the capacity to publish and to garner such attention and to generate policy 'impact' may be related to the presentation of clear-cut findings. Media organisations often report on scientific findings in a way that emphasises the most attention-grabbing aspects while ignoring nuance or ambiguity; and this may then be folded back into the scientific process with researchers either producing work that fits this mould, or if it does not, emphasising those aspects of their work that can be presented accordingly.[30] Private sector businesses also conduct their own research when launching products with possible health effects and often support research that contests public health claims. Tobacco manufacturers, for example sought to conceal evidence of a link between smoking and lung cancer.[31] More recently the alcohol and food industries have sponsored researchers who argue that physical inactivity and not food intake is the primary cause of the 'obesity epidemic'.[32] Elsewhere, however, producer interests may profit from public health research and legislation that stimulates the demand for their products as when the diet and health foods industries mobilise claims about relationships between obesity, ill health, and longevity to stimulate a demand for diet plans and more recently for dieting drugs.[33] Though the coalitions and their motivations vary, a broad range of public and private actors thus perceive their interests through a discursive formation premised on the validity of a linear or 'simple' model of causation that grants to epidemiologists and/or social statisticians the capacity to identify the behaviours conducive to better health.

The subsequent rush to policy generated by these power effects, the tendency to 'police the truth', and the reluctance to revise such 'truths' when confronted with contrary data may be detected right across the domain of lifestyle governance. In the case of passive smoking, for example, the existence or magnitude of the health threat *was not* established when public health professionals aligned with anti-smoking activist groups to demand extensive regulation over the use of tobacco in public and private spaces.[34] In subsequent years evidence on the role of passive smoking remained inconclusive, but contrary data was

[30] Kolderup Hervik, S., Kolderup Hervik, A., and Thurston, M. (2021) 'From Science to Sensational Headline: A Critical Examination of the Sugar as "Toxic" Narrative', *Food, Culture and Society*, 25 (3): 505–19.

[31] Collin, J., Lee, K., Gillmore, A. (2004) 'Unlocking the Corporate Documents of British American Tobacco: An Invaluable Resource Needs Radically Improved Access', *The Lancet*, 363: 1746–7; Gruning, T., Gillmore, A., and McKee, M. (2006) 'Tobacco Industry Influence on Science and Scientists in Germany', *American Journal of Public Health*, 96: 20–32; World Health Organisation, *Tobacco Industry Interference with Tobacco Control*, Geneva: WHO.

[32] Gillmore, A., Savell, E., and Collin, J. (2011) 'Public Health, Corporations, and the New Responsibility Deal: Promoting Partnerships with Vectors of Disease?', *Journal of Public Health*, 33 (1): 2–4.

[33] Oliver, J. (2006) *Fat Politics*, New York: Oxford University Press.

[34] Berridge, V. (2011) *Marketing Health: Smoking and the Discourse of Public Health in Britain, 1945–2000*, Oxford: Oxford University Press.

suppressed and those responsible for it were often marginalised or accused of having been corrupted by the tobacco industry. In the UK specifically, the combination of pressure from anti-smoking campaigners and a radical subgroup within the public health profession influenced by the discourse of social medicine generated a sustained campaign to shift the emphasis away from discouraging private consumption through taxes on tobacco (where health risks were clearly established) to a disciplinary approach focussed on eliminating smoking through the surveillance and management of public and private spaces.[35]

This pattern may now be repeating itself for the tobacco substitute vaping where despite the absence of systematic evidence connecting the practice to second-hand or passive health risks, proposals are now being considered by nation-states and bodies such as the European Union to ban vaping in all public and private spaces where people gather.[36] For alcohol consumption while there is a well-established link between persistent heavy drinking and serious liver conditions, there is little or no consistent evidence to support the guidelines for recommended daily intake issued by many public health authorities and international bodies such as the World Health Organisation (WHO) that have informed policies such as minimal-unit pricing.[37] Finally, with nutrition and diet, many public health authorities rushed to issue guidance against diets high in saturated fats when only weak associations with high cholesterol and heart conditions were apparent. Though some authorities now seek to revise that guidance, this is taking place decades after research questioning this association first came to light, and during which time those conducting the research in question were subject to disciplinary marginalisation by much of the public health profession.[38] More recently, a similar rush to policy and the marginalisation of dissenting views appear to be unfolding in the context of demands for regulating the sugar content of food and drink and for the alleged health risks associated with the consumption of 'ultra-processed' foods.[39]

From the standpoint of freedom and pluralism, the issue here is not that those advancing a particular behavioural-environmental conjecture about health and longevity are necessarily 'wrong'. Rather, it is with an institutionalised and quasi-monopolistic power/knowledge regime or strategic codification that aligns a form of scientific rationalism with state power to push or to mould subjects into believing certain things, to live in certain ways, and to submit to a combination of state-imposed and self-imposed controls, *irrespective* of whether there is a solid

[35] Ibid.

[36] European Union (2021) *A Cancer Plan for Europe*, European Commission.

[37] Fitzpatrick, M. (2001) *The Tyranny of Health: Doctors and the Regulation of Lifestyle*, London: Routledge.

[38] Teicholz, N. (2023) 'A Short History of Saturated Fat: The Making and Unmaking of a Scientific Consensus', *Current Opinion in Endocrinal Diabetes and Obesity*, 30 (1): 65–71.

[39] Kolderup Hervik et al., 'From Science to Sensational Headline'.

basis for these actions. The analysis offered here thus problematises discourses and institutions that may attribute 'too much' responsibility for health status either to personal decisions; to those of private businesses; or that grant power, resources, and positionality to those who claim an ability to manipulate 'social structure' or 'choice architecture' to produce 'better outcomes'. In Foucauldian terms, the public health *dispositif* influences how subjects experience their health and freedom, and it is these power effects that might be questioned from a sceptical position that emphasises greater humility and toleration of difference in the face of complexity and uncertainty.

Normalising health and lifestyle

A second set of threats to freedom and pluralism concern not only the direct and indirect restrictions on choice arising from overconfidence in a scientistic model but also from the normalising and disciplinary techniques and tactics of government often deployed in conjunction with such models. The incorporation of 'disease-based' metaphors into the social construction of lifestyle choices has allowed what were previously framed as largely private concerns to be turned into matters for the public gaze. These strategies are most evident in the mobilisation of overlapping contagion and externality narratives to govern a raft of consumption practices. In the context of tobacco, for example, *any* instance of smoking in the company of non-family members is now routinely described as a physical 'invasion' of other peoples' spaces akin to a form of 'pollution', and in many countries this has led to smoking bans in collective spaces—with discussions in some jurisdictions now advocating bans in private homes to protect the interests of children.[40] For alcohol, as well as for the consumption of fatty and sugary foods, the pollution is considered cultural in form and operative through a mimetic contagion effect where the presence of people engaging in these behaviours or of companies advertising or promoting them is presented as an undue temptation to deviate from 'healthy behaviour'.[41] Appropriated and repurposed by behavioural economics, the strategic logic of a pollution/externality and social contagion discourse extends from making normative judgements about conflicts of value *between* persons to those *within* persons with the current desires of people to consume in an 'unhealthy' manner described as 'imposing a cost' on their 'future selves'—a cost demanding public attention and 'rectification'.

Recognition that consumption decisions are not purely private, that they have a social component or involve potential external effects, need not itself

[40] European Union, *A Cancer Plan for Europe*.
[41] Kolderup Hervick et al., 'From Science to Sensational Headline'.

constitute a threat to freedom and pluralism. On the contrary, if externalities are framed as interpersonal conflicts between (or within) subjects who hold differing valuations of specific practices and their attendant risks, then so long as decision rights are assigned to one or other party it would remain possible for a process of bargaining and mutual adjustment to occur across these practices.[42] Those in possession of a right to smoke might, for example, be 'bought-out' by those preferring a smoke-free setting and vice versa. Alternatively, where bargaining or negotiation costs are excessive and where some form of third-party decision may reduce these costs and their attendant conflicts, then hierarchical authorities ranging from nightclub owners and restaurateurs through to shopping mall proprietors and to local authorities may specify different rules governing the practice of smoking in the presence of others with people selecting the rules under which they wish to associate.[43]

Crucially, however, the scope for this pluralism and toleration of difference is likely to be overwhelmed whenever the behaviours in question are open to strategic construction as 'life threatening' or as prone to 'contagion effects' that generate 'health emergencies'. Such narratives provide fertile ground for the deployment of moralising distinctions or 'dividing practices' between those judged 'perpetrators' of the emergency or contagion and those depicted as its 'victims'. In these circumstances, toleration between differing subjective evaluations of the possible trade-offs between health and non-health goals may be replaced by a highly judgemental approach that targets a specific set of behaviours. This strategic moralising may be applied with equal vigour against the promotion or advertising of targeted products or behaviours with consumers constructed as the hosts or 'victims' of 'disease', products such as tobacco and fatty or sugary foods described as 'toxic agents' or sources of 'infection', and advertisers and businesses construed as 'disease vectors'. The strategic mobilisation of these dividing practices is, for example, evident in the way that public health campaigners have increasingly adopted a 'perpetrator versus victim' discourse which pits the interests of 'Big Alcohol' and 'Big Food' against those of consumers, much in the way that anti-tobacco campaigners previously framed 'Big Tobacco' as the enemy of uninformed smokers.[44]

From a Foucauldian or postmodern liberal standpoint, the deployment of such constructions may be understood as a form of discursive entrepreneurship where what were described in chapter 3 as 'externality entrepreneurs' use the prestige of epidemiology and/or economics to mobilise scientific justifications for what may be attempts to secure power, positionality, and/or resources at the

[42] Coase, R. (1960) 'The Problem of Social Cost', *Journal of Law and Economics*, 3: 1–44.

[43] Meadowcroft, J. (2011) 'Economic and Political Solutions to Social Problems: The Case of Second-Hand Smoke in Enclosed Public Space', *Review of Political Economy*, 23 (2): 233–48.

[44] Kolderup Hervick et al., 'From Science to Sensational Headline'.

expense of others. This process is often played out in elite-level confrontations, where public health professionals construct themselves and are constructed by parts of the media and by politicians as 'protectors' of consumer interests from the predatory actions of corporate elites in the alcohol, food, and tobacco businesses.

Public health narratives focussed on contagion and externality effects may, however, also act as a stimulant to discourse elsewhere in society and may interact with more decentred power relations. The latter may be witnessed in the way that narratives around alcohol, diet, and obesity frequently interact with class- or status-based framings. Consumption practices often associated with low-income groups may be disproportionately targeted for public health interventions where discourses of contagion/externality or concerns for welfare and capability may reflect a paternalistic 'cynicism of power' that speaks 'for or above' those concerned. Obesity is for example often taken to reflect a subjects' character, with the prevalence of 'fatness' in lower income groups frequently attributed to laziness or an inability to exercise 'responsible' health choices given a lack of education or intellectual sophistication. Alternatively, lifestyle epidemiology may be deployed to conceal feelings of revulsion or disgust by some members of higher status or higher income groups for choices and bodily forms or comportments that fail to meet their aesthetic standards and which may represent an attempt to impose those standards on others.[45] There are in this regard, strong historical echoes between contemporary lifestyle epidemiology and the class and social status dynamics associated with the passage of sanitary legislation in the latter part of the nineteenth century. While improvements in basic sanitation through the introduction of public sewerage systems were beneficial across income and class differentials, in many instances those in working-class neighbourhoods experienced the sanitary movement as a form of social discipline. The relatively poor did not necessarily wish to spend scarce income or leisure time on cleansing activities, with sanitary legislation and the norms it proliferated perceived as primarily of benefit to those in higher or middle-income groups.[46]

The combined effect of these discursive and entrepreneurial 'dividing practices' appears to be producing an amoeba-like growth of micro-disciplinary or 'pastoral' controls with a regulatory environment that now goes far beyond the provision of basic informational requirements for consumers to an all-encompassing safetyist narrative that purports to speak 'for them'. In the case of tobacco consumption, for example, in addition to health warnings on packaging, almost all advertising has been eliminated, and in the United Kingdom

[45] Oliver, *Fat Politics*, chap. 3.
[46] Wohl, A. (1984) *Endangered Lives: Public Health in Victorian Britain*, London: Routledge.

specifically, there are now bans on vending machines and requirements for retailers to hide all tobacco products from public view. Combined with bans on smoking in public places, the experience of the freedom to consume tobacco is now not dissimilar to that which faced gay men under the Sexual Offences Act of 1967—where homosexual acts were permitted between consenting adults—but only in private, lest public visibility of gay sexuality have a contagious effect on 'normal' males by encouraging them to experiment with their bodies. A similar dynamic is now spilling out to the regulation of food and alcohol promotion and consumption with governments considering advertising bans and restrictions on where retailers can display high-fat or high-sugar products in their stores.[47] Indeed, the chair of the UK Food Standards Agency has recently gone so far as to suggest that bringing cake into work environments should be treated in the same way as passive smoking—because it imposes a dangerous 'harm' on those who suffer from 'weakness of will'.[48]

What matters here is that the institutionalisation of these scientised and moralised categories may have profound effects on how people see themselves and how they experience their choices notwithstanding the weakness of any evidence with respect to the effects on health and longevity. People may pay higher prices or experience feelings of guilt and shame in settings where products are adorned with warnings or made more difficult to access.[49] Alternatively, even when evidence is much clearer and widely known, as with first-hand tobacco smoke, the possibility that people might be willing to sacrifice a few extra months or years of life for the mere pleasure of smoking or to risk entering places where others smoke, or simply that they may enjoy consuming high-fat or high-sugar foods, may be experienced very differently when these acts are presented as a form of contagion or externality, damaging to others as well as to their 'future selves'. Similarly, in such a discursive setting the notion that there might be a legitimate consumer interest in having access to certain consumption goods at affordable prices is erased from view. When attempts are made to make people feel guilty about what they consume and/or to present them as dupes of corporate marketing, the cost of expressing opposition to lifestyle regulation may be experienced as prohibitive.

None of this implies that all regulations pertaining to smoking, alcohol, or the consumption of various foods are unnecessary and/or reflect an equal threat

[47] Department of Health and Social Care (2020) *Tackling Obesity: Empowering Adults and Children to Live Healthier Lives*, London: UK Government, July.

[48] Sylvester, R., and Smyth, C., Cake in the office should be viewed like passive smoking expert warns, *The Times*, 19 January 2023, https://www.thetimes.co.uk/article/times-health-commission-office-cake-sugar-passive-smoking-5s3bzb3dn?fbclid=IwAR3zvKCCMDSl4LLQcrI9Y5xwua5J2A1UBdlIDg19Hi2SitUdnbQtsTSvNEs.

[49] Kolderup Hervick et al., 'From Science to Sensational Headline'. See also Bell, K., McCollough, L., Salmon, A., and Bell, J. (2010) 'Every Space Is Claimed: Smokers Experience of De-Normalisation', *Sociology of Health and Illness*, 32 (6): 914–29.

to freedom. Constraints on fraudulent claims and exposing the manipulation of scientific research by large businesses are entirely compatible with a framework within which people may exercise their freedom. Rather, the intention here is to highlight the strategic logics where the interaction among the power of organised expertise, state power, and more decentred power relations may narrow options to the point where people may experience a form of 'over-government' that limits their scope to exercise agency over their style of life and death.

Lifestyle, power/knowledge, and constitution of the self

In addition to the normalising quality of lifestyle epidemiology highlighted thus far, still further dangers arise from the conception of the self that dominates the public health *dispositif* and the technologies of government deemed appropriate to the 'administration' of this self. These dangers are most apparent at the intersection between the discourse of social medicine and that of behavioural economics. In their different ways these narratives posit the existence of a 'true' or 'underlying' self, waiting to be revealed or liberated by the appropriate public health policies.

The first problem to note about this specific discourse coalition is that it grants cognitive and informational capacities to lifestyle practitioners that it does not grant to those for whom the relevant changes in choice architecture are designed. It thus introduces significant scope for paternalistic acts of misrecognition through a regulatory power/knowledge that speaks 'for and above' its targets. In the case of social medicine, the discourse echoes long-established socialist tropes suggesting that market economies stultify freedom by providing people with goods that do not meet their 'genuine needs'. As such, it neglects to explain how the practitioners of this expertise have been able to escape from these processes and to identify in a 'neutral' or 'power-free' manner what preferences and needs people would or should express were it not for the effects of history, culture, and commercial marketing.

Behavioural economics is more forthcoming in this regard but suffers from many of the same deficiencies. It claims to help agents achieve their own subjectively defined and expressed goals by measuring how far their 'revealed preferences' say for alcohol or fatty foods, depart from their 'underlying preferences', and to design 'nudges' that will properly align these preferences. Though it challenges the accuracy of neo-classical welfare theory as a description of how people act, behavioural economics holds to the neo-classical model of rationality as a normative ideal of how they *should* act.[50] In principle, this requires a highly individualised process of 'correction' or 'treatment' with the

[50] On this, see, e.g., Rizzo, M., and Whitman, G. (2019) *Escaping Paternalism*, Cambridge: Cambridge University Press.

specific 'incentive' or 'nudge' tailored to each subject's level of information, their preferences and beliefs, and the extent and character of their cognitive departures from neo-classical rationality. Sin taxes on fatty foods should, for example, be higher for those suffering from short-term bias and or for those who already exceed a certain weight threshold.[51] A key challenge here, however, is that even when judged against its own model there is ample scope for the 'libertarian paternalist' gaze to result in acts of misrecognition because there may be 'rational' reasons for subjects to depart from the neo-classical 'ideal'. Once contextual factors such as environmental and cognitive constraints are properly accounted for, then it may not be 'rational' for actors to have a fully consistent preference ordering or for them to be immune to framing effects of various kinds. The knowledge required to design nudges that on balance improve rather than worsen an individual's capacities to pursue their ends is likely to be highly contextual and thus largely inaccessible to external regulatory agencies. A more inclusive approach to rationality would recognise that though people may be subject to biases, they may still be more familiar with their own preferences, values, and context than external observers.[52] Moreover, even if external parties can spot decision-making biases better that those subject to these biases, this does not preclude the possibility of people choosing their own mentor or 'pastor' for this purpose. Different behavioural experts have different views on the appropriate responses to cognitive bias, so there seems little reason to grant public regulators authority over those whose behaviour they seek to judge—a monopolistic privilege scarcely distinguishable from traditional paternalist assertions that experts know better than subjects what values and preferences they *should* have.

Given the significant transactions costs in tailoring nudges to match individual requirements, public health policies tend to target populations in general. The 'whole population' or bio-political model of lifestyle epidemiology might thus be thought to reduce the risks of an unduly disciplinary and normalising discourse that targets specific individuals and groups. Nonetheless, this model raises a different set of problems because for any set of individuals better placed to achieve their subjectively defined goals following a public health intervention such as a sin tax, there are likely to be others for whom it will be more difficult to pursue their respective goals. Those suffering from short-term bias may, for example, benefit from a nudge that reduces their immediate propensity to consume fatty or sugary foods, but those who have an exaggerated view of the risks involved may lose out on what could be beneficial and pleasurable acts of consumption.[53] Either way, there is little reason to believe that lifestyle intervention

[51] Delmotte, C., and Dold, M. (2022) 'Dynamic Preferences and the Behavioural Case Against Sin Taxes', *Constitutional Political Economy*, 33: 80–99.

[52] Ibid.

[53] Ibid.

will work in a 'neutral' manner that does not use its power to favour one set of ends over others.

Important though these difficulties are, a more significant problem follows from the constitution of the self by the public health *dispositif* as an 'impaired soul' or 'broken machine'. This construction, expressed in different form by social medicine and behavioural economics, presupposes the existence of a 'power-free' or 'autonomous' agent waiting to be revealed when all social 'distortions' are lifted or when the self is 'repaired' by an appropriately informed 'choice architect'. On a Foucauldian view, however, since there is no real or authentic self 'outside' of power any identification of the constituents of such a self should be understood as a power/knowledge claim. Instead of 'liberating' subjects from power or 'fixing' their broken rationality, freedom requires that people retain sufficient scope to *reshape themselves* not in accordance with an underlying, essence, truth, or rationality but as part of a creative, experimental, and open-ended process of *self-constitution* where their preferences may evolve in often unanticipated ways. It follows that while the revealed preferences of subjects should not be interpreted as their 'real' preferences as in orthodox neo-classical welfare theory, neither should they be understood as 'uncorrected' or 'impaired' preferences, as in social medicine and behavioural economics.

For Foucault, though there can be no escape from power, the self-constituted individual is one who recognises their potential subjection and finds ways of acting on themselves by engaging critically with the institutions, disciplines, and discourses in which they are embedded to create something new or different. Subjects do not have real or true preferences 'outside' of those generated by their entanglements in markets, civil society, and the state, but they may exercise their agency by experimenting with techniques they find within these entanglements to reconstitute their values and to generate and be exposed to previously unthought of possibilities. This type of freedom is threatened, not by the existence of power-relations per se—such as, for example, cultural norms and standards that value some body shapes and comportments more than others—but by strategic codifications or alignments between decentred power relations and state authority that narrow the scope for subjects to witness alternatives and to think and to act differently.

Crucially, many ideas for nudging subjects within the public health *dispositif* threaten to narrow pluralism of thought and action in precisely this way. While there is no 'nudge-free' or 'interference-free' position against which the freedom of subjects can be judged, there is a non-trivial distinction between choice environments that emerge unintentionally from the push and pull of multiple agents seeking to exert influence and positionality over others in plural and often contradictory ways, and those where the discourse coalitions that manage to capture public agencies are able to use sovereign state power in an attempt to manipulate choice architecture. Thus, while chocolate and cake manufacturers may use marketing techniques that mould decisions in one direction, those in the leisure, fitness, and health industries may seek to mould them in a different direction. Subjects may exercise their freedom by spotting gaps or ambiguities between these different technologies of government, but these gaps may be narrowed or closed in a context where sin taxes, mandatory health warnings, or more diffuse or decentred forms of 'guidance' are codified and given formal authority by public health agencies.

Far from providing people with tools to counteract the potentially narrowing effect of these normalising and disciplinary techniques, the public health *dispositif* seeks to combine public authority with the deliberate use of such techniques to manipulate subjects into what it determines as their best interests. Recognising that people are often sensitive to normative social pressure, it aims to use these decentred pressures towards behavioural conformity in combination with cognitive biases to advance population-level improvements in health and welfare. One illustration of this tendency is the use by nudging agencies of so-called spotlight effects that seek to magnify cognitive illusions where subjects may overestimate the extent to which others in their environment pay attention to their conduct.[54] Public information and social media campaigns, phone apps, and associated tracking devices are used to generate the sense, real or imagined, of being under observation by a peer group and encouraging compliance with the observer's gaze.

From a Foucauldian perspective, such techniques should not necessarily be judged in a negative light, and indeed they may be utilised as part of a process of self-constitution. A subject who has understood that social pressure to participate in after-work drinks has contributed to their alcohol dependence might, for example, join a group such as Alcoholics Anonymous or subscribe to a phone app that places them in a situation where there is a countervailing gaze that discourages their drinking. There is, however, a crucial distinction between choosing to submit to such a gaze by opting into an app that sends out warnings whenever one enters a public bar and say a state monopoly digital currency linked to a social credit scheme that requires corporations to track retail purchases for the purpose of shaming people into conformity with publicly approved behaviours. Where the former involves the exercise of personal agency, the latter involves a conscious effort to combine monopoly public power with a decentred surveillance model that narrows the scope for such agency. For better or for worse, 'surveillance capitalism' uses digital technologies to track in ever-increasing detail the purchasing decisions of consumers either directly or by selling data to advertisers to better cater to the relevant consumer preferences.

[54] For example, Sunstein and Thaler, *Nudge*, 54–5.

By contrast, a public health *dispositif* operating through a corporatist surveillance state adopts the now familiar tactic of 'governing at a distance'—recruiting private and civil agencies to restrict access to 'non-approved' sources of information,[55] and requiring corporations to mould and to discipline their consumer subjects in accordance with state approved behaviours.

Problematising the public health *dispositif* II: The governance of infectious diseases

The foregoing analysis does not imply that pluralism and freedom over lifestyle governance have been eliminated in contemporary liberal societies but highlights the processes through which a set of overlapping discursive and non-discursive practices may be narrowing the strategic field within which individuals exercise powers of choice and self-government over health-related conduct.[56] It will be the contention in what follows that similar narrowing processes; the erasure of complexity and uncertainty in favour of a scientistic managerialism; the widespread recourse to normalisation strategies; and the construction of subjects as incapable of exercising agency without expert assistance were witnessed in more extreme form during the COVID-19 pandemic. That experience suggests that the interlocking technologies of government central to the lifestyle *dispositif* may have been folded back into this more traditional aspect of public health policy.

The erasure of complexity and uncertainty

Though epidemiologists may discern the general principles through which a virus such as COVID-19 spreads and may use modelling exercises to simulate a range of possible outcomes, the precise manner of spread through a population will depend on a host of context-specific factors that may be inaccessible to scientists or experts and that cannot be captured by statistics. While they are natural science phenomena, epidemiological problems should not be understood as the 'simple' physics type. Rather, infectious diseases such as COVID-19 might be better understood as complex phenomena that exhibit often *unpredictable* responses to differences in geography, weather, and public policy interventions.

[55] Alshamy, Y., Coyne, C., Hall, A., and Owens, M. (2023) 'Surveillance Capitalism and the Surveillance State: A Comparative Institutional Analysis', GMU Working Paper in Economics, No. 23-10, https://ssrn.com/abstract=4361776 or http://dx.doi.org/10.2139/ssrn.4361776.

[56] This section draws on Pennington, M. (2023) 'Foucault and Hayek on Public Health and the Road to Serfdom', *Public Choice*, 195: 125–43.

With complex phenomena, there is a significant 'knowledge problem' in understanding not only the epidemiology of viruses such as COVID-19 but also how human expectations will be changed by the pattern of events or by policy interventions, and this problem may be especially severe in a context of heterogenous individuals whose actions cannot be reduced to those of a representative agent. Such uncertainties multiply when the health consequences in question extend to the trade-offs between the possible reduction of deaths from a virus following measures such as 'lockdown' and the possible increase in deaths arising from illnesses that might go undiagnosed or untreated because of such measures. In addition to the trade-off between deaths from these different sources, there are also costs to be considered in terms of possible deteriorations in people's mental health as well as increases in domestic violence that may accompany prolonged periods of confinement and social isolation. Away from these health-related trade-offs there is likely to be considerable uncertainty over the extent to which the damage inflicted by the uncontrolled spread of a virus is matched or outweighed by the scale of the socio-economic costs such as impairments to children's education following school closures and the accumulation of public debt associated with measures that might seek to contain it.[57]

Far from emphasising the importance of pluralism and reflexivity in the face of these complexities, the public health response to COVID-19 in many liberal democracies appears to have been driven by processes that sought to *undermine* pluralism and reflexivity. Notably, the opinions of epidemiologists and economists, as well as civil society groups, who challenged what became the dominant narrative in favour of 'lockdowns' or radical 'social distancing' measures saw their circulation restricted. Public health agencies and governments often worked 'at a distance' in 'partnership' with social media channels such as Twitter, Facebook, and YouTube to exercise disciplinary power, placing 'warnings' on advice that questioned WHO guidance or that of local public health authorities.[58] Neither were these disciplinary pressures confined to individuals—with countries such as Sweden and in the United States, jurisdictions such as South Dakota and Florida, routinely condemned for not following the dominant narrative that favoured extreme social distancing.

These Foucauldian power tactics appear to reflect the process discussed previously where professional bodies narrow the range of opinion to protect the authority of a power/knowledge complex that might be undermined by the

[57] For a more detailed discussion see Pennington, M. (2021) 'Hayek on Complexity, Uncertainty and Pandemic Response', *Review of Austrian Economics*, 34: 203–220.

[58] Berenson, A. Covid and the New Age of Censorship, *The Wall Street Journal*, 7 December 2020, https://www.wsj.com/articles/covid-and-the-new-age-of-censorship-11607381415. Beachum, L., and Bellware, K. YouTube removed Trump advsier's video for minsinformation. He compared it to Thirs World Censorship, *Washington Post*, 17 September 2020, https://www.washingtonpost.com/nation/2020/09/17/scott-atlas-youtube/).

absence of a more unitary stance. In the case of the pandemic response the *appearance* of a coherent body of opinion was generated by the leading public health officials in government agencies such as the Center for Disease Control and Prevention (CDC) in the United States and Scientific Advisory Group for Emergencies (SAGE) in the United Kingdom. These officials had the public and media platform to specify what 'the science' says; a message that was then enforced through the more decentred actions and inactions of agents within the relevant professional networks, as well as through politicians, the media, and civil society. Such actions and inactions were, however, not necessarily driven solely by 'the science' but by the flow of events and how these were discursively constructed by actors in society at large.

Crucially, these examples show that the operation of discursive power is not wholly a 'top-down' phenomena but may reflect an interaction effect where the options available to top-down public health actors such as CDC or SAGE officials are structured by a more decentred complex of events, institutions, and the discourses in general circulation. In the specific case of the COVID-19 pandemic, preparedness advice from bodies such as the WHO and SAGE was that 'lockdown' measures were undesirable or ineffective and the initial response in countries such as the UK stuck to this line.[59] It was only *after* the Italian and then the Spanish administrations imitated the 'lockdown' response first adopted in China, soon followed by others, and the subsequent clamour from many parts of civil society and the media that policy changed—and was presented as required by 'the science'.[60] Of particular significance here was the widespread circulation of 'worst-case scenario' models predicting mass fatalities that were then taken up and represented by the media to the public. In this instance, pressure towards convergence on 'lockdowns' was arguably driven by the deployment of emergency narratives and a highly precautionary, risk-averse or safetyist stance that has become a hallmark of the wider public health *dispositif*, with large sections of the populations in question *demanding* restrictions on themselves and on others more severe than those thought credible or workable by many of the relevant

[59] World Health Organisation (2019) *Non-Pharmaceutical Health Measures for Mitigating the risk and impact of Epidemic and Pandemic Influenza*, Geneva: WHO; Department of Health and Social Care (2011) 'UK Influenza Pandemic Preparedness Strategy', London: UK Government, https://www.gov.uk/government/publications/review-of-the-evidence-base-underpinning-the-uk-influenza-pandemic-preparedness-strategy.

These reports refer to pandemic influenza and may not be thought relevant to COVID-19. Crucially, however, lockdown measures were advised against for scenarios with death rates between 200,000 and 300,000 per fifteen weeks (Department of Health and Social Care, 2011). No country, *irrespective of the policy adopted*, experienced such death rates from COVID-19.

[60] For a content analysis of COVID-19 media framing see Ogbodo, J., Onwe, E., Chukwu, K., Nwasum, C., Nwakpu, E., Nwankwo, S., Nwamimi, S., Elem, S., and Ogbaega, N. (2020) 'Communicating Health Crisis: A Content Analysis of Global Media Framing of Co-Vid 19', *Health Promotion Perspectives*, 10 (3): 257–69.

experts. It may have been the greater institutional separation of the public health bureaucracy in Sweden from media and political pressure that accounted in part for its *relative* insulation from these more decentred forces. In the latter instance pluralism was limited from the top down, as officials coordinated a strategy that *rejected* lockdowns as *not* supported by 'the science'—notwithstanding pressures from some localities for such measures to be implemented.[61]

Note, the suggestion here is not that lockdowns were necessarily 'wrong' or that other strategies such as the Swedish approach, or the focussed protection model advanced by the signatories to the Great Barrington Declaration,[62] were 'right'. Rather, what has been emphasised is how the institutionalised defence of scientific rationalism may stifle debate and reflexivity through a combination of top-down and bottom-up disciplinary dynamics. In many countries, as soon as opinion had sufficiently aligned, professional public health bodies coordinated both internally and with external agents, such as media outlets, to close down the range of opinion about different ways of governing and to marginalise dissenting individuals, scientists, and jurisdictions, even in situations where evidence was at worst non-existent or at best highly contestable.

Normalisation and pandemic response

A second set of similarities between the governmental techniques adopted by lifestyle epidemiology and those deployed during the COVID pandemic response were the frequent recourse to normalisation strategies and the circulation of externality and emergency narratives. The problem of 'imposed costs' or 'externalities' occurs whenever there are *conflicting* subjective evaluations of risks. In the context of infectious diseases, those reluctant to social distance may harm others, especially those with underlying health conditions. Nonetheless, those wanting to eradicate infections may also harm those with vulnerabilities to economic or other forms of distress arising from 'excessive' public health concern. In standard welfare economic discourse, the focus is on identifying externalities, measuring them, and devising mechanisms that will internalise costs—activities which it is assumed can and will be carried out in a neutral manner by professional economists, politicians, or judges acting separately or in concert.

The Foucauldian/postmodern liberal perspective, however, questions the capacity to generate and to process the relevant 'data' in a neutral manner. When there may be little or no objective data to assess the size or direction of externalities or whether private actions are already sufficient to internalise

[61] Bylund, P., and Packard, M. (2021) 'Separation of Power and Expertise: The Tyranny of Experts in Sweden's Co Vid 19 Responses', *Southern Economic Journal*, 87 (4): 1300–19.

[62] https://gbdeclaration.org/.

them,[63] 'externality entrepreneurs' may fill the vacuum, strategically constructing whom to *brand* as the moral *wrongdoer*, depending on where they believe the greatest reservoir of support in the media, civil society, and politics may lie or where it might be generated. Thus, in the case of COVID-19, though not as prominent as epidemiologists in public discourse, many economists publicly supported lockdown measures[64] in the absence of *any* relevant cost-benefit data and notwithstanding the fact that welfare economics offers no clear guidelines on the wisdom of these or any other policies in this regard.[65]

Instead of viewing the management of disease as an interpersonal conflict between subjects who perceive risk differently, the circulation of contagion and externalities narratives also enabled a *moralisation of* distinctions between those labelled as 'perpetrators' of harm and those described as 'victims'—that ran in *one direction.* When these normalising tactics are mobilised by public and private agencies to discipline and 'correct' those considered perpetrators, then this objectivation process may activate a subjective experience of 'moral deviance' for those concerned. These tendencies were evident in political and media discussions of COVID-19 response where citizens resisting lockdown regimes were routinely demonised in public and media commentary as 'selfish', 'ignorant', or 'lacking in community spirit',[66] as well as being subject to fines and a complex apparatus of public and private surveillance. Indeed, the 'spotlight' effects often advocated by behavioural economists in the context of lifestyle epidemiology were explicitly deployed to generate social pressure in favour of lockdown policies and to delegitimise those who resisted them.[67]

Now of course, there may be some diseases that present such enormous threats to life and health that they might be considered analogous to a 'war scenario', and where it would be far-fetched to consider restrictions on what can be said and done as the manifestation of a normalising society. The problem here, however, is that such clear-cut cases may be the exception rather than the rule. With COVID-19 it was far from self-evident that health risks even to the most vulnerable elderly people, significant though they may have been, outweighed

[63] On the problem of quantifying these see Lesson, P., and Rouanet, L. (2021) 'Externality and CoVid-19', *Southern Economic Journal*, 87 (4): 1107–18.

[64] *Financial Times*, 4 April 2020, https://www.ft.com/content/e593e7d4-b82a-4bf9-8497-426ee e43bcbc

[65] Boettke, P., and Powell, B. (2021) 'The Political Economy of the Co Vid 19 Pandemic', *Southern Economic Journal*, 87 (4): 1096–116.

[66] See, e.g., comments by the UK secretary of state for health, Mason, R. Hancock accues those still socialising in UK of being 'very selfish' *The Guardian*, 23 March 2020, https://www.theguardian.com/politics/2020/mar/23/hancock-socialising-uk-slowing-coronavirus-effort.

[67] Coyne, C., and Yatsyshina, Y. (2020) 'Pandemic Police States', *Peace Economics, Peace Science and Public Policy*, online, https://www.degruyter.com/document/doi/10.1515/peps-2020-0021/html; Hannah, M., Hutta, J., and Schemann, C (2020) 'Thinking Through CoVid 19 Responses with Foucault: An Initial Overview', https://antipodeonline.org/2020/05/05/thinking-through-covid-19-responses-with-foucault/.

lost family interaction inflicted on them by radical social distancing. From a plural rationalities or subjectivist perspective, it may have been no less reasonable for an eighty-year-old woman to want to take their chances with the virus and continue seeing loved ones than it was for a similarly situated person to wish for themselves and others to self-isolate. Similarly, for some subjects in lower income groups with limited access to outdoor space and lacking the material or cultural resources to homeschool their children, it may not have been unreasonable or selfish to want to have considered the long-standing effects on their children's mental health and long-term educational development—the consequences of which have subsequently shown to be profound.[68]

The point here is that decisions to favour one side or another in such conflicts are not necessarily 'wrong' or 'inefficient' but that they may generate or reflect the strategic deployment of governing discourses and techniques that *limit pluralism* and block or bias the consideration of opportunity costs. Graphic presentations by politicians and the media of people dying in hospital beds combined with statistical models and contagion narratives were deployed strategically in many countries to galvanise support for COVID-lockdown measures, in a context where many conditions that have subsequently gone untreated and the severe mental health challenges that have followed them were less amenable to presentation via such imagery or statistical inferences. Such biases may also have reflected class or status differentials, with many of those who propagated these narratives and policies relatively insulated from many of the relevant costs.

These problems appear to have been most pronounced in unitary governance structures that imposed a single 'solution'. Nonetheless, even in more fractured governance regimes where in theory 'different sides' could have been taken in different places, the deployment of contagion narratives, the pressures towards conformity of professional and public opinion discussed previously, and moral certainties about who was in the 'wrong' often coalesced to overwhelm that pluralism. The latter dangers may be especially pronounced in any discursive context where 'war' narratives and metaphors are commonplace. As Walter Lippman once explained:

> The war spirit identifies dissent with treason, the pursuit of private happiness with slackerism and sabotage, and on the other side obedience with discipline, conformity with patriotism. Thus, at one stroke war extinguishes the difficulties of planning, cutting out from any individual any moral ground on which he might resist the execution of the official plan.[69]

[68] On these, see, e.g., Centre for Social Justice (2023) *Two Nations: The State of Poverty in the UK*, London: CSJ.

[69] Lippman, W. (1936) *The Good Society*, New York: Grosset and Dulop, 67.

Undermining agency

The final similarity to note between the practices of lifestyle epidemiology and the COVID-19 response was the use of discursive concepts that downplayed the scope for private agency and the deployment of techniques that might further diminish the scope for that agency. Specifically, the focus on a contagion that demanded social distancing combined with a discourse depicting agents as prone to free-riding constructed an inexorable logic where draconian intervention by central government agencies *was the only option*. By so constructing these problems, the cultural heterogeneity and the plural or subjective rationality of the relevant agents may thus have been neglected, with differential individual and cultural propensities to free-ride or to perceive issues as having a collective goods structure erased from view. While it does not rule out scenarios where collective goods would be insufficiently supplied through decentralised mechanisms, the Foucauldian/postmodern liberal perspective questions such essentialist understandings. Whether a good has collective good properties and whether this compromises the viability and efficiency of a pluralist model may be *culturally contingent*. In the context of pandemics, it may be that the governance challenge does not equate to a *singular* collective action problem but involves a *plurality* of localised collective action problems—the structure of which may vary according to the cultural characteristics and beliefs of the populations concerned.

Seen through this lens the apparent unwillingness of public bureaucracies, public health experts, much of the media, and public opinion to countenance such pluralism may have reflected the now routinised dominance of pastoral discourses that privilege the role of public regulators in speaking 'for and above' subjects and that denude the potential for the latter to exercise more localised agency. On the one hand, the contagion and externality discourse provided 'externality entrepreneurs' in public health bureaucracies and interest groups with a communicative resource to secure additional power and resources at the expense of other actors. On the other hand, the institutionalisation of a discursive formation within public organisations and the media that depicts the structural properties of infectious diseases as large-scale collective action dilemmas, reinforced by the circulation of emergency/contagion narratives, may have worked to *produce* a subjectivity of helplessness on the part of many citizens—a situation where self-governance was experienced as a practical impossibility and where those concerned demanded that controls be imposed on themselves and on others. Indeed, far from helping subjects consider different possibilities in responding to the pandemic, there is evidence that public health agencies deliberately used behavioural techniques to *panic* the population into supporting the measures adopted. As one scientist from the UK pandemic advisory group subsequently explained:

> In March 2020 the government was very worried about compliance, and they thought people would not want to be locked down. There were discussions about fear being needed to encourage compliance and decisions were made about how to ramp up the fear.[70]

To problematise the use of such techniques is not to imply that there might have been satisfactory responses to the pandemic that allowed more room for individual agency. Rather, it is to suggest that dominant public health discourses may have worked to influence what was considered true about the requirements of pandemic response *irrespective of whether they were true*. Behavioural techniques that emphasised the need to correct 'faulty' understandings of risk may have prevented individuals and communities from discovering whether they might have crafted satisfactory responses without recourse to centrally imposed and disciplinary solutions. As the previous pages have shown, such techniques have become the hallmark of the public health *dispositif*.

Resisting the public health *dispositif*

The forgoing analysis has highlighted the processes through which alignments or strategic codifications between state power and more decentred forms of power may be working to suppress freedom and pluralism. While it would be inaccurate to describe this state of affairs as one of domination, the prevailing scientistic and managerialist approach to public health represents a significant threat to freedom nonetheless, and one that may require some form of resistance if the space within which subjects may be exposed to alternative ways of thinking and of being governed is to be preserved or expanded.

An important element of any such strategy is likely to entail a refusal of scientific narratives that attribute excessive responsibility for health status to individual choices. Now, it may seem strangely incongruent for an approach describing itself as *liberal* to question the responsibility of individuals in this way. Those adopting such a stance typically consider themselves *critics* of liberalism precisely because in their view the latter attributes 'too much' responsibility for personal outcomes to the fiction of an autonomously choosing subject.

[70] Rayner, G. Use of fear to control behaviour in Covid crisis was 'totalitarian' admit scientists, *The Telegraph*, 14 May 2021, https://www.telegraph.co.uk/news/2021/05/14/scientists-admit-totalitarian-use-fear-control-behaviour-covid/.

Left Foucauldians and advocates of social medicine, for example, argue that with its preference for statistical risk profiles to 'guide' consumers towards 'healthier choices', lifestyle epidemiology legitimates and sustains 'neo-liberal' discourses that 'responsibilise' subjects for their health in ways that allow governments to escape greater responsibility for financing and structuring an environment within which people might live healthier lives.

On a postmodern liberal view, however, resisting the discourse of 'health responsibility' *does not* imply rejecting the value of individual choice, and neither does it provide justification for the transfer of responsibility for lifestyles to government agencies. What it may require is the cultivation of a properly sceptical attitude towards scientistic models that claim to identify a more, or less, precise set of behaviours to be adopted in the name of health and against which individuals or their governments might be judged or held to account.

In terms of individual lifestyle decisions, this scepticism is compatible with the adoption of some broad yet simple rules of thumb that caution individuals against extreme practices around alcohol, food, tobacco, and sedentary lifestyles. In the context of state action equivalent rules might discourage public guidance that favours prescriptive dietary regimes or subsidises specific food stuffs and industries. Similarly, where governments have facilitated the creation of transport models that privilege the private car and made it harder for people to exercise by walking or cycling, then attempts to counteract these effects may contribute to greater pluralism. Though not rejecting government action in this limited sense, a resistant discourse most certainly would oppose *wholesale* efforts to engineer changes to people's lifestyles such as their 'food environments' through synoptic models of government control—models implicitly or explicitly favoured by the social medicine perspective. If health is understood as a complex rather than a simple phenomenon, then the notion of 'responsibilising' government agencies for people's health is worthy of as much if not greater scepticism than 'neo-liberal' strategies that 'responsibilise' individuals for their health status. The social medicine perspective would grant even greater power and positionality to a class of public health experts not only to 'guide' or to 'nudge' decision-makers but also to plan much of the environment within which people live their lives in a manner overriding the diverse and situated knowledge of those concerned. The process of multiplying disciplinary and bio-political controls presented in this chapter illustrates how rapidly a positive rights or capabilities discourse can generate a dynamic that progressively squeezes out the space for personal agency, overriding the desires and preferences of subjects in the name of promoting 'their freedom'.

Seen in this light, an important way of reframing how people experience the governance of lifestyle may be to move towards a genuinely *entrepreneurial* understanding of the challenge that maintaining health presents. Though Left

Foucauldians and social medicine theorists routinely describe approaches that assign probabilities for ill health to specific behaviours as 'neo-liberal',[71] these approaches are better understood as managerialist or technocratic and are anything but entrepreneurial in character. An entrepreneurial approach would recognise that where health outcomes reflect a complex constellation of factors, exercising choice over lifestyle governance may allow people to have a sense of agency in their lives while also recognising that many outcomes may be beyond their or anybody else's capacity to predict or to control. If human health is part of a voyage of exploration where nothing is static, then people might exercise their creative capacities in a process of adventure and agonistic struggle rather than seeking to live according to mechanistic rules. While people may use such rules to give shape to their lives, choice matters precisely because it allows subjects to engage actively with the world around them, constituting themselves by exercising judgement in a context of genuine uncertainty rather than one of calculable risk.

An entrepreneurial counter-discourse around public health would thus emphasise that granting room for choice over lifestyle may empower people to make the most of whatever agency they have *without* any suggestion that they can be held responsible for all that happens to them. It may also allow for a greater degree of empathy for those who come to experience ill health than a scientistic model that attributes health outcomes to calculable causes and that seeks the submission of subjects to a panoply of disciplinary or bio-political controls, often for no discernible reward. Such a discourse would allow people to experience their freedom and health differently by reducing feelings of guilt, responsibility, or shame should they succumb to unforeseeable or uncontrollable events. This view should not, however, be confused with a fatalist stance that denies the possibility of improvements in scientific knowledge such as, for example, various gene therapies that may improve both longevity and quality of life. Rather, it implies that whatever improvements are generated in this regard, new and unanticipated problems will arise in their wake which will themselves generate the need for new and often *divergent* practices of freedom.

A corollary of adopting this entrepreneurial and open-ended approach implies resistance against the one-dimensional 'healthism' and 'safetyism' which sees people imposing restrictions on themselves and their willingness to support state-imposed limits on others. The implication of such pastoral framings is that uncertainty can be minimised through submission to greater regulatory control. Even on its own terms, however, if people seek to avoid uncertainty either through their own actions or those of public authorities, the result may not be a safer or less uncertain world but one where subjects have no experience of

[71] For example, Mayes, C. (2016) *The Bio-Politics of Lifestyle*, London: Routledge.

navigating *ineradicable* uncertainties and developing the capacities to deal with or adapt to them. A resistant discourse would thus refuse the binary between 'safety' and 'danger', emphasising instead that there may be no safety without exposure to danger. It would also challenge the potentially oppressive presence of rules that while promising to prolong people's lives may simply deprive them of valuable experiences and interactions while they are alive. Though it was undoubtedly an extreme case, there could be no clearer instance of the latter tendency than denying many elderly persons in the final stages of their lives the right to interact with family members by pandemic-induced policies justified in the name of 'protecting health'.

A Foucauldian or postmodern liberal alternative to the scientistic narratives that dominate contemporary public health discourse might thus seek to cultivate an 'aesthetics of life and health' that allows the challenge of balancing health concerns with other valued goals to be approached in varied and open-ended ways. One important example of such an aesthetic is provided by the 'body positive' movement that has emerged in recent years to challenge an unduly normalising approach to body weight associated with both scientistic approaches to obesity and pressures to conform to an aesthetic of 'thinness' propagated by the fashion and beauty industries. Body positive groups such as those involved in the Body Image Network provide a setting within which people can debate and discuss different approaches to dietary governance to avoid potentially dangerous eating excesses without succumbing to an obsessive or disciplinary focus on achieving a specific body mass index or conforming to prevailing stereotypes of male or female beauty.[72] The presence of these groups and the changes in attitudes they have prompted have increasingly fed into commercial practices with a growing number of fashion and beauty outlets now catering specifically to the body positive market. Such movements need not be construed as being in direct opposition to an 'oppressive' medical profession or the 'body fascism' of the conventional fashion and beauty industries but as a creative force that helps subjects develop new practices of freedom and to negotiate their way through the thicket of normative pressures in their lives.

The example of the body positive movement also challenges another binary within contemporary public health debates. Many critics of approaches that emphasise the importance of personal agency brand them as being excessively 'individualistic' or as having an overly 'heroic' understanding of entrepreneurship—suggesting that they neglect the opportunity for more

[72] Beausoleil, N. (2009) 'An Impossible Task? Preventing Disordered Eating in the Context of the Current Obesity Panic', in Wright, J., and Harwood, V., eds. (2009) *Bio-Politics and the Obesity Epidemic*, New York: Routledge. See also Bacon, L. (2010) *Health at Every Size: The Surprising Truth About Your Weight*, Dallas, TX: Benbella Books; Heyes, C. (2007) 'Foucault Goes to Weightwatchers', *Hypatia* 21 (2): 126–49.

collective forms of resistance where subjects exercise a 'care of the self' in a setting of community-based collective action.[73] Others maintain that the values of body positivity are a manifestation of a 'neo-liberalism' that places the onus on subjects in dealing with how they experience their bodies rather than placing the responsibility on 'society' to change its normalising attitudes towards those concerned.[74]

There is, however, nothing in the Foucauldian or postmodern liberal stance that need reduce an entrepreneurial narrative of health to an atomised, narrowly individualistic, or 'heroic' conception of the subject. Team production is as important an aspect of market activity as more individualised modes, and so too group-based activities may be as much a part of resistance to normalising public heath narratives whether these emanate from science or from commerce, as may be forms of self-help. Whether they engage in resistance to power privately or through social movements, what matters is that group-based entities or their representatives are not empowered to act 'for or above' the individual. Entrepreneurial freedom does not exclude collective action from its armoury of resistance techniques. Rather, it recognises that the potential for such action can only be perceived through creative acts of individual agency as subjects *choose* to resist on their own or by joining in concert with others. Such acts of individual and collective resistance may entail a 'care of the self', cultivating a personal sense of self-esteem, but they may also contribute incrementally to the transformation of the normative pressures resisted as those who subscribe to such norms are alerted to alternative ways of thinking about health and beauty and how they may impact the experience of others.

Maintaining a space where this individual and collective resistance to normalising public health imperatives may be exercised may also require challenging attempts to further centralise governance arrangements and where possible to introduce greater competition into the production of public health discourse and regulation. An excessive belief in scientistic expertise tends to generate or sustain support for monopolistic organisations that then act as arbiters of a unitary scientific 'truth'. Those empowered with such authority are in turn shielded from the feedback and reflexivity that comes where there are rival centres of decision-making authority. As with the macroeconomic management models discussed in chapter 3, once centralised governance structures or 'big players' are empowered to police the truth by closing-down nodes of opposition through legislative authority, then the harder it becomes for those subjected to this power to conceive of alternatives to the explanatory categories of the *dispositif* and the more decentred exercises of power it sustains. In the context

[73] For an example, see Mayes, *The Bio-Politics of Lifestyle*, esp. chaps. 7 and 8.
[74] Cooper, C. (2016) *Fat Activism: A Radical Social Movement*, Bristol: HammerOn Press.

of the COVID-19 pandemic, for example, while many countries chose to adopt lockdown arrangements, others such as Sweden and United States' jurisdictions, such as Florida and North Dakota, followed a different path, allowing for a gradual spread of the virus through the population. It remains unclear which, if any, of these approaches 'worked best', but absent such dissident, marginalised, or heterotopic models, then the scope for subjects to conceive of alternatives to the dominant narrative would have been reduced if not eradicated as opportunity costs or counterfactuals would have been suppressed or hidden from view. It follows that attempts to assert greater central control or harmonisation of public health policies in otherwise federal or decentralised government systems, or at the international level, efforts to instantiate 'global governance' by empowering institutions such as the WHO to enforce common policies, may require resistance. A fractured governance regime, though it cannot guarantee pluralism of thought and action, may increase the possibility that subjects will be exposed to alternative ways of governing their health and lifestyles and sustain an atmosphere of generalised scepticism towards the power/knowledge claims of organised science and other corporate groupings.

Away from this, efforts might also be made to break the quasi-monopolistic powers generated by the large-scale state financing of public health research. The latter has typically been justified on the grounds that private funding allows for the corruption of the scientific enterprise as for-profit companies sponsor research reflecting their own commercial imperatives rather than a commitment to scientific 'truth'. Yet, the experience of the public health *dispositif* shows that when governments are 'big players' in the market for truth, either funding the research themselves or in partnership with business and/or using it to inform their rules and regulations, then those researchers who do not conform to the prevailing political wisdom are likely to find themselves disciplined and marginalised. Similarly, large-scale public funding may exacerbate tendencies towards 'herd behaviour' where once a dominant coalition leverages the distribution of public revenue, it can exercise a combination of agenda setting and disciplinary power over much of the research ecosystem, narrowing the scope for alternative voices to be seen and heard.[75]

It is unlikely that such dynamics can be entirely removed from any system, but a decentralised model combining competitive for-profit industry research with not-for-profit philanthropic alternatives may contain them. Where the claims of any for-profit or not-for-profit organisation can be contested by those of rivals, then regardless of whether the research is conducted out of commercial

[75] For a discussion of these dynamics in the context of the nutritional research discussed earlier see Taubes, G. (2007) *Good Calories, Bad Calories: Challenging the Conventional Wisdom on Diet, Weight Control and Disease*, New York: Knopf.

self-interest, professional or political self-aggrandisement, or the public-spirited pursuit of scientific endeavour, the push and pull across rival networks of power may help weaken the claims of any one network. It may also work to sustain a generalised scepticism that vaccinates subjects against those who would police the conditions of their life and death.

7

Bio-Power and the Political Economy of Ecological Order

The Sustainability *Dispositif*

Introduction

Where discourses of social justice and public health governance appear to be proliferating a network of bio-political constraints that may limit pluralism and freedom, what will be referred to in this chapter as the *sustainability dispositif* is a constellation of parallel discourses with the potential to develop still more totalising dynamics of pastoral control. Though ecological problems such as loss of species diversity and anthropogenic climate change are real phenomena, the grids of intelligibility through which they are currently conceptualised imply a potentially unprecedented expansion in the terrain of surveillance, normalisation, and regulation that seeks to make the entire earth subject to an ecological pastorship.

The analysis that follows presents a critical political economy focussed on the confluence of discourses that generate and sustain this *dispositif*. The critical examination of these discourses and the institutional practices to which they have given rise does not deny the potential seriousness of ecological challenges but aims instead to question the underlying epistemic assumptions, showing that certain narratives and the strategic logics that connect these discourses with sovereign state power and more decentred forms of power may weaken freedom and pluralism. Specifically, it will be argued that dominant environmental discourses rely on a scientific naturalism and an explicit or implicit positivism that erases the significance of socio-ecological complexity; these discourses moralise interpersonal conflict in ways that threaten ethical pluralism; they essentialise the character traits of both people and their environments; and they are prone to a 'politics of catastrophe' that generates a disciplinary logic often associated with states of war. The discussion concludes by suggesting some discursive-institutional possibilities for resisting the sustainability dispositif while recognising that there may be some environmental conflicts that cannot be addressed without a potentially unchecked form of this ecological 'bio-power' coming to fruition.

Foucault and Liberal Political Economy. Mark Pennington, Oxford University Press. © Mark Pennington 2025.
DOI: 10.1093/9780197690550.003.0007

Discourses of ecological order

Contemporary environmental social movements are characterised by perspectival diversity and the absence of any sovereign or ruling point of view. Nonetheless, there are discernible confluences between these movements and the discourses through which they define and pursue their goals that have played a significant role in shaping the social construction of ecological dilemmas and the growth of what might be referred to as the contemporary 'bio-political state'. Though they have no specific date of origin, the discursive components that inform this state were crystallised in the Brundtland Report, *Our Common Future*, first published in 1987, which projected the concept of 'sustainable development' on a global scale.[1] Prior to this the construction of ecological dilemmas emerged in a more decentred vein from the activities of multiple environmental campaign groups, media commentaries, and documentaries, alongside the activities of natural and social scientific analysts working for government bodies and international agencies. In subsequent decades sustainability memes and concepts have spread via the publications and statements of international organisations and in various treaties and accords. In 2015, for example, the United Nations General Assembly adopted Agenda 2030 listing seventeen sustainable development goals, alongside 269 sustainability indicators and 169 sustainability targets for its member states. The currency of this *dispositif* is also evident in the 'action plans' now put forward by nation-states and regional groupings, such as the European Union, to meet the relevant targets. These plans have also spawned legislative and regulatory action by sublocal authorities mediated through mechanisms such as the UN Local Agenda 21 process and the more recent Agenda 2030.

Most of these international arrangements are voluntary, but they have been widely adopted by many countries to inform a regulatory framework in which national, regional, and local agencies seek to align on environmental goals and targets. Increasingly, key aspects of the discourse have also been adopted by businesses and corporations as they negotiate a strategic regulatory field infused with sustainability memes and a market environment where consumers and environmental NGOs exert pressure on them to abide by specific practices—notably through the proliferation of environmental, social, and governance (ESG) initiatives. The latter represent a confluence of both 'top-down' and 'bottom-up' forces. In the former instance national governments, aligned with international statements, agreements, or treaties, produce formal guidelines about the production and consumption processes compatible with sustainable development; while in the latter pressure groups, NGOs and private businesses lobby

[1] World Commission on Environment and Development (1987) *Our Common Future*, Oxford: Oxford University Press.

for changes both to the content of the guidelines and for specific interpretations of the rules, standards, and procedures required to meet them. Within this context, it is possible to discern three discursive or narrative frames that either individually or by way of shifting discursive alliances constitute the sustainability *dispositif* and what might be referred to in Foucauldian terms as a ruling 'environmental governmentality'.

Discourses of ecological equilibrium

The first of the three discourses constituting this 'environmental governmentality' draws on a scientific naturalism prevalent early in the twentieth century and witnessed in the then-emergent science of ecology. The status of this naturalism remains deeply controversial with an important *motif* in ecological discourse being the subordination or mastery of nature by modernist science—a science held to have had damaging consequences both for the natural world and for humanity alike.[2] Notwithstanding this tension, a central theme in the strategies of many campaign groups has been the use or appropriation of scientific naturalist concepts to highlight the damaging consequences of human interventions in environmental systems.

According to the paradigm dominating much of twentieth-century environmental thought, ecological systems typically exist in or have a tendency towards a stable equilibrium. This was initially expressed in the 'balance of nature' concept which suggested that outside exogenous shocks, such as volcanic eruptions, nature was unchanging or with any changes being so small and slow as to be indistinguishable from a state of rest.[3] Subsequent ecological science abandoned the idea of equilibrium states, recognising instead a less static view of ecology where change is generated endogenously but where the relevant changes are framed as a series of evolutionary adaptations leading towards a longer term equilibrium state.[4] This teleological understanding came to be expressed in concepts such as ecological succession and climax ecology. Though natural systems are not stable, according to this discourse endogenous changes within them, such as droughts, fires, or the influences on habitats by the breeding or predatory patterns of various species, proceed through a series of 'law-like' stages culminating in a 'climax

[2] On this see, e.g., Alford, C. (1985) *Science and the Revenge of Nature*, Gainesville: Florida University Presses; Gorz, A. (1975) *Ecology as Politics*, London: Pluto Press.

[3] For a history of this concept, see Egerton, F. (1973) 'Changing Concepts of the Balance of Nature', *Quarterly Review of Biology*, 48 (2): 322–50.

[4] Following Worster, D. (1909/77) *Nature's Economy: A History of Ecological Ideas*, Cambridge: Cambridge University Press.

equilibrium', the parameters of which are determined by relatively stable climatic or other background conditions.[5]

Viewed through this equilibrium lens, outside of major convulsions, such as geological shifts, the main source of instability or 'disorder' within ecological processes is human 'intervention' in naturalistic laws.[6] Ecological orders are closed systems that operate in an otherwise stable or stationary state and with human action in the form of resource use, agricultural and industrial production framed as a source of exogenous shocks.[7] This discourse does not, however, necessarily see *all* human action in these terms. In recent incarnations the concept of the Anthropocene recognises that most 'natural' systems are intertwined with human activity, with many ecological phenomena seen as the product of a complex *co-evolution*.[8] Alongside this recognition is a less teleological understanding of ecological systems, which appreciates non-linearity and disequilibrium. Nonetheless, what is emphasised in modern systems ecology is the scale of the dynamism wrought by human action since the Industrial Revolution and the possibility that this scale of change may exceed certain thresholds. It is the emphasis on 'thresholds', 'limits', or 'tipping points' that is centred in the discourse of 'sustainable development'.[9]

In systems ecology, resources are seen as fixed in composition and quantity with concepts such as 'sustainable yield' or 'optimal population' used to guide decision-making via statistical modelling and the identification of the human actions that should be controlled or curtailed and those considered 'unsustainable'. Modelling focuses on aggregate variables measuring non-renewable resource stocks, the absorptive capacity of waste sinks, the populations of various species, and with interactions between these statistical categories used to predict or to simulate systemic effects. These exercises informed highly influential reports such as the Limits to Growth publications of the 1970s and 1980s that

[5] Clements, F. (1936) 'Nature and the Structure of Climax', *Journal of Ecology*, 24 (1): 252–84—for the notion of climate-centred equilibrium. Tansley, A. (1939) 'British Ecology During the Past Quarter Century: The Plant Community and the Ecosystem', *Journal of Ecology*, 27 (2): 513–30—considers other background factors in climax equilibrium as well as climate.

[6] For example, Soule, M. (1985) 'What Is Conservation Biology', *Bio Science*, 35 (11): 727–34.

[7] Odum, E. (1964) 'The New Ecology', *Bio Science*, 14 (7): 14–16; Odum, E. (1969) 'The Strategy of Eco-system Development', *Science*, 164: 252.

[8] Use of the term 'Anthropocene' was first popularised by Crutzen, P., and Stoermer, E. (2000) 'The Anthropocene', *Global Change Newsletter*, 41 (May): 17–18—see also, Kareiva, P., and Marieva, M. (2012) 'What Is Conservation Science', *Bio Science*, 62 (11): 962–9; Ruddiman, W. (2013) 'The Anthropocene', *Annual Review of Earth, and Planetary Science*, 41: 45–68.

[9] For example, Steffen, W., Crutzen, P., and McNeill, J. (2007) 'The Anthropocene: Are Humans Now Overwhelming the Great Forces of Nature?', *Ambio*, 36 (8): 614–21: See also Rockstrom, J., Steffen J., Noone, K., Persson, A., Stuart Chapin, F., Lambin, E., Lenton, T., Scheffer, M., Folke, C., Schellnhuber, H., Nykvist, V., de Wit, C., Hughes, T., Van der Leeuw, S., Rodhe, H., Sorlin, S., Snyder, P., Costanza, R., Svedin, U., Falkenmark, M., Karlberg, L., Corell, R., Fabry, V., Hansen, J., and Foley, J. (2009) 'A Safe Operating Space for Humanity', *Nature*, 461: 472–5.

identified potential 'crisis' or 'emergency' scenarios.[10] More recently, they have been witnessed in the reports of the International Panel on Climate Change (IPCC) which set out a range of scenarios for 'safe' and 'unsafe' levels of anthropogenic climate disturbance.[11] Elsewhere, NASA's vision for a new 'earth system science' seeks to simulate the entire earth system and how its component elements will evolve across multiple time scales. The European Union's 'Destination Earth' project also aims to develop a digital view of the earth to develop a stimulus-response model which can predict the interaction between natural systems and human activity.

Crucially, in all these discursive constructions, human populations cannot be left to their own devices to moderate, change, or adapt their behaviour without guidance from those with access to the relevant scientific expertise.[12] People in general are constructed as lacking the necessary data to understand how their localised actions may impact the ecological systems on whose health they depend and/or as lacking the incentives or value orientation to act in accordance with the relevant limits. It follows that they must be constrained by regulatory controls or behavioural inducements devised by ecological scientists and managers who are positioned to have the appropriate knowledge and values.[13]

Discourses of economic equilibrium

Though they differ in important respects, the equilibrium narrative of systems ecology has many parallels with economic discourses of environmental governance. The dominant paradigm in environmental economics is that of neo-classical welfare theory.[14] This perspective departs from systems ecology in questioning the 'limits to growth' narrative. From a neo-classical standpoint, resources of various kinds can *always* be substituted for one another such that materials consumed in the process of production have been used efficiently if the outputs they generate are judged to be of greater value than the inputs used to produce them. It follows that human-created capital, such as factories, technology, and the goods they produce, may substitute for the loss of 'natural

[10] Meadows, D., Randers, J., and Behrens, W. (1972) *The Limits to Growth*, New York: Universe Books; Meadows, D., and Randers, J. (1992) *Beyond the Limits: Confronting Global Collapse, Envisioning a Sustainable Future*, Post Mills, VT: Chelsea Green.

[11] International Panel on Climate Change (2018) *Global Warming of 1.5 Degrees C: An IPCC Special Report*, Geneva: IPCC.

[12] Lovejoy, T. (1989) 'The Obligations of a Biologist', *Conservation Biology* 3(4): 329–30.

[13] Bierman, F. (2014) *Earth System Governance: World Politics in the Anthropocene*, Cambridge, MA: MIT Press.

[14] Notably, Mishan, E. J. (1981) *Introduction to Normative Economics*, Oxford: Oxford University Press; Baumol, W., and Oates, W. (1975) *The Theory of Environmental Policy*, Englewood Cliffs, NJ: Prentice Hall.

capital'.[15] Calculations of the relevant values may in turn be reflected in market-generated prices or in governmental substitutes for such prices.

In this 'weak sustainability' discourse economic systems are understood to secure an efficient equilibrium when all Pareto-improving or welfare-enhancing opportunities for individuals or organisations have been exhausted. Departures from such equilibria are explained as institutional failures associated with the characteristics of environmental goods. 'Market failures' or 'decentralisation failures' reflect the 'non-excludability' of goods, which allows actors to impose costs or externalities on others and/or secure access without paying the costs for producing or sustaining the goods in question.

This focus on external or unaccounted costs is compatible with an ethical focus on protecting negative rights of persons and property from unwanted 'interference', and where those who are 'interfered' with might secure some form of compensation or redress. In practice, however, most environmental economists work with an aggregative utilitarian frame that aims to equalise private and 'social costs' rather than one that conceives of externalities as disputes or boundary crossings between subjects who hold to different and perhaps incommensurable values. One reason for this follows from the belief that bargaining or transaction costs between individuals may be 'too high' such that a 'welfare maximising' or 'cooperative' solution must be imposed on the relevant parties from *outside*.[16] The latter conceptualises a two-stage process whereby economic experts first calculate and assign a welfare-maximising value to environmental goods and then select the most efficient mechanism to secure this value. The choice between using 'incentives', such as taxes or subsidies, to induce the desired behavioural and technological changes indirectly or the deployment of direct regulation to mandate the production techniques or modes of consumption to deliver the desired outcome depends on a comparative assessment of the costs of monitoring and enforcing these alternatives in different settings.[17]

Neo-classical welfare theory remains the dominant perspective in environmental economics but has increasingly coalesced with what was initially a counter-discourse known as 'ecological economics'.[18] The latter challenges the

[15] For example, Warford, J., and Pearce, D. (1993) *World Without End: Economics, Environment and Sustainable Development*, Washington, DC: World Bank; Beckerman, W. (1995) 'How Would You Like Your Sustainability Sir: Weak or Strong? A Reply to My Critics', *Environmental Values*, 4 (2): 167–79.

[16] The 'Stern Review' described anthropogenic climate change as the 'greatest market failure the world has ever known'—see Stern, N. (2007) *The Economics of Climate Change*, Cambridge: Cambridge University Press.

[17] Mishan, *Introduction to Normative Economics*; Baumol and Oates, *Theory of Environmental Policy*.

[18] Pioneers include Daly, H. (1977/1991) *Steady State Economics*, Washington, DC: Island Press; Cobb, J., and Daly, H. (1989) *For the Common Good*, Boston: Beacon Press; Martinez Allier, J., and Schlupmann, K. (1987) *Ecological Economics: Energy, Environment and Society*, Oxford: Blackwell.

contention that there are no limits to growth owing to the substitutability of assets, suggesting instead that certain forms of 'natural capital' are *irreplaceable.*[19] Rather than seeing human action as an exogenous intervention, ecological economics frames such action as part of complex *interdependencies* constrained by the second law of thermodynamics and the concept of entropy. This perspective recognises that economic processes transform available energy into unavailable or waste energy.[20] While joining neo-classicism in rejecting Malthusian claims that humanity may 'run out' of resources such as food, minerals, or energy, ecological economics emphasises the possibility that as humans 'solve' scarcity constraints they may exceed various 'systemic limits', including the capacity of the earth's atmosphere to assimilate wastes. The discourse thus combines the language of modern systems ecology with that of mainstream neo-classical theory, referring to ecological 'producers' and 'consumers', concepts such as 'sustainable yield' and 'energy budget efficiency', and the importance of maintaining 'critical natural capital'. Within this context, the carrying capacity of the earth is seen to provide a biological or law-like constraint through which to govern human action.[21] Economic growth must stay within these 'limits' or must be 'decoupled' from processes that deplete natural capital.

Instead of the neo-classical emphasis on incremental modifications within a linear system, the concept of 'strong sustainability' in ecological economics emphasises non-linear processes and the possibility of socio-ecological collapse when 'tipping points' are reached. This understanding aligns with interpretations of the Anthropocene that while recognising the co-evolution of humans and ecology also considers risks from the scale of human-induced change. With uncertainty about when various 'tipping points', crises, or ecological emergencies may be reached, the discourse emphasises a highly risk-averse or precautionary stance with the focus on maintaining a 'steady state' economy[22] or in some cases favouring 'de-growth'.[23] On this understanding 'emergency situations' or 'existential threats' require a radical extension of the neo-classical concept of externalities to include the full-cost pricing of 'ecosystem services' such as climate and biodiversity—a pricing that should reflect the high-risk premium ecological economics ascribes to these services. Within this context,

[19] Neumayer, E. (2007) 'A Missed Opportunity: The Stern Review on Climate Change Fails to Tackle the Issue of Non-Substitutable Loss of Natural Capital', *Global Environmental Change*, 17 (3–4): 297–301.

[20] Georgescu-Roegen, N. (1971) *The Entropy Law and the Economic Process*, Cambridge, MA: Harvard University Press.

[21] For an early articulation see Boulding, K. 'The Economics of the Coming Spaceship Earth', in Jarrett, H., ed. (1966) *Environmental Quality in a Growing Economy*, Resources for the Future, Baltimore, MD: John Hopkins University Press.

[22] Daly, *Steady State Economics.*

[23] Kallis, G., Kerschner, C., and Martinez Alier, J. (2012) 'The Economics of De-Growth', *Ecological Economics*, 84: 172–80.

insurance metaphors are frequently invoked to suggest that while there is no certainty of ecological collapse, environmental controls reduce the likelihood of such collapse and reflect a 'better safe than sorry' strategy.

Though highly precautionary in this regard, this construction also justifies radical interventions to shift the socio-economic trajectory, including a strong preference for 'missionary' government policies[24] to galvanise public and private actors in the shift to clean technologies such as renewable energy and decoupling from carbon-intensive production, or in still more radical narratives towards a new socio-economic model based on 'de-growth'. In contexts where radical uncertainty about future trajectories may paralyse decision-makers, preventing them from moving towards more sustainable paths, bold government actions are seen as necessary to break out of path-dependent dynamics and to build a critical mass of confidence about the direction of socio-economic change. In this sense, the ecological economics discourse is heavily influenced by Keynesian constructions that envisage sovereign state power as a 'steering mechanism' that enables private agents to negotiate coordination problems and other uncertainties.

Discourses of ecological democracy

Where the systems ecology and economic discourses favour an expert-centred conception of environmental governance, a third set of discourses assert the importance of collective democratic sovereignty or control over socio-ecological systems. These narratives do not question the potential for ecological crisis, and neither do they challenge economic understandings of market and decentralisation 'failures'. Rather, what they challenge is the focus on scientific or expert forms of control combined with a generalised suspicion of 'uncontrolled' market institutions.

The critique of expert rule and of markets in ecological democracy has both an epistemic and an ethical component. The former, instead of centring knowledge in expert managers or in the price system, emphasises multiple and differently situated 'stakeholders' who must be empowered to communicate different forms of know-how through participation in public dialogue. On this account, scientific expertise and markets are incapable of reflecting the complexity of socio-ecological interrelationships and of taking account of knowledge that cannot be expressed scientifically or in the form of exchange ratios.[25]

[24] Mazzucato, M. (2021) *Mission Economy: A Moon-Shot Guide to Changing Capitalism*, London: Allen Lane; Pettifor, A. (2019) *The Case for the Green New Deal*, London: Verso.

[25] Dryzek, J. (1992) 'Ecology and Discursive Democracy: Beyond Liberal Capitalism and the Administrative State', *Capitalism, Nature, Socialism*, 3 (2): 18–42; Dryzek, J. (1996) 'Foundations for Environmental Political Economy: The Search for *Homo Ecologicus*?', *New Political Economy*,

The ethical component of this ecological stakeholderism focuses on the dangers from an excessively instrumental value orientation with modernist science and market institutions challenged for their treatment of human and non-human subjects as manipulable means to the achievement of managerial goals such as efficiency or economic growth. On this view, scientific experts and the growth imperatives of market economies fail to respect subjects as agents with goals of their own and as potential contributors to a dialogue not only about efficient means but also about the ethical status of different ends and their contribution to various common goods.[26] In principle this critique is compatible with a negative rights discourse where individuals are enabled to 'speak for themselves' rather than having their views overridden by scientific planners. In practice, however, ecological democrats frequently reject negative rights and private property on the grounds that the individualist value orientation they presuppose is incompatible with the *essentially* collective character of environmental goods. This suspicion of private property also follows from an interpretive grid that sees environmental problems as in large measure the products of cultural pressures within capitalism for subjects to judge themselves and others according to their capacity to consume and what it sees as the social injustice of the relevant inequalities of wealth and status.

In advancing a more reflexive and communitarian conception of collective rationality, these discourses favour the extension of participatory democracy and deliberative control to cover multiple interactions between human and ecological systems. The hubris of scientific expertise must be reined in through participatory mechanisms that subject its claims to contestation. Similarly, markets must be 'kept in their place' by a collective sovereignty lest they 'corrupt' environmental goods through bias towards the rich and the privileging of instrumental, self-interested, and consumerist orientations.[27] There is a corresponding hostility towards the idea of environmental assets being subject to private ownership and commodification, and a preference for restricting market relationships to a relatively small scale with suspicion of complex global trading relationships that exceed the capacity for states or lower level jurisdictions to exercise deliberative control.[28]

The preference for small-scale interactions combined with scepticism of science and technology in this discourse overlaps with the strongly precautionary

1: 27–40; Fischer, F. (2000) *Citizens, Experts, and the Environment: The Politics of Local Knowledge*, Durham, NC: Duke University Press.

[26] Dryzek, 'Ecology' and 'Foundations'.
[27] Dryzek, 'Ecology' and 'Foundations'.
[28] Dryzek, 'Ecology' and 'Foundations'. See also Anderson, E. (1990) 'The Ethical Limitations of the Market', *Economics and Philosophy*, 6 (2): 179–205.

approach of systems ecology and the more radical versions of ecological economics that favour a 'stationary state', or 'de-growth'. The neo-classical view that the choice between environmental taxes and direct regulation should result from a cost-benefit calculation is, however, rejected in favour of a moralised or expressive preference for regulations or mandatory product specifications as better placed to instantiate the 'common good'.[29] While emphasising localised forms of community control,[30] the focus on having a collective mission is also applied at higher levels of decision-making and overlaps with ecological modernisation and/or degrowth narratives that favour state-led missionary policies to achieve socio-ecological transformation on multiple different scales.[31]

The sustainability *dispositif*

It should be evident that though there are tensions between these discursive streams, there are also significant overlaps between them that allow public agencies, social movements, pressure groups, and private businesses to deploy discursive constructs and to forge the strategic alliances that work to produce and reproduce the constituent elements of a sustainability *dispositif*. First, there is a common grid of understanding focussed on 'limits', whether to current models of economic growth or moral limits to the kinds of relationships deemed commensurate with environmental protection. These narratives are accompanied by a focus on the potential for 'crisis' or 'emergency' should the relevant limits be breached. Second and relatedly, there is a common focus on solutions that involve some form of centralised or sovereign 'guidance' regarding either an aggregate notion of welfare or the 'common good' or what is 'socially responsible'. Though there is disagreement about who should exercise this role, the perceived need for a 'common mission' organised or guided by states or deliberative bodies is shared throughout. Third, there is a tendency towards an essentialisation of goods, people, or institutions. Environmental economics essentialises people by constructing human actors as selfish rational actors, while for ecological democracy the essentialisation applies to private property and capitalist markets, which by their very nature are considered to encourage or produce instrumental and egoistic forms of conduct. Finally, and overlapping with all these themes the *dispositif* is suspicious of 'unguided' market institutions and outcomes—and

[29] Dryzek, 'Foundations'.
[30] For example, Fischer, F. (2017) *Climate Crisis and the Democratic Prospect*, Oxford: Oxford University Press.
[31] For example, Hathaway, J. (2020) 'Climate Change, the Intersectional Imperative and the Opportunity of the Green New Deal', *Environmental Communication*, 14 (1): 13–22.

indeed of *any* decentralised processes not subject to some form of technical or moral shaping.

Problematising the sustainability *dispositif*

The discursive alignments underpinning this 'environmental governmentality' are, when seen from a Foucauldian or postmodern liberal perspective, best understood as *correctional dispositifs*—new incarnations or mutations of a 'pastoral power', which while not necessarily 'wrong' in all circumstances are pregnant with threats to freedom. To properly situate and to understand the character of these threats, however, it is important to specify what a critical approach to these discourses and their favoured institutions entails, and why they might endanger an open-ended process of ethical self-creation and self-governance.

In their different ways Foucault and postmodern liberals might easily be dismissed as contributors to 'anti-environmental' schools of thought. Foucault himself said and wrote little about the environmental movement, but his attitude towards ecology appears to have been one of indifference if not outright hostility. Darier, for example, reports that whenever Foucault was taken to visit a scenic landscape or vista, he protested—'my back is turned against it'.[32] More broadly, many within the environmental movement fear that postmodernist concepts lead to a corrosive relativism that undermines *any* scientific claims about environmentally damaging actions and moral judgements about those responsible for them. In the case of liberal political economy meanwhile, the emphasis on the growth-promoting qualities of open market economies is often aligned with a totalising and radically cornucopian stance that sees no environmental dangers in the permanent expansion of human populations and the economic processes required to sustain them.[33] The latter perspective has been interpreted by many critics as little more than an apology for financial and industrial capitalist interests who have benefitted from what these critics see as a regime of relatively unregulated market interactions.[34]

It will be the contention here, however, that such dismissals are unwarranted. A Foucauldian or postmodern liberalism *neither* favours *nor* opposes 'environmentalism' per se but offers a critical political economy sceptical of scientific naturalism and positivism, open-ended in its account of possible environmental governance practices, and wary of the threats to freedom from aggregative

[32] See Darier, E. (1996) *Discourses of the Environment*, Oxford: Blackwell, 5–6.

[33] This position is most closely associated with Julian Simon—e.g., Simon, J. (1996) *The Ultimate Resource 2*, Princeton, NJ: Princeton University Press. See also Lomborg, B. (2001) *The Sceptical Environmentalist*, Cambridge: Cambridge University Press.

[34] For example, Oreskes, N., and Conway, E. (2010) *Merchants of Doubt*, New York: Bloomsbury.

conceptions of welfare that attempt to assert purposive, pastoral control over self, society, and environment.

Destabilising ecological naturalism and ecological equilibrium

The first element of a problematisation of the sustainability *dispositif* in this regard follows from deep scepticism of equilibrium analyses both on grounds of descriptive inaccuracy and in providing normative benchmarks for judging socio-ecological relations. Specifically, the suggestion that ecosystems generate stable equilibria is informed by a mathematical formalism borrowed from the discourse of physics and engineering and from concepts of thermodynamics and control. In recent years, however, this perspective has been seriously undermined. Far from tending towards predictable processes of succession or climax, historical research has revealed ecological systems to have no discernible telos such that the notion of a stable natural state with which humans should not 'interfere' is called into doubt.[35] In place of a relatively stable 'balance of nature' operating in accordance with underlying laws, the emphasis now is on change, disequilibrium, and unpredictability. Where the systems ecology perspective operates with a mechanistic and teleological view of nature with species responding predictably to background conditions in closed communities, this new disequilibrium systems ecology understands ecological processes as closer to a shifting mosaic or kaleidoscope where patterning processes though discernible are at most temporary.[36]

On this more dynamic understanding, ecological concepts, and categories such as 'tropical rainforest' and 'savanna' are not defined by a stable species mix but are characterised by constant flux in species composition. Neither are these environments as long established and fragile in the face of human action as the equilibrium perspective might imply—in many instances they are relatively new incarnations, continually decomposing and recomposing in response to both natural and human-induced change.[37] Elsewhere, the inability of ecologists

[35] Worster, D. (1994) *Nature's Economy: A History of Ecological Ideas*, 2nd edn, Cambridge: Cambridge University Press.

[36] Botkin, D. (2012) *The Moon in the Nautilus Shell: Discordant Harmonies Reconsidered*, Oxford: Oxford University Press; Kricher, J. (2009) *The Balance of Nature: Ecology's Enduring Myth*, Princeton, NJ: Princeton University Press. See also Ruhl, J., and Salzman, J. (2010) 'Gaming the Past: The Theory and Practice of Historic Baselines in the Administrative State', *Vanderbilt Law Review* 64 (1): 1–57; Sullivan, S. (1996) 'Towards a Non-Equilibrium Ecology: Perspectives from an Arid Land', *Journal of Biogeography*, 23 (1): 1–5; Wiens, J. (1984) 'On Understanding a Non-Equilibrium World: Myth and Reality in Community Patterns and Processes', in Strong, D., Simberloff, D., Abel, L., and Thistle, A., eds. (1984) *Ecological Communities: Conceptual Issues and the Evidence*, Princeton, NJ: Princeton University Press;

[37] See previous note.

to discern differences in functioning between so-called heirloom and invaded ecosystems has destabilised categorisations of 'native' and 'invasive' species, which presuppose the existence of largely closed and equilibrated ecological 'communities' threatened by the arrival of human or non-human 'outsiders'.[38]

What all these analyses point towards is a more postmodern emphasis on dynamism, disequilibrium, and unpredictability that questions the idea of human action or intervention as a uniquely destabilising force. While some contributors to systems ecology and ecological economics recognise processes of co-evolution and non-linearity, they maintain that the unprecedented scale of human activity is creating the possibility of systemic tipping points that threaten sustainability.[39] Yet, it is precisely the suggestion that human action *alone* is the source of such unpredictable shifts that the disequilibrium ecology perspective undermines. Tipping points that result in radical shifts are part of an open-ended process where new ecosystems are constantly emerging and old ones destroyed. Studies of rapid desertification and soil erosion, for example, which had previously been thought to reflect human mismanagement, now suggest that human impacts are often dwarfed in their effects by those of dynamic and often unstable biophysical processes.[40]

From the disequilibrium standpoint, *both* human *and* ecological systems generate 'innovations' or 'mutations' that may have beneficial or damaging qualities. Though these innovations generate risks for the human and non-human occupants of current socio-ecological niches, they also have the potential to generate resilience and adaptiveness to unexpected events whether natural or human in origin. Moreover, as soon as human action is endogenised within the process of ecological motion, then agency-oriented concepts such as entrepreneurship and technological innovation, which continually challenge and push the boundaries of 'carrying capacity', must be accounted for. This is why the highly precautionary stance adopted by the discourse of ecological economics and ecological democracy is problematic. It is possible to accept that there may be current limits to human population and economic growth based on the capacity of natural systems to assimilate wastes while also recognising that further technological progress may enable humans to *transcend* those very limits. Seen in this light, adopting a precautionary approach and forestalling, or blocking,

[38] On this, see, e.g., Sagoff, M. (2009) 'Who Is the Invader?', *Social Philosophy and Policy*, 26 (2): 26–52.

[39] Dryzek, J. (2014) 'Institutions for the Anthropocene', *British Journal of Political Science*, 46: 937–56.

[40] Thomas, D., and Middleton, N. (1994) *Desertification: Exploding the Myth*, Chichester: Wiley; Fairhead, J., and Leach, M. (1996) *Misreading the African Landscape: Society and Ecology in a Forest-Savanna Mosaic*, Cambridge: Cambridge University Press; Stott, P. (1997) 'Dynamic Forest Ecology in an Unstable World', *Commonwealth Forestry Review*, 76 (3): 207–9; See also Forsyth, T. (2003) *Critical Political Ecology*, London: Routledge.

technological changes in favour of a stationary state *may* reduce systemic risk, but failing to adopt such technologies and forsaking economic growth may also increase exposure to known and unknown sources of naturally occurring as well as human-induced risks. Recognising system-level limits, therefore, does not speak decisively either in favour of a position seeking to restrict economic growth or of one that valorises it. The Foucauldian/postmodern liberal view challenges this binary, suggesting that *both* these positions amount to totalising acts of faith in the ability to scientifically predict what the future holds and the capacity to evaluate that future in advance of its emergence.

To destabilise the concepts of ecological equilibrium, closed systems and limits in this way should not, however, be taken to imply that people have no reason to conserve habitats or species or to seek to protect them from unwanted change. Subjects may resist change for aesthetic reasons; to seek repose from the tumult of the market economy; or to preserve identities connected to a heritage of social norms, rhythms, and routines entwined with the landscapes where they live. All that the disequilibrium perspective implies is that such actions cannot reliably be justified in naturalistic or scientific terms. Ecological and human interactions may be ordered in multiple different ways, none of which should necessarily be seen as more, or less, natural than another.

Similarly, this postmodern attitude must not be confused with a totalising cornucopian ethic that values entrepreneurial dynamism above all else. Postmodern liberalism appreciates that subjects may exercise their freedom by *resisting* or *refusing* the normalising pressures in market economies for innovation, growth, and consumption as part of a strategy of ethical self-creation and of self-governance. Those favouring de-growth, an anti-consumerist or monastic life, the continuation of traditional farming methods, or working for organisations that seek to rewild previously cultivated lands may be engaged in Foucauldian 'practices of freedom' and the pursuit of a particular 'aesthetics of the self', and such freedom requires institutions and rights that facilitate the exercise of these practices. Equally, however, other subjectivities may engage their freedom through entrepreneurial innovations that seek to open hitherto unthought of possibilities and to pursue 'limit experiences' against those that would constrain them within naturalistic categories. Maintaining freedom and pluralism thus requires a discursive and institutional space allowing for the push and pull of Apollonian traditions and discourses that exhibit reverence for established ways of being with Dionysian forces that challenge them.

It is, however, the possibility of such coexistence that is threatened by the limits narratives currently centred by the sustainability *dispositif*. The suggestion that these 'limits' are *objectively* definable produces an emphasis on identifying *the* sustainable option or options through scientific technique—whether a sustainable rate of economic growth, human population, or biodiversity. Yet, once it is recognised that categorisations such as 'sustainable use' are socially constructed, then it should be apparent that the 'policing' of these categories will reflect and may give rise to Foucauldian power effects. Specifically, instead of creating more space for freedom and the coexistence of plural and perhaps incommensurable aesthetics, values, and understandings, the discourse of ecological limits generates a normalising imperative which grants currency to the idea of a true 'ecological self' that respects 'nature' and a 'deviant self' that fails to do so. Rather than seeing different orientations towards nature and to economic activity as alternative practices of freedom, those challenging the relevant limits may be judged 'guilty' by the ecological pastorate of quasi-criminal breaches of naturalistic laws, labelled as ecological destroyers, and considered appropriate targets for social discipline.[41]

There is also a tendency in these narratives to speak 'for and above' human subjects, seeing them as uniquely vulnerable to or ignorant of the ecological consequences of their actions unless they are subject to pastoral control. The possibility that people may have the potential to build resilience in the face of change, whether natural or otherwise, and who might willingly partake in a voyage of exploration into the ecological unknown is never really considered. This orientation also leads to a systemic propensity to downplay or ignore the extent to which social interactions that proceed without pastoral intervention can adapt to problems of resource scarcity. One such example is the phenomenon of 'de-materialisation', where dynamic market processes have in many instances effectively decoupled resource consumption from economic growth to the point where not only do they use fewer resources to produce any given unit of output, but where they also increasingly use fewer resources *overall*. Nonetheless, since there is no identifiable pastor or pastorate that can take credit for having 'guided society' to the appropriate path, successes of this kind are often ignored or deliberately erased from public recognition by those manoeuvring within the sustainability *dispositif*.[42]

The power exercised by pastoral and precautionary narratives is also witnessed in the propensity to favour efforts to halt or, as in some de-growth narratives, to *reverse* human-induced environmental change rather than to emphasise possibilities for adaptation and co-evolution in the face of such change. Though they are not mutually exclusive, adaptation strategies are often constructed as both *riskier and morally inferior* to initiatives aimed directly at reducing human impacts.[43] The very need to adapt is held to reflect the

[41] For an illustration of how expansive the concept of 'ecological crimes' might be, see, e.g., Lynch, M., and Long. M. (2022) 'Green Criminology: Capitalism, Green Crime and Justice and Environmental Destruction', *Annual Review of Criminology*, 5: 255–76.

[42] Adler, J., 'Introduction', in Adler, J., ed. (2023) *Climate Liberalism: Perspectives on Liberty, Property and Pollution*, London: Palgrave/Macmillan.

[43] For a discussion see Forsyth, *Critical Political Ecology*.

consequences of ignorance or a prior 'disrespect' for nature, while a preference for adaptation is constructed as unduly risky and as avoiding responsibility for such ethical error. As the former vice president of the United States once put it:

> Believing we can adapt to just about anything is ultimately a kind of laziness, an arrogant faith in our ability to react in time to save our skin.[44]

Wherever such a discourse becomes institutionalised and aligned with state power, however, the notion that natural processes may themselves generate a need for adaptation may be hidden from view, and as subjects become the targets of a pastoral power that seeks to bring them 'into line with nature', the scope for people to self-constitute and to exercise different practices of freedom may be seriously undermined.

Ecological bio-power and ecological normalisation

If the concept of an equilibrated nature where human action is the primary source of instability is problematic from the standpoint of both science and of human freedom, then so too is the notion of a sovereign capacity to consciously value, manage, or control processes of socio-ecological evolution. The sustainability *dispositif* seeks to integrate multiple dimensions of life into a purposeful, calculative, and administrative apparatus that gathers and produces statistics about natural resources, populations, energy budgets, and economic yields to manage society in accordance with naturalistic laws. Moreover, since 'the environment' is the setting where *all* human action takes place, it promises an ever-expanding terrain of normalisation, surveillance, and intervention where everything from people's morality to the layout of their towns, transport, water- and land-use systems, and their consumption habits are considered legitimate targets for a 'green gaze' that 'shepherds' subjects towards ecologically benign ends. Indeed, in its more totalising manifestations *all life forms* and the *entire planet* are constituted as manageable and knowable objects falling under the gaze of a socio-ecological pastorship.[45] Though the constituent discourses within the *dispositif* differ in their understanding of who should exercise this bio-power, the possibility and desirability of exercising purposive pastoral control over others is assumed throughout.

[44] Al Gore in 1992 quoted in Pielke, R. (1999) 'Nine Fallacies of Floods', *Climatic Change*, 42 (2): 413–38.

[45] Luke, T. (1995) 'On Environmentality: Geo-Power and Eco-Knowledge in the Discourses of Contemporary Environmentalism', *Cultural Critique*, 31: 57–81.

On the view advanced here, however, this reasoning is deeply problematic from both a scientific and from a normative or ethical standpoint. Scientifically, it reflects a synoptic delusion that erases the complexity of the ordering phenomena in question and the role of human agency within such phenomena. Historical experience shows that socio-ecological systems do not evolve in linear fashion, and the number of elements and the character of their interaction may be too vast to be comprehended by any scientific or democratic pastorate. While not denying the possibility of expert knowledge per se, the post-foundational view of science informing this Foucauldian or postmodern liberal critique highlights instead the inadequacies of a positivist, managerialist, or deliberativist conception of that expertise.[46] Ecological observers may, for example, understand the principles of avian murmuration that generate an 'orderly' flock of birds without being able, either individually or collectively, to access the highly localised conditions that drive the adjustments of individual birds and to predict in detail how specific flight formations will unfold. Similarly, predator-prey relationships where the growth of certain species may create new niches for others may be comprehended in *general* terms by trained ecologists without implying a capacity to predict the dynamics of any specific evolution. Such problems will multiply wherever the complex interaction effects at issue also include co-evolution with processes of creative human agency, interpretation, and valuation.

Seen in this light, it is important to question the powers granted to discursive and non-discursive practices premised on predicting the evolution of highly fluid and non-linear socio-ecological states and of assigning quasi-objective values to these different states of the world. The discourse coalitions between neo-classical and ecological economics presuppose a scientific expertise that can detect and quantify the value of ecological services according to some objective metric of socio-ecological welfare held to exist *outside* of the diverse, changing, and often incommensurable beliefs of those who use, consume, and conserve, as well as innovate with, environmental assets and who in the process continually *transform* their character and value. On the view advanced here, however, no pastoral bio-power can survey and represent the multiple and often contradictory interpretations of localised socio-environmental conditions both now and in the future, and there is no unitary scale of values or interpretations to judge what is more, or less, important, or more, or less, 'sustainable'. From a normative standpoint, while they are unlikely to succeed in achieving the level of control they proclaim as necessary, the institutionalisation of these eco-managerialist discourses may operate nonetheless to suppress pluralism of thought and action

[46] Wermer, W. (2023) *Epistemology of the Human Sciences: Restoring an Evolutionary Approach to Biology, Economics, Psychology and Philosophy*, London: Palgrave.

and may generate significant power effects in terms of how different actors perceive themselves and how they are perceived as subjects.

As noted in the case of public health governance, what economists describe as externalities arise whenever conflicting evaluations of risks come into contact. In contexts where there are no objective data to assess the size or direction of such costs or the extent to which private or communal action already considers them, then Foucauldian power/knowledge claims may predominate with scientistic classifications and evaluations justifying the assertion of power and positionality over others. Historically, for example, colonial and postcolonial authorities routinely deployed statistical categorisations and social welfare or utilitarian concepts to justify the seizure of assets from Indigenous peoples whether to create national parks, forest reserves, or to halt what were classified as 'destructive' local practices in precisely these terms.[47] These actions both reflected and produced a sense of epistemic superiority amongst their practitioners while contributing to the political and economic marginalisation of those who were subject to them. In the United States meanwhile, in the early part of the twentieth century nearly half of the land area of the western states was nationalised and subject to principles of 'scientific resource management', often on the grounds that private actors were either 'too ignorant' or 'too greedy' to consider all relevant cost-benefit margins and to manage the assets sustainably.[48]

Against these modernist narratives historical research has shown that private landowners, farmers, and horticulturalists, working in a context of largely negative rights to property and contract, have often attempted to incorporate site-specific, transitory, and tacit understandings of the shifting value of ecological processes, including pollination, pest control, and drainage functions through dynamic contracting arrangements in ways that have *not* been considered by scientists and ecological economists who see these systems as prone to 'market failure'.[49] Granting experts who deploy eco-system services narratives the authority to 'correct' such 'failures' by, for example, imposing environmental taxes might thus be seen as a form of 'police power' that suppresses or minorises the knowledge of property owners, market participants, and local jurisdictions in

[47] For example, Agrawal, A. (2005) *Environmentality: Technologies of Government and the Making of Subjects*, Durham, NC: Duke University Press; West, P., Igoe, J., and Brockington, D. (2006) 'Parks and Peoples: The Social Impact of Protected Areas', *Annual Review of Anthropology*, 35: 251–77; Neuman, R. (1998) *Imposing Wilderness: Struggles over Livelihood and Nature Preservation in Africa*, Berkeley: University of California Press.

[48] Libecap, G. (2007) 'The Assignment of Property Rights on the Western Frontier: Lessons for Contemporary Environment and Resource Policy', *Journal of Economic History*, 67 (2): 257–91; Libecap, G. (1981) *Locking up the Range: Federal Land Controls and Grazing*, San Francisco: Pacific Research Institute for Public Policy.

[49] Sagoff, M. (2011) 'The Quantification and Valuation of Ecosystem Services', *Ecological Economics*, 70: 497–502.

the name of a socio-ecological 'truth'—in much the same way that socialist economic models routinely marginalised or demonised those whose actions departed from centrally approved planning targets. In the case of ecological taxes, for example, the greater the discrepancy between the 'tax prices' imposed by experts and politicians and the market prices negotiated between producers and consumers, the more likely it may be that the producers and consumers concerned will be driven out of business or pushed into illicit trades and exposed to criminal or disciplinary sanction—with corresponding implications for their subjectivity.

Environmental taxes need not of course be necessarily disciplinary in this way; they do allow some room for their targets to continue choosing preferred production techniques or consumption practices within the parameters set by the tax. Elsewhere, however, economic and ecological expertise is increasingly being used in an explicitly disciplinary mode with managerial experts specifying what they judge to be the ecological practices commensurate with greater local, national, or even global environmental 'goods' and deploying normalisation strategies to mould subjects in the relevant direction. Disciplinary narratives of this kind have become commonplace in recent years with governments from the Netherlands to Sri Lanka adding layers of regulation—such as biodiversity offsets, set-aside requirements, organic farming mandates, and in some cases compulsory purchase schemes—onto farmers, horticulturalists, and landowners. The European Union's proposal for a 'farm to fork' strategy, for example, aims to 'redesign' the entire food production system by reducing the use of pesticides and fertilisers, increasing organic production, and bringing consumers dietary habits 'into line' with those specified by national dietary authorities and the parameters of their respective 'food environments'.[50] Though they will undoubtedly benefit some producers and consumers, these schemes threaten the livelihoods of others while constructing some land-use practices and dietary habits and the subjects who engage in them as 'backward' or 'progressive' with respect to sustainability goals.

The suggestion here is not that the relevant valuations are *necessarily* 'wrong' or that those of farmers, horticulturalists, and consumers are 'right'. Indeed, many of these actors may have previously been the beneficiaries of power relations and governmental schemes, such as the European Union Common Agricultural Policy, that have heavily subsidised agribusiness at the expense of consumers, taxpayers, and habitats. Rather, the contention is that the increasingly routine privileging of expert valuations is contrary to a Foucauldian pluralism of rationalities where those with *different* and perhaps *incommensurable* understandings of socio-ecological problems might associate through

[50] https://food.ec.europa.eu/horizontal-topics/farm-fork-strategy_en.

persuasion, bargaining, and consent. Expert-centred discourses and the 'dividing practices' they deploy empower some actors to speak 'above others' and 'on behalf' of ecological interests, while the others concerned are increasingly subjected to a regulatory gaze that may activate a subjectivity of moral-ecological deviance.

Crucially, the suppression of pluralism in this regard may not be altered when attempts to implement an ecological pastorship are conducted by majorities or their representatives in democratic fora. In the context of highly interdependent socio-ecological systems, the magnitude and complexity of the interaction effects between millions of agents may not be comprehended by any sovereign or pastoral gaze, including one organised on deliberative democratic lines. Given the impossibility of consulting all those affected in some way by multifarious and interdependent decisions, in practice such deliberation will be delegated to appointed experts and elite representatives from those designated as 'stakeholder' groups who claim to speak 'for' environmental, business, or labour interests. The context-specific knowledge of multiple individuals and organisations seeking to innovate and adapt to their local circumstances as they see best may thus be diluted or suppressed as third parties are increasingly empowered to veto private or localised decision-makers.

This narrowing process need not be a purely top-down phenomena. The categories, indicators and statistics centred in the *dispositif* may also be taken up and reinterpreted by multiple private, civil, and public actors and deployed in an attempt to secure power or advantage in a more decentred vein. Non-governmental organisations, the media, local public agencies, private companies, and consumers may push from below, demanding the production of data to distinguish 'good' from 'bad' ecological behaviours and to influence the relevant 'dividing practices', and as these circulate, they may determine which actors are listened to and heard in formal regulatory arenas and democratic fora alike. The latter dynamic may best account for the increasingly widespread use by businesses of external environmental 'stakeholder panels' to assess their progress with respect to various 'sustainability indicators'. Though frequently dismissed by environmental campaigners as corporate 'greenwashing', many enterprises now engage in this ESG reporting, either as a *defensive* strategy to avoid more direct legal intervention in their affairs or to comply with the guidance issued by regulatory agencies,[51] and as they do, they reinforce the disciplinary categories propagated within the *dispositif*.

The threat to free agency and pluralism here comes not from this disciplinary power per se but, as in the case of the social justice and public health *dispositifs*,

[51] Chelli, M., and Gendron, Y. (2013) 'Sustainability Ratings and the Disciplinary Power of the Ideology of Numbers', *Journal of Business Ethics*, 112: 187–222.

from a strategic context where private or local decision-making operates under the shadow or threat of direct regulatory action or legal disadvantage. When local jurisdiction and negative rights to property and freedom of contract are perceived as secure, individuals and firms will still be subject to attempts by private and civil actors to 'conduct their conduct'—but they will also retain significant scope to resist this pressure if they believe they can use their knowledge to secure better outcomes for themselves and their contractors and/or customers by acting differently from what the majority of external 'stakeholders' prescribes. By contrast, in a discursive-institutional arena where the failure to fall 'into line' with the demand to 'buy local' or to use only 'sustainable suppliers' may lead to statutory regulation, then the scope for resistance against these normalising imperatives may be narrowed, and individuals and enterprises may bend towards the dominant or consensus position even if they do not believe in its stated goals. In this way, disciplinary power 'governs at a distance', narrowing pluralism of thought and action even when there is no formal legal prohibition or direct regulation in place. As in the social justice and public health *dispositifs,* this power masks many of its effects. It works through guidelines or codes that while, not specifying approved conducts or behaviours, silently empower the policing of producer and consumer behaviour by campaign groups, the media, and politicians with subjects moving into line with what they perceive to be approved standards lest these or other standards be imposed on them through formal regulation.[52] Such power effects are capillary in nature, with organisations working not only to impose the relevant standards on themselves but also on multiple other actors in their supply chains through certification schemes and audits, as well as on those who consume the products through various eco-labelling initiatives.[53] In other contexts, private companies may also develop standards and codes in anticipation of future regulation to be better placed to shape that regulation or to buy the support of politicians and public agencies.

In effect, the doctrine of ecological stakeholderism places enterprises under permanent surveillance and uncertainty with respect to their decision rights, which may lead them to either support dominant narratives as a

[52] On this process see, e.g., De Sombre, E. (2000) *Sources of International Environmental Policy: Industry Environmentalists and US Power*, Cambridge, MA: MIT Press; Garcia-Johnson, R. (2000) *Exporting Environmentalism: US Multinational Chemical Corporations in Brazil and Mexico*, Cambridge, MA: MIT Press; Prakash, A., and Potoski, M. (2006) *The Voluntary Environmentalists: Green Clubs, ISO 14001, and Voluntary Environmental Regulation*, Cambridge: Cambridge University Press.

[53] Bartley, T. (2003) 'Certifying Forests and Factories: States, Social Movements and the Rise of Private Regulation in the Apparel and Forest Products Fields', *Politics and Society*, 31 (3): 433–4; Cashore, B., Auld, G., and Newsom, D. (2004) *Governing Through Markets: Forest Certification and the Emergence of Non-State Authority*, New Haven, CT: Yale University Press.

defence mechanism/reputational device or alternatively to be recruited into these discourses for private ends—by, for example, endorsing environmental standards and regulations that raise competitors' costs and that marginalise competitors as 'bad actors'. Such 'cynicisms of power' may include the creation of 'baptist and bootlegger' coalitions where moralistic or normalising campaigns are exploited by business and labour interests to limit competition.[54] There have been numerous examples of such alliances in the context of trade negotiations with allegations of 'ecological dumping' routinely deployed by business and labour interests in richer nations to restrict imports from poorer countries.[55]

These alliances may also arise through the attempts of corporate managers to reduce their accountability to shareholders. Where direct financial accountability provides a relatively clear indication of managerial success or failure, requirements to balance profits and losses with multiple environmental and social 'indicators' may shield managers from effective shareholder scrutiny and allow them to shift responsibility for managerial failures to the ethical requirement to meet social and environmental demands. In effect, ESG schemes and the broader discourse of deliberative democratic stakeholderism from which they emanate multiplies the number of principals to whom managers must be accountable, and in the process dilutes their accountability to shareholders. The existence of diverse and often conflicting stakeholder constituencies may allow managers to pick the stakeholder coalition that best aligns with their own interests and to conceal from view failures of financial governance. With most ESG schemes negotiated by large corporate and financial interests in conjunction with environmental NGOs and various public and international regulatory agencies, the institutionalisation or strategic codification of stakeholder narratives thus points away from pluralistic, open, and competitive markets and towards processes of increasing managerial discretion, corporatism, and cartelisation.[56] As power relations and markets thus become rigidified and as contrary framings and narratives may be suppressed, subjects constrained within these limits may increasingly fail to think or to act in opposition to the routinised conducts they generate.

[54] Yandle, B., and Buck, S. (2002) 'Bootleggers, Baptists and the Global Warming Battle', *Harvard Environmental Law Review*, 26 (1): 177–229. In Yandle and Buck's account Baptists in Prohibition era America were those who campaigned on moralistic grounds for prohibition, while bootleggers opportunistically saw the opportunity for higher profits in the illicit markets generated by prohibition.

[55] For example, Lal, D. (2006) *Reviving the Invisible Hand*, Princeton NJ: Princeton University Press.

[56] Bainbridge, S. (2023) *The Profit Motive: Defending Shareholder Value Maximization*, Cambridge: Cambridge University Press, 87.

Bio-political essentialism, emergency normalisation, and missionary ecological governance

The limitation of difference and pluralism highlighted thus far may also be reflected and reinforced by the discursive prevalence of a bio-political essentialism. In line with its public health counterpart, the sustainability *dispositif* constructs many environmental issues as large-scale collective action dilemmas that preclude reliance on decentralised or competitive forms of governance. The suggestion that environmental problems transcend territorial boundaries, combined with discourses emphasising the ubiquity of free-riding, constructs a totalising logic wherein intervention by government agencies and often central government agencies *must* be invoked if ecological disaster is to be avoided. While some ecological democrats emphasise the greater effectiveness of small-scale actions where subjects identify most with their immediate surroundings, the centrality of collective action 'failures' to the *dispositif* provides a strategic option for multiple parties to act as 'externality entrepreneurs' portraying issues as trans-boundary collective action dilemmas because this may afford opportunities for interest groups and for bureaucracies to secure power and resources.

This is not to imply that satisfactory decentralised solutions are necessarily available but is to stress that the prevalence of this bio-political essentialism may influence what is considered true about ecological challenges *irrespective of whether it is true*. Ostrom's work, for example, shows how many top-down schemes for natural resource management have ignored or erased the historical achievements of localised communities in managing assets effectively and have often contributed to the disempowerment of many such actors by public bodies. Elsewhere, writers in the 'market environmentalist' tradition have unearthed multiple historic cases where private entrepreneurs have found ways of 'fencing' environmental assets, bringing them within the scope of consensual commercial exchange—examples often forgotten or inconceivable to those operating in an elite policy discourse dominated by narratives of 'inherently public goods'.[57] The suppression of market-centred possibilities is in turn reinforced by the moralistic and censorious hostility to commerce evident in the pastoral discourse of ecological democracy. When currency is granted to a narrative suggesting not only that markets *cannot* adequately supply certain goods but that it is also 'unnatural' or 'morally corrupting' to allow goods such as ecosystem services to be subject to buying and selling, then even if there are opportunities for market processes to operate in these domains, they may not be explored.

[57] Anderson, T., and Libecap, G. (2014) *Environmental Markets*, Cambridge, Cambridge University Press; Anderson, T., and Leal, D. (2015) *Free Market Environmentalism*, New York: Palgrave.

These threats to pluralism are amplified by the 'emergency' or 'crisis' narratives surrounding the concept of sustainability. The construction of a 'politics of necessity' or of 'catastrophe' in these discourses assumes critical significance here because when an actor or group of actors can be described as threatening the future of a population, an ecosystem, a species, or habitat, then those concerned are unlikely to be seen as parties to be bargained with but as ethical 'wrongdoers' who must be punished, silenced, or marginalised. Wherever environmental problems are described as threatening survival, then the bio-political or pastoral justification of protecting 'the whole' or 'the community' from the 'irresponsible' actions of subsets of individuals or groups may generate a combination of disciplinary and sovereign powers that suppress diversity of thought and action. Instead of viewing environmental problems as disputes between subjectivities who perceive risks differently and that may be open to two-way bargaining,[58] the circulation of emergency narratives enables a *moralisation* of distinctions that flow in *one direction*. The effect of these discourses in contemporary societies appears to be evident in the growing proportion of people expressing a combination of extreme psychological distress about 'the state of the planet' with a willingness to countenance increasingly authoritarian institutional responses. Recent studies suggest that over three-quarters of younger people consider the future to be 'frightening' and half of European youth believe that authoritarian regimes are better placed to address environmental challenges.[59]

These logics and tactics of power may be reinforced by discourses of 'missionary government' that favour restructuring political economies either on 'ecological modernisation' or 'de-growth' lines. For their advocates, if governments take bold action investing and regulating to chart a clear course towards sustainability, then this will give confidence to multiple civil and private actors to engage their ingenuity to follow suit. The strategic logic of adopting this 'missionary position', however, points towards a form of 'disciplinary government' that institutionalises the suppression of dissent and any counter-narratives. The idea of missionary government is that public authorities can reduce private agents' uncertainty, encouraging them to invest in environmentally sustainable forms of production and consumption by staking out a clear stance for the future and then sticking to it in the longer term. This commitment means, however, that the views of those who might question the chosen mission or propose an alternative to the favoured direction are likely to be suppressed lest hearing them undermines the very confidence that adopting the 'missionary position' is supposed to generate in the wider population. To be coherent, a mission-oriented

[58] Coase, R. (1960) 'The Problem of Social Cost', *Journal of Law, and Economics*, 3: 1–44.

[59] Hickman, C., Marks, E., Pihkala, P., and Clayton, S. (2021) 'Climate Anxiety in Children and Young People and Their Beliefs About Governmental Responses to Climate Change', *The Lancet: Planetary Health*, 5 (12): 863–73.

government must place its subjects on something like a permanent 'war footing' that prevents 'too many' alternative visions of sustainability from seeing the light of day. As noted in chapter 6, a similar dynamic may be operative within the public health *dispositif* where professional associations routinely close down debate and marginalise dissenting voices to maintain public confidence in the competence and reliability of professional expertise—even when the evidence in favour of a particular course is far from clear.

These processes have important parallels with those described in Hayek's *Road to Serfdom*, where in the absence of anything resembling an objective social welfare function or agreement on the contents of a unitary plan, attempts to engage in large-scale planning may mutate into more, or less, brutal power struggles as rival interests seek to impose their subjective and partial perspectives on others. Once authority has been established over the cacophony of conflicting voices, then the standard tactic in such situations is to demonise subsequent dissidents as 'enemies of the people' or in this instance of 'the planet'. Though its advocates claim that the form of missionary government they have in mind is compatible with open and democratic institutions, significantly, all the examples they present as alleged successes of what missionary governments can achieve have hailed either from non-democratic and authoritarian regimes, such as China, or from authoritarian or non-democratic enclaves within otherwise liberal political orders, such as the US military-industrial complex.

None of this denies the possibility of genuine ecological emergencies that are analogous to war and that *may* justify the exercise of 'missionary powers' like those that may be required in a military campaign or on a battlefield. What it does suggest, however, is that the centrality of crisis narratives to the sustainability *dispositif* makes it *more likely* that these constructs will be appropriated by those seeking some form of power or political-economic advantage *irrespective of whether the emergencies are real or discursively generated.* Emergency and missionary narratives may be mobilised to block or limit resistance, producing and reproducing a form of groupthink or herd behaviour, and in the process preventing subjects from exposure to other ways of being governed.

The sustainability *dispositif* and the tragedy of climate change

The threats to pluralism and freedom of agency from a potentially totalising 'environmental governmentality' are perhaps nowhere more pronounced than in the context of anthropogenic climate change. One reason for this is that discursive constructions of global climate have themselves played a significant role in the formation of the sustainability *dispositif.* Scientific naturalist concepts of equilibrium and carrying capacity have been at the forefront of climate analysis, as have attempts to place econometric valuations on future climate states. Policy discussions have also been framed in terms of possible 'tipping points' or 'systemic limits', giving rise to constructs such as 'climate emergency' or 'climate crisis'. These narratives have in turn been mobilised by a range of public, private, and civil actors to demand radical or missionary action to ensure that greenhouse gas emissions are curtailed. The centrality of climate change to the sustainability *dispositif* has also been folded back into the analysis and understanding of multiple other socio-ecological problems, with responses to these challenges now routinely constructed in terms of their contributions to reducing greenhouse emissions. Authority is thus increasingly granted to the category of the 'global climate' to guide, direct, and to discipline an ever-expanding domain of human actions.[60]

The Foucauldian or postmodern liberal perspective put forward here does not question the natural science underlying the analysis of anthropogenic climate change, and neither does it suggest that specific responses to climate change are 'wrong'. On the contrary, it recognises that climate change is real and possibly dangerous and presents serious institutional and decision-making challenges at multiple different levels. From a critical standpoint, however, what matters is that alternative cultural and social scientific constructions of climate change and of the possible responses to it are far from neutral in terms of their Foucauldian power effects. Different discourses of climate change governance and their alignment with the sovereign powers of states and, increasingly, international bodies may produce different positionalities and subjectivities, some of which may be more amenable to pluralism and to freedom, while others may be deeply ambiguous or downright threatening to that freedom.

Climate change and government by statistics

The first set of dangers to highlight here are associated with the discursive power granted to scientific naturalist analyses of climate change which imply that there are knowable and quantifiable limits to human intervention. As early as 1988 the world's governments committed themselves to measures that would ensure 'the conservation of climate as part of the heritage of mankind' and to 'make every effort to prevent detrimental effects on climate and activities which affect the ecological balance'. In subsequent years these commitments were manifested in the creation of the International Panel on Climate Change (IPCC), the Framework Convention on Climate Change, and the Convention of the Parties (COP).[61]

[60] For a detailed analysis of this process see Hulme, M. (2023) *Why Climate Change Isn't Everything*, Cambridge: Polity.

[61] Hulme, M. (2020) *Climate Change*, London: Routledge, 197.

Crucially, the assumption projected by all such global initiatives and institutions is that the global climate is a 'knowable object' that can be managed by governments and that it is technically possible for those with the relevant scientific expertise to identify the measures that will facilitate such management. Though there is no suggestion in the *dispositif* that governments are capable of directly controlling the climate per se, there is an assumption that by purposefully manipulating technologies, patterns of mobility, and consumption and their effect on greenhouse gases that certain climate changes might be avoided. This narrative is evident in the commitment made at the COP meeting in Paris in 2015 and reaffirmed at the Glasgow meeting in 2021 to take all necessary steps to ensure that temperature rises stay well below 2°C above preindustrial levels and to pursue efforts to limit any increases to 1.5°C.

In any chaotic, complex, or non-linear system such as the global climate, however, it may not be possible to discern whether the adoption of specific policy measures can be causally linked to observable trends in temperatures because these observations may reflect the consequences of previously accumulated emissions as well as naturally occurring perturbations. Put simply, it may not be possible to 'stop' climate change because in a disequilibrium and non-linear system there can be no 'going back' to a previously 'undisturbed state'. Moreover, the climate effects of policy decisions that may lead to an increase or decrease in emissions in the near to medium term simply cannot be assessed in a context where any such consequences may not be apparent for decades to come.

The danger here then arises from a 'government by statistics' and a discursive formation where short- to medium-term variations in temperature and related weather events and simulations of future such events operate as a form of disciplinary bio-power over human subjects. Just as macroeconomic models that evaluate the performance of 'the economy' against the ideal of a 'stable rate of growth' may generate or produce constant demands for 'treatments' and 'interventions' whenever there are departures from such stability, so scientific naturalist representations that emphasise climate stability or equilibrium may operate as a disciplinary frame justifying multiple policy interventions whenever departures from 'normal' climate conditions are observed. Subjects may thus become enmeshed in a maze of policies, taxes, and regulatory initiatives with highly contestable and uncertain consequences for future climate states and their relationship to different states of human welfare. Furthermore, the institutionalisation of a discourse focused on statistics and climate managerialism may in turn work to *produce* subjects who enforce this discipline on themselves—interpreting different localised weather-related events in terms of the success or failure of climate policies or the lack thereof and demanding further exercises of this pastoral power by 'climate managers' in response to such events.

A related power effect of this *dispositif* may be a pronounced bias towards mitigation initiatives. The notion that climate change is open to clearly defined technical 'solutions' that might deliver greater 'stability' may centre efforts on the search for such solutions rather than on adaptation and resilience in the face of potentially uncontrollable change. The focus of the climate governance apparatus is on limiting changes within the climate system, and this gaze may divert attention away from any relationships between such changes and the various trade-offs that affect how people live. Among such trade-offs is the possibility that economic growth may increase resilience against extreme weather events whether natural or human induced—as suggested by declines in the number of climate-related deaths during a period when both emissions *and* temperatures have risen.[62] Moreover, insofar as attention is given to climate adaptation, the *dispositif* may also understand this through a 'predict and control' grid that grants currency to the capacity of modellers to forecast the type and location of future climate events and hence to guide public and private investments and regulatory decisions that may impact adaptive capacity. The dominance of these positivist-managerialist constructs may conceal from view that the aggregate classifications they target are not 'real' phenomena but social constructs—forecasts and projections that may have little relationship to the highly varied and continually evolving adaptive challenges that people and businesses may experience in their daily lives.

The latter problem is perhaps best illustrated by the privileged position granted to the integrated assessment models (IAMs) that attempt to predict the 'social welfare' implications of different climate change scenarios and that are projected by international groups such as the IPCC and reported in media narratives to drive policy in this regard. These econometric simulations attempt to model an unbounded set of possibilities concerning the quantities and costs of different resources; the opportunity costs of different methods of energy production; the contribution to welfare of technologies not yet invented and how these will be affected by alternative climate change policies in the near and distant future; and the balance across the years between mitigating risks from climate change by restricting emissions and adapting to reduce the impact of harms resulting from such change. Within this context, some critics have suggested that biases within these models may lead to underestimating the likely costs of climate change and overestimating mitigation costs,[63] while others maintain that IAMs are likely to

[62] Formetta, G., and Feyen, L. (2019) 'Empirical Evidence of Declining Vulnerability to Climate-Related Hazards', *Global Environmental Change*, 57: 1–9; see also Lomborg, B. (2020) 'Welfare in the 21st Century: Increasing Development, Reducing Inequality, the Impact of Climate Change and the Cost of Climate Change Policies', *Technological Forecasting and Social Change*, 156: 1–35.

[63] Ackerman, R., De Canio, S., Howarth, R., and Sheeran, K. (2009) 'Limitations of Integrated Assessment Models of Climate Change', *Climate Change*, 95: 297–31.

overestimate the costs of climate change while underestimating the costs of mitigation.[64] Similar uncertainties surround attempts to estimate the 'social cost of carbon', with estimates ranging from a few dollars per ton to hundreds or even thousands of dollars per ton.[65] Still other critics object that focussing on narrowly economic valuations or conceptions of risk ignores other dimensions of human welfare such as those pertaining to health and social injustices, including the loss of valued ways of life owing to climate change itself or the consequences of having to adapt to it.[66]

On the view advanced here, however, the fundamental problem with *all* such models is that their results are driven by highly subjective and perspectival power/knowledge claims about possible mitigation costs and the 'damage function' associated with different levels of climate disturbance that may be unknowable. The different model specifications and assumptions underlying IAMs vary so markedly that, as one leading economic analyst puts it, the models 'can be used to generate almost any result that the analyst desires'.[67] These are entirely speculative functions because economists do not know enough about the multiple interaction effects that may affect the socio-economic costs of climate change decades, let alone centuries, ahead.[68]

Such problems would be reproduced in any attempt to use alternative aggregates that incorporate health or social justice metrics. Thus, while carbon-fuelled technological progress in the United States, the United Kingdom, and Western Europe may now be generating costs for other countries facing the prospect of climate change, many such countries have also received benefits from these emissions by way of access to capital and technology that may have *lowered* their own emissions relative to any base line that had required them to develop equivalent technologies on an 'early adopter' basis. There is, however, no 'unbiased' statistical procedure to work out counterfactuals of how much 'worse' or 'better-off' the inhabitants of the 'Global North' might be than those of the 'Global South' if the former had produced fewer greenhouse gases.[69]

The critical point here is that few if any aggregate indicators or combinations thereof are likely to have or to have had any clear relationship with the unfolding decisional contexts and complex trade-offs between conflicting values that

[64] Lomborg, 'Welfare in the 21st Century'.

[65] Tol, R. (2018) 'The Economic Impacts of Climate Change', *Review of Environmental Economics and Policy*, 12 (1): 4–25.

[66] Dotson, K., and Whyte, K. (2013) 'Environmental Justice, Unknowability and Unqualified Affectability', *Ethics, Place and Environment*, 18 (2): 55–79.

[67] Pindyck, R. (2013) 'Climate Change Policy: What Do the Models Tell Us', *Journal of Economic Literature*, 51 (3): 860–72.

[68] Pindyck, R. (2022) *Climate Future: Averting and Adapting to Climate Change*, New York: Oxford University Press.

[69] See, e.g., Posner, E., and Sunstein, C. (2007) 'Climate Change Justice', *Georgetown Law Journal*, 96: 1565–1612.

confront and have confronted a diversity of differently situated agents. Replacing one aggregate variable with another or adding on multiple and perhaps contradictory 'indicators' to generate a 'basket of indicators' does no more than institute a different set of 'governing statistics'.

This problem may also apply to attempts to move beyond a 'fine-tuning' approach to climate policy to the development of broader brush approaches that conceive of climate change mitigation as a kind of insurance scheme against catastrophic risk.[70] Econometric simulations are no better placed to assess the comparative costs of insuring against climate risk versus insuring against other catastrophic risks such as the possibility of asteroid strikes, nuclear terrorism, or bioterrorism where the relevant probabilities are highly uncertain or simply unknown. Though supportive of vigorous climate mitigation measures on catastrophe avoidance grounds, many of those concerned are forced to recognise that weighting the parameters relevant to discerning which catastrophic risks should be prioritised amounts to little more than subjective speculation.[71] Seen in this light, the centring of statistical aggregates and simulation modelling in climate change discourse grants to econometricians and statisticians precisely the kind of totalising epistemic power experienced under systems of central economic planning—*on a global scale.* Notwithstanding the failure of such models at the subglobal level, in a discursive arena saturated with macroeconomic modelling motifs and where the decisions of public bodies, corporations, and citizens may already be habituated to a form of 'government by statistics', these models may exercise a significant disciplinary effect on governments as well as the subjects over whom they rule.

The problem of distinguishing the 'real' from the 'statistically generated' is especially profound in the climate change context because many features of the governance problem preclude the generation of realised counterfactuals against which the utility of econometric modelling exercises might be judged. Econometric techniques attempt to cope with problems of missing data through proxy measures or simulations—but the capacity to 'test' the value of these very simulation techniques as guides to action depends on whether the problem at hand allows for comparisons with other decision-making methods to be made. In the case of the former planned economies, for example, it was not econometric modelling that identified its weaknesses but the polycentric

[70] For an example of the 'insurance' argument see Pindyck, R. (2021) 'What We Know and Don't Know About Climate Change and Implications for Policy', *Environmental and Energy Policy and the Economy*, (2): 4–43.

[71] For recognition of this point see Martin, I., and Pindyck, R. (2015) 'Averting Catastrophe: The Strange Economics of Scylla and Charybdis', *American Economic Review*, 105 (10): 2947–85. See also Pindyck, *Climate Future*. Note, Pindyck, who has produced the comprehensive critique of IAM models discussed above, offers little or no reason why economists might nonetheless be any better placed to discern the opportunity costs of alternative catastrophic insurance scenarios.

or heterotopic character of the international order that revealed differences in outcomes between economies governed by econometrically simulated prices in comparison to those governed by the data produced in actual though imperfect markets. Indeed, many enthusiasts for 'planometric techniques' continued to predict that the systems based on such principles were on track to outstrip market economies, just a few years before the planned economies of Eastern Europe collapsed.[72]

In other contexts, an important way of coping with radical uncertainty is to hedge bets, that is, fracturing or dividing decision-making authority; allowing for comparative trial-and-error data production, which facilitates reflexive learning across decision-making units; and that may reduce or disperse systemic risk. In the context of climate change governance, however, the indivisibility of the global climate system and the length of the relevant evaluative time frames preclude such an option. If governments introduce taxes or regulations guided by econometric models, then while it may be possible for politicians and citizens to judge the performance of such models with respect to the forecasted short-term costs of mitigation or adaptation measures, it may not be possible for them to judge how these compare with the projected longer term economic costs or benefits as these are manifested under future technological and climate states. This is why the epistemic challenge of climate governance is far more pronounced than was the case for the problem of ozone depletion. In the latter case, cheap substitutes for chlorofluorocarbons were readily available, and the severe negative consequences arising from destruction of the ozone layer were clear and proximate. Moreover, the effects on the ozone layer from reducing emissions could be tracked over a relatively short period. For climate change, however, the time frame within which it may be possible to discern any stabilisation effects from reducing emissions is likely to be much greater with forecasts about the potential socio-economic consequences of alternative climate change policies correspondingly more tenuous.

These seemingly essential characteristics of the climate system may also make it harder to subject the power/knowledge claims of those who seek to govern people in the name of climate stability to critical scrutiny. This was probably a key factor that allowed those in the fossil fuel industry who had a material interest in sowing doubt about the phenomenon of anthropogenic climate change to continue to exert an influence on public opinion for many years after the thesis became widely established in the scientific community. Equally, however, it must be recognised that there is now a vast apparatus of industrial interests, universities, research institutes, and national and international regulatory

[72] Levy, D., and Peart, S. (2011) 'Soviet Growth and American Textbooks: An Endogenous Past', *Journal of Economic Behaviour and Organisation*, 78 (1–2): 110–25.

agencies that have a professional and economic stake in the expansion of research on climate change mitigation and that support the development of specific alternatives to fossil fuels. While the thesis of anthropogenic climate change must be taken as a given, this should not be the case with respect to the scientistic claims circulated in the media from climate experts and economists professing an ability to forecast the socio-economic costs of alternative climate change scenarios and the technologies that might contribute significantly to a reduction in greenhouse emissions. It is, however, the propensity for those in the governing climate apparatus to use their disciplinary powers to shut down alternative problem constructions that may entrench this emergent system of bio-power.

Climate change, missionary government, and emergency normalisation

In Foucauldian or postmodern liberal terms these features of the climate change dilemma may make it difficult for those subject to different climate change effects, policies, and governance regimes to be exposed to or to understand the possibilities of their being 'governed differently', and this problem may be exacerbated by the centring of 'emergency' and 'crisis' narratives in the sustainability *dispositif.* The strategic deployment of emergency narratives conveys a message that there is 'no time' for further debate about the appropriate course to take and that decisive action is required even if this closes down alternative voices, constructions, and understandings. Indeed, some have gone so far as to suggest that democracy itself might need to be suspended in favour of authoritarian bio-political climate measures.[73]

Given the global character of climate change, some limits on pluralism seem inevitable because insofar as countries decide individually or collectively to opt strongly for reducing emissions this will limit the parameters within which their subjects are permitted to act. What matters, however, is that emergency narratives may lead to a *further narrowing* of options with respect to *how emissions might best be reduced.* The centrality of missionary discourses in the *dispositif* and the need for unity and common purpose they espouse are of particular concern here. The narratives of ecological economics and ecological democracy are hostile to price-centred approaches such as carbon taxes or emissions-trading regimes. Though the relevant prices are centrally determined—either through taxes or quantity restrictions which can then be sold in the form of permits—rather than market determined, these indirect or bio-political forms of regulation still

[73] For example, Mittaga, R. (2021) 'Political Legitimacy, Authoritarianism and Climate Change', *American Political Science Review*, 116 (3): 1–14.

allow relatively more scope for actors at multiple levels (governments, firms, and consumers) to choose how they respond to the relevant 'signal' according to their own circumstances and purposes—by innovating in unspecified ways to find fossil fuel substitutes or continuing to invest in and to use such fuels if they are able and willing to pay a compensatory price for doing so. Catastrophising emergency narratives are, however, now increasingly deployed to suggest that there is 'no time' to allow markets and other decentralised processes to generate a new mix of energy sources in response to such signals. In this framing, governments must commit resources to restructure energy markets in the direction determined by technological experts in favoured energy sectors. Yet, wherever governments seek to centrally determine priorities such as, for example, investment in solar or wind rather than nuclear power or vice versa, the effect is to block realised counterfactuals and thus conceal the possible opportunity costs of these actions. Precisely because they block counterfactuals in this way, the institutionalisation of missionary narratives may intensify the grip of the power/knowledge complex surrounding climate change mitigation initiatives with those who have a professional and economic stake in support of specific technologies or sectors eager to suppress any heterotopic spaces that might undermine their claims to authority and expertise.

The latter limitation on pluralism is reinforced in a context where overlapping narratives favour a highly moralised approach that deploys disciplinary 'dividing practices' to celebrate the ethical credentials of certain technologies and behaviours while demonising others. Ecological democracy and social justice narratives, for example, are often deployed by actors who reject approaches such as carbon taxation and emissions trading not only because they might be 'too slow' in an emergency but also because they are *insufficiently normalising.* Instead, these discourses favour expressive standards and targets that distinguish ecologically 'good' behaviours from 'bad' behaviours across multiple decisional domains. Though international agreements such as the COP 2021 in Glasgow continue to emphasise a role for carbon-pricing schemes, missionary narratives and a disciplinary approach have gained traction to the point where it is increasingly the case that market adjustments are tolerated only insofar as they generate a normatively approved energy or consumption mix. Here 'bad' behaviours include, among others, fossil fuel extraction and production, air travel, driving combustion cars, low-density housing construction, and eating meat and dairy. In a context where governments are showing increasing interest in using 'big data' technologies to track and to monitor multiple behaviours, these developments could rapidly morph into a disciplinary 'social credit' regime where surveillance techniques are used to generate reputational 'sustainability scores' for citizens and businesses which will then be used to ration access to services such as international travel.

The tragedy here is that while climate change represents a significant threat to humanity—a threat with the potential to fall disproportionately on those who have contributed historically least towards it, the discursive and non-discursive practices of the sustainability *dispositif* may now be morphing into a form of disciplinary 'climatism' where the confluence of government by statistics, government by emergency, and government by missionary normalisation has the potential to be profoundly illiberal in its effects—and on a global scale.[74]

Resisting the sustainability *dispositif*

If the sustainability *dispositif* is pregnant with threats to pluralism and freedom, then what options or strategies might be available to those seeking to maintain pluralism and freedom in the face of this system of power?

The first point to stress here is that the Foucauldian/postmodern liberal perspective is deeply sceptical of naturalistic categories. Sustaining freedom may require destabilising the idea of a true 'ecological self' that stays within natural 'limits' and creating spaces for subjects to constantly rework their relations with themselves and with others, both human and non-human, in complex and varied ways. Such freedom does not preclude subjects from drawing on elements within the *dispositif* to create an 'environmental aesthetics of the self' and resist the power of materialistic or consumerist discourses elsewhere in market capitalist economies. Nonetheless, it does require the maintenance of spaces where people can create themselves in different ways through more entrepreneurial and consumer-oriented discourses and practices that are not unduly tied either to scientific naturalism or to democratic stakeholderism.

One opportunity for those seeking to conserve such freedom may be to draw on cultural-discursive trends in contemporary societies that might challenge the power of a potentially totalising 'green gaze'. The social movements that have questioned essentialisms based on sex, sexuality, and race have been at least partly successful in unsettling naturalistic identities and highlighted significant uncertainties in scientific constructions that raise wider doubts about using science as the basis of public morality. Those who have experienced a loosening of the disciplinary hold over their identities by naturalistic concepts may thus be sensitive to the dangers represented by a potentially totalising ecologism. Though the Foucauldian/postmodern liberal conception of the self is open to ambiguity and does not require strict consistency between all beliefs, at the very least it would be odd for those who have successfully rolled back the frontiers of scientific naturalism to acquiesce with the imposition of a new form of that

[74] Hulme, *Why Climate Change Isn't Everything.*

naturalism operating in the name of ecological sustainability. Discursive entrepreneurship highlighting such tensions may thus help forge alliances that can preserve spaces where subjects are able to shape the relationships among themselves, the socio-economic order, and ecological processes in more pluralistic and creative ways. The type of 'environmentalism' envisaged here is one that recognises different and conflicting environmental aesthetics and attitudes towards economic growth emergent from different histories and traditions and the role for bargaining and dispute resolution in facilitating cooperation across these differences.

Similar opportunities may arise through the exposure of gaps and contradictions within the *dispositif* itself. One such opportunity might be afforded by the narrow attitude towards reflexivity evident in ecological democratic and stakeholder discourses. These emphasise the import of social communication processes in exposing subjects to alternative problem constructions and understandings, yet they reduce the exercise of reflexivity to democratic settings and are hostile to private property, commerce, and trade—especially long-distance trade—all of which afford important opportunities for cooperation and communication across difference that can prompt changes in how subjects see themselves, their relations with others, and their environments. Tourism, for example, while it may not immerse people in the complexity of the societies visited, is still an important source of exposure to alternative ways of living and being governed. Though tourism may reflect and may act as a stimulant for consumerism, such exposure may also alert people to traditions and practices that de-emphasise consumerism or towards different consumption practices. Green hostility towards consumerism and travel here is particularly unfortunate because the goods people consume and how they are consumed are important aspects of their subjectivity. People are not necessarily passive consumers but may use different forms of consumption to actively craft an identity or environmental aesthetic for themselves in ways that may be unduly constrained by bureaucratic and majoritarian fora—and this may include the negotiation of new forms of environmental subjectivity not confined to naturalistic categories. Defending the right to travel and challenging attempts by public authorities to ration travel may thus represent an important focal point for resistance against the scientistic and moralistic excesses of an emergent ecological pastorate.

A similar discursive niche may be opened by challenging anti-commodification narratives in green discourse and their propensity to normalise 'good' and 'bad' behaviours. An important value of market institutions is that subjects who value the same goods *differently* can nonetheless find grounds for compromise across difference. If an individual or group owns a stretch of forest or waterway valued as a site of ecological significance, they may turn down monetary offers from those who would use the site for recreational purposes. Alternatively, the relevant owners may accept such offers if the money concerned enables them to secure their ecological aesthetic more effectively—perhaps tolerating some disturbance in exchange for revenues that enable the purchase of additional sites perceived to be under still greater threat. While all societies have background cultural norms setting some limits on what can be bought and sold, wherever it is legitimate for subjects to own assets such as land or water and to exclude others from using them—as is the case in most liberal societies—then it is far from clear why they should be constrained from exchanging these rights in markets.[75] Green fears of a totalising 'commodification' may themselves be depicted as a totalising discursive projection that erases the differentiated meanings that subjects routinely attach to their decisions in market settings. Decisions to accept or refuse offers in markets may reflect all manner of personal identifications, historical attachments, and cultural meanings that may be inaccessible to third parties whether econometricians or majorities of other citizens. The right to sell one's house or one's pets does not mean that people see their houses or pets as 'mere commodities' to be sold to the highest bidder. On the contrary, 'owning' such 'commodities' is often associated with deep meaning for those concerned.[76]

Green hostility to the private sphere may also be challenged on similar lines. Negative rights to property and contract allow entrepreneurs to engage in 'permission-less innovation' but the enforcement of such rights also affords critical space for subjects to resist what may be experienced as negative consequences from an excessive focus on growth by refusing inappropriate offers. While specific market economies may have imperatives to grow, there is no *essential* tendency for market economies to grow, and negative rights to property, whether individual or communal, may provide the space within which subjects can *refuse* growth-oriented narratives. Individually or by pooling their resources in voluntary associations, people may, for example, sacrifice material goods to buy land to preserve it from development and to engage in re-wilding exercises. Creative opportunities may thus arise for discursive entrepreneurs and social movements to communicate the value of property rights as tools that provide subjects with the space to resist normalising imperatives whether these come from a materialist or from an ecological naturalist direction. Ownership rights are critical because they afford the space for minorities to develop resistant readings of socio-ecological situations and to act on them accordingly. Irrespective of whether any one individual, group, or organisation is best placed to read any specific socio-ecological 'sign', a regime dispersing decision-making authority across many individuals, groups, and jurisdictions is likely to generate

[75] On this see, e.g., Brennan, J., and Jaworski, P. (2015) *Markets Without Limits*, London: Routledge.
[76] Ibid.

a higher level of reflexivity than one focussed on arriving at and policing singular democratic decisions.

While postmodern liberalism does not maintain that private property and markets are necessarily appropriate for all environmental conflicts and challenges, it emphasises the important role these institutions might play as part of a shifting mosaic of arrangements that may also include local communal property and some public property, as well as various mixed or hybrid regimes that are neither fully private, communal, nor public. Given the complex and shifting character of socio-ecological relations and of human subjectivity, the elements of this mosaic should be open to incremental decomposition and recombination, allowing new forms of property ownership, regulation, and dispute resolution to evolve. When the character and direction of externalities is subject to flux, then there needs to be scope for institutional entrepreneurs to craft new governance arrangements in diverse and changing ways that allow subjects the greatest amount of room to 'speak for themselves' and not to be 'spoken for'. Such institutional entrepreneurship can be driven by individuals, civil associations, and social movements, and their deployment of different discourses in seeking to communicate different trade-offs may facilitate bargaining between alternative environmental aesthetics, lifestyles, and belief systems on different scales. What matters is that institutional reflexivity implies an ongoing willingness to experiment with market-based or 'commodified' forms of valuation and co-ordination in this process—a commitment threatened by alliances between scientistic and normalising green discourses that either rule out or seek to constrain markets on the grounds that they are corrupters of ecological 'truth'. In a cultural-discursive context where negative rights to property retain cultural resonance, entrepreneurs might emphasise that while people should not be forced into 'commoditising' their environment neither should they be prohibited from expressing their environmental subjectivity by participating in markets and trade.

Away from these possibilities there are important non-discursive institutional factors operating within contemporary liberal political economies and in the broader international order that might contain the power of the sustainability *dispositif*. Perhaps the most important limitation on an unconstrained ecological governmentality arises from the fact that the world lacks a global administrative infrastructure to project and enforce global governance solutions to environmental challenges. Relative to the more fractured and decentralised governance regime that currently prevails, a global governance approach would homogenise environmental standards and practices in ways severely limiting the capacity for subjects to observe and to learn from different approaches to environmental valuation and regulation. Many, if not most, environmental challenges are not obviously global in scale, falling within the purview of nation-states, lower level jurisdictions, or property owners within such states—none of which may be willing to be subjected to a global ecological sovereignty. Correspondingly, the division of decision-making power between these different states, jurisdictions, and owners sustains a degree of polycentricity or institutional pluralism that may continue to generate Foucauldian heterotopias for the ownership, regulation, and valuation of environmental assets in ways that limit the disciplinary reach of any global green gaze. This fractured authority also provides an important institutional check against those forms of 'scientism' that imply the existence of clear-cut scientific 'solutions' to environmental challenges. The very different approaches adopted regarding the regulation and governance of genetically modified organisms in Western Europe, which has adopted a highly precautionary stance, and the United States, which has been much more permissive, is an important illustration of this institutional and regulatory pluralism that helps destabilise any suggestion that the risks and trade-offs associated with socio-ecological innovation are susceptible to a singular scientific 'truth'.

Some of the same institutional pressures may also explain the effective abandonment of a global governance response to anthropogenic climate change. Following the breakdown of the Copenhagen climate talks in 2009, the Paris Agreement of 2015 saw a move away from attempts to build globally agreed and legally binding obligations to reduce emissions to a 'pledge and review' regime where countries decide for themselves the extent to which they will reduce emissions according to the costs they are willing to bear, and where there is no binding commitment to a particular target. Arguably, this approach is more in tune with the complexity of the climate change problem. Though it cannot address the unresolvable problem of generating reliable knowledge on the socio-economic costs and benefits of *future* climate states, it may be better placed to allow for experimentation and reflexivity across multiple jurisdictions and actors to allow an assessment of the short- to medium-term costs associated with different emissions reduction targets and the different means adopted to meet these targets.[77] Moreover, by exposing consumers, firms, and governments to alternative ways of governing, such approaches may also minimise the possibility of an excessively normalising climate regime by reducing the likelihood of freezing people into a moralised view of *necessary* rules and behaviours.

Nonetheless, as the COVID-19 pandemic showed, there remains a pronounced danger, both within and across nations, that the power currently exerted by catastrophic bio-political narratives may overwhelm this polycentrism and pluralism even in the absence of a formal global governance regime. For those perceiving climate change as an existential threat, emergency normalisation

[77] Ostrom, E. (2009) *A Polycentric Approach to Coping with Climate Change*, Washington, DC: World Bank.

and a war footing are precisely what is required with all the attendant risks to pluralism and human freedom from a disciplinary surveillance state. The recent ruling by the European Commission on Human Rights that the state of Switzerland is breaking the rights of its citizens by choosing not to implement net-zero policies with sufficient haste—a governmental stance endorsed by the Swiss electorate in a referendum—is perhaps illustrative of these totalising dynamics.[78] The problem here is not with the liberal principle that a court seeks to respect rights that set limits on what majorities can decide but with the claim to know what protecting those rights entails in a setting where there is no obvious mechanism to discern the costs to the respective parties.

On the view advanced here, whether climate change is worthy of a response such as net zero simply cannot be established.[79] Given the radical nature of uncertainty in complex non-linear systems, all that can be said is that there are grounds to be wary of those who would exercise power over others through claims to predict the future. The postmodern liberal stance on climate change is thus strictly diagnostic and not prescriptive. It recognises that climate change could represent an 'emergency' for humanity, and part of the tragedy is that we cannot tell whether the limits people choose to impose on themselves, or are imposed on them by others to address this challenge, are necessary. In the context of what may or may not be catastrophic risks, the contribution to the preservation of freedom derived from such scepticism is itself highly uncertain. Both in terms of risks to freedom and in terms of the risks arising from the exercise of their freedom, human societies are proceeding on an exploration of the unknown—and the unknowable.

[78] https://www.bbc.co.uk/news/science-environment-68768598.

[79] Most recent studies suggest a low probability of catastrophic climate change—defined as an indefinite reduction of global consumption by as much as 50%—with an estimated probability of 0.01 that temperatures may rise 4.5°C above preindustrial levels—see, e.g., Cox, P., Huntingford, C., and Williamson, M. (2018) 'Emergent Constraint on Climate Sensitivity from Global Temperature Variability', *Nature*, 553: 319–22.

8

Bio-Power and the Political Economy of Crime and Punishment

The Law and Order *Dispositif*

Introduction

The preceding chapters examined three different but interrelated *dispositifs* that may narrow the scope for people to exercise creative agency and their exposure to alternative modes of government. The discursive coalitions underpinning these power/knowledge complexes deploy pastoral or bio-political narratives that construct people and populations as knowable and manageable objects. Though there are grounds to question the epistemic capacity to manage complex human phenomena in this vein, the institutionalised belief in these modes of governance may generate multiple power effects constraining the capacity of subjects to exercise their freedom.

This chapter turns to what might be considered the apex of these overlapping pastoral or correctional *dispositifs* in contemporary political economies—the government of crime and punishment. Though there are important differences within and across countries, the attempt to manage crime and to maintain order is widely seen as one of the most important functions of liberal administration. Private individuals, interest groups, the media, and politicians routinely deploy discourses of 'law and order' to justify multiple interventions to manage the behaviours from which 'society must be defended'.

The analysis presented here does not downplay the significance of crime or deny the existence of trade-offs between private and public security and the protection of personal liberties. Rather, it uses the Foucauldian or postmodern liberal perspective to problematise underlying social constructions that influence how crime is experienced in ways that may tilt towards potentially *illiberal* forms of 'over-government'. Specifically, the discourses constituting the contemporary law and order *dispositif* are part of a wider governmental continuum that seeks to survey, monitor, and regulate an ever-expanding array of conducts through a stimulus-response grid. These controls while not necessarily 'wrong' in all cases may exercise power effects that engulf people in a network of state-imposed and

Foucault and Liberal Political Economy. Mark Pennington, Oxford University Press. © Mark Pennington 2025.
DOI: 10.1093/9780197690550.003.0008

self-imposed controls *irrespective* of any contribution they may make to private and public security.

The chapter begins by outlining the primary discourses constituting what will be referred to in this case as the 'law and order' *dispositif*. It proceeds to critique the possible power effects that may be generated by this *dispositif*: first in the context of day-to-day crime control measures, and second with respect to measures associated with defence against terrorism. It concludes by exploring possibilities to open greater space for people to exercise their freedom in relation to the crime control practices that govern contemporary societies.

Discourses of crime and punishment

The social construction of crime and punishment is not historically stable. In *Discipline and Punish* and in *Security, Territory and Population*,[1] Foucault documents a shift away from a construction where the exercise of often brutal and highly public forms of justice reflected the sovereign's right to impose order on 'his domain' and towards a model where crime control was part of a broader set of governmental 'technologies' or 'police powers' targeted at the 'welfare of the population'. Outside of crimes against the sovereign, earlier periods tended to see crime as a matter of dispute resolution between private parties, but with the emergence of the Enlightenment era criminality increasingly came to be constructed as a 'public' or 'social concern'. These trends coincided with the gradual takeover and eventual monopolisation of the policing, prosecution, and punishment functions by state agencies. Though perpetrated against individuals, criminal acts were reconfigured as violations against the social or public body—a body whose representatives had the authority not only to identify and to punish criminal behaviour but also to engage in 'social legislation' to reduce its prevalence.[2] 'Police power' and the emergent notion of 'public policy' were thus entwined in a model of social regulation which aimed to secure 'orderly' conditions conducive to the health, wealth, and safety of 'the population', with the legitimacy of states linked to their perceived ability to deliver these improvements.[3]

This basic construction has remained largely intact since the late nineteenth century and has operated through overlapping disciplinary and bio-political

[1] Foucault, M. (1975) (hereafter MF) *Discipline and Punish*, New York: Vantage. MF (1977/2007) *Security, Territory and Population*, New York: Palgrave.

[2] Pasquino, P. 'Criminology: The Birth of a Special Knowledge', in Burchell, G., Gordon, C., and Miller, P., eds. (1991) *The Foucault Effect: Studies in Governmentality*, Chicago: University of Chicago Press.

[3] Garland, D. (1990) *Punishment and Society: A Study in Social Theory*, Oxford: Clarendon Press.

technologies. In the case of discipline, the target is the individuals who have committed acts defined as crimes and the attempt to remould their behaviour. Examples include prison sentences, re-education programs, and probation systems that seek to monitor behaviour and to 'correct' it in line with law-abiding norms. With respect to bio-power the targets are background socio-economic conditions such as income levels, access to education, family structures, the prevalence of alcohol or drug consumption, and architectural design that might be correlated with the incidence of crime and with interventions designed to alter those conditions to reduce criminality. These technologies have often worked in conjunction with one another, but the balance reflects the shifting coalitions between the different disciplinary and bio-political frames or discourses constructing the problem of crime in the public imagination. Three such frames that have contributed to and are evident in the contemporary law and order *dispositif* are identified below.

Penal welfarist discourses of crime and punishment

Penal welfare discourses rose to prominence in the later part of the nineteenth century and were part of the new scientific discipline of criminology.[4] Where early governmental efforts to address crime had focussed on deterrence, favouring a graduated but fixed set of 'tariffs' for specific offences whether in the form of fines or prison sentences, crime control came increasingly to be colonised by an expert-centred discourse that analysed its underlying causes in scientific terms.

Early scientific criminology concerned itself with the classification of criminal 'types', such as 'the delinquent', that could be distinguished in their constitution and behaviours from population-level norms. The emphasis here was on a positivistic identification of the biological, physiological, or psychological traits correlated with criminal conduct and in situating individuals within these classificatory grids. In addition to punishment and protective functions, the focus was one of 'treatment' or 'correction' for the underlying pathologies or abnormalities.[5]

Classification of 'born criminals'[6] in this discourse was closely aligned with the rise of eugenics and its identification of the biological or genetic types

[4] Garland, D. (1985) *Punishment and Welfare: A History of Penal Strategies*, Aldershot: Gower; Garland, D. (2001) *The Culture of Control: Crime and Social Order in Contemporary Society*, Oxford: Oxford University Press.

[5] Horn, D. (2003) *The Criminal Body: Lombroso and the Anatomy of Deviance*, London: Routledge.

[6] Lombroso, C. (2006) *Criminal Man*, trans. Gibson, M., and Hahn Rafter, N., Durham, NC: Duke University Press.

'predisposed' towards criminality and the prescription of treatments, such as sterilisation and other efforts to discourage reproduction. As eugenics fell from favour, owing in part to its association with the Nazi program of 'social hygiene', greater emphasis was placed on psychological abnormalities related to the individual's family background or personal history.[7] The focus on specific 'types' of individuals was retained with some subjects classified for treatments that could return them to a 'normal' and law-abiding state, while others such as psychopaths were considered largely beyond treatment and suitable only for detention and permanent surveillance. This individualising discourse matched the chosen sentence or punishment to the specific 'type' of subject identified, with indeterminate sentencing arrangements deemed suitable for a regime where expert criminologists classify criminals, examine in detail their case histories, propose correctional measures, and observe their effects through continuous surveillance.

The emphasis on the individual as the object of scientific attention retained significance throughout the twentieth century but over time came to be supplemented, and in many cases superseded, by discourses on the 'social' causes of crime which continue to be influential today. Criminal propensities were no longer located in the genetic or psychological dispositions of specific individuals but in societal conditions that generated criminal psychologies and behaviours. Some such theories understand criminality as a form of learned or habituated behaviour imitated or picked up from others through socialisation and contagion effects often associated with class or other demographic characteristics.[8] Elsewhere, however, a more influential discourse identifies background social conditions such as rates of poverty, unemployment, or the character of urbanisation that might be linked to criminality. Just as the social medicine approach to public health referenced in chapter 6 focuses on the relationship between poverty and ill health, so this 'social' analysis correlates criminality with statistical indices of deprivation. Criminal 'types' are considered most likely to have been brought up in conditions of poverty or to have experienced inadequate parenting—itself a symptom of poverty. Initially these analyses focussed on absolute poverty, but in the postwar era attention increasingly turned to concepts of 'relative deprivation' and inequality, with crime perceived as a reaction against

[7] Eugenic theories of crime have not entirely died out—for a more recent example of a eugenic approach see, e.g., Ellis, L. (2008) 'Reducing Crime Evolutionarily', in Duntley, J., and Shackleford, T. (eds.) *Evolutionary Forensic Psychology: Darwinian Foundations of Crime and Law*, Oxford and New York: Oxford University Press. Arguably, the influential work of Hernstein and Murray is also flavoured with eugenic themes—see Herrnstein, R., and Murray, C. (1994) *The Bell Curve: Intelligence and Class Structure in American Life*, New York: Free Press.

[8] Durkheim, E. (1982) '*The Rules of Sociological Method, and Selected Texts on Sociology and Its Method*', trans. Hall, W., London: Macmillan; Tarde, G. (1962) *The Laws of Imitation*, trans. Clews Parsons, E., Gloucester, MA: Peter Smith.

the inability of lower income individuals to achieve what was visibly available to those with greater opportunities and resources. While punishment and protection of the public retains a short-term role within this interpretive grid, the long-term solution to criminality is placed in social policy interventions such as income redistribution, better education, and social service provision to reduce both absolute and relative poverty.[9]

Though diverging in their interpretations of the causes of crime, the component discourses of penal welfarism unite in questioning the responsibility of individual actors. For biological or psychological approaches, it is not the criminal's 'fault' that they are socially maladapted, and neither can the subject be expected to rectify their deficiencies without expertly guided 'treatment'. Similarly, for socio-structural explanations individuals cannot be held responsible for the structural conditions leading them towards criminality or for altering these circumstances. Rather, it is the role of organised expertise to design the state interventions that will produce socio-economic settings less conducive to crime. Individual- and society-centred criminology may thus be understood as complimentary discourses in that they construct crime control as integral to the broader operation of the welfare-regulatory state. Social workers, psychologists, psychiatrists, welfare agencies, and socio-economic planners are positioned as having access to the necessary knowledge to manipulate crime-inducing variables and to produce a 'stable and well-ordered society' governed by social scientific expertise.

Economic discourses of crime and punishment

Penal welfare narratives were dominant for most of the postwar period, but by the later part of the twentieth century they were increasingly challenged though never entirely replaced by alternative discourses. One such discourse is associated with the 'economic' approach to crime. Instead of targeting specific 'types' of individuals or groups, these narratives consider *all* human agents as potential perpetrators of criminal acts. Inspired in part by the Chicago school, they extend the concept of the rational, utility-maximising individual, which neo-classical economics deploys to understand the logic of market interactions and apply it to *all* social situations.[10] Agents are understood to calculate the benefits derived

[9] Cloward, R., and Ohlin, L. (1960) *Delinquency and Opportunity*, New York: Free Press; Downes, D. (1966) *The Delinquent Solution*, London: Routledge—for a discussion see Garland, *Culture of Control.*

[10] Becker, G. (1968) 'Crime and Punishment: An Economic Approach', *Journal of Political Economy*, 76: 19–217; Becker, G. (1974) *Essays on the Economics of Crime and Punishment*, New York: National Bureau of Economic Research, distributed by Columbia University Press; Ehrlich, I. (1972) 'The Deterrent Effect of Criminal Law Enforcement', *Journal of Legal Studies*, 12

from committing an act such as theft relative to the likelihood of their being apprehended and the costs associated with fines, imprisonment, or other forms of punishment. While not denying that socialisation, cultural norms, or social class may affect the propensity to break the law, this discourse maintains that 'at the margin' *all* such decisions will reflect a calculation of costs and benefits. As such, the 'economic approach' is not dissimilar to early Enlightenment and utilitarian perspectives on crime and punishment, such as those of Beccaria and Bentham who favoured a graduated set of punishments or tariffs tailored to the seriousness of the crime in question.[11]

What is distinctive about the economic approaches that gained influence in the late twentieth century, however, is their analysis of crime through an 'optimisation' lens. Decisions to criminalise activities as well as decisions over how and to what extent crimes should be prosecuted are considered through a cost-benefit frame.[12] The total eradication of crime is not necessarily desirable on this view because the costs from seeking to reduce criminality may be higher than the respective benefits. Just as there is a welfare-maximising equilibrium for the individual considering whether to commit criminal acts, so too those seeking to protect themselves from crime must balance the benefits from avoiding becoming a victim of crime against the costs of providing private and/or public security and the infrastructure of courts and prisons. 'Social welfare' with respect to crime control is achieved when all relevant cost-benefit margins are accounted for.

This economic narrative makes no judgements as to whether current definitions of crime, observed crime rates, and responses to them are in fact 'socially optimal'. In contexts where public and media concerns about high and rising crime levels have been at the fore, however, a variant of this discourse has been widely deployed to suggest that reductions in criminality require 'raising its price'—typically through greater investment in surveillance and detection and increases in the tariffs for multiple offences. This analysis has played a significant role in debates across much of the Western world since the late 1970s with increased public and private surveillance combined with longer and fixed-term prison sentences becoming an important feature of public policy.[13]

(2): 289–332; Ehrlich, I. (1981) 'On the Usefulness of Controlling Individuals: An Economic Analysis of Rehabilitation, Incapacitation, and Deterrence', *American Economic Review*, 71 (3): 307–22.

[11] Beccaria, C. (1775/1992) *An Essay on Crimes and Punishments*, 2nd edn, Boston: International Pocket Library; Bentham, J. (1970) *An Introduction to the Principles of Morals and Legislation*, ed. Burns, J., and Hart, H., London: Athlone Press.

[12] For example, Posner, R. (1973) *Economic Analysis of Law*, Boston: Little, Brown; Posner, R. (1985) 'An Economic Theory of the Criminal Law', *Columbia Law Review*, 85 (6): 1193–1231.

[13] For a detailed discussion see Garland, *The Culture of Control*. See also, Simon, J. (2007) *Governing Through Crime*, Oxford: Oxford University Press.

Many innovations in crime prevention such as surveillance cameras and the formation of gated communities have their origins in the private sector, but underlying most economic narratives is the assumption that crime control is largely a matter for public authority—or at least a function that must be organised primarily through state agencies in conjunction with private and civil actors, owing to multiple external effects and collective action problems that would otherwise lead to an 'undersupply' of 'law and order'. State agencies must be entrusted with collecting data about the prevalence of crime through, for example, the formulation of 'risk profiles' indicating where crimes are more or less likely to occur and to allocate policing resources accordingly. Nonetheless, public choice narratives of bureaucratic failure associated with state monopolies have also directed attention towards the incentive structures *within* criminal justice systems. Seen through this lens criminal justice actors may not put the public welfare in controlling crime above their private interests if the incentives aligning these interests are inadequate. One consequence of this narrative has been an emphasis on the development of performance indicators often associated with the 'new public management' movement that seek to promote accountability for public expenditure. Target setting for arrests, clear-up rates, prosecutions, and other performance metrics have thus become a hallmark of contemporary policing and criminal justice—especially in the Anglophone world.[14]

Though departing from discourses of penal welfare in important respects, economic discourses also overlap with these narratives in significant ways. First, the penal welfare focus on inequality as a 'structural' cause of crime is compatible with a rational choice analysis of 'incentive structures' with the income or employment status of potential offenders seen as part of a 'utility function' which determines their opportunity costs of criminal acts. Second, the economic approach as reflected in the concept of social welfare is potentially extensive in the range of behaviours it regulates. Whether an agent is allowed the freedom to engage in a particular act will depend on an aggregate social welfare calculation such that *any* private action which has 'externality' effects is potentially open to public regulation or criminalisation. Third, economic narratives share with penal welfare the assumption that crime must be addressed or managed through the application of appropriate professional expertise. The primary difference between the respective discourses is that where penal welfarism sees the relevant expertise to reside with welfare state agencies, economic narratives see the expertise as the property of 'risk profilers' and 'crime managers' who can design optimal 'incentive structures' that reflect the 'price' of crime and the efficient arrangement of policing and criminal justice services.

[14] Garland, *Culture of Control*; Simon, *Governing*.

Communitarian discourses of crime and punishment

Where penal welfare and economic discourses see crime control as primarily a responsibility of the state, communitarian discourses draw on a 'co-production' lens which comes in both conservative and social democratic specifications. Efforts to reduce crime are conceived as a shared responsibility between the sovereign state and citizens, where the latter are understood to be the members of distinct 'communities'.

For communitarian discourse it is the responsibility of the state and its agencies to punish crime through a retributive approach. Where penal welfare frames the criminal justice system as rehabilitative, and where economic narratives see it as setting a menu of 'prices' for different offences, communitarian discourse understands crime and punishment in largely expressive terms, with the punishment function conveying a highly moralised evaluation of the conducts defined as criminal. This lens overlaps with economic approaches in that retribution is seen to have an important deterrent effect.[15] Nonetheless, it prioritises the moral revulsion of the organised community about crime *in general* through a commitment to specific types of punishment, notably a preference for imprisonment over fines because of the expressive message prison conveys.[16] This communicative dimension is also apparent in concerns about the victims of crime relative to perpetrators. Expressing the community's moral repugnance towards criminal conduct means centring the experience of victims over concern for criminal rehabilitation—with sentencing prioritising the victims desire to feel protected from future criminal acts. The latter inflection coincides with a 'warehousing' model of incarceration—with the function of prison to protect potential victims of crime rather than to 'cure' or to 'treat' the criminal.

Nonetheless, communitarian discourses also claim to address the underlying 'social causes' of crime, and here they overlap significantly with both penal welfare and economic narratives. There is a shared focus on identifying the 'criminogenic' environments considered more likely to produce criminal conduct and the public interventions that can address the relevant causal connections between crime and social conditions. 'Risk profiling' is common to these narratives, with statistical analyses deployed to highlight the prevalence of crime across localities and correlating this with background variables such as drug use, the proportion of single parent families, ethnic composition, rates of

[15] On this, see, e.g., Wilson, J., and Herrnstein, R. (1985) *Crime and Human Nature*, New York: Free Press. Arguably, Wilson and Herrnstein's narrative traverses all three of the discourses set out here—they suggest that some personality 'types' may be more disposed to crime in a manner similar to earlier personality theories of crime; they emphasise increasing the likelihood of capture and tougher sentencing to disincentivise crime according to a rational choice logic; and they emphasise an expressive element to punishment in accordance with communitarian narratives.

[16] Scruton, R. (1984) *The Meaning of Conservatism*, London: Macmillan.

unemployment, and dependence on welfare payments. 'Community profiling' is also favoured to target areas where policing may need to be increased and to identify the sites for public intervention to address the social causes of crime. Within this context, conservative narratives attribute causality to a generalised moral breakdown arising from the decline of religious socialisation, the effects of increasing sexual permissiveness in the family unit, drug use, and decreasing levels of 'social cohesion' and personal responsibility brought about by a combination of multiculturalism and the welfare state.[17] 'Broken windows' and 'zero-tolerance' policing approaches to low-level antisocial behaviours considered as 'gateways' to more serious crimes are exemplary of this approach.[18] While placing less emphasis on the traditional family and the effects of multiculturalism, social democratic discourses share with conservative narratives concerns about declines in social cohesion or solidarity which they associate with the effects of a hyper-individualistic market economy.[19] Educational interventions in the home and in parenting skills are prioritised alongside social service provision targeted at the unemployed to ameliorate problems the discourse associates with inequalities in access to welfare services and education.[20]

Though recognising a critical role for the state in punishing crime, communitarian discourses also emphasise the role of individuals and communities in taking steps to protect themselves from crime by installing locks, alarm systems, and surveillance cameras; educating children about the risks of crime; and the formation of community protection associations that monitor localities for behaviours thought to correlate with criminality. This 'responsibilisation' strategy also requires that associations, such as neighbourhood watch groups, sports clubs, local public agencies, schools, and employers, are actively involved in inculcating and enforcing the values and attitudes that reduce the likelihood of people turning towards criminal conduct. State action is not absent in this approach, however, but operates 'at a distance', facilitating or 'enabling' communities to engage in both protective and preventive functions.[21] Enabling actions include the provision of parenting education centres, support for local authorities in identifying the family settings most likely to generate criminality, lifestyle advice, and environmental planning and architectural services that seek to design crime 'out' of social spaces. These are often combined with a new

[17] For example, Mead, L. (1986) *Beyond Entitlement: The Social Obligations of Citizenship*, New York: Free Press.

[18] Wilson, J., and Kelling, G. (1982) 'Broken Windows', *The Atlantic Monthly*, March, 29–38.

[19] For example, Etzioni, A. (1993) *The Spirit of Community: Rights, Responsibilities and the Communitarian Agenda*, New York: Crown; Giddens, A. (1994) *Beyond Left and Right: The Future of Radical Politics*, Cambridge: Polity.

[20] Finn, D. (1997) 'Labour's New Deal for the Unemployed', *Local Economy*, 12: 247–58.

[21] Rose, N. (1996) 'The Death of the Social? Reconfiguring the Territory of Government', *Economy and Society*, 25 (3): 327–56.

public management emphasis on incentivising police services to engage in co-production strategies with communities to meet targets for arrests and clear-up rates.

The law and order *dispositif*

The discursive constructions set out above have been evident across the liberal democratic world but with the overlaps and coalitions brokered between the different narratives varying across time and place. Anglophone societies have, especially since the late 1970s, moved towards a strategy combining the deterrent and protective functions of targeted policing and incarceration that owes much to a reading of the economic approach, with a communitarian conservative narrative that emphasises the retributive and protective value of prison to victims and the attempt to identify the community profiles and situational settings most susceptible to crime.[22] The focus on mass incarceration in the United States is widely considered an outlier,[23] but the movement towards greater surveillance and longer prison sentences has also been apparent in the United Kingdom and Australia, though in both these countries the legacy of penal welfare has been more resilient. Here communitarian discourses have also reflected a more social democratic tone. In the United Kingdom for example, the Labour administration of 1997–2010 pursued a 'tough on crime and tough on the causes of crime' approach, combining an emphasis on improved detection and increased sentencing with welfare and community 'enabling' services focused on 'at-risk' groups such as single parent families and the unemployed.[24] Elsewhere, continental European societies have been influenced by both conservative and social democratic communitarianism in a general context that has moved away from penal welfare towards a focus on deterrence and protection. Penal welfare has retained greater influence in Nordic countries, but there too there has been a shift towards an economic narrative combined with one that emphasises co-production of crime control and prevention on communitarian lines.[25]

These shifts in the discourse coalitions that have governed crime give the appearance of flux, but important though this fluidity has been there are also significant and often overlooked commonalities between the constituent discourses, which have remained stable throughout and on which different mixes of policies

[22] Garland, *Culture of Control.*

[23] Simon, J. (2014) *Mass Incarceration on Trial*, New York: New Press.

[24] Driver, S., and Martell, L. (1997) 'New Labour's Communitarianism', *Critical Social Policy*, 52: 27–46.

[25] Borch, C. (2015) *Foucault, Crime and Power: Problematisations of Crime in the Twentieth Century*, London: Routledge—for a focus on Denmark.

and techniques of government have been assembled. It is these background assumptions that represent the core of what is described here as the law and order *dispositif*.

The first stable assumption across this *dispositif* is a broadly positivist project of identifying the causes of crime or 'risk factors' through a predictive, stimulus-response grid and the identification of the policy 'treatments' that will address these causes. Though differing in their understanding of the relevant causal factors and necessary treatments, each of the discourses contributing to the emergence of contemporary criminal justice regimes maintains that the nature of criminality and/or of 'criminogenic' situations can be understood or 'known' through the application of the appropriate social scientific technique and expertise.

Second, the focus on scientific understanding is reflected in a shared belief that knowledge of how to control crime is available primarily to those in possession of the relevant professional expertise. Even discourses emphasising a role for communities as part of co-production strategies give priority to professional crime experts in identifying and engaging the relevant communities to shape the crime control response. 'Community' in the law and order *dispositif* is not an organic or bottom-up phenomenon, but one that must be *created* by government through the delineation of geographical and territorial boundaries, demographic profiling, and funding regimes that seek to consciously 'build' a community identity.[26]

Third and relatedly, all the relevant discourses assume that criminal justice functions are primarily the responsibility of state agencies that either govern crime directly through the passage of legislation and regulation or who 'govern at a distance' by inducing other parties to act in ways commensurate with the goal of providing security. What has been referred to as an 'animator state'[27] or an 'enabling state' operates a form of government that engages families, citizens, schools, and professions all of which are to be 'mobilised' and 'steered' towards law and order objectives—either through the provision of funds, the design of incentives, the creation of community identities, or some combination of these strategies.

Finally, and perhaps most important, there is a stable and shared conception across the *dispositif* that crime should be understood as part of a broader biopolitical or pastoral agenda for public policy to address what are constructed as 'social problems' that require publicly guided collective action to improve the 'welfare of the population' through processes of directional intelligence and institutional design.

[26] Rose, 'The Death of the Social?'.
[27] Donzelot, J., 'The Mobilisation of Society', in Burchell et al., *The Foucault Effect*.

Problematising the law and order *dispositif*

Insofar as long-run evolutionary processes provide some guidance about the parameters within which societies are ordered or governed, then it is reasonable to assume that all societies require mechanisms for protecting person and property against transgressors. Historically, there have not been any functioning societies, or at least none that have survived for long without institutional arrangements, that protect people from violence and theft. The critique that follows, therefore, does not question the need for crime control measures per se. Rather, it attends to the assumptions underlying the suite of overlapping narratives that continue to frame discussions around crime in largely liberal societies and the potentially illiberal 'power effects' of these discourses and their associated institutions.

Crime, complexity, and bio-power

The first set of background assumptions to be problematised here is the contention that there are underlying or stable causes of crime that can be discovered through social scientific methods and that law enforcement and penal measures best suited to address criminality may be similarly discerned. These ontological and epistemological premises are evident across all discursive constructions that seek to correlate crime rates and recidivism rates with other 'variables' such as levels of unemployment or inequality, demographic profiles, arrest rates, and length of sentences. They are also reflected in informal but widely circulating narratives holding politicians accountable for providing 'solutions' to criminality. It is this mechanistic or scientistic understanding in both academic accounts and their interplay with journalistic, 'folk', or popular constructions that underpins the law and order *dispositif*.

Though it does not reject the existence of causal factors explaining criminality, the Foucauldian or postmodern liberal perspective offered here interprets these 'causes' not in mechanistic terms but as historically and culturally contingent. Instead of seeing crime as a 'simple phenomenon' that can be 'known' through a stimulus-response grid, criminality is understood to have complex and fluid causes such that its prevalence may not be subject to law-like prediction and pastoral control. On this view, what count as criminogenic situations may vary depending on the cultural-discursive symbols, meanings, and routines that generate different motives, strategies, and perceptions of the costs and benefits of criminality and the efforts to counter it. Understanding what are defined as criminal acts and why agents may or may not choose to participate in them requires access to the meanings and theories guiding their actions and how these change in response to their experiences of crime. Such a view does not deny that personal psychology, demographics, levels of inequality, or the likelihood of arrest and punishment *may* be linked to the incidence of crime in specific cases. It does, however, question any mechanical or law-like relationship between crime rates and other such variables. Those committing crime and those seeking to avoid it are understood to be culturally constituted and creative actors whose decisions are not mechanically linked to a background set of 'causes'.

It follows that while many factors centred by the law and order *dispositif* may be relevant to the incidence of crime, the complexity of their interaction with these decentred cultural processes may not be accessible to social scientific observers and public policy practitioners. If crime is a complex phenomenon, then it may not be possible to anticipate how it will be impacted by changes in human beliefs and behaviours over time—including those induced by policy interventions. Different individuals and communities with varying social attitudes, time horizons, and belief systems may respond to crime control measures and the spread of news about these policies in different ways—some of which may counteract the intent of the relevant policies.[28] If, for example, people come to believe that increases in neighbourhood policing and surveillance are in the offing, they may reduce their own investments in security. Similarly, if those intending to commit crimes come to believe that specific offences are to be targeted by the authorities or private agents, they may shift their activities into fields thought less likely to be detected. There are thus significant 'knowledge problems' in understanding how multiple expectations and strategies surrounding criminality will be changed by unfolding events and policies, and these may be especially pronounced in a context of heterogenous agents whose responses cannot be reduced to those of a statistically 'average' actor.

Seen through this lens the different notions of crime control centred in the law and order *dispositif* may be subject to a bio-political 'pretence of knowledge' which erases the complexity of the targeted phenomena. Penal welfare, for example, especially the variant which understands crime to be structurally related to social inequality, unemployment, and the extent of welfare state provision, implicitly or explicitly presupposes that criminologists working in conjunction with planners and regulators have the epistemic capacity to manipulate socio-economic environments to produce the levels of income inequality, the structures of employment, and the inter- and intra-community relations conducive to reductions in crime. The often unspoken assumption here is that contemporary welfare state capitalism exhibits *insufficient* socio-economic control,

[28] Cameron, S. (1989) 'A Subjectivist Perspective on the Economics of Crime', *Review of Austrian Economics*, 3 (1): 31–43; See also Harcourt, B. (2007) *Against Prediction*, Chicago: University of Chicago Press.

and instead of focussing control efforts on those committing crimes, society 'as a whole' should be subject to expert socio-economic regulation on bio-political lines.

With the failure of centrally managed economies to deliver material welfare and their routine criminalisation of subjects for plan-disrupting actions, this socialist approach has never gained significant traction in predominantly liberal societies, and even the more modest, social democratic penal welfare evident in the law and order *dispositif* has receded in influence. The narratives that have gained at its expense are, however, scarcely less scientistic or mechanistic. Economic discourses, for example, attempt to assign 'prices' reflecting the costs of different crimes to other actors and to design 'incentive structures' that will deter offenders at minimal cost, but the prices and incentives concerned are not derived from a process accounting for the dispersed, subjective, and fluid understandings of those who will be subject to them. Rather, they are mechanistic projections derived from statistical categories which assume a predict and control model that may misrecognise what influences decisions to participate in criminal acts—much in the way that the statistical accounting methods used in the formerly planned economies often bore no relationship to the economic circumstances facing producers and consumers. The statistical probability of being caught for an 'average' individual may, for example, have little relevance to decisions to participate in crime if those concerned subjectively rate their abilities to avoid detection as superior to those who are arrested—much as movements in markets are driven not by 'representative agents' but by entrepreneurs who believe they have knowledge that will enable them to 'beat the market' and who may shape its future trajectory. Similarly, an increase in the average arrest rate, while it may deter some would-be transgressors, may prompt more entrepreneurial and creative criminals to change their methods in ways that allow them to carry out a similar or possibly greater number of crimes.[29]

More generally, aggregate statistics such as arrest rates may mean very little to those who have no experience of criminal activity with expectations only acquired through the act of committing crime as subjects try out different techniques and as they experience various degrees of stress or pleasure from taking risks with their freedom and/or social status.[30] People may not know whether they have a 'taste' for crime until they have 'tried it'—much as consumers and workers may not know that they have a taste for other 'goods' or forms of employment until they have experimented with them—and once they have acquired or developed such a 'taste' their experience of crime and expectations about the risk of capture may diverge significantly from those of any statistically 'average' criminal.

[29] Cameron, 'A Subjectivist Perspective'.
[30] Ibid.

Similar problems afflict the calibration of punishment methods to deter criminality. While actual or potential criminals may be deterred by specific punishments such as the possibility of imprisonment, others may experience punishment differently.[31] The effect of imprisonment may be, for example, to solidify what was previously an uncertain identification with crime as the social stigma and reduction in legitimate opportunities that may be associated with a prison record, and the scope for learning more about criminal methods from other prisoners may tilt the 'incentive structure' towards committing future offences. Similarly in some gang-based cultures members may use periods of imprisonment to 'prove themselves' to their peers, and prison itself may be experienced as a form of 'education centre' for the acquisition of criminal expertise.[32] Elsewhere, young offenders who lack social support networks or access to services may experience little deterrent effect from the threat of imprisonment.[33] Indeed, it is possible they will commit crimes to access such networks and services, much as some individuals may join the army in search of the regimentation and security offered by military life. In all such cases, however, the cultural meanings and the resultant balance of forces decreasing or increasing the supply of criminal acts may be inaccessible to external observers, and neither is such a balance likely to be stable.

In view of these difficulties, it may not be surprising that the criminological search for the causes of crime has yielded little in the way of clear-cut results.[34] Over the twentieth century and especially in the postwar period, *all* liberal societies saw a significant increase in rates of recorded crime—a trend that has only recently reversed—but the causes of these increases and the more recent decreases remain shrouded in ignorance. Penal welfare explanations focussed on background structural factors such as levels of poverty, inequality, and unemployment as drivers of crime do not account for rising crime rates during long periods when poverty levels declined, inequality was stable or falling, and unemployment was low.[35] Deterrence or rational choice theories focused on changing incentives have fared little better with significant increases in recorded crime occurring during periods when there was little if any change in the severity of punishment regimes.[36] Similarly, communitarian explanations focussed on

[31] For example, D'Amico, D. (2015) 'Knowledge Problems and Proportionality', *Criminal Justice Ethics*, 34 (2): 131–55.

[32] Skarbek, D. (2014) *The Social Order of the Underworld: How Prison Gangs Govern the American Penal System*, Oxford: Oxford University Press, 141.

[33] Cameron, 'A Subjectivist Perspective'.

[34] For the UK specifically, Marris concluded from a review of 300 studies that the evidence base does not provide any significant guidance on the 'true' causes of crime—see Marris, R. (2003) *Survey of the Research Literature on the Economic and Criminological Factors Influencing Crime Trends*, London: Home Office. For a discussion of this and international comparisons see, e.g., Ormerod, P. (2005) *Crime, Economic Incentives and Social Networks*, London: Institute of Economic Affairs.

[35] Marris, *Survey*; Ormerod, *Crime, Economic Incentives*.

[36] Marris, *Survey*; Ormerod, *Crime, Economic Incentives*.

the destabilising effects of rapid technological and cultural change cannot account for the fact that earlier historical periods, and notably the period after the Industrial Revolution, witnessed similar if not greater rates of socio-cultural change but without concomitant increases in criminality.[37]

Cross-country variations also show little if any association with background variables and policies. The United States, for example, exhibits higher levels of income inequality and provides fewer welfare state services than either Britain or Sweden, but overall it experiences lower population-adjusted levels of crimes against property and person than the latter two countries.[38] Violent crime rates are higher in the United States, but these are heavily concentrated in some of the larger metropolitan areas, with many rural localities seeing minimal crime of any kind. Within-country variation is also significant, but here too there appears to be little that links criminality to predictable differences in policies and institutions. In the United States specifically, metropolitan areas exhibit huge differences in crime rates, but these fail to track substantial differences in the policy regime. There is, for example, little to suggest that the prevalence of 'broken windows' policing consistently tracks recent declines in crime with cities that have resisted this strategy experiencing similar declines.[39] Some econometric studies suggest that increasing incarceration rates may have played a role in reducing crime rates[40] by removing from circulation 'super-predators' that commit a disproportionate share of offences, but these are hard to disentangle from other influences such as increased private surveillance and shifts in relative prices such that goods that were once high-value targets for burglary (e.g. televisions, CD players, and computers) are no longer seen as worth the risk. There is also the possibility that mass incarceration may have contributed to criminality by intensifying processes of family and community breakdown.[41]

Though positivist criminology, *judged on its own terms*, would seem to have had little success in isolating specific causes of crime and the measures most likely to address them, it is important to emphasise that for the post-foundational and pragmatist social science of a Foucauldian or postmodern liberalism even if stable historical identifications could be established, this would not imply that these relationships will hold in the future or that associations that hold in some places are relevant to others. If, for example, a historical association were to be found between lower murder rates and the presence of capital punishment, this would not necessarily imply that capital punishment

[37] Marris, *Survey*; Ormerod, *Crime, Economic Incentives*

[38] Ibid. See also Garland, *Culture of Control*, 208.

[39] Harcourt, B. (2001) *The Illusion of Order: The False Promise of Broken Windows Policing*, Cambridge, MA: Harvard University Press.

[40] For example, Levitt, S. (2004) 'Understanding Why Crime Fell in the 1990s: Four Factors That Explain the Decline and Six That Do Not', *Journal of Economic Perspectives*, 18 (1): 163–90.

[41] Simon, *Governing*. Vitale, A. (2017) *The End of Policing*, London: Verso.

is *the* solution to lowering the murder rate. It could be that there are multiple other potential ways of governing violent crimes that have yet to be tried out and that were they to be experimented with might destabilise any relationship between the prevalence of murder and the presence or absence of the death penalty.[42] Similarly, it does not follow that if gun ownership were to correlate with lower levels of crimes against person and property in one country that allowing gun ownership would reduce levels of crime in another country or jurisdiction. Elsewhere, if police numbers correlate with lower levels of reported crime, this would not mean that increasing numbers in a cultural context where the police are perceived as a hostile force, as in some US cities where 'military-style' policing is experienced negatively by minority communities, would exercise a similar effect. The extent to which variables such as gun ownership or police numbers contribute to reductions or increases in criminality may depend on complex contingencies and interaction effects with cultural norms and decentred meanings that are unlikely to be picked up by even the most sophisticated multivariate analyses.

The relative absence of strong criminological findings set out above and problems of complex and contingent causation does, however, raise the question of why public discussions of crime and punishment are often conducted *as if* such data were available or attainable. On a postmodern liberal view, it may be hard to detach answers to this question from the potential Foucauldian power effects arising from the discourse coalitions and power/knowledge complexes that continue to govern crime. What unites these narratives with each other and with the discursive coalitions examined in previous chapters is adherence to bio-political or pastoral constructions that conceptualise human populations as knowable, aggregate objects that can be subject to deliberative control. Where these narratives predominate, they may produce subjectivities whose perceived interests generate a strategic logic reproducing criminological debates couched in these very terms. Though they are not necessarily created to benefit specific interests, once these discourses are established in the public imagination and entwined with political authority, it may be difficult for concepts not expressed in the language of a stimulus response grid to gain a foothold. It is, for example, hard to envisage contemporary politicians seeking re-election in a context shot through with bio-political conceptions of crime control telling voters that they 'do not know' or are 'unsure' about the causes of crime and or the appropriate policy responses to it. Similarly, it may be difficult for law enforcement and criminal justice agencies seeking to increase their budgets to express a lack of confidence in their ability to control criminality. There is a whole network of police

[42] D'Amico, D. (2017) 'The Counter-Revolution of Criminological Science: A Study on the Abuse of Reasoned Punishment', *Erasmus Journal for Philosophy and Economics*, 10 (1): 1–40.

unions, prison officers, and private contractors whose job security and social status depend on the assumption that what they do is in some sense 'effective'.

Pastoral security *dispositifs*, though differing in the specific causes of crime they identify, may also select for relatively simple and highly visible analyses or proposals to address public demands that 'something must be done'—demands that may themselves be generated by the *dispositif* and that may bring to the fore experts and/or political actors who cater to them. By contrast, those understanding criminality as a complex and shifting phenomena may fare less well in competition with those who target visible problems with targeted solutions. There are, of course, many criminologists who are aware that data on criminality do not point in a specific direction and who refrain from policy recommendations.[43] Nonetheless, in a discursive environment infused with both expert and popular expressions of a scientistic 'will-to know', the less circumspect may be more likely to seek and to garner attention. Similarly, media outlets may be prone to publicise studies that appear to pinpoint a clear causal link between crime and specific policies while ignoring the many studies that show no such connections—and politicians seeking electoral advantage may respond to such studies with rhetorical policy initiatives such as being 'tough on crime and tough on the causes of crime'.[44]

Within this context, the direct influence of social scientific theories on public understandings should not be overemphasised. It seems unlikely that, for example, support for increasing prison sentences has been generated by a widespread awareness of neo-classical economic analyses of the 'price of crime' and perhaps more likely that this reflects the popularisation of simplified versions of these theories by political entrepreneurs, which have been taken up or recirculated by the media, anti-crime campaigners, and law enforcement agencies.[45] What matters is that such entrepreneurs may be favoured in a broader discursive setting primed towards 'stimulus-response' reasoning and the powers of directional intelligence, and where there may be little if any reward in terms of influence, power, and prestige for those deploying concepts that question such reasoning. These power effects may be especially pronounced in the field of law and order; the provision of which is widely seen to be *the* fundamental responsibility of sovereign government—even by conservatives and classical liberals who are otherwise sceptical of government regulation and control. To openly contemplate the possibility that the political authorities may not in

[43] See, e.g., Marris, *Survey*, and much earlier Martinson, R. (1974) 'What Works?—Questions and Answers About Prison Reform', *The Public Interest*, 22–54. The latter analysis was highly influential especially in sociological circles, inspiring the 'nothing works' doctrine.

[44] On this see, e.g., Vitale, *End of Policing*.

[45] For example, Blakely, J. (2019) 'The Hermeneutics of Policing: An Analysis of Law and Order Technocracy', *Critical Review*, 31 (2): 160–78.

fact know how to 'control' crime through the exercise of directional intelligence might be perceived to undermine and potentially shatter one of the most important legitimating foundations of the modern administrative state and the multiple interests entangled with it.

Government by crime statistics

Further power effects may be generated by the mode of communication characteristic of bio-political discourses on crime and criminality and the strategies of government they may produce. In Foucault's understanding bio-political discursive formations are often premised on the production of statistical data which purport to 'make visible' various phenomena, with the subsequent policy interventions allowing those in authority to signal to others that they are fulfilling their pastoral role in a bid to maintain their status and access to resources.[46] All the overlapping discourses contributing to the law and order *dispositif* centre the production of crime statistics in this respect so that they might be correlated with other 'variables', such as rates of poverty (penal welfare), arrest and conviction rates, sentencing levels (economic discourses), or cultural demographics (communitarian discourses). Within this context, most public knowledge of crime is derived from official statistics and their circulation in the media and political debate. Insofar as these statistics enable law enforcement agencies and citizens to identify where problems of criminality are most pronounced and to allocate resources accordingly, then few would question that the production of these data may be of public and private benefit. One recent example of a statistical aggregation system used for such purposes is the CompStat model that has been adopted by many US cities, which continually updates reported crimes and maps them, thus identifying crime 'hotspots'.

The problem here, however, is that while information about such hotspots may be valuable on some dimensions, the circulation of these and other statistics in a discursive setting that presupposes actions by politicians, the police, or other public agencies are directly responsible for measurable changes in reported crime may also generate unintended consequences and power effects. It may, for example, inform 'governing at a distance' strategies where subjects are disciplined or held to account through targets and 'performance indicators' with government officials, police officers, and crime managers at various levels judged against statistical measures of criminality in their jurisdictions.[47]

[46] MF, *Security, Territory and Population.*

[47] Muller, J. (2018) *The Tyranny of Metrics*, Princeton, NJ: Princeton University Press; see also Mau, S. (2019) *The Metric Society*, Cambridge: Polity.

These managerial techniques may induce politicians, police chiefs, and lower level officers to 'game' the statistics and divert their energies towards meeting targets or metrics that may detract from other aspects of police work, and they may favour classifications and responses to such data that insulate their access to public funds. They may, for example, reclassify crimes to remove them from the official record or classify them as lower level offences less likely to generate public attention and concern. Evidence from the US and UK indicates that crimes such as house break-ins and theft have been downgraded (to trespassing and lost property respectively) because this may enable the police to reduce the statistical prevalence of more serious crimes.[48] Elsewhere, the use of statistics on arrest rates may lead to similar cynicisms of power. If a higher rate leads to plaudits and financial rewards from managers and politicians, then police officers may respond by increasing arrests for easily targeted and minor misdemeanours rather than attend to more serious and/or more difficult to solve cases. The outcome may be a systemic underproduction of police activities that may have greater value to citizens and systemic overproduction of what may be less valued crime prevention services.

The potential mismatch between how crime is experienced by people 'on the ground' and the perceived structure of rewards facing government agents, police officers, and crime managers may provide a further analogy with the operation of 'planned economies' where producers often responded to quantitative output targets rather than attending to the qualitative value of the relevant outputs. Where subjects under socialism had no effective way of signalling through their purchasing decisions the relative value placed on the quality of different goods, so subjects in the law and order *dispositif* have no easy way of communicating to the producers of criminal justice services the qualitative value they place on addressing some crimes in relation to others or how they view specific experiences of policing or crime prevention. Economic narratives on crime which imply the existence of an 'optimum' level of protection and prevention are especially problematic in this context because in a society characterised by technological innovation and by diverse, changing, and potentially conflicting cultural values, there is unlikely to be any such optimum, and the data pertaining to the multiple and perhaps contradictory social constructs on crime and crime control which affect its 'price' are not accessible to any single agency or group. On this view, public agencies may be no better placed to decipher the price of crime than they are to decipher the price of anything else.

Neither do police officers and crime managers face direct competition from those who may read crime statistics differently or from those who might devise crime reduction strategies that eschew the use of statistics entirely. Law

[48] Muller, *The Tyranny of Metrics*; Mau, *The Metric Society*.

enforcement agencies monopolise the production and construction of statistics on crime and may thus manipulate the relevant data to protect incumbents. These power/knowledge games may also exercise important subjectivation effects—on law enforcement officers who may come to see themselves as beholden to bureaucratic managers and statistical targets rather than innovating to better serve citizens—and on the latter who may lose faith in crime statistics—ceasing to report crimes that have been downgraded in importance.

The use of statistical classifications to inform predictions of where crimes are most likely to be committed and the 'types' of subjects most likely to commit them may generate still further processes of subjectivation. These appear to have been especially pronounced with the experience of 'racial profiling' and 'broken windows' policing in the US but also in the UK and Europe where big data and algorithmic techniques which attempt to identify 'criminogenic situations' or groups are increasingly used for predictive purposes. Health, education, crime records, demographics, and multiple forms of surveillance may be deployed to make both person-based and environmental- or community-based predictions. While these techniques are often depicted as neutral developments enabling 'crime managers' to improve decision-making, the algorithms may reproduce the perspectival biases and incentives of those working within the relevant law enforcement apparatus. They may, for example, reflect a focus on easy to detect street crimes such as prostitution rather than harder to detect cases of fraud or 'white-collar' crime.[49]

'Looping effects' where algorithmic data reflect the propensity to subject certain people, groups, or locations to higher levels of policing and to make more arrests may also generate predictions that intensify these very phenomena. In the US context, for example, 'hotspot data' appear to replicate historical police efforts that have targeted poor, African American, and Latino neighbourhoods for surveillance and for practices such as stop and search.[50] Similar problems of misrecognition may arise in the context of broken windows and zero-tolerance policing, where what may look to be statistically similar crime environments are in fact experienced very differently by those in the localities concerned. While the presence of graffiti in a neighbourhood may, for example, correlate with the incidence of other property-related crimes, the experience of that graffiti may vary significantly between those neighbourhoods where it is perceived as a form of hipster street art and those where it is perceived as a sign of lawlessness and a threat to the safety and security of residents and visitors alike.[51] It is precisely these subtle differences in culturally constituted meanings, however, that are

[49] Harcourt, *Against Prediction*.

[50] Ferguson (2017) *The Rise of Big Data Policing: Surveillance, Race, and the Future of Law Enforcement*, New York: New York University Press.

[51] Blakely, 'Hermeneutics of Policing'.

unlikely to be recognised by algorithmic models. When the latter are deployed by commercial retail platforms such as Amazon to encourage future purchases through targeted advertisements based on previous purchases and statistical patterns, the consequences of any misrecognition may amount to little more than minor irritation for their customers. In the context of criminal justice, however, if the deployment of machine algorithms leads to invasive stop-and-search procedures where misrecognition involves the targeting and arrest of often innocent parties, then the subjectivation effects may be correspondingly more profound. Specifically, there is a possibility that the use of these techniques may generate a self-fulfilling prophecy with path dependencies becoming even more pronounced if those subjected to these methods respond through increasing levels of hostility towards the criminal justice system.

This analysis does not imply that it is 'wrong' to try to predict instances of criminality or to use statistical profiles or algorithmic techniques to do so. On a Foucauldian or postmodern liberal view, there can be no 'stereotype-free' or 'power-free' realm in the construction of crime and punishment any more than there can be power-free constructions in any other aspect of social life. The human mind works through the classifications and stereotypes it receives from the surrounding culture, with these classifications evolving as the mind engages creatively with its environment and as it confronts anomalies or unanticipated events. Citizens and the police alike will thus inevitably use routinised constructions of social situations and other people, including those based on physical appearance, style of dress, bodily comportment, and neighbourhood characteristics, to anticipate vulnerability to crime in specific settings and to take precautionary steps. Thus, long before the advent of algorithmic models, police forces routinely used past experiences of criminal behaviour to predict and respond to future criminality by, for example, targeting tourist hotspots which may have been associated historically with the prevalence of pickpocketing by younger demographics.

On the view advanced here, however, what matters is whether any given set of power/knowledge constructions can be subject to challenge and reconfiguration in ways that might produce new understandings of crime and possible ways of governing or responding to it. Within this context, algorithmic methods aggregate *existing* patterns of social interactions, as well as the biases and understandings built into them, rather than generating new social constructs and alternative ways of governing or responding to the issue in hand. This is not necessarily problematic in settings such as a competitive market where entrepreneurs must continually revise their predictions of consumer behaviour as those concerned are exposed to previously unthought of possibilities by the actions of new market entrants that may destabilise previous patterns and thus change the data that might be fed into a machine-learning formulation. In the context of crime control measures, however, what is problematic is the insertion of algorithmic techniques into a power/knowledge setting that may narrow the scope for the resultant power effects to be disrupted or subject to challenge in an equivalent way. The monopolistic position of public law enforcement agencies limits the extent to which pre-existing biases and power effects can be challenged by actors who understand the problem of crime and how to respond to it differently. In such circumstances the use of algorithms by law enforcement may represent a 'governmentalisation of stereotyping' that reproduces existing social constructions of crime, crime control, and the subject positions associated with it. The profiling of racial minority communities in the United States, for example, far from protecting people's freedom from criminal acts, may have entrenched practices that are experienced by the subject populations as a form of oppressive unfreedom and as a direct threat to their person and property.[52] Such problems may also be exacerbated by the fact that in large-scale democracies many of those who may vote in favour of such tactics may live elsewhere and may not be subject to or aware of their effects.[53]

Bio-power, cultures of control, and the criminalising society

The problematisations thus far have focussed on the epistemic difficulties of subjecting crime prevention to a directional intelligence and on the 'power effects' arising from a scientistic 'government by crime statistics'. In addition to these issues, however, alignments between the discourse coalitions constructing crime control in bio-political or pastoral terms with public authority may also lead to a species of governmental 'overreach', narrowing the scope for subjects to constitute themselves as self-governing agents. Existing Foucauldian work problematising this dynamic conceives of the law and order *dispositif* as a set of disciplinary and bio-political techniques that extend an insidious 'culture of control' into many aspects of subjects' lives.[54] From the management of family life and schooling through to community governance, welfare services, and architectural design, the strategy of 'governing through crime' presents itself as a contribution to the 'welfare of the population' through the management of security risks.[55] Each of the discourses within the *dispositif* focuses on specific causes or risk factors, with the emergent narrative coalitions emphasising multiple risks that require monitoring and management. In both Europe and in the United

[52] Alexander, M. (2010) *The New Jim Crow*, New York: New Press.

[53] Fegley, T., and Murtazashvili, I. (2023) 'From Defunding to Refunding Police: Institutions and the Persistence of Policing Budgets', *Public Choice*, 196: 123–40.

[54] See also Garland, *Culture of Control* and Borch, *Foucault*.

[55] Simon, *Governing*.

States, for example, rather than have a narrow focus on inculcating basic norms of civil interaction, public policy guidance filtered down through the education system, social services, and amplified by mass media has propagated a model where parents, educators, and increasingly employers are encouraged to monitor children or employees for behavioural and environmental 'risk factors' that might be 'predictors' of future criminality while simultaneously emphasising the risks that may lead to their becoming victims of crime.[56] These bio-political narratives are often accompanied by the deployment of 'war' metaphors with government-organised 'wars on crime' heightening public awareness of criminality and leading to a potentially stifling form of 'over-government' as multiple aspects of life become targets for precautionary or safetyist crime prevention initiatives.

The Foucauldian or postmodern liberal perspective offered here does not demur from this critique. Nonetheless, it adds to this understanding of potential 'over-government' and a 'culture of control' by analysing the strategic logics that connect the discursive and non-discursive practices of the law and order *dispositif* to the much wider and interlocking 'cultures of control' examined in this book. What unites the *dispositifs* of social justice, public health, and environmental sustainability with that of law and order is a set of pastoral constructions multiplying the private behaviours and exchanges between consenting adults that are subject to a bio-political gaze. These narratives bring forth 'externality entrepreneurs' who diagnose the allegedly negative 'social consequences' of 'unregulated behaviours'; identify the 'perpetrators' and 'victims'; and propose different combinations of disciplinary, bio-political, and sovereign government to manage them. Rather than seeing the relevant issues as private problems or as matters of dispute resolution between parties with conflicting preferences, issues are framed as 'social problems' where private actions must be publicly regulated for their effects on aggregates such as the 'common good', 'social welfare', or 'social cohesion'. What emerges from these narratives is an increasing range of actions that become liable to criminal sanction if disciplinary and bio-political techniques fail to deliver the desired results. It may be for this reason, that the growth of the bio-political regulatory state has coincided with a significant expansion in the number of activities that are *criminalised*.[57] In the United States, for example, in the period 2000–2007 alone the US Congress created over 450 new crimes, mostly unrelated to acts of violence or theft, at a rate of more than one per week.[58] Just as the discursive alignments between bio-political *dispositifs* and sovereign state authority may lead to a form of 'over-regulation', so too they

[56] Ibid.

[57] On this see, e.g., Larkin, P. (2013) 'Public Choice Theory and Over-Criminalisation', *Harvard Journal of Law and Public Policy*, 36 (2): 715–93.

[58] Ibid., 725.

may lead to a dynamic of 'over-criminalisation'—a process with power effects that may then fold back into the law and order apparatus in ways limiting the scope for subjects to give themselves their own rules of governance.

One salient example of this dynamic is illustrated by the 'war on drugs,' where historically the criminalisation of consumption, production, and dealing has been closely aligned with bio-political narratives targeting the 'social consequences' or 'externalities' of private actions. In the United States, for example, during the Progressive era, drug use was framed as a contributor to wider problems of 'crime and disorder' as well as a threat to 'public health', with users considered more likely to engage in violent crimes, such as theft, murder, and rape. These bio-political framings corresponded with a push from the medical and public health professions to 'medicalise' more areas of life, converting what had been considered 'private vices' into 'public policy' problems that required technocratic or managerial solutions and a class of bureaucratic experts to administer a form of 'social hygiene'. Subsequent wars on drugs were instigated by the Nixon, Reagan, and Clinton administrations—and these contributed to the phenomena of mass incarceration with the US prison population quadrupling between 1977 and 2009[59]—and with up to 40% of that population convicted of drug-related offences.[60] Similar trends, though less pronounced and from a lower base, have been evident across Europe and in Australia.

Though the criminalisation of drug use has often been constructed as a strategy to reduce wider levels of criminality, as with other forms of bio-political regulation discussed in this book, these benefits are far from self-evident. It is, for example, possible that constraints on the legal supply of drugs may have increased prices on the black market to a level where those who continue to use the prohibited substances resort to crimes such as theft and violent assault to secure the funds to sustain their habits. The absence of contract enforcement procedures may also have led to violence between the partners to illicit trades, and the control of supply by criminal gangs may have precipitated violent 'turf wars' like those during the Prohibition era in the United States. Finally, the imprisonment of individuals for drug offences may have introduced them to new techniques and wider cultures of criminality to draw on when released which may have increased recidivism.[61]

For the reasons articulated earlier, owing to the complexity of the interacting factors and decentred cultural meanings that may contribute to criminality, it cannot be established whether the criminalisation of drugs and other activities,

[59] Simon, *Mass Incarceration*, 18.
[60] Ibid.
[61] For discussions see Duke, S., and Gross, A. (1993) *America's Longest War: Rethinking Our Tragic Crusade Against Drugs*, New York: GP Putnam's Sons; see also Simon, *Governing*, and Vitale, *End of Policing*.

such as prostitution, proscribed for similar reasons have iatrogenic effects on the incidence of other crimes in a stable or universal way. *Irrespective* of any direct or indirect effects on the total level of crime, however, there are likely to be significant power effects arising from bio-political measures that criminalise what might otherwise be voluntary transactions between consenting adults.

The first and perhaps most obvious of these power effects is that logics of criminalisation may create new subjectivities as consenting acts are classified as criminal and as the individuals concerned may to varying degrees come to see themselves as criminals. Second, and perhaps more important, because acts such as using and trading drugs are consensual, they may require significantly higher levels of intrusive surveillance and enforcement *relative to crimes against person and property*. Where the potential victims of non-consensual crimes are likely to undertake their own precautionary measures and to report transgressions, those engaging in 'consensual crimes' are unlikely to monitor or report themselves to the authorities. Third, the growth of the necessary surveillance apparatus, either from other private citizens or from public authorities, may result in multiple acts of misrecognition, as many who are monitored and apprehended for suspected participation in consensual crimes may be innocent of them—an experience which may generate further subjectivation effects. Though such misrecognition may be accidental, it may also reflect 'cynicisms of power' where specific individuals or groups are targeted by members of the public or law enforcement agencies to exert power over them and to extract political or economic advantage. Fourth and relatedly, when the designated crimes may be committed by large numbers of citizens, law enforcement agencies may try to reduce monitoring or surveillance costs while meeting arrest and conviction goals by focussing on easily targeted groups.

Arguably, all these power effects may have been generated by the war on drugs and to a lesser extent the prosecution of other consensual crimes such as prostitution. In the US context specifically, anti-drug campaigns have been accompanied by a significant expansion of surveillance activities by law enforcement, many of which have led to tensions with minority communities that perceive themselves to have been targeted for political reasons or in accordance with racial stereotyping, and this may have contributed to the development of a 'siege mentality'. These powers have also been deployed disproportionately against poorer communities even though recreational drug use may be equally prevalent in more affluent neighbourhoods. Stop-and-search powers are also frequently associated with abuse and corruption as law enforcement officers are placed in a position where they can extract bribes from those they apprehend. Elsewhere, the discretionary power of law enforcement officers in policing the sale of drugs has often been engaged by drug gangs to protect their 'turf' from competitors.[62]

[62] Ibid.

Irrespective of whether behaviours such as drug use or commercial sex are criminalised as a crime control measure (because they are thought to correlate with the prevalence of other crimes), or whether criminalisation is justified as part of another bio-political strategy (e.g. improving public health), a logic of expanding surveillance, control, and potentially arbitrary power may be set in train, reducing the space for people to choose or fashion the rules that shape themselves as individuals. As indicated in previous chapters, this tendency towards 'over-regulation' and in this case 'over-criminalisation' may be especially pronounced when there is an alignment between discourses that exhibit a scientistic 'will to know' with positive rights commitments that continually override individual decisions in the name of securing some population-level outcome or pattern. In the specific context of law and order however, implicit, or explicit commitments to a wider positivistic or scientistic frame where virtually *any* action can be correlated or linked as a 'risk factor' to some undesirable state of the world may be folded back into the *dispositif* such that both positive *and* negative rights commitments may generate a similar spiral as externality entrepreneurs vie to produce new categories of 'social ills' and their 'victims' and 'perpetrators'.

Consider in this context, the proliferation of 'hate speech' laws. While it has long been recognised that incitements to violence against specific individuals or groups may precipitate breaches of rights to the person and property of those concerned, a new generation of legislation defines the concept of hate to encompass multiple 'micro-aggressions', which do not incite violence but may generate social exclusion as those exposed to them experience feelings of offense or insecurity. Expressions deemed to show 'signs' of misogyny, racism, homophobia, or transphobia are increasingly seen as predictors or 'risk factors' for wider exclusionary conducts that must be regulated as a form of 'crime prevention'. Consequently, there is now a push to expand the domain of surveillance, monitoring, and criminalisation to include examples of 'offensive speech' made not only in public or semi-public settings, such as social media accounts, but also to *any* space—including private homes.[63]

Many of these laws reflect the power of social justice discourses that proffer positive rights to social inclusion, but they have also been reinterpreted in negative rights terms as reducing the risk of violence against person or property, with those who commit micro-aggressions also considered *more likely* to resort to *actual* violence against their targets. In one of the more radical cases, draft Canadian legislation proposes the possibility of *preventive* 'house arrest' for actors who might be considered likely to engage in 'hateful conduct' *in the*

[63] Cook, J. Hate crime law: Force for Good to Recipe for Disaster, BBC Scotland News, 14 March 2024, https://www.bbc.co.uk/news/uk-scotland-68570614.

future—as judged by the content of their previous statements. Those suspected in this regard would be subject to curtailments such as electronic tagging, being required to refrain from the consumption of intoxicating substances, and being confined to their homes during specified periods.[64] Though there is little or no evidence that does in fact link micro-aggressions to actual violence, this trend may be indicative of processes examined in earlier chapters where the alignment of a scientistic attitude with public authority progressively closes down the space within which subjects are able to think, act, and even speak differently.

The suggestion here is not that it is 'wrong' for individuals and organisations to make their own 'risk assessments' of whether certain forms of speech may constitute a prelude to criminal action and to avoid persons and settings accordingly, but it is to highlight the pronounced dangers to freedom of action and expression from a 'statification' or 'governmentalisation' of such 'sign reading' in a monopolistic public security apparatus.

As one Foucauldian analyst puts it,

> For what situation is there of which one can be certain that it harbours no risk, no uncontrollable or unpredictable chance feature? The modern ideologies of prevention are overreached by a grandiose technocratic rationalising dream of absolute control of the accidental understood as the irruption of the unpredictable. In the name of this myth of absolute eradication of risk, they construct a mass of new risks which constitute so many targets for preventive intervention . . . Yet throughout the multiple current expressions of this tranquil conscience, one finds not a trace of any reflection on the social and human costs of this new witch hunt.[65]

Problematising the law and order *dispositif*: Terrorism and counterterrorism

The previous section sought to problematise dominant discursive and non-discursive responses to 'everyday' criminality. Similar issues may arise, however, from the framing and response to 'emergency' crime prevention initiatives under the banner of counterterrorism. The issues raised by terrorism and the wider dynamics of international order are far too vast to be considered in detail here. Nonetheless, it is worth drawing out the possible parallels between the

[64] Matza, M. Canada intorduces sweeping new online safety rules, BBC News, 27 February 2024, https://www.bbc.com/news/world-us-canada-68409929; Coen, S. Canada considers house arrest for people at risk of committing hate crimes, *The Telegraph*, 3 March 2024, https://www.telegraph.co.uk/world-news/2024/03/07/justin-trudeau-canada-legislation-hate-crimes-free-speech/.

[65] Castel, R. 'From Dangerousness to Risk', in Burchell et al., *The Foucault Effect*.

dangers to freedom highlighted by the Foucauldian or postmodern liberal stance in the context of crime and punishment with those that may be relevant to counterterrorism initiatives.

Terrorism comes in different forms, ranging from internal attacks by the citizens of a state designed to overthrow a particular regime or to induce policy change, to attacks by external agents or their proxies attempting to destabilise a government, or to extract political concessions from it. Internal terror includes the actions of nationalist, ethno-separatist, and/or religious groups, as well as the ideologically motivated terror of communist and fascist organisations. External terrorism refers to violence against private citizens and public institutions within a state by non-citizens—though it may also involve the collaboration of non-citizens with those of the target state. The most prominent examples in recent years have been associated with radical Islamist groupings such as al-Qaeda and ISIS; and in the wake of the attacks of September 11, 2001, these have been the primary focus of counterterrorism initiatives in many liberal democracies. For present purposes attention will focus on attempts to curtail terrorist actions by *external* agents.

Though these is no one-to-one correspondence with the coalitions that govern everyday crime, the discourses governing terrorism share with these narratives a bio-political analysis of terrorism as a 'knowable' phenomenon that can be managed through appropriate interventions. These include a combination of measures designed to reduce the likelihood of people sympathising with terrorist causes, those that seek to deter individuals who have acquired terrorist sympathies, and measures designed to protect citizens from people who intend to commit terrorist acts.

The discursive and non-discursive practices targeted at the supply of terrorist sympathisers are nested within broader bio-political grids focused on economic development and the emergence of liberal democratic institutions. In these constructions, external terrorism is associated with 'unstable' political regimes or 'failed states' characterized by large numbers of poor people, high levels of corruption, limited access to democratic forms of representation, and a tendency by some towards religious fundamentalism or radical movements that profit from blaming their condition on more prosperous nations—especially when there is a legacy of colonial rule. These narratives encompass an 'aid-focused' discourse not dissimilar to penal welfare which sees the solution to external instability as involving extensive programs of international income redistribution and macroeconomic management administered by organisations such as the International Monetary Fund, the World Bank, and various UN affiliates;[66]

[66] Stiglitz, J. (2003) *Globalisation and Its Discontents*, New York: W. W. Norton and Sachs, J. (2005) *The End of Poverty*, New York: Penguin are examples of this narrative.

a rational choice or economic narrative which privileges the role of these international agencies not for narrowly redistributive purposes but to tie development aid to the 'redesign' of institutions that create 'incentive structures' conducive to general prosperity; and finally an overlapping narrative of 'good governance' focused on building identities through education and cultural programs that foster support for liberal democratic institutions such as open markets and democratic elections.[67] For the most part these discourses and the coalitions between them try to achieve their pastoral goals through financial inducements. In some instances, however, elements of them have been invoked to support military interventions such as the post-9/11 invasions of Afghanistan and Iraq by the United States and its allies.[68]

In addition, contemporary counterterrorism discourses also emphasise an important role for deterrence, drawing loosely on a rational choice frame. The focus here is on predominantly negative sanctions that 'raise the price' of terror, to the point where fewer such acts are committed. 'Raising the price' includes killing the perpetrators or imposing lengthy prison sentences on them. It may also include military attacks on states thought to harbour or support terrorists, and the imposition of economic sanctions against governments or specific individuals associated with terror groups. In the aftermath of 9/11, the use of overwhelming force by the US government in Afghanistan and the launch of the 'war on terror' to hunt down members of the al-Qaeda network might all be interpreted through this discursive frame.

The final component of the discursive and non-discursive practices directed towards terrorism is a protective one focused on tracking and surveillance of those known to have committed terror in the past or who appear to be terrorist sympathisers. These methods include actions such as phone tapping and increasingly involve the use of predictive modelling and profiling techniques to identify the environmental situations or patterns that correlate with terrorism so that perpetrators might be intercepted. The latter methods assume that individual irregularities in behaviour become regular over 'large numbers' such that successful predictions can be made from the analysis of 'big data' sets about the type of persons or situations (travel patterns, money transfers, and communications networks) associated with terror events.[69]

[67] Both the rational choice and 'good governance' narratives are loosely associated with the 'Washington Consensus' and in a form that re-emphasises redistributive mechanisms what is now referred to as the 'Post-Washington Consensus'.

[68] Boot, M. (2002) *Savage Wars of Peace: Small Wars and the Rise of American Power*, New York: Basic Books; Kagan, R. (2012) *The World America Made*, New York: Vintage Books.

[69] McCue, C. (2005) 'Data Mining and Predictive Analytics: Battlespace Awareness for the War on Terrorism', *Defence Intelligence Journal*, 13 (1–2): 47–63.

Problematising state-building as counterterrorism

Though recognising a role for states in pursuing counterterrorism initiatives, the Foucauldian or postmodern liberal perspective is sceptical nonetheless of any suggestion that terrorism is a scientifically 'knowable' phenomenon that can be managed through appropriate 'treatments'. While states may hit upon overseas aid packages, facilitate the redesign of social institutions and incentives, or build identities that reduce the supply of terrorists, the complex interactions contributing to these outcomes fall largely outside the grasp of any directional intelligence. If there are 'knowledge problems' limiting the pastoral powers exercised by states over domestic populations, these may be of a similar if not greater magnitude for efforts to exercise such power over the inhabitants of other nations.

In the context of state-building initiatives dominant bio-political discourses construct the world outside of existing liberal democratic states as 'disordered' and in need of expert 'steering' or 'guidance'. Instead of understanding human institutions as complex, dynamic assemblages of actors with often contradictory goals and knowledge which may evolve in unanticipated ways, problems of poverty or poor governance are perceived through a simple or linear mode of reasoning that can distinguish 'orderly' from 'disorderly' states and where there is a singular route to an 'orderly' outcome discernible through sovereign reason. On the view advanced here, however, just as domestic socio-economic planners may lack the context- and time-specific knowledge to plan resource allocation effectively, so too attempts to induce changes to the institutions and practices of other nations are likely to misclassify or misrecognise the complex entanglements of power generated by culturally situated agents pursuing localised strategies for political or economic advantage. The factors contributing to the emergence of violence-reducing institutions cannot easily be discerned or transferred from one context to another. Even if it were possible to 'reconstruct' or 'reverse-engineer' the emergence of broadly liberal institutions in say Britain or the United States, it does not follow that such a route is applicable elsewhere. The consequences of attempting to intervene or to 'treat' other societies in these circumstances may be twofold.

First, it is unlikely that interventions, whether in the form of aid packages, military engagement, or some combination of these, will 'work' systematically as anticipated by the interveners. In the context of development aid, meta-analyses suggest that the supply of aid has been largely ineffective in promoting growth and poverty reduction.[70] Most of these studies rely on comparative static and

[70] Doucouliagos, H., and Paldham, M. (2009) 'The Aid Effectiveness Literature: The Sad Results of 40 Years of Research', *Journal of Economic Surveys*, 23 (3): 433–61.

econometric techniques, which from the post-foundational standpoint espoused here are unlikely to be sufficiently sensitive to the complex situations within which aid is embedded and of the potentially positive or negative effects that may transpire in specific cases. Nonetheless, there is little to suggest that even where aid may have improved outcomes that the relevant causal mechanisms are known and that what emerges from aid-based interventions can be separated from largely accidental or contingent background factors. In the context of military intervention meanwhile, far from reducing terror, three of the most recent examples of military state-building in Afghanistan, Iraq, and in Libya appear to have generated negative unintended consequences with new terror groups unexpectedly emerging from the dynamics that followed the violent removal of incumbent regimes.[71]

It should also be emphasised that without access to the specific meanings and beliefs of those concerned there may be few grounds to connect growth and prosperity per se with reductions in the prevalence of violence. Dominant state-building discourses tend to postulate a mechanistic relationship between prosperity and peace when the experience of the twentieth century showed that some of the most economically 'advanced' societies are capable of terrible acts of war. It seems unlikely, therefore, that the prevalence of terrorism can be linked mechanically to states of prosperity, desirable though these states may be. The al-Qaeda network was for example, led by wealthy subjects from one of the most prosperous states in the world.

Second, while they may not 'work' as intended by their designers, attempts to engage in state-building initiatives may exercise discursive power effects. First, the widespread classification of 'failed states' and the attempt to 'treat' such states may generate or perpetuate a paternalistic sense among elites and large sections of the citizenry of the intervening entities that they are morally or intellectually 'more advanced' and possess a right to speak and intervene 'over and above' the expressed interests of other peoples. Just as mechanistic economic discourses may generate a self-perpetuating demand for interventions in economic processes perceived as 'disorderly' (see chapter 3), so discursive frames interpreting existing liberal democracies as uniquely 'orderly' realms may generate a near permanent demand for more, or less, invasive 'treatments' in other societies that do not conform with a liberal democratic 'blueprint'. Second, the elites and the citizenry subjected to the relevant interventions may come to see themselves either as passive recipients of external assistance or, alternatively, they may feel compelled to define themselves as 'freedom fighters', resisting quasi-imperial or colonial rule. Though these subjectivation processes should

[71] Coyne, C. (2022) *In Search of Monsters to Destroy: The Folly of American Empire and the Paths to Peace*, Oakland, CA: Independent Institute.

not themselves be construed in mechanistic terms eliminating the scope for individual or collective agency, where relations between peoples come to be framed through a state-building grid, the scope for the subjects of states who engage in these initiatives and their targets to find alternative ways of relating to one another may be significantly narrowed.

Problematising deterrence as counterterrorism

Similar issues arise with deterrence narratives focused on subjects who have already developed terrorist sympathies. A Foucauldian or postmodern liberal perspective does not dispute that those inclined to commit acts of terror are strategic, goal-pursuing agents who may be sensitive to incentives. What it questions is the capacity of any group of external agents to assess the character of these incentives and the relevant margins of adjustment to systematically 'design' the 'right' incentive structures.

Most deterrence narratives work on the assumption that increasing the punishment level by killing terrorists, imposing lengthier prison sentences on those who aren't killed and subjecting them to extreme punishment environments, or, in the case of state-sponsored terror, the threat of military intervention and economic sanctions decreases the likelihood of violence. The problem here, however, is that the direction of any marginal changes to behaviour prompted by such initiatives may be far from universal or predictable. In the case of radical Islamist groups, for example, where actors may be embedded in belief systems that see it as a moral duty to fight against those they perceive as disdainful of Islam, then the risk of a hefty prison sentence may count for very little. Indeed, it may even increase the likelihood of a potential perpetrator attempting to commit an atrocity in situations where being caught for 'taking on the enemy' may increase their social status and/or sense of self-esteem. Even the prospect of death may not work unequivocally as a deterrent in contexts where the beliefs of the protagonists perceive what awaits them in the afterlife as a form of reward for taking on moral enemies during their time on earth.[72]

In the context of interventions against states the effects are also far from unambiguous. While military strikes against a state supporting terror may work as a deterrent, they also risk increasing the likelihood that others will join the terror cause, especially so if military action inflicts casualties on innocent bystanders. The wars in Afghanistan and Iraq and the retaliatory strikes by the state of Israel

[72] See, e.g., Frey, B. (2004) *Terrorism: Stick or Carrot*, Cheltenham: Edward Elgar.

against Palestinian terrorists such as Hamas, far from reducing incentives to join terror groups, may have recruited more subjects to their cause.[73] More generally, conducting highly visible 'wars' against states that may support terror groups may have pronounced subjectivation effects that build a coherent identity among the wider citizenry of the targeted state in ways increasing the pool of would-be terrorists. Similar problems arise with non-military economic sanctions, where the penalties inflicted on the community at large may work to build an oppositional subjectivity towards those blamed for imposing the resultant hardships while bolstering identifications with the ruling regime.

It is tempting to think that such problems may be confined to negative deterrence and that an approach that tries to diffuse terrorism through positive incentives or rewards for those who move away from violence may have greater chances of success.[74] Here too, however, there may be significant knowledge problems in calibrating the relevant inducements in ways that secure the desired effects. Depending on the context, attempts to offer 'pay-offs' to actors for committing to peace may induce 'moral hazard' by encouraging those targeted with such benefits to 'come back for more'—threatening to resume attacks if the stream of benefits is discontinued. Elsewhere, the offering of inducements might be perceived as 'bribes' and in the context of religiously motivated groups as further evidence that those offering bribes are 'corrupt' and worthy of punishment.[75]

From a Foucauldian or postmodern liberal standpoint, one of the potential merits of rational choice discourses is that they refuse to engage in potentially normalising distinctions between subjects and behaviours deemed 'rational' as opposed to those that are 'irrational'—even where factors such as religious belief and national or ethnic identity are concerned. To the extent they adhere to these principles, however, these narratives lose much if not all their supposed 'predictive power' because the character of the incentives that face agents and what is in fact rational will vary according to highly contingent circumstances of time and place. There is unlikely to be an optimal mix between negative and positive incentives or at least not one discernible to external actors. The problem is, however, that in contexts where political leaders are socially constructed as able to exercise conscious control over phenomena such as incentives to terrorism, they may be prone to scientistic interpretations of these narratives that produce multiple acts of misrecognition.

[73] Coyne, *In Search of Monsters*.

[74] Frey, *Terrorism*, makes the case for a 'positive deterrence' approach.

[75] Ibid. Frey is sensitive to some of these problems but unwilling to recognise the damage they do to 'scientific' versions of rational choice theory that use predictive power to inform public policy.

Problematising prevention as counterterrorism

Issues of misrecognition are also relevant to counterterror initiatives focussed on detection and interception. Profiling and big data methods assume that acts of extreme violence follow definable patterns that while not discernible to individual analysts may be identified by algorithmic techniques that can discover the types of persons and behaviours that foreshadow violence. Where spying has long been deployed by security services to track specific terror suspects, these newer methods now operate on the secret surveillance or profiling of large numbers of people by acquiring travel information, monitoring airline bookings, and biometrics to pick out the 'information signatures' correlated with the propensity to violence.

To problematise such techniques is not to dispute that acts of violence *may* exhibit patterns over a specific period and that knowledge of these *may* be useful to organisations such as airlines and counterterror agencies in the short term. What is questionable, however, is whether the capacity to identify previous patterns of conduct enables better predictions about the character of future terror events in the medium to longer term. The assumption underlying the discourses within which these methods are often situated is that by collecting more and better data, previous uncertainties about the types of persons and situations that are a prelude to violence might be eradicated or at least reduced to manageable proportions. On the view advanced here, however, there is unlikely to be a fixed or bounded set of terror 'types' or 'tactics' that can be 'searched' and 'discovered' in this way. Rather, terrorism like crime in general might be better understood as a complex and open-ended phenomena, where the relevant subjectivities and modes of action continually evolve as those intent on committing violent acts respond *creatively* to new technologies and attempts to track them down.

Uncomfortable as it may be to conceive of terrorists as entrepreneurial agents, once this step is made, the notion of managing terror as a form of calculable or probabilistic risk may need to be replaced with a recognition of radical uncertainty.[76] Where entrepreneurial action in commercial settings destabilises existing production and consumption models, so creative action by those intent on doing harm to a society for whatever reason is likely to generate new terror tactics unanticipated by modelling that looks for patterns in *pre-existent* 'data'. The attacks of September 11, 2001, for example, far from conforming to established knowledge about the most likely profile of terrorists and their preferred methods significantly broke from these patterns. More recently, the mass slaughter of Israeli citizens by the Hamas group on 7 October 2023 appears to have taken

[76] For a discussion of radical ignorance or radical uncertainty in this context see Aradau, C., and Van Munster, R. (2011) *Politics of Catastrophe: Genealogies of the Unknown*, London: Routledge.

one of the most security conscious nations in the world by complete surprise. Of course, the subsequent response of the security apparatuses may reduce the likelihood of similar attacks, but as opportunities may be narrowed on these margins and as the capacity for terror groups to utilise emerging technologies such as artificial intelligence against the security apparatus itself develops, innovation is likely to shift to new and unexpected dimensions.

Set against the difficulties of tracking a constantly evolving security target, the likely subjectivation effects from treating terrorism as a predictable phenomenon must also be considered. The widespread use of profiling and mass surveillance techniques on religious or ethnic identifiers may risk stoking or creating subjectivities sympathetic towards terror groups or hostile towards the security apparatus. Equally, the institutionalisation of a surveillance state often relies on the maintenance of a 'state of fear' or 'war' similar to those discussed in the public health and sustainability *dispositifs.* The tendency of these 'missionary' and 'catastrophising' narratives is to create a dynamic that centralises political authority and the imposition of ever-more prescriptive controls that promise better health, ecological protection, or in this instance greater security. By homogenising the security response however, this process may insulate the counterterror apparatus from challenge, curtailing the scope for subjects to experience alternative modes of governance that may do better—or at least no worse in terms of security and that may come at a 'lower price' in terms of maintaining privacy and freedom.

Resisting the law and order *dispositif*

The problematisations set out in this chapter do not imply that all the measures adopted under the law and order *dispositif* are necessarily 'wrong'. Rather, they question the 'taken-for-granted' assumptions on which many discursive and non-discursive crime control practices are grounded and how these may narrow the scope for subjects to find different ways of 'governing themselves'. Envisaging alternatives to the status quo may be especially challenging in this context because the parameters of a crime control model monopolised or directed by public agencies have been in place for such a prolonged period. It is important therefore to set out what attempts to 'destabilise the present' with respect to this aspect of government in contemporary liberal societies might entail.

The first point to emphasise is that resistance to the law and order *dispositif* does not imply an ability to escape from all its categories and technologies but to find creative recombinations that can continually refashion approaches to crime and punishment in ways sensitive to differences in circumstances of time and place. If people are to constitute themselves as self-governing agents, then there needs to be rules and institutions that reduce the likelihood of others resorting to crime and to secure some level of protection for person and property. Though the Foucauldian or postmodern liberal perspective is highly sceptical of positivist, stimulus-response models, this is not incompatible with following basic rules that experience suggests may have *some* effect on the level of crime in *any* society. Without endorsing the comprehensive social engineering of penal welfare discourses, for example, it seems reasonable to assume that provision of a minimum social safety net or basic income may reduce the need for people who lack the means to support themselves to resort to criminal acts. Similarly, though it may be beyond the scope of crime managers to design optimal deterrence and crime prevention as envisaged by rational choice discourses, those demonstrating a willingness to kill or maim may need to be imprisoned, and there must be a level of detection that gives would-be criminals reason to believe they might be caught and punished. Finally, no system that protects persons from crime can rely entirely on public authorities without the active participation of the persons themselves as emphasised in communitarian and co-production narratives. A free and self-constituting subject is one who can craft for themselves at least some of the practices of government that may reduce their vulnerability to crime, and this implies developing capacities to engage in localised judgements of risks either individually or in concert with others.

Away from these basic rules of thumb, however, if subjects are to have more space to govern themselves, approaches to criminal justice may need to be reconfigured in ways that reduce intrusive surveillance, that tailor crime control to specific contexts, and that afford significant latitude for innovation. Resistance to the law and order *dispositif* may thus require cultivating a scepticism of scientistic and paternalistic criminologies that speak 'over and above' those they govern.

A central aspect of any such resistance may require contesting the widespread criminalisation of consensual or 'victimless' behaviours. If external surveillance operates as a constraint on the capacity of subjects to self-govern, then criminalising choices that do not directly infringe on the person and property of others is particularly problematic. First, because it represents a form of institutionalised paternalism and ethical policing which objectivates many who engage in acts such as drug taking, gambling, and commercial sex as 'incapable' of making the 'right' decisions and/or as being morally 'deviant'. Second, because it requires an apparatus of tax-funded policing, profiling, surveillance, and incarceration that impinges on the freedoms of those who do not engage in these behaviours as well as the freedoms of those who do.

To favour decriminalisation does not of course imply that these activities will be 'unregulated' or 'power free'. Decentred disciplinary powers within families, firms, and voluntary associations exercised by those with moral, aesthetic, or instrumental objections will continue to affect where and when these behaviours are practiced. Moreover, there will always be disputes between subjects engaged in legalised transactions that may require public adjudication. What matters, is that *relative* to the status quo, decriminalising consensual crimes may *reduce* the extent of this moral policing and make it more sensitive to circumstances of time and place. Though there may remain social pressures against commercial sex, most employers are, for example, unlikely to institute costly internal surveillance systems to monitor whether their employees paid for sex or were paid for sex the night before work. Even when a subject's performance at work may be affected by their actions outside the home, surveillance is unlikely to be universal. While many employers may be concerned about the effects of drug consumption outside of work, depending on the field, others may be more relaxed, and some employers in music and the performing arts may even encourage these particular 'limit experiences'.

If over-criminalisation threatens subjects' capacities for self-constitution, then resistance against the strategic logics pushing towards the surveillance and criminalisation of ever-more behaviours by a stream of 'externality entrepreneurs' may also require resistance. These entrepreneurs are produced by broader bio-political formations that seek to evaluate, regulate, and potentially criminalise multiple decisions according to what they claim will improve the 'welfare of the population'. The Foucauldian or postmodern liberal stance thus diverges from analyses locating the pathologies of contemporary criminal justice in 'neo-liberal' discourses that emphasise the protection of negative rights to property and contract. For left Foucauldians such rights depend on an apparatus of state violence. Far from a mythical regime of 'natural liberty', economic deregulation *requires a strong and often draconian penal state* to pay for the inequality, economic insecurity, and crime that a 'deregulated' market economy brings—with the growth of the contemporary penal state the effect of the retreating welfare-regulatory state.[77] Left Foucauldians are thus concerned to 'deregulate' the criminal justice system by being more generous to the 'victims' of the 'free market' while favouring an *extension* of the welfare state and public

[77] Harcourt, B. (2011) *The Illusion of Free Markets*, Cambridge, MA: Harvard University Press. Harcourt's argument offers a twist on the claim of Karl Polanyi that the 'free markets' ushered in prior to the Industrial Revolution represented a form of social engineering supported by state violence—see Polanyi, K. (1944) *The Great Transformation*, Boston: Beacon Press.

Polanyi's historical claims have since been widely criticised with the historical literature suggesting that 'free markets' long *predate* the state. What has changed across historical periods is how participating in such markets has been experienced—with some periods and their associated discourses condemning market activity and others coming closer to a celebration of it. In the specific context of the Industrial Revolution, far from a radical transformation, the more positive attitude towards market institutions and practices appears to have been an emergent property from centuries of incremental change. For a summary of this literature see Hejeebu, S., and McCloskey, D. (2000) 'The Reproving of Karl Polanyi', *Critical Review*, 13 (3–4): 285–314.

regulation over rights to property and contract. By contrast, the Foucauldian postmodern liberal approach advanced here refuses *both* the welfare-regulatory state *and* the penal surveillance state, seeing these systems as closely entwined in an overlapping nexus of 'correctional pastoral power'. There are two reasons for this refusal.

First, because like penal welfare before it, left Foucauldian analysis erroneously assumes that it is possible for socio-economic regulation to manipulate private interactions to produce distributions of income and social status that will reduce the prevalence of crimes through the exercise of a directional gaze. There is an irony here in that analysts who have offered some of the most compelling critiques of scientism and 'cultures of control' in the penal surveillance state[78] implicitly or explicitly seem to favour a far wider model of socio-economic regulation and surveillance that would rely for its success on similarly scientistic assumptions—and one that would expand the scope of normalising surveillance far beyond what may be required to protect largely negative rights.[79]

Relatedly, construing the expansion of the penal surveillance state as the flipside of economic deregulation mistakenly assumes that contemporary political economies have in fact been deregulated. It is true that during the 1980s and 1990s the pace of regulatory growth slowed, redistribution was reined in, and there was some liberalisation of international trade and labour markets. These developments have, however, been outpaced by the growth of new social expenditures and the tide of normalising regulation and criminalisation related to social justice, public health, and environmental protection documented elsewhere in this book. While these controls may not be as extensive as some left Foucauldians desire, the direction of travel during the last century has been shaped by discourse coalitions that have significantly *expanded* the scope of a pastoral-regulatory apparatus that has criminalised an increasing number of behaviours or placed them on the border of criminality. Setting aside the persistence of consensual crimes such as drug use and prostitution, states that spend between a third and a half of their subjects' output on social programs—that regulate everything from land use to the size of sugary drinks, and that increasingly try to control speech through criminal law—cannot plausibly be described as 'nightwatchman states' narrowly focused on protecting private property and incarcerating the destitute.

[78] See, e.g., Garland, *Culture of Control*. Harcourt, *Against Prediction* and *Illusion of Free Markets*.

[79] Garland, who critiques the 'culture of control' surrounding crime, argues instead for politicians to 'embed social controls, regulate economic life, and develop policies that will enhance social inclusion and integration'. And, to ensure that 'moral regulation and social control are extended to the mainstream process of economic decision-making and market allocation—not confined to the world of offenders and claimants', *Culture of Control*, 203.

Second, it is false to portray the case for economic liberalisation as trying to restore a 'naturalistic' or 'power-free' social order. Systems of property, contract, and markets require rules, but their development and enforcement though not 'natural' may arise in a decentred or polycentric vein through the interaction of individuals, firms, and civil associations.[80] In competitive sports for example, individuals and teams submit to the disciplinary regulations of leagues, while the organisers of the relevant leagues often try to fashion rules that may increase the attractiveness of their sport over alternatives in the same sport or other sports.[81] Few if any such 'policing mechanisms' are created or enforced by sovereign state law, and many markets, such as stock exchanges, have historically operated 'club-based' models of regulation to 'conduct the conduct' of commercial transactors in a similar vein.[82] In some cases these have operated in the 'shadow of the state' with government granted charters, but elsewhere they formed 'outside' of any public supervision.

It remains an open question whether the introduction of sovereign state law increases the effectiveness of protections to persons and property relative to these private and community governance technologies, but it is inaccurate to maintain that the enforcement of property and contracts *requires* state violence. The *Lex mercatoria*, for example, emerged historically in large measure as merchants sought to *escape* the powers of centralised states and to constitute their own dispute resolution mechanisms. Many aspects of this system are still operative with most international commercial transactions governed *outside* of state law through private arbitration, with those who refuse to be bound by its terms unlikely to find willing partners to trade.[83] Such environments, while by no means 'free' from disciplinary power, tend to *limit* this discipline to conducts that smooth bilateral transactions between culturally varied parties. They are also forms of 'law' oriented towards dispute resolution between transactors where transgressions are dealt with through fines and restorative justice. Such models have even emerged in what might be thought the least auspicious circumstances, with informal norms of property, contract, and private or community arbitration

[80] Dekker, E., and Kuchar, P. (2023) 'Markets and Knowledge Commons: Is There a Difference Between Private and Community Governance?', *Public Choice*, online, https://doi.org/10.1007/s11127-023-01099-0.

[81] For a discussion see Pennington, M. (2011) *Robust Political Economy: Classical Liberalism and the Future of Public Policy*, Cheltenham: Edward Elgar, chap. 4.

Harcourt cites the rules for sporting competitions as evidence for what he describes as the 'preposterous idea of a "free" or "un-regulated" market', *Illusion of Free Markets*, 196. As such, Harcourt seems unaware that the development and enforcement of such rules has in most cases little or no association with sovereign law. Many who argue for 'free markets' do not dispute that they require rules—but they do contest the claim that the rules must necessarily come from state-provided law.

[82] Stringham, E. (2015) *Private Governance*, Oxford: Oxford University Press.

[83] Leeson, P. (2008) 'How Important Is State Enforcement for Trade', *American Law and Economics Review*, 10 (1): 61–89.

found to govern the property rights of inmates and the supply and distribution of contraband in contemporary prisons.[84] In other words, the notion that 'law and order' is an inherently 'public good' that *must* be supplied by the state is an historical social construct and not a 'necessary' or 'natural' feature of social organisation.

None of this implies that it is possible or desirable to replace all the penal and regulatory roles occupied by contemporary states. Rather, it is to make the case for innovation and the search for creative combinations drawing on historical and contemporary experiences that highlight different possibilities for defining and governing crime in a more liberal manner. One such model might combine support for a basic income guarantee that secures subjects a cushion against the effects of socio-economic change, with efforts to rollback prohibitions on consensual behaviours and a much greater reliance on decentred governance mechanisms to address possible externalities to regulate socio-economic life in more pluralistic and less criminalising ways. This stance might be supported by strategic alliances between victims' rights and prison reform movements, resisting a bio-political frame where crimes are judged to have been committed against 'state and society', and towards something closer to a tort model that seeks recompense for individuals whose rights to person and property have been infringed. Apart from the war on drugs, one factor that may have driven the phenomenon of mass incarceration is that when they are not directly compensated for the harms done to them, victims or their representatives often feel they have no option other than to push for incarceration if justice is to be done. Though many criminal justice systems provide limited forms of compensation, there may be much greater scope to move towards a model where offenses such as thefts are handled in civil instead of criminal courts and with monetary compensation awarded to victims rather than imprisonment as the primary form of punishment.[85] Those who cannot afford to pay the relevant damages might be required to work to 'pay off' their debt to the individual or organisation concerned while remaining outside of prison or under some form of supervision.

While caution should be exercised, such movements might also explore whether violent crimes such as assault, domestic abuse, and rape might be approached in a similar vein—with some feminist analysts and campaigners now recognising the potential damage done to both victims and their assailants by the incarceration model.[86] Not only might such approaches offer a greater sense of agency for crime victims by offering them the scope to be directly

[84] Skarbek, *Social Order of the Underworld*.

[85] Ferguson, R., and Witcher, M. (2022) *Black Liberation Through the Marketplace*, New York: Emancipation Books.

[86] See, e.g., Gruber, A. (2021) *The Feminist War on Crime: The Unexpected Role of Women's Liberation in Mass Incarceration*, Oakland: University of California Press.

compensated for more of the damage suffered, they might also give guilty parties greater agency by keeping them out of prison and affording greater latitude to reconstitute themselves as subjects.

Given the scepticism of totalising projects evinced here, resistance towards current models of crime control might also focus on reducing the tendency towards centralisation and monopolisation of crime prevention services. Many criminal justice models are highly centralised, and even those operative within federal/decentralised regimes are often steered in a particular direction by 'governing at a distance' mechanisms such as the financial inducements distributed by the US federal government to pursue the war on drugs.[87] The advantage of decentralised or polycentric models, where localities largely devise and fund their own criminal justice regimes, is that they may expose subjects to alternative ways of governing crime and reduce the likelihood of monopolistic power/knowledge complexes suppressing alternatives.

A still more radical possibility might be to move towards models of 'police choice', where the contractual principles informing the security practices found in some private and gated communities are extended outside of the middle-class areas where these are concentrated with public police funds redistributed to neighbourhood groups or community associations in poorer localities. These initiatives might be spurred by minority communities that have historically borne the brunt of intrusive policing, working alongside fiscal conservatives sceptical of the efficiency of public sector monopolies. In the United States, for example, many African Americans do not favour 'defunding the police' but wish to have more agency over how policing is conducted. A 'police choice' movement might thus secure a significant change in power dynamics, where instead of criminal justice bureaucracies choosing who and how they police, neighbourhood associations would be empowered to choose who polices them and how. The aim of such resistance would not be to make the moving target of crime necessarily more predictable or solvable but to give subjects greater scope to adapt and to respond to its evolving forms and to constitute themselves as 'self-governing' rather than 'governed' subjects in their relationships to crime and punishment.

What such resistance might entail or seek to achieve in the context of terrorism and counterterrorism is perhaps harder to envisage. One of the difficulties of countering precautionary narratives, whether on public health, ecological sustainability, or security grounds, is that they justify restraints on freedom by claiming that whatever outcomes do in fact transpire would have been worse had the controls they favour not been instituted. In a climate of fear and in the absence of realised counterfactuals these techniques and logics

[87] Fegley and Murtazashvili, 'From Defunding to Refunding Police'.

are hard to 'disprove'. At the very least, however, liberal resistance movements that destabilise bio-political narratives that justify monopolistic public control over everyday criminality in the manner set out above may also prompt greater scepticism of discourses that promise citizens security by empowering their governments to intervene overseas and to engage in mass monitoring and surveillance at home.

Conclusion

In the years since his untimely death from HIV/AIDS in June 1984, Michel Foucault has exercised probably more influence on intellectual life, especially in the Anglophone world, than any other philosopher or social theorist. Multiple fields in the human and social sciences from sociology and psychology, to the history of ideas, linguistics, and literary theory bear the imprint of his work or interpretations of it. This influence has not, however, been felt or at least not to anything like the extent it should have been in the tradition of liberal political economy.

By opening a conversation between Foucault and a postmodern discourse in liberal thought, this book has sought to develop a reconstituted liberal political economy embracing key Foucauldian themes while also seeking critically to inform those themes. Part I set out the elements of this postmodern liberalism to include a culturally situated individualism; a philosophy of social science sceptical of socio-economic positivism and the efforts at conscious social control it fosters; and a conception of freedom as an open-ended process of self-creation in the face of power—a freedom threatened by 'strategic codifications' between decentred and state-centric forms of power. Part II drew on this perspective to offer problematisations of overlapping bio-political or pastoral *dispositifs* that combine a socio-economic scientism, a belief in the capacity of directional intelligence to 'correct' pattern anomalies, and a managerial approach to risk, all of which may narrow the scope for subjects to exercise their freedom.

The power exercised by these *dispositifs* is reflected in the continual expansion of social expenditure and regulation in contemporary capitalist welfare states. Significant though this growth is, it may underestimate the extent of the managerial and self-surveillance mechanisms proliferated by the 'government at a distance' strategies that now 'partner' the public, private, and civil sectors in the pursuit of numerous 'social objectives'. What emerges from this process is a political economic order characterised by quasi-monopolistic networks of regulatory power that, while not eliminating the scope for agency, close down the freedom of subjects to think, act, and even speak differently. While this process might be taken as a reflection of the 'endogenous imperialism of the state',[1]

[1] Foucault, M. (hereafter MF) (1978–79/2008) *The Birth of BioPolitics*, New York: Palgrave/Macmillan, 187.

Foucault and Liberal Political Economy. Mark Pennington, Oxford University Press. © Mark Pennington 2025.
DOI: 10.1093/9780197690550.003.0009

it is important to recognise that it is *not* the inevitable or law-like outcome of having a state per se—a view that Foucault refers to as 'state phobia'.[2] Rather, if states are conceptualised as institutions with no stable 'essence', this imperialistic logic must be understood as part of a process where sovereign power has become tethered to or captured by bio-political or pastoral discursive formations.

If the narrowing of spaces where people can exercise their freedom arises from codifications of these pastoral discourses in state institutions, then these alignments may need to be destabilised. The counter-pastoral discourse offered in this book is thus libertarian in orientation, favouring a regime of open markets and fractured political and economic authority. It draws on an anti-foundationalist social science which appreciates the coordinating but kaleidic qualities of market processes embedded in competing systems of formal and informal rules. While it favours open markets, it allows room for ongoing localised experimentation with non-market forms of coordination to contest its 'truth claims'. At the global level this is exemplified by the co-existence of predominantly market economies with anti-capitalist spaces, such as those provided by Cuba, North Korea, and Venezuela. Globally, there is no sovereign authority empowered to enforce a conception of socio-economic 'truth', and the aspiration of postmodern liberalism is for the practices *within* sovereign states to come closer to this global arrangement. Unlike the latter, however, it recognises a role for a minimal state or centre to maintain the framework of law within which the process of experimentation unfolds. Such a centre would not rule on the content of socio-economic truth but maintain a framework of predominantly negative rights which allows different conceptions of truth to coexist.

If one were to outline a political-institutional vision corresponding with this stance it would be close in spirit, if not in detail, to the 'meta-utopia' set out in the final third of Robert Nozick's *Anarchy, State and Utopia.* The latter framework is not tethered to the deontological, rights-based foundation that occupies the earlier parts of Nozick's treatise. Rather, it offers a radically open and perhaps postmodern vision of a society with

> a wide and diverse range of communities which people can enter if they are admitted, leave if they wish to, shape according to their wishes; a society in which utopian experimentation can be tried, different styles of life can be lived and alternative conceptions of the good can be individually or jointly pursued.[3]

Recast in the language of a postmodern liberalism, such a framework would allow competition between multiple 'technologies of government'—a

[2] Ibid., 188–91.
[3] Nozick, R. (1974) *Anarchy, State and Utopia*, New York: Basic Books, 307.

competition which would produce a diversity of subjects and which would offer many opportunities for those subjects to be exposed to alternative ways of being governed and to recreate themselves through acts of self-constitution.

Attractive and inspiring though this vision of a liberal and pluralistic society may be, an important implication of a Foucauldian approach is that such a vision should not be imposed on others 'from above'. Though Foucault has often been portrayed by critics as evading normative questions, this view misconstrues the concerns that inform his philosophical stance. As indicated throughout this book, Foucault clearly *does* engage with normative questions, but his reluctance to situate these engagements in an overarching political vision stems from recognising the dangers arising from attempts to *implement* such a vision and especially to do so in ways which speak 'for or above others'.[4] While there may be good reasons to favour some normative visions and discourses over their competitors, *all* normative visions may be dangerous if those who try to implement them ignore their potential power effects. Where David Hume suggested that political institutions should build checks and balances against the abuse of power by assuming that 'all men are knaves',[5] Foucault's perspective suggests that normative theorising should proceed on the basis that all discourses are potentially 'dangerous'.[6]

In the context of a postmodern liberalism while there are strong social scientific grounds to favour a liberal market economy and to believe that pastoral controls must be loosened if freedom is to be expanded, this liberalism must not fall into the same trap as revolutionary 'left' movements that seek to 'liberate' others by seizing the apparatus of state power. Such movements cannot hope to implement their visions without resort to violence because the subjectivities they seek to 'liberate' are the *products* of power and will not simply submit to those who claim to have discovered 'truth'. Revolutionary movements and vanguard parties evince an arrogance that they alone are in possession of the knowledge to 'reconstruct' society in an emancipatory direction, and they ignore the multiple cynicisms of power unleashed by concentrations of political authority. Neither are such tendencies the preserve of the political 'left'. They are also evident in the imperialistic attitude that has informed the militaristic 'state-building' initiatives that have sought to 'export' liberal capitalism and democracy to contexts where they are often experienced not as 'liberating' but as the alien imposition of colonial powers.

[4] For a discussion on the relationship between Foucault and normative theory in this regard see Kolodny, N. (1996) 'The Ethics of Crypto-Normativism: A Defence of Foucault's Evasions', *Philosophy and Social Criticism*, 22 (5): 3–84.

[5] Hume, D., 'Of the Independency of Parliament', in Miller, E., ed. (1985) *Essays, Moral, Political and Literary*, Indianapolis, IN: Liberty Press.

[6] MF (1983) 'Afterword', in Dreyfus, H., and Rabinow, P. (1983) *Michel Foucault: Beyond Structuralism and Hermeneutics*, Chicago: University of Chicago Press.

A postmodern liberalism must therefore strive to avoid overly totalising or global forms of critique when addressing the power/knowledge complexes that it understands may constrain people's freedom. Though it cannot avoid an engagement with state power, it must engage creatively at multiple levels to cultivate a scepticism of the bio-political *dispositifs* that sustain it and to foster alliances in the world of ideas and practical political economy that might open new spaces where these pastoral discursive formations can be incrementally challenged and undermined.

In the realm of ideas this may require building new discursive coalitions. Traditionally, liberal political economy has drawn extensively on discourses from economics and political science, and the postmodern liberalism set out here is no exception. Though it does not abandon the idea of a 'science' of political economy, the interpretive, evolutionist, and anti-foundationalist perspective it works from is radically at odds with the scientific naturalism that now dominates economics and political science and that reinforces a social engineering approach to public policy. As such, there may be room to cultivate new coalitions with discourses in the humanities that have traditionally been sceptical of theories and methods that imitate the natural sciences.

Disciplines, such as cultural studies, though influenced by Foucault and postmodernism have either eschewed political economy approaches or drawn on those much closer to Marxism or the 'critical theory' of the Frankfurt school and their constructions of commercial societies as inherently exploitative and alienating.[7] Nonetheless, there may be scope to engage these disciplines from a liberal perspective by showing that there is a postmodern political economy that understands market processes and their entanglements with politics not as mechanistic and closed equilibria but as radically open texts, fuelled by the imaginations of entrepreneurs, workers, consumers, and civil associations engaged in a creative drama of profit and of loss—both monetary and psychological.[8] This is a political economy that accounts for the productive and coordinative advantages of economies that have seen incomes increase by *thirty-fold* since the Industrial Revolution[9] and that understands commercial societies

[7] For example, Eagleton, T. (2011) *Why Marx Was Right*, New Haven, CT: Yale University Press; Eagleton, T. (1996) *The Illusions of Post-Modernism*, Hoboken, NJ: Wiley-Blackwell; During, S. (1999) *The Cultural Studies Reader*, London: Routledge; Osteen, M., and Woodmansee, M., eds. (1999) *The New Economic Criticism: Studies at the Intersection of Literature and Economics*, London: Routledge.

[8] See, e.g., Kukathas, C. (2009) 'The Capitalist Road: The Riddle of the Market from Karl Marx to Ben Okri', in Cantor, P., and Cox, S., eds. (2009) *Literature and the Economics of Liberty*, Auburn, AL: Ludwig Von Mises Institute; Lavoie, D., and Chamlee-Wright, E. (2001) *Culture and Enterprise*, London: Routledge; McCloskey, D. (1998) *The Rhetoric of Economics*; McCloskey, D. (2010) *Bourgeois Dignity: Why Economics Can't Explain the Modern World*, Chicago: University of Chicago Press.

[9] McCloskey, D. (2016) *Bourgeois Equality*, Chicago: University of Chicago Press.

not as sanitised, equilibrated machines or 'power-free' arenas with a 'harmony of interests' but as domains of contestation, struggle, and creative exchange. It recognises that while they do not deliver any overarching notion of justice, the dynamism of these societies may offer more room for people to constitute themselves as subjects than discursive and non-discursive practices, Marxist or otherwise, that promise freedom by subjecting economic and cultural life to the discipline of 'conscious social control'.

Elsewhere, there may be room for productive conversations with those from multiple social constructionist perspectives in the humanities and social sciences who are concerned about promoting pluralism and cultural fluidity but who tend towards a normative preference for deliberative democratic models of socio-economic organisation. If cultural interchange and fluidity is seen as beneficial and enriching, then perhaps such approaches might be persuaded of the connection between this fluidity and entrepreneurial creative destruction and to recognise that innovation in business, science, culture, or the creative arts has rarely emerged from an institutionalised rule by deliberative committees.

In the context of practical political economy, rather than adopt a state-centric model of social change, a postmodern liberalism would encourage bottom-up resistance movements fostering 'counter-pastoral' subjectivities that draw on the experiences of those individuals and civic associations who embrace uncertainty, dynamism, and enterprise while tolerating and cooperating with those who favour security, stability, and tradition. Rather than seeking to seize the state apparatus and to 'privatise' governmental functions, it would use the energy of these resistant social movements to refuse the continual expansion of public surveillance into the private and civil spheres and build *new* spaces of private and community governance outside of the state. From crypto-markets to mutual aid, from crowdfunding to online learning networks, it would create entrepreneurial heterotopias that spread and grow from person to person and from institution to institution through a bottom-up spontaneous order based on innovation, imitation, and reflexive learning that incrementally shrinks the *relative* size of the pastoral state.

There has been no suggestion here that Foucault ever endorsed this normative vision or the techniques that may be best placed to advance it. Throughout his life, he steadfastly refused to align with *any* of the dominant paradigms in political thought and indeed revelled in the multiple, contradictory interpretations of his work that were expressed by numerous critics and followers. As he explained in a late interview:

> I think I have in fact been situated in most of the squares on the political checkerboard, one after another and sometime simultaneously: as anarchist, leftist, ostentatious or disguised Marxist, nihilist, explicit or secret anti-Marxist,

> technocrat in the service of Gaullism, new liberal etc. . . . None of these descriptions is important by itself; taken together, on the other hand, they mean something. And I rather like what they mean.[10]

The posthumous publication of *The Birth of BioPolitics* lectures has prompted a renewed and at times fevered debate about whether Foucault did in fact come to endorse a liberal political stance prior to his death. This book has not contributed to that debate. If persuasive, however, its arguments suggest that Foucault's commitments should perhaps always have been liberal.

[10] MF 'Polemics, Politics and Problematisations', in Rabinow, P., ed. (1984) *The Foucault Reader*, New York: Pantheon, 383.

Index

For the benefit of digital users, indexed terms that span two pages (e.g., 52–53) may, on occasion, appear on only one of those pages.

Note: Page numbers in bold indicate an overarching discussion.